THEY COULDN'T HAVE
DONE BETTER

THEY COULDN'T HAVE DONE BETTER

THE STORY OF
THE DORSET REGIMENT
IN WAR AND PEACE
1939–67

Christopher Jary

They couldn't have done better.

Brigadier George Wood OBE MC
describing the 2nd Dorsets' performance at Kohima, 1944

Published in September 2014
Copyright © Christopher Jary 2014

ISBN 978-0-9929033-0-5

Typeset in 11pt Celeste by Bookcraft Ltd,
18 Kendrick Street, Stroud, Gloucestershire GL5 1AA

Printed and bound in the UK by Henry Ling Limited, The Dorset Press, Dorchester DT1 1HD

CONTENTS

The generosity of everyone listed here made this book possible.

SPONSORS

Thomas Bamlet

Tony Barron

Charles Baxter

Robin Betts

David Bredin

Bill Bullocke

Gerald Burnett

Harry Chandler

Frank Cottam

Geoff and Joan Cullington

John Curl

Mike Davis-Sellick

Philip Deane

David Downton

Richard Drax

Robin Fraser

David Gargrave

John Gaye

Ade Harris

Peter Harris

George Hendrick

Pat Hendrick

Babs Holloway

Elizabeth Hunter

William Hurrell

Philip James

Mick Jarrett

Alexandra Jary

Nick Lee

Roger Lidgley

David Laughrin

Franey Matthews

Mo and Julia Mee

Ken Miles

Derek Mogg

Geoff Nicholls

Andrew and Monica Nickell

William Osmond

Colin Parr

Mike Richardson

Robin Price

Bob Roberts

Vince Rogers

Paul Roper

Adrian Rouse

Bin Roy

Nigel Spink

Martin Stanley

Christopher Stephenson

John Tinsley

Shelagh Wenham

John Wilsey

George Winslet

Simon Young

MAPS

The author and publishers are very grateful to Peter Turner,
whose skill and hard work produced our twenty maps.

Colour Plates

Photographs and Drawings

The Home of the Dorsets: The Keep, Dorchester

FOREWORD

This book completes the written history of the Dorset Regiment from the raising of the 39th Foot in 1702 until the last Dorset cap badge was removed from the order of battle 265 years later as the Dorset TA became part of the Wessex Volunteers. Much has been written before but Christopher Jary and Nick Speakman are to be congratulated on drawing the strings together and recording the story of members of the Regiment and its battalions both during the 1939–45 War and the subsequent years of the Cold War and National Service. But hotter wars still went on in Korea, Malaya, Kenya, Aden, and Oman, to name but a few, and in all of these the Dorsets were represented as the stories here tell.

All regiments feel that they are uniquely better than others and some are not backward in saying so. That has never been the Dorset style, which has been described by others in many different ways but some qualities are constantly repeated. Modest, understated, a quiet good humour and a close-knit confidence between all ranks, a sense of being rooted deep into their county and all those special qualities so well summed up by Padre Gus Claxton MC in the Regimental Collect written on the bloody battlefield of Kohima. *Grant that we who bear arms in the Dorset Regiment will endure as our Fathers did before us with steadfast courage.* This they certainly did as this history shows. The Dorsets have always done the business in such a way that others coming from other units, arms, counties or even Dominions, such as the Canloan Officers, have not only been made to feel warmly welcome but have quickly absorbed that special Dorset ethos so well summed up in Cliff Lloyd's story in his Foreword.

Those of us who joined the Dorsets in the 50s were quickly aware of the quality and depth of battle experience that still existed amongst those of the Regiment who were still serving. Not vain-glorious tales of derring-do, but the quiet confidence and humour of experienced men who knew the reality of the battlefield exemplified by the Military Medals worn by two Warrant Officers and the Military Crosses worn by six Field Officers of the 1st Battalion in Minden in 1956 and from whom we learnt much and which, in our turn, we passed on to others. Techniques, equipment and operational capabilities change, but the nature of men and the underlying truths of battle do not, and that was what the Dorsets taught us and our successors in the Devon and Dorsets and now the Rifles.

Great regiments do not die; they evolve, taking with them the best of all that has gone before. For a little period of time those who serve give something of themselves to that continuing thread that started in Ireland over 300 years ago and even now carries on into the future. I commend this wonderful book to all those who love Dorset, or who have served, or whose relatives have served, in the Dorset Regiment or their predecessors of the 39th or 54th Foot or their successors since. There is much to reflect on within it.

WHO'S AFEAR'D?

Colin Shortis
The Dorset Regiment 1953–58
Major-General and Colonel of The Devon and Dorset Regiment 1984–1990

Lieutenant Colin Shortis

FOREWORD

Private Cliff Lloyd

In 1938 I joined the Gillingham detachment of the Territorial Army with my friends Fred Gay, John Gifford and Charlie Butt. For the next year, as war came closer, we met at the Drill Hall on Tuesday and Thursday evenings and practised rifle drill, map reading and marching. Sunday mornings were spent on the rifle range at Eccliffe.

Early in September 1939 I was cutting cheese at the International Stores, where I worked, when Sergeant Jim Whitmarsh, in uniform, burst through the doors. "You're wanted at the Drill Hall straight away," he said. That was my call up.

At the age of ninety-five, and seventy years on, it's difficult to remember the thoughts I had in time of war. It is easier to remember the sights of death and destruction and what might have been. A combination of good training and comradeship got me through difficult times. I do feel I was lucky, though.

At Éterville I was inches away from a sniper's bullet. At Hill 112 I was knocked out by shrapnel, again inches away from serious injury if not death. Even when I came round and was crawling my way towards what I hoped was safety, I could have been shot by the enemy. When crossing the Neder Rijn, under German fire, I could have perished as did many of my comrades. Having crossed the river I was again in a vulnerable position when it was obvious that we were surrounded by German troops. The Commanding Officer's order "Dorsets cease fire!" saved my life along with many others.

Subsequent imprisonment in a POW camp was a different situation again. Prisoners were not subjected to the ill treatment suffered by POWs in Japanese camps, but life was difficult at times and possible death was not far away. There was only one meagre food ration daily. When I became ill from an infection in my hand and refused to work, the guard put a round in his rifle. That was a frightening experience! However, medical treatment was eventually given and I recovered. The best day was when I heard someone shout "The gates are down, we are free!" But, even then, as we marched away from the camp the future was unknown until we reached an American road-block.

The eventual return home brought much relief to my family and fiancée. I returned to my old job but, in view of my recent POW experience, got fed up with customers complaining about food and rationing so I changed jobs. The discipline experienced in the army has helped me through life and even today I am independent, needing only minimum help from my family.

I am proud to be a member of the Dorset Regiment, which has been a very important part of my life, and I am very pleased that the last part of our story has been told in this new book.

Cliff Lloyd

Private

4th Battalion, The Dorset Regiment 1938–45

AUTHOR'S INTRODUCTION

This book began one morning in the autumn of 2012 when I asked Colin Parr and Charles Cooper (two recent, kindly and knowledgeable curators of the Keep Military Museum) where I might find the final volume of the History of the Dorset Regiment. They told me that the History's several volumes ended in 1939. Although there were battalion war histories, they explained, no one had completed the Regiment's story from 1939 until the amalgamation in 1958. A week or two later Nick Speakman (another dynamo behind the Museum) asked if I might like to finish the job. I have no idea whether these two conversations were in any way connected, but the suggestion came at a good moment for me. Earlier that year I had found myself unexpectedly free to follow a new path. Now Nick, Colin and Charles were offering one.

Thanks to them, I have spent the last eighteen months on an enthralling and inspiring journey in excellent company. As I read and wrote, several of my companions, long dead, became a vibrant presence. Leaders in the mould of Colonel Steve, Knocker White and Speedy Bredin, whose devotion to their soldiers and their Regiment shone through their every deed and utterance. Fearless soldiers like William Evans, Sam Thompson, Yorky Seale, Snagger Highett, Joe Symonds, Clive Chettle and Ronald Macnamara. Humourists like Willie Hayes and Knocker White, who seem to have retained their sense of fun even in the darkest hours of battle. Selfless men – Gus Claxton, Joe Chamberlin, Kenneth Prebble, Henry Jesty, Denis Bounsall, Harold Apps and a host of heroic Dorset stretcher bearers – who repeatedly risked their own lives to save others. And countless young men who patiently and bravely did their duty, giving their lives in the process. One of them was twenty-year-old Leslie Willimott, who died in pain and alone in the jungle where even Joe Chamberlin, his Battalion's devoted Medical Officer, could not reach him. Such men, such qualities and such sacrifices should not be forgotten.

Sometimes, reading their words, I could hear their voices. First-hand accounts are almost invariably better than histories, and this book would have been immeasurably poorer without Ivor Ramsay's arresting memories of the retreat to Dunkirk, Jack Coogan's colourful descriptions of the siege of Malta, George Beadle's vivid account of the campaign in Sicily, Knocker White's dazzling history of the 2nd Battalion and Tom Cattle's evocative memories of Burma. These are just a handful of examples that stand out. There are many others, and it is these participants' contributions that have breathed life into this story of their Regiment.

I have had the great pleasure of meeting and writing about some of the surviving Dorsets, most of them National Servicemen, whose memories helped bring to life their post-war experiences in Hong Kong, Korea and Minden. As my lengthy Acknowledgements section demonstrates, this has been a team effort. Far too many people have helped with this book for me to be able to list them again here. I should, however, like to thank Peter Turner, who drew every one of the twenty maps that help tell this story, and Colin Parr and John Murphy, who helped so much in choosing and copying the many pictures we have included. My daughter, Vicky Johnson, has edited and proof-read the whole thing, showing great patience in a demanding task and with a particularly irritating author. Helen Jones at the Keep Museum helped often, and her husband Steve gave up a Saturday to take some of the photographs. But one name stands out. Nick Speakman commissioned the book, advised me throughout its writing, helped research it, helped choose the maps and pictures, raised the money to produce it, introduced me to lots of people who shared their memories, jollied me along and stood for me as a constant reminder of two things: what it means to be a good regimental officer and what it means to be a Dorset. I have been buoyed up throughout by the hospitality, help and kindness I have met from Colin, his recent successor Chris Copson and the staff and volunteers at the Keep. And finally I have been privileged by Cliff Lloyd and Colin Shortis each providing a foreword. As the senior surviving Dorset, General Colin has provided characteristically dynamic support.

I shall always be grateful for having been offered this chance to complete the story of the Dorset Regiment. It has been an honour. I only hope that, with all the help I have received, I have come somewhere near to doing their proud story justice.

Christopher Jary
Frampton–Mgarr–Fontvieille–Rome
November 2012–May 2014

THEY COULDN'T HAVE DONE BETTER

In our heart of hearts believing
Victory crowns the just ...

Thomas Hardy

The 1st Dorsets arriving on Malta June 1939

The 2nd Dorsets taking part in the Aldershot Tattoo June 1939

THE 2ND BATTALION, FRANCE AND BELGIUM 1939–40

1914 REVISITED

THE OUTBREAK OF WAR

At 0445 on Friday 1st September 1939, as German aircraft, tanks and infantry erupted across the Polish border, Neville Chamberlain's policy of appeasing Hitler's Germany exploded in his face. Two days later Great Britain's guarantee to Poland propelled her, inadequately prepared, into a war on a scale unprecedented even by the slaughter of 1914–18.

The war would cost sixty-three million lives. It would be fought in the air, over battlefields, heavily defended cities, distant oceans, deserts, mountains and jungles; and it would end with the dropping from the air of two bombs of a power unimaginable on that Friday in 1939. It would be fought at sea, guarding Britain from invasion across the English Channel and North Sea, shepherding precious convoys across an Atlantic patrolled by U-boats, supplying Stalin's Russia in frost-bitten convoys to Murmansk, in the cauldron of the Mediterranean, and in the sweltering Pacific, where the war would finally end in cataclysmic triumph six years after this ominous and inauspicious beginning. And it would be fought on land between huge armies across three continents – throughout Europe, in North Africa and across large tracts of Asia.

Despite huge technological advances, the Second World War still involved immense conscript armies. The infantry remained foremost on the battlefield in both prominence and casualties. The main body of Britain's infantry was her county regiments. Dorset would be represented on the battlefield by four infantry battalions, who between them would fight first in France, then on Malta, on Sicily and in Italy, in India and Burma, and through France, Belgium and the Netherlands into Germany. Dorset soldiers would be involved from the first to the last – starting with Gort's humiliating retreat through Belgium and France to the beaches at Dunkirk, and ending in Monty's triumphant advance across the plains of North West Germany. They would fight in some of the bloodiest battles – Festubert, Agira, Regalbuto, Kohima, the advance to Mandalay, the D-Day landings, the Normandy bocage, Arnhem, Geilenkirchen and the Rhineland. And they would leave more than a thousand of their friends in war cemeteries from Imtarfa to Calabria, from Kohima to Mount Popa, and from Bayeux to Bremerhaven.

Great Britain's declaration of war on 3rd September 1939 found three of the Dorsets' four battalions in the south of England. The 1st and 2nd were the Regiment's Regular Army battalions while the 4th and 5th were Territorial Army units made up of part-time volunteers.[1]

Only the 1st Battalion were overseas, garrisoning a tiny, sleepy, colonial backwater in the central Mediterranean. In June 1939, they had left India and been despatched – rather to their surprise – to Malta. They had a new commanding officer, Lieutenant-Colonel Ivan de la Bere. In the First World War de la Bere had transferred to the Royal Flying Corps at about the same time as another Dorset officer, Arthur Tedder. While Tedder had stayed with the RFC to become a founder member of the RAF in 1918, de la Bere had been severely wounded before returning to the Dorsets to resume soldiering. He was appointed to command the 1st Battalion soon after their arrival on Malta. For the 1st Dorsets Malta provided a pleasant contrast to the harsh life on the North West Frontier and, despite their disappointment at not having returned home, the troops had enjoyed a relaxing summer in a warm climate remote from the threats and alarms of northern Europe.

The other Regular battalion, the 2nd, were at Aldershot. With the 2nd Royal Warwicks and the 1st Cameron Highlanders, they were in 5 Infantry Brigade, in the 2nd Division of I Corps. Having spent long years in India, Egypt and Palestine, the Dorsets' officers and men had had ample experience policing an empire. Now they would be among the first to have to fight a modern, mechanised war. Their senior officers were brave, experienced men. Colonel Eric Stephenson, known as Colonel Steve, had been commissioned in 1910. In the First World War he had fought in Mesopotamia and France with the Dorsets and the Seaforth Highlanders, returning with three Military Crosses and a mention in Despatches. He had recently succeeded Charles Woodhouse as CO of the 2nd Battalion. His Second-in-Command, Major Dayrell Stayner, had just returned from serving in India with the 1st Battalion. He had been an Acting-Major in the 1st Dorsets in 1918 and twice

---

1   The 3rd Battalion, once the Militia and then the Special Reserve, had not been revived after the First World War.

Colonel Steve DSO MC

mentioned in Despatches. Several of the company commanders were veterans of France and Flanders, and one of them, Major Bob Goff, as a young subaltern in late 1917 had won a Military Cross leading a raid on the German trenches. Like Stayner, Goff was fresh from service on the North West Frontier. Although the First World War had ended more than two decades earlier, the Battalion's senior officers' experience defeating the Kaiser's army would serve them well in their first encounters with Hitler's.

Both the Territorial Army battalions were in Dorset. Since 1920 the Dorsets had had only one Territorial battalion, the 4th, but, as the TA belatedly doubled in size in the summer of 1939, a duplicate battalion was raised. The 5th, which had been created for the First World War and disbanded after the Armistice, was recreated. The 4th and 5th were now brigaded together in the 43rd Wessex Division. The declaration of war found the 4th at Weymouth, recruiting from the north and west of the county and receiving the influx of men who had been sent telegrams mobilising them for war. The 5th were at Poole, recruiting from South and East Dorset, trying to piece together a new battalion and prepare for a world war. Commanding the 4th was Lieutenant-Colonel Donald Baxter, a veteran of the Great War with a Military Cross. The 5th were under the command of a very distinguished 60th

Rifles officer, Lieutenant-Colonel Sir John Lees DSO MC, a Dorset baronet of South Lytchett Manor, who had previously commanded the 4th Dorsets.

During their 1939 summer camp at Corfe Castle the 4th Dorsets had taken part in an exercise in which the 2nd Battalion of the Grenadier Guards held a position which the Dorsets were required to capture. Although it was expected that the part-time soldiers of a county regiment would stand little chance set against some of the cream of the Regular Army, it was thought that their training might benefit from the encounter. In the darkness the poachers and countrymen of the 4th slipped between the Guards' positions and appeared suddenly in their rear, having stolen various prominent bits of the Guards' equipment – helmets, caps and worse – which they now displayed in triumph. Five years later at Arnhem, the Colonel of the 2nd Grenadiers, by then a lieutenant-general, would remember his men's humiliation at the hands of the 4th Dorsets and ask for their help. His name was Frederick, but he was known as *Boy* Browning.

From September 1939 the part-time soldiers of both battalions were embodied to serve full time for so long as *the emergency*, as it was euphemistically called, lasted. Those pre-war Terriers who survived would find themselves serving six years or more but, sadly, many would not live to see their victory.

Over the next six years the Regular and Territorial Dorsets of these four battalions would be supplemented and succeeded by conscripts and volunteers who, but for the war, would never have joined the army. Men from the Durham Light Infantry, the Essex Regiment, the Bedfordshire and Hertfordshire Regiment, the Wiltshire Regiment, the East Surrey Regiment and from many other regiments – including the Royal Artillery – would serve as Dorsets. Men who came not from Dorset but from other parts of the British Isles – Irishmen, Scots, Yorkshiremen, Brummies, Londoners and Welshmen – would wear the Dorset cap badge. Some would even come from another continent; the twenty-four Canadian officers who joined the Regiment simply became *Canadian Dorsets*. That so many from such varied backgrounds would be absorbed into the Regiment so completely and would fight so well with such courage would provide solid proof of the subtle but robust inclusivity of the regimental system. As their fathers had done twenty years before, these civilian soldiers, beside their Regular and Territorial comrades, would add a new chapter to the history of the Dorset Regiment, new honours to its Colours and a fresh lustre to its reputation.

THE PHONEY WAR

The 2nd Battalion were the first Dorsets to go to war. Their advance party, under Major Stayner, left Aldershot at 0500 hours on 13th September. Five days later, their Colonel was taken ill and had to remain in England. Next day the Battalion's mechanised transport left for France. On 23rd September 1939, the main body of the Battalion entrained from Aldershot to Southampton and crossed, as their fathers had done twenty-five years before, to France. Mid-afternoon on 5th October found them at Rumegies on the French-Belgian border and, within a couple of hours, they were visited by the Commander-in-Chief of the British Expeditionary Force (BEF), Lord Gort.

Gort's BEF faced an impossible task. A relatively small force, they found themselves under command of a much larger French army who, since their courageous and costly performance in the First World War, seemed to have lost the will and capacity to fight. Gort's role – balancing the political requirement of maintaining good relationships with our principal ally and obeying his French superiors with protecting the kernel of the British Army and trying to follow sensible military principles – was contradictory and precarious. Nor, despite his extraordinary courage, selflessness and dedication, was he the right man for the job. His performance as a regimental officer in the First World War remained a legend and he was widely admired, but his rapid promotion before the war had been for political, rather than military, reasons. A leader who depended on personal example and a grasp of detail, he lacked the experience, understanding and temperament to make a great commander.

After twenty-five years of imperial policing and political penny-pinching on defence, the BEF were among the first to pay the price. They arrived in battle with little experience or training in modern, combined arms warfare, no effective armour, and few and inadequate anti-tank weapons. They stood little chance against the blitzkrieg tactics of Hitler's Luftwaffe and panzer divisions. Their hopes of holding any German advance depended on two factors: their making good use of any interval before the German onslaught to train their troops in what was to be required, and their French allies standing firm on their flanks. The senior commanders of Gort's BEF were a mixed bag. Some – Alan Brooke, Harold Alexander and Bernard Montgomery – excelled. Others, including some very brave men, would not survive the test of modern battle. Among these were the commanders of I Corps and 2nd Division in the Dorsets' chain of command, both of whom would be taken ill and replaced during the BEF's retreat to the sea.

Some divisions, including the 2nd Division, used the time bought by the Phoney War constructively and trained hard; some did not. Gort's staff and command set-up did little to prepare itself for war, while their Commander-in-Chief's attachment to detail resulted in complicated, inefficient command systems that would fail in battle. Gort was forced to commit to the French strategy of occupying the French-Belgian frontier until any German attack and only then moving forward to engage the Germans in Belgium. The cause of this was political: the Belgians would not allow French or British forces into Belgium. Against the evidence of history, their King believed that, providing they remained neutral, the Germans might not invade. The result of this delusion was a disastrous French plan in which the British and French would await the German invasion before advancing through country they had not been able to reconnoitre to fight an invading enemy on ground he had chosen.

The Dorsets found themselves on the south of the British front, living in empty houses and barns. Here, at Rumegies, they spent a great deal of time and energy fortifying their positions, occupying blockhouses and digging new positions in ground where, in the wet weather, their spades hit water after two or three feet. On 15th October they suffered their first fatality when twenty-nine-year-old Private George Foot of B Company died at the Military Hospital in Douai of pleurisy and peritonitis. On the 17th General Sir John Dill, soon to become Chief of the Imperial General Staff but now commanding I Corps, visited the Battalion. On 31st October Colonel Stephenson arrived, now fully recovered from his illness, and resumed command.

The soldiers of 1939 heard frequent echoes of their fathers' experience in 1914 – the difficulty of digging trenches in the sodden ground, the sluggishness of the mail from home, the strangely pronounced French towns, trying to sleep on a chill autumn night under a single blanket, sudden flaps causing leave to be postponed, and long periods of boredom and discomfort tinged with homesickness and apprehension about the future. The men of 1914 and 1939 also shared an anxiety about enemy spies or, as they were known in the Second World War, *fifth columnists*.

On 1st November C Company reported to Battalion HQ the arrest of a fifth columnist who had been caught snooping around their blockhouse. Bespectacled and wearing army battledress, this fifth columnist was found on closer inspection to be wearing his collar back to front. Thus entered, stage left and slightly unexpectedly, one of the central characters of the 2nd Dorsets' long drama: Captain The Reverend Gus Claxton of the Royal Army Chaplains' Department. He would serve with them throughout the campaign in Belgium and France and then throughout the next one in India and Burma. He too would prove to be a First World War

Major Bob Goff inspecting his men's feet, France 1940

echo – of padres in the Woodbine Willie mould. Once, he entertained the men by playing the piano, unapologetically because there was no other piano, in a brothel in Lille. And he would win the respect and affection of the whole Battalion, together with a Military Cross.

Just before Christmas came yet another First World War echo. Bob Goff's D Company was exchanged with a company on the Maginot Line to gain experience of a livelier part of the front. The 2nd Royal Norfolks had asked specifically for a company from the 2nd Dorsets because of the two battalions' unique relationship formed in Mesopotamia in 1915. Both horribly under strength, the Norfolks and Dorsets had combined and fought for some time as a single unit – *the Norsets*. Now the Norsets were briefly resurrected, and D Company had the opportunity to hold and patrol an area close to the enemy.

In the New Year the Brigade was re-organised with a TA unit, the 7th Worcesters, replacing the 2nd Royal Warwicks. At the Dorsets' Battalion HQ Peter Brind succeeded Howard Cowie as Adjutant. Brind had served in India with the 1st Battalion but had joined the 2nd Battalion just as the war began. He will reappear in our story as Second-in-Command of the 1st Dorsets in 1944, before winning a

DSO commanding the 2nd Devons in the closing stages of the war in Germany. Cowie returned to England, but he too will reappear in a later chapter to take the 4th Dorsets to Normandy.

After a flap in April when the Germans invaded Norway, things quietened down sufficiently in May for Brigadier Gerald Gartlan to take leave in England. The new Adjutant, Peter Brind, did the same. Meanwhile, Colonel Steve took over temporary command of 5 Brigade while once again Dayrell Stayner stood in as CO of the 2nd Dorsets. Thus it was that none of them were occupying their usual chairs when the storm broke on 10th May 1940.

That single day saw two events, one in London, the other in Belgium, that ended the Phoney War and changed world history. In London Chamberlain resigned after a humiliating debate in the House of Commons. At a meeting with his two possible successors, Winston Churchill and Lord Halifax, Chamberlain asked which of them should succeed him. While Churchill remained silent, Halifax observed that it might be difficult for him to lead the country from the House of Lords. Thus the leadership of the British government and of the free world's fight against Nazism passed to the right man for the feeblest of reasons. From that day the conduct of the war would be transformed. Decisiveness and resolute military action replaced self-delusion and political dithering. In the next five years there was not a British serviceman – from the Chief of the Imperial General Staff to the most junior private soldier in the Dorset Regiment – whose life would be unaffected by this transfer of power.

While this quieter drama played out in Westminster, across the Channel the Germans declared their own abrupt end to the Phoney War, bursting into the Low Countries, their bombers flattening the way for their tanks and infantry. For the second time in twenty-five years Germany had invaded Belgium on her way to attack France. And now the BEF complied with the French plan to advance through Belgium to meet and halt the German advance.

BLITZKRIEG

By 13th May the Dorsets were dug in on the Divisional Reserve line west of the River Dyle near Wavre, ten miles south of Louvain. This was the southern-most position on the far right of the BEF, and the Dorsets therefore found a French Algerian division on their right. Colonel Stephenson, who had commanded the Brigade's move into Belgium, now returned while Dayrell Stayner left to take command of the 8th

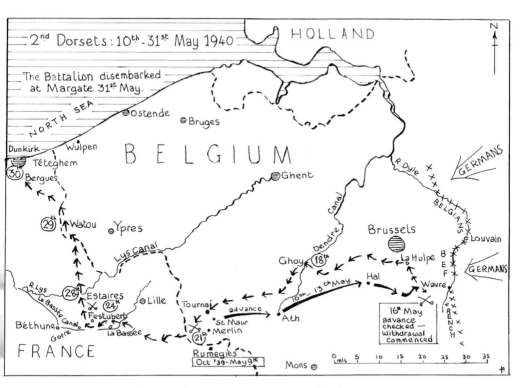

2nd Dorsets' Campaign, France and Belgium 1940

Lancashire Fusiliers. On the 15th, German aircraft bombed and machine-gunned the Dorsets' positions while their troops launched an attack on the Algerian unit beside them. When the Algerian defence weakened, the Dorsets sent D Company and a section of Bren gun carriers up to plug the gap developing on their right. By the evening enemy infantry had turned their attentions to the Dorsets' positions and were engaging their two forward companies.

Echoes of 1914 persisted. At 0130 hours on 16th May the Battalion began a fighting retreat reminiscent of the withdrawal from Mons twenty-five years earlier. Bob Goff's D Company were last out and escaped just in time. At La Hulpe the Battalion dug in to defend a frontage of 3,000 yards. After some inconclusive contact with the advancing enemy, they were ordered to move again to the area of the race course south of Brussels. Next morning they were ordered to retreat another twenty-four miles to Ghoy, west of Brussels. Progress was slow because the roads were crammed with refugees and with Algerian soldiers who, having lost their officers, were heading west. Meanwhile Major Goff, leading a mixed force of carriers and 25mm anti-tank guns, protected the approaches to a bridge on the Battalion's route.

By the early hours of 18th May the Dorsets were dug in on the line of the Dendre Canal, near Ghoy. Early that afternoon a German reconnaissance unit carried out a probing attack on the Battalion's front. It was repulsed by machine gun and mortar fire, which knocked out a German machine gun position. Meanwhile, their supporting field regiment of the Royal Artillery brought down a heavy concentration of fire on a German mechanised transport park which they had spotted in a wood east of the canal. At 1800 hours a warning order was received for another withdrawal next day.

The Battalion pulled out next morning, nearly losing their new padre, who was found fast asleep by the Signals Officer in a last-minute check before leaving the position. Their retreat was covered by a force of Bren gun carriers under Lieutenant Oner Bray[2] and a platoon of A Company under Platoon Sergeant-Major Ted Giles. This small force fought a brave defensive action throughout the morning, Bray winning a Military Cross and Giles a Distinguished Conduct Medal, before successfully disengaging and following the main body of the Battalion.

Second Lieutenant Ivor Ramsay of C Company described the retreat.

It was a warm day and we marched on and on. The further we went the more people were to be seen. They brought jugs of water, milk or beer to the roadside. It was a job to keep the troops going as they tended to queue up for a drink. As we went the RE [Royal Engineers] were blowing up bridges behind us, with tremendous roar and columns of dust visible for miles. Periodically the Bosche came over and bombed and machine-gunned the route. I had a feeling of intense rage at these show offs doing their steep dives and climbs and thinking themselves no end of fellows.

Everyone was tired before we started and as the long march continued we became footsore and painfully stiff. As I was in the rear of the Company I was kept hard at it trying to keep the stragglers going. The majority of these were men who had not been on training: mess staff, sanitary orderlies etc.

At about one o'clock we halted, pretty well all in. It was at a crossroads where a bomb had burst a short time before. It had blown in a house and killed four gunners, literally blowing them to pieces and plastering bits of them over the walls of the house and in the branches of a tree.

We waited over an hour at this place and then learnt that RASC lorries were waiting for us about a mile further on. We limped up to them and crammed everyone in.

---

2   Despite being a good shot, Hubert Bray had earned his nickname, Oner, by scoring only one hit on the ranges reputedly after a liquid lunch.

As the French army on the Dorsets' right collapsed, the next four days followed the same exhausting and depressing pattern: painfully sluggish retreats along roads crammed with army transport and pathetic, straggling columns of Belgian refugees trying to escape the relentless and sometimes brutal invaders. Most upsetting was the spectacle of Tournai, which they had left only a few days before and which now was ablaze and littered with the corpses of civilians killed by the Luftwaffe's bombing and strafing.

Ivor Ramsay vividly recalled the large grass space previously used as a children's playground and for football, where *now there were well camouflaged gun positions and a long trench filled with infantry... it was a lovely summer evening and the sun was setting. One expected to see people strolling about or playing cricket, with houses flung open to the balmy air. Instead this silence, broken and empty houses with shuttered windows and the pervading smoke.*

During the 21st, while they were in brigade reserve at St Maur, the Dorsets suffered thirty casualties from heavy German shelling. Major Sam Symes led the Battalion, and Captain Chips Heron and Ivor Ramsay, marching together, met Second Lieutenant John Asser riding in one of the carriers. In Ramsay's words, Asser *was understudying Oner as carrier commander* and... *had a slight wound in the head.*

They lost more men from shelling the next day at Merlin, where a fighter strafed Battalion HQ, and they finally arrived, via La Bassée, at Festubert on 24th May. On the way they had marched past the bodies of French women and children who had been machine-gunned by low-flying German aircraft. The sight hardened the Dorsets' resolve just as their Division were asked to stand and fight a rearguard action to allow retreating British troops to cross the La Bassée canal before all the bridges were blown.

La Bassée and Festubert were already inscribed in blood in the Regiment's history. Here, at Pont Fixe, on 13th October 1914, the 1st Dorsets had fought a heroic defence at a cost of 460 casualties. Now, a quarter of a century later on 25th May 1940, an already exhausted and heavily outnumbered 2nd Battalion would be asked to emulate their courage by holding the position to allow other units to escape.

THE BATTLE OF FESTUBERT

The war diary described the positions occupied by the Dorsets.

The Battalion dug in on the line of the La Bassée-Bethune Canal on a frontage of nearly 4,000 yards, being responsible for three bridges, two of which were completely destroyed and one partially destroyed. 8th Lancashire Fusiliers were on the right and the 7th Worcestershire Regiment on the left. The position was held with B, A and C Companies forward... Heavy casualties were suffered during the day from shelling. Enemy co-operation [artillery observation] aircraft were over the Battalion position at an average height of 2,500 feet during the hours of daylight. Any movement by day appeared to be quickly observed, and accurate shelling followed with little delay.

When rifle and machine gun fire failed, the Dorsets propped up anti-tank rifles to fire at the German spotter aircraft.

Supplies were not getting through. Mortar and artillery shells were running short and the Dorsets were on half rations, which they supplemented with the produce of local farms and gardens. After their long retreat, they were tired,

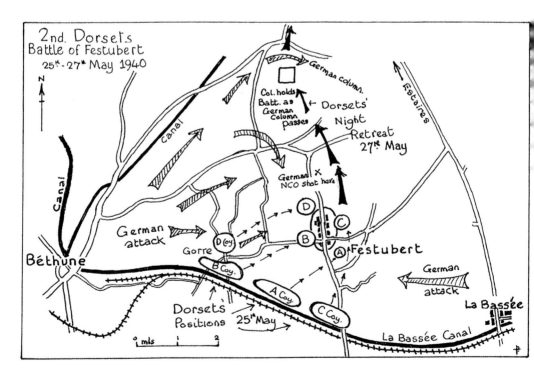

Battle of Festubert 25th–27th May 1940

hungry and dirty. Opposite them, across the canal, were two motorised battalions of the 4th Panzer Division. On 25th May they mustered 960 fighting soldiers against the Dorsets' 380. They were supported by two panzer companies each with twelve tanks, against which the Dorsets had two 25mm anti-tank guns and eight Boys anti-tank rifles, which were almost entirely useless.

The Battalion were very thinly stretched over a huge, featureless area north of the canal. Their historian, Colonel Knocker White, tells us that *A Company took a mile of front... C Company continued the line for another fifteen hundred yards... It was about two and a half miles from Battalion Headquarters to B Company and about a mile or so down the road to C Company... the country was exceedingly open, so flat indeed as practically to deny to the defenders the power of movement in the open by day, but the situation in Gorre was quite tricky. B Company were widely extended in Gorre village, with two platoons up on the canal. Owing to the defection of the French and the failure of the Lancashire Fusiliers to reach the canal, their right flank was wide open... by 1100 hrs D Company were on the move to Gorre to stop this gap on the right. Bob Goff's D Company had a pretty rough passage across the open, losing fifteen men.*

Shelling also took a heavy toll. Battalion HQ, occupying a First World War German pillbox, was hit, and the Adjutant, Peter Brind, who had rushed back from leave in London to rejoin the Battalion, was wounded and evacuated. Oner Bray took over and young John Asser in turn stepped into his shoes to command the Carrier Platoon. That evening the bulk of HQ Company and soldiers who were not essential to the defence were withdrawn. A Company was out of contact with the rest of the Battalion from noon until midnight, when contact was restored.

During the night of 25th/26th May patrols were sent out to provide early warning of any German attack or raid. Meanwhile, three men defending the Gorre brewery – Sergeant Jimmy James and two Irishmen, Privates Thomas Tabb and James Sinnott – swam the canal with grenades strapped to their heads to gather intelligence by searching the bodies of a German machine gun team on the far bank. All three men returned unscathed and were recommended for the Military Medal. Sadly, twenty-two-year-old James Sinnott was killed next day and, as a result of a bureaucratic misinterpretation of the meaning of the word *posthumous*, his award was reduced to a mention in Despatches, which was gazetted nearly two years later.[3]

---

3   During the Second World War only the VC, GC and mentions in Despatches could be awarded posthumously. Sinnott's award was not, however, posthumous because he was not killed winning it.

On the following day the warm weather changed to heavy rain. Having been up all night siting his positions, Ivor Ramsay was soaked through. Taking off his drenched battledress, he donned the only other uniform he had with him: his khaki drill best. Then he had breakfast. *Soon after I had finished Major Molloy came round. As always he was most cheerful and seemed to be enjoying himself. He remarked 'This is the life, isn't it?' He had been visiting our platoons and was on his way to A Company. He stopped with us for about three quarters of an hour. We were very happy to see him. Not only because it gave us a chance of hearing the wider picture. He chaffed me about my smart uniform and asked had I put it on to go to church. I realised it was Sunday.*

Early that morning enemy shelling wounded an officer and three more men, and the Luftwaffe dropped leaflets across the 2nd Division's front, urging the British to surrender because they were surrounded. At 0900 some German troops advanced, screened from the Dorsets' rifles by a party of French women and children. On the flank, however, a single Bren gun was able to fire without endangering the civilians. Six Germans were killed. Throughout the day the German artillery and mortars kept up their shelling, and the field gunners and the Dorsets' mortars retaliated. Ivor Ramsay was hit in the eye by a splinter from a mortar bomb. Beside him Lance-Corporal Walker was wounded in the back while Private Smith, the Company cook, lost a thumb and another man was shell-shocked. The Dorsets' Mortar Platoon hit a French ammunition train behind the German positions south of the canal. The huge explosion killed and wounded some Germans and wounded nine more Dorsets, bringing their casualties for the two days 25th and 26th May to sixty.

At 0430 on the 27th the SS Totenkopf Division crossed the canal about 1,000 yards on the Dorsets' right and established a bridgehead on what had been the Lancashire Fusiliers' forward positions. Two platoons of D Company and some Vickers guns of the Argyll and Sutherland Highlanders' Company moved across to Gorre Wood to support B Company. Here they were able to engage the enemy as they advanced 800 yards away. The SS retaliation – with mortars and machine guns – was rapid, inflicting twenty-five casualties. At 0730 Battalion Headquarters were bombed by the Luftwaffe. Meanwhile, the field gunners shelled the canal where German combat engineers were trying to erect a crossing that could be used by medium tanks. By 0930 hours the Germans had succeeded, and heavy weapons were able to cross the canal.

At 1000 B Company were attacked on their open right flank but Sergeant Walter Cooper of the Bren Gun Carrier Platoon arrived with two carriers full of ammunition. Chips Heron, a pre-war TA officer, led a gallant attack with the two carriers, inflicting heavy casualties on the enemy and blocking their attempt to outflank the Battalion. Later that morning, when the enemy tried again to outflank their position, Sergeant Cooper repeated Heron's tactic with similar success. Happily both men survived to receive, respectively, a Military Cross and a Distinguished Conduct Medal.

Also at 1000 the rest of the carriers were sent out under their new commander, John Asser. Embroiled in a heavy engagement south-east of Loisnes, they lost one carrier and their brave young platoon commander. The son of a retired Dorset Regiment Brigadier-General, John Asser was just nineteen years old.

At noon 17 Platoon were sent up to the north-west of Gorre Wood to forestall yet another threatened attack on the Battalion's right rear. During this action the German machine guns knocked out 17 Platoon's supporting machine gun section from the Argylls.

Two Platoon Sergeant-Majors, both called Brown, distinguished themselves in this bitter defensive battle. Reg Brown commanded a platoon in B Company and held on for ten hours under heavy shell fire and during several fierce attacks. Meanwhile, Sidney Brown's platoon in S Company was on the canal defending a crossing. Under shell and machine gun fire, they drove off two German attempts to cross. At the end of the battle both Browns successfully extricated the survivors of their platoons and both later received the Distinguished Conduct Medal.

Platoon Sergeant-Major Sidney Brown DCM

Throughout the morning and well into the afternoon, and at great cost, the Dorsets continued to hold the German advance. By lunchtime their communications had broken down both with Brigade Headquarters and also within the Battalion itself. On their right the 8th Lancashire Fusiliers had been overrun and their new CO, Colonel Dayrell Stayner, had been forced to surrender.[4] A few survivors managed to escape capture and join the Dorsets during the day. By early afternoon the Germans had widened their bridgehead across the canal by over a mile. The Dorsets were being outflanked and would not be able to hold on much longer.

Having received a warning order at 1430 to withdraw, at 1515 Colonel Steve finally received the order: *You will hold Festubert unless attacked, when you will withdraw fighting.* He at once ordered his rifle companies to withdraw to an inner defensive perimeter in Festubert village. Two old hands, Bob Goff and Sam Symes, commanding B and D Companies, managed to surmount the problems of poor communication and withdraw their companies from contact. During the withdrawal D Company lost two Platoon Sergeant-Majors, Meakin and Bowles, while the runners of B Company ran into advancing enemy troops from whom they only just escaped. Sadly, Harry Meakin was killed, but John Bowles recovered, to be mentioned in Despatches and commissioned. Under heavy mortaring, Private Harold West scurried about tending the wounded and winning the first of several Military Medals earned during the war by the Dorsets' heroic stretcher-bearers.

At 1645 hours, before they were in their new positions, the men of B and C Companies had to beat off another German infantry assault with armoured support. For the loss of two anti-tank rifles, the Dorsets drove off the attack. But less than an hour later another German unit attacked, supported by twelve tanks. Met by a hail of artillery, anti-tank, machine gun and rifle fire, the Germans again withdrew, leaving three of their tanks blazing. But the attack had cost the Dorsets another of their anti-tank rifles and eight of their precious carriers.

At 1800 the Dorsets' surviving vehicles withdrew under the command of a new officer, Lieutenant Hugh Wyllie. On the road they ran into a German armoured unit and almost all, including Wyllie, were captured.

Half an hour later, after the Battalion had begun thinning out its forward positions to withdraw from Festubert, the Germans launched yet another attack with tanks and infantry. Breaking into Festubert village, according to Colonel White, they were *held up by D Company's road block reinforced with some Royal Warwicks and Royal Irish Fusiliers, but continued to fire straight down the village street. The*

Company's one remaining anti-tank weapon, a Boys rifle, was knocked out imme-
diately, but the company commander moved the remainder of D Company into an
orchard on the left of the road, and for a quarter of an hour an intense close-quarter
battle was fought, both sides firing point blank at each other, at the end of which time
the Boche decided to pull out. Bob Goff had been slightly wounded in the head before
this last attack developed but, despite this, he continued to fight his company with the
utmost gallantry. Any hesitation on his part or lack of steadfastness on the part of the
company would have left that part of the perimeter wide open...

Having lost three tanks in that attack, at 1930 the Germans tried again, this time
with just infantry. This final attack was again repulsed with machine gun, mortar
and small arms fire.

By dusk the Dorsets found themselves surrounded and by-passed by the German
forces now advancing westwards behind them. But, having reached the Estaires
road, 4th Panzer Division paused. The 2nd Battalion's heroic defence had cost
them 308 casualties: forty killed, 110 wounded and 158 prisoners of war. One
of those taken prisoner – thirty-eight-year-old Sergeant Snowy Mullins who had
served nineteen years in the Regiment – recognised the senior Wehrmacht officer
who captured him as Erwin Rommel. Mullins and his fellow Dorset prisoners
of war now faced five long years in captivity; but they fared better than the 2nd
Royal Norfolks and 2nd Royal Warwicks, who together had 180 prisoners of war
murdered by the SS on 27th and 28th May.

ESCAPE AND EVACUATION

It was now that Colonel Steve led the break-out by the 245 survivors of his
Battalion and forty men of other units, including Worcesters, Argylls, Royal Irish
Fusiliers and Royal Warwicks. Following the gaunt figure of their Colonel, they
slipped quietly into the darkness, away from Festubert. Compass in hand and with
Major Tom Molloy by his side, Colonel Steve now personally navigated and led the
remnants of his Battalion – across fields, round houses and farms, across fences
and roads travelled by the advancing Germans. At 2330 hours, when challenged
by a German soldier, Stephenson, flanked by two soldiers with rifles and bayonets,
ordered them to bayonet the man. When they hesitated, the Colonel quickly shot
him with his revolver. Inexplicably, the pistol shot evoked no response from the
German's comrades and the Dorsets were able to move on. At 0115, when they
reached a main road and found it jammed by a German motorised column making

slow progress, all 285 men crouched silently by its side for forty-five minutes until the column had finally passed and they could move on.

At 0200 it began to rain heavily. Half an hour later they reached the first of two canal crossings and Oner Bray and John Peebles swam the canal twice to reconnoitre before the main body could cross, with those who could swim shepherding the non-swimmers through the deep water.

They reached Estaires at 0500 on 28th May to find Sappers preparing to blow up the bridge, and the remaining British troops evacuating the town. After a halt of three hours they marched on another twenty miles to Watou. The whole exhausting day was spent on the march, which Colonel White later described vividly.

The going on this day was pure hell. Feet soaked from the drenching of the night before and boots in ribbons after the fierce marching of the past few weeks, and, finally, the rough, hard road down which they now had to continue the withdrawal in torrential rain...

They arrived at 2100 hours to find that their escape had come as a complete surprise to the rest of the BEF. In turn, they were astonished to hear for the first time that units of the BEF were already being evacuated from Dunkirk. Gort, a man of immense courage but limited vision placed in an impossible position by Anglo-French politics, had nonetheless grasped and acted on the reality of the situation. Ignoring orders from the War Cabinet and appeals from his French allies, and bolstered by three stalwarts, Brooke, Montgomery and Alexander, he resolved to save the BEF. Faced by the most important decision of his life, he got it right.

Within half an hour, parties of the Dorsets were moved in precious lorries north-west to Bergues, just below Dunkirk. On the afternoon of 29th May the Battalion assembled on the line of the Furnes Canal near Téteghem, where they remained until the evening of the following day. Leaving a party of twenty men under Second Lieutenant Peter Stephenson – a distant cousin of the Commanding Officer known throughout the Battalion as Young Steve – to guard the bridges, the Battalion now marched with all their platoon weapons through Dunkirk. Twenty-year-old Stephenson and his men slipped safely away from the canal and, catching alternative transport, rejoined the Battalion a few days later. We will encounter Young Steve again, much later in this story and in unexpected circumstances.

Not far away another Dorset was also helping to form the rearguard. On 29th May, Company Quartermaster Sergeant William Trusler found himself commanding about thirty men holding the northern bank of the canal running north-east from Wulpen. Undeterred by heavy enemy mortar fire, his men brought accurate rifle

The evacuation from Dunkirk

fire to bear on enemy machine gun positions and on various parties trying to cross the canal. Recommended by the Officer Commanding Number 2 Reception Camp for a Military Medal, Trusler was later mentioned in Despatches.

Meanwhile, Colonel Steve led his Battalion into the port. Ivor Ramsay, who, despite his eye wound, had remained with his Company, later described the scene.

On the beach was a mass of wrecked vehicles; many more had been driven out into the sea forming piers to help embarkation. There were a number of dead horses. It was dusk but we could see a destroyer beached and broken in two, very close in.

We were formed up five deep and tacked on to the end of a long serpentile procession. Then bit by bit we advanced along the beach. In these perfect sands were huge bomb craters as well as innumerable smaller ones as well as shell holes. The soft deep sand must have saved a vast number of lives. On a rocky shore the casualties would have been terrific.

Every five or ten minutes the Germans shelled the harbour. As we got near the mole a salvo came whistling over to land not so far away. Everyone was a bit edgy, being herded together and hardly making any progress, with the evidence of the effects of bombardment all around.

A voice said 'It's all right, they are not shelling you, only the dock yard. How many men have you got here?'

We saw it was the Brigadier, wearing his red hat. Yesterday he told us that he had been ordered off, and to his regret would not be able to see us embark. However, here he still was, radiating confidence.

We got onto the mole and seemed to go a long way on it. One of the Embarkation Staff Officers came fussing up and gave some order that I could not hear, to the effect that we were to split up. The CO was at our head, and we remained as we were. The ESO started swearing at us, until the CO told him to shut up and stop talking tripe. 'I am not going to split up my Battalion.' So we carried on.

A little further and another of this fraternity said 'Now it's absolutely essential to double after this point.' It was where the mole debouched from behind a moored or sunken ship. The CO continued to lead quietly on. The ESO screamed at us till once again told in unmistakable language to shut up. As the CO remarked later 'What the hell did he think would be achieved by doubling in the dark out towards the end of a shell-broken mole?'

We continued to walk steadily on till we could go no farther, and there we sat down in our close packed ranks and waited for four or five hours. The mole had started as concrete and later changed to a wooden structure, with every now and then a gap made by a shell hit. While we waited we were entertained by fireworks. We would see the flashes of the German guns, then hear the whistle of the shells, then the explosions. Many went into the water, but frequently one would land on the mole, then there would be the call for stretchers. Tom Molloy was a tower of strength organising and helping to embark the wounded.

Aircraft activity was constant, and we watched the tracer curling up towards them. The sea itself was full of the most astoundingly brilliant phosphorescence which illuminated the passage of boats.

At last our ship came alongside and we boarded her. The Dorsets, some of the Camerons and one or two odds and ends. As I went alongside the deck an unperturbed voice said 'I think we must have got on the wrong ship. This one's sunk already.'

One of the crew was passing at the time, and overheard the speaker, Major Symes, who was looking down what appeared to be a flooded hold, where phosphorescent water could be seen swilling about. 'Don't worry about that, sir. This is a mud dredger.'

We went below and managed to get some bread and cheese. One of the friendly crew was asking us – would we believe it? They had not even been issued with steel helmets to come over. But we were feeling completely safe within steel walls. Responsibility was no longer ours.

Soon afterwards we moved off, and I went on deck, and looked back at blazing Dunkirk with the silent tracer shells soaring gracefully up. No longer our concern. I went below and fell asleep on the floor.

While most of the 2nd Battalion's survivors disembarked at Margate at 0830 on 31st May, at least one of them had been left behind. Private Alf Finch, a pre-war Territorial with the 4th Battalion, had only joined the 2nd Dorsets in April. During his embarkation leave he and his young fiancée had been married in Sherborne Abbey. At Dunkirk he had been seconded to the Provost staff directing the evacuation and, when the last ship had gone, Finch and his detachment were told to find their own way home. Hitching a ride on a cattle truck, they reached St Malo and caught the last boat to England, arriving on 16th June. But his adventures were far from over. We will meet Alf Finch again.

Colonel Steve's Battalion were part of a defeated army which, unlike the BEF of 1914, had been forced to withdraw from the European mainland. They had been sent to war ill-equipped, with obsolete weapons and with senior officers and staff inadequately trained in modern warfare. They had been committed to a plan which could not work. They had been let down by allies who, twenty-five years earlier, had fought like tigers but who now ran away. They had faced a well-equipped, professionally trained modern army which had already rehearsed its blitzkrieg tactics in Poland. The British Army as a whole had some hard lessons to absorb before it would be able to meet that enemy again on equal terms. But for the Dorsets there was some solid reassurance. Despite the pathetic inadequacy of their anti-tank weapons, despite their woeful lack of armoured support, despite the craven unreliability of their allies and despite the breakdown of their divisional and corps commanders, they had met the Germans head-on in battle at Festubert and seen them off time and again.

The brief, disastrous campaign in Belgium and France had cost them forty killed. Two thirds of their original strength had been killed, wounded or captured, but the 2nd Battalion had won new honours for the Regiment: three Military Medals and four Distinguished Conduct Medals, Military Crosses for Chips Heron, Oner Bray and John Peebles, and OBEs for Majors Sam Symes and Bob Goff, for whom the DSO might have been a more fitting reward. Finally, there was a hard-won DSO for the middle-aged man who had taken them to war, commanded them so success-fully in battle and then, despite exhaustion, led the survivors through the German lines safely home. Having held the enemy at Festubert, Colonel Steve had managed to save more of his soldiers than any other commanding officer in the 2nd Division and had set a standard of professionalism and devotion to his men which future Dorset colonels would have to work very hard to match.

A Strange Honour for a Dorset

But these medals earned by the 2nd Battalion were not quite the first to be won by Dorsets in the Second World War. The first – by a whisker – was an award to an ex-Dorset officer and, curiously, it was a Bar to the Distinguished Flying Cross.

Three weeks after the return of the 2nd Battalion, the *London Gazette* contained the following announcement:

Air Ministry, 21st June, 1940

ROYAL AIR FORCE

The KING has been graciously pleased to approve the undermentioned awards, in recognition of gallantry displayed in flying operations against the enemy:—

Awarded a Bar to the Distinguished Flying Cross
Pilot Officer Louis Arbon STRANGE, DSO, MC, DFC (78522), RAF Volunteer Reserve.

Pilot Officer Strange was detailed to proceed from Hendon to Merville to act as ground control officer during the arrival and departure of various aircraft carrying food supplies. He displayed great skill and determination whilst under heavy bombing attacks and machine-gun fire at Merville, where he was responsible for the repair and successful despatch of two aircraft to England. In the last remaining aircraft, which was repaired under his supervision, he returned to Hendon, in spite of being repeatedly attacked by Messerschmitts until well out to sea. He had no guns in action and had never flown this type of aircraft previously, but his brilliant piloting enabled him to return with this much needed aircraft.

The award of a Bar to a DFC so early in the war was unusual – there had barely been time to win one award, let alone two. But what made it unique were the previous awards won by this apparently very junior RAF officer. In reality, Louis Strange was far from junior and he was not a young man. Originally commissioned from the Dorset Yeomanry into the Dorset Regiment in July 1914, he had flown with the Royal Flying Corps in the First World War and reached the rank of lieutenant-colonel. He had become a legend in May 1915 after falling out of his aircraft having unstrapped his harness to change the magazine on his Lewis gun during a dogfight. His aircraft suddenly turned upside down and he was left swinging below it, suspended from the jammed magazine. Somehow he had found the strength to swing his feet back into the cockpit and to right the aircraft. He was a lucky – and agile – man. Between the wars he had returned to his family's farm at Worth Matravers but, when he tried to rejoin the Royal Air Force in 1939, he was allowed to do so only as a Pilot Officer in the RAFVR. Louis Strange would serve throughout the Second World War and return to Purbeck, aged fifty-four, as a Wing Commander.

MALTA 1939-42 G.C.

Valletta's Grand Harbour by John Worsley

2

The 1st Battalion, Malta 1940–43

The Station of the Cross

1940

The events in France that had engulfed the 2nd Battalion now precipitated the 1st Battalion, 1,300 miles away on sleepy Malta, into battle. For the nine months since the outbreak of war, the jackal Mussolini had been hesitating. Despite scenting the rich pickings he might snatch by joining Nazi Germany's war with Britain and France, he wanted first to see how the more powerful beasts fared in their encounter in France. The collapse of the French army and the BEF's evacuation from Dunkirk finally decided him. On 10th June 1940, Italy declared war on Great Britain and on the already defeated France. Malta, which a year earlier had seemed to the 1st Dorsets a forgotten colonial backwater, was hurled suddenly, utterly unprepared, into the front line of world events.

When the 1st Dorsets had arrived from India in June 1939, Private Bill Chutter,[1] a battalion signaller, had been struck by the contrast with the North West Frontier: *It seemed like transferring into heaven.* Until the spring of 1940 the Battalion's activities were restricted to garrison duties, training and sending small parties afloat on Royal Naval contraband patrols, but on 17th April the Malta Garrison had been ordered to man the island's defences. The four British infantry battalions – the 1st Dorsets, 2nd Devons, 2nd Royal Irish Fusiliers and 2nd Queen's Own Royal West Kents – divided between themselves the task of defending Malta, the Dorsets assuming responsibility for the south-eastern quarter below Valletta. By 1700 hours on the 17th the Battalion was occupying its war stations on Malta's east coast at St Thomas Bay near Marsascala and Marsaxlokk. The names of these towns provide a clue to the nature of the Battalion's charge. In Maltese *Marsa* means harbour, and the island's east coast contained a number of little ports, ranging from tiny fishing ports to the naval flying boat base at Kalafrana.[2]

---

5   Bill Chutter celebrated his hundredth birthday in May 2014.
6   Maltese is a form of Arabic but it is written in the Latin alphabet, creating some peculiarities, such as x being pronounced *sh* and q usually being silent.

The island's geography determined her fate. In the central Mediterranean, south of Sicily and east-south-east of Tunis, the tiny island – 122 miles square and smaller than the Isle of Wight – dominated the sea and air routes between Italy and North Africa. Any craft steaming or flying between the two must pass within range of aircraft, surface ships or submarines operating from Malta's four airfields and two enormous natural harbours. Mussolini knew that, to supply his million-strong army in Libya and expand his North African empire by attacking the British in Egypt, he must first clear a safe passage across the Mediterranean by capturing or neutralising Malta.

The geography that made Malta strategically important also left her desperately vulnerable. At the outset of war, she lay almost totally unprotected within eighty miles of Mussolini's Sicilian airfields. At the beginning of her three-year siege, Malta's defences totalled thirty-four heavy and twenty-two light anti-aircraft guns, four Sea Gladiator fighters (which were there by accident), four submarines and a few other light surface vessels.

Malta is a mix of cultures and her people a blend of races. Across the centuries any civilisation traversing the Mediterranean – Greeks, Phoenicians, Romans, Arabs, Turks, French and British – came to Malta and left their mark. In 60 AD, St Paul's shipwreck there, when under guard on his way to Rome to face trial, began

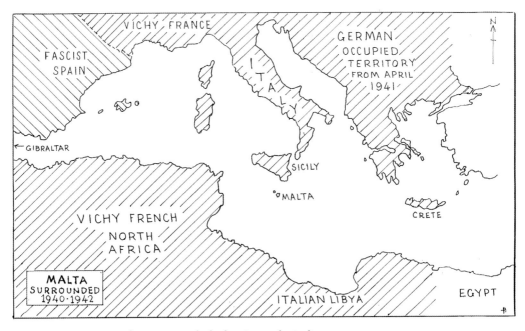

Malta Surrounded: the Central Mediterranean 1940–42

the conversion of the Maltese to Christianity centuries ahead of most of Europe. The Maltese remained a devout race whose Roman Catholic faith bound them closely together. Geographically, Malta might be African, but religiously, culturally and politically, her people looked north to Europe. Before the war many Maltese had felt an affinity with their nearest neighbour, Roman Catholic Italy. Mussolini's attacks would change their attitude: the Maltese people would throw in their lot with the British and pay a heavy price.

Geologically, the three islands – Malta, Gozo and tiny Comino – are reminiscent of the rocky, djebel terrain of Northern Tunisia. Their landscape is striking, rather than pretty. The overall impression is yellow. Yellow rocks, yellow buildings and a yellow light from a sun which is gentle for most of the year but which, from June to September, can create a relentless, blazing heat relieved only by the wind from a sea which is never far away. Gozo, Malta's vegetable garden, is greener but, during the fierce summer, even there the grass dries out and turns to dust-coloured scrub. In the rural villages of Malta and Gozo, the scattered small stone houses with flat roofs, the ubiquitous cacti, stone walls and goats recreate a biblical landscape.

Malta's old capital, Mdina, was built in traditional Arab style, its high walls and tall, yellow stone houses and churches forming narrow, shady passages to avoid the summer sun. Built as a fortress on a high hill in the centre of the island, Mdina commanded spectacular views across the island. To the north lay Malta's north coast, whose western stretch offered an invading army some inviting beaches on which to land. On the plain below Mdina lay RAF Takali, a fighter airfield, and beyond it the town of Mosta with its enormous dome. On a hill to the north-east stood the modern capital, Valletta, flanked by its two enormous harbours, Marsamxett and Grand Harbour. Below, to the east, was Malta's main airfield, RAF Luqa, which was large enough to accommodate bombers as well as fighters. A couple of miles beyond lay the other airfields, Hal Far and Safi, and beyond those the Royal Naval base at Kalafrana. This was the sector that the 1st Dorsets were now ordered to defend.

To the south-west of Mdina the land was less populated. Peppered with rocks and stone walls, it was mostly farmland, which stopped abruptly at the precipitous cliffs that characterised Malta's south coast. Towards the western tip three small beaches offered potential sites for a landing, but all were dominated by surrounding high ground, including Marfa Ridge, the high, north-western tip of the island.

Malta had been besieged before. Four centuries earlier the Knights of St John, supported by the Maltese people, had withstood one of the bloodiest sieges in history. Even by the standards of 1565, both sides – the Knights supported by the

Maltese, and the Turks – behaved barbarously, but it is worth recalling that the entire population of Gozo had been abducted to become Turkish slaves. When the Knights finally emerged victorious, they built a new capital, named after their leader, La Vallette. With her future defence in mind, Valletta was built on a high promontory between Malta's two natural harbours: Marsamxett Harbour beyond her west walls and Grand Harbour to the east. Massive fortifications dominated its high walls, which towered over the sea. Yet the Knights still contrived to build a beautiful, modern, European city. Designed on a grid pattern, its principal streets ran north-south, crossed by a succession of smaller streets running only east-west. Its houses, all built at the turn of the 16th century, were baroque. It was a capital to be proud of, whose ancient defences would serve the Maltese well in the modern

Malta GC

siege that was beginning now. And her foundations – the massive expanses of limestone below them – would convert readily into enormous air raid shelters to protect her population against the weight of the 20th century weaponry that would be hurled down on them.

Over the next three years the island's civilian population, its own servicemen of the King's Own Malta Regiment and the Royal Malta Artillery, and its British defenders – sailors, soldiers and airmen – would together confront and surmount unimaginable hardships and deprivation. Parts of Malta, notably the three old cities of Senglea, Cospicua and Vittoriosa to the east of Valletta's Grand Harbour, would become some of the most heavily bombed places on the face of the earth. Blasted from their homes, people would first be driven to live underground and then starved almost to the point of surrender. Although the island would remain a perpetual, painful thorn in her enemies' side, only a few inhabitants would have the chance to hit back at their relentless attackers. Malta's vital contribution to ultimate victory in the Mediterranean theatre lay in her continued resistance, and her Maltese and British inhabitants' unique courage lay in their dogged refusal, whatever the cost, to give in.

The Italian assault began at dawn on 11th June 1940, when the bombers of their Regia Aeronautica launched the first of eight raids that day. Their principal target was Grand Harbour, but Malta's airfields were also bombed. The eighth and heaviest raid came in the evening and fell on the dockyard. Despite the barrage put up by the few anti-aircraft guns defending the harbour, twenty-two civilians were killed. Two civilian dockyard workers, one Maltese, one British, won George Medals for continuing their dangerous work throughout the bombing. In the last of these raids Verdala Barracks, behind Cospicua, were hit and several houses demolished. Fifteen Dorsets in the barracks were injured by splinters and flying debris, but thirteen of them returned to duty immediately after receiving medical treatment.

Between 11th June and the end of the month the Dorsets' war diary recorded no fewer than fifty Italian raids. Fuller and more descriptive than the professionally terse, often uninformative war diary was the illicit diary begun that day by one of their soldiers, Private Jack Coogan. The first entry – for 11th June – read:

That day I was in the sangar [observation post] *looking out for hostile planes. On the morning of Tuesday at seven o'clock I heard the air raid alarm go up. Then you could hear the droning of the enemy planes coming in. I looked above and could see eight fighters with two bombers. When they had reached the harbour they released their bombs. I thought that Malta took her first air raid with a good heart. All told, Malta had eight air raids. Damage not known.*

Two days later the 1st Battalion's war diary recorded *eight further air raids over Malta by day.* During the last raid of the day a Royal Navy launch, returning to Grand Harbour having beached an impounded Italian merchantman a couple of miles east of the harbour entrance, was accidentally hit by a shell from a coastal battery. From one of their concrete sangars lining the rocky shore near Xghajra, three Dorsets, Lance-Corporal Edward Read and Privates Richard Munday and Jack Bagge, saw the launch sink some distance out and her crew floundering in the water. Each of them swam out twice, between them rescuing five sailors, despite the treacherous currents and themselves nearly drowning through exhaustion. Six months later the *Times of Malta* reported the award of the newly instituted George Medal to each of the three men. The report was incorrect. Although they had been recommended for the GM, the recommendation had been reduced to a King's Commendation apiece. Nearly nine years later, however, their Commendations were cancelled and each finally received a George Medal. Their awards were thus the first and the last army gallantry awards won during the siege of Malta and the first and last of sixty-seven won by the 1st Dorsets in the Second World War.

Their citation reads:

During an evening raid by enemy aircraft on Malta, in 1940, several motor launches were observed to be in difficulties, and personnel were seen to be swimming for the shore about a quarter of a mile out. Lance Corporal Read and Privates Munday and Bagge immediately entered the water and swam out, each bringing back a survivor. Privates Bagge and Munday swam out again, each bringing in another survivor, and were followed by Lance Corporal Read who had observed that Private Bagge was in difficulties. Together they brought back a third survivor; Private Munday was by this time practically exhausted. By reason of this prompt and gallant action, five persons were saved.

For the first couple of weeks the island's principal defence was its inadequate anti-aircraft guns. Its sole air defence – and a much-needed boost to morale – appeared in the form of three obsolete, ex-Fleet Air Arm, Gloster Gladiators. The Maltese characteristically nicknamed these relics *Faith*, *Hope* and *Charity* as they saw them daily taking to the skies, often vainly trying to intercept Italian bombers they could hardly catch. But on the evening of the 22nd one of the Gladiators found itself positioned high above an Italian reconnaissance aircraft. With the advantage of height and surprise, its pilot George Burges closed in high above Valletta and sent the enemy aircraft spinning in flames into the sea. The Dorset war diarist recorded this first victory with satisfaction, adding that two of the Italian crew had baled out and been taken prisoner. The next day's diary entry described Burges's second even more remarkable kill, a Macchi fighter, which had been escorting the bombers.

Meanwhile, Malta's pitiful air defence had been strengthened by the addition of eight Hurricanes which, en route to Egypt, were abruptly diverted to join the garrison's strength. On 3rd July a third enemy aircraft was brought down and on the 4th low-flying Italian aircraft strafed the airfield at Hal Far. On the 6th two more aircraft were shot down, but Verdala Barracks was hit again.

On 7th July the Battalion suffered its first fatal casualty when twenty-five-year-old Private Arthur House, from Sparkford in Somerset, was accidentally shot and killed at Zabbar. Three days later two enemy aircraft were destroyed but one of them crashed on men of B Company and three were badly burned.[3] Two of them, Private George Le Provost and Lance-Corporal Maurice Malcolm, later died of their wounds. House, Le Provost and Malcolm were the first of some thirty 1st Battalion men to die during the siege of Malta and of more than 330 to lose their lives in the Second World War.

For the infantry on Malta the siege was falling into the pattern it would maintain until the end. They would spend their lives dodging bombs, repairing bomb damage, filling in holes on runways and roads, rescuing people and salvaging food or equipment from bombed buildings, manning observation posts and trying to maintain their training for when they might be called on for operations elsewhere. And all the time they prepared to repel an invasion – from sea or air – that happily never came. If stoicism and steadiness under bombardment are two of the principal qualities of the infantryman, the men of the Malta garrison would demonstrate them to an unprecedented extent. Few opportunities arose for them to hit back, but one chance came on 16th July, when a light machine gun in C Company's Headquarters brought down an enemy aircraft. It was a doubly dramatic incident in which both the enemy aircraft and Flight-Lieutenant Peter Keeble's Hurricane, which had been shot down in the dog-fight, crashed within a few yards of the Company. Sadly both pilots were killed.

---

7   An engine plate from this aircraft, a three-engined Savoia-Marchetti bomber, was picked up at the scene by a stretcher-bearer attending the wounded and is now in the archives of the Keep Museum, Dorchester.

While the army and RAF prepared and manned the island's defences, the Royal Navy was able to act offensively. Admiral Cunningham's fleet encountered the Italian battle-fleet and, directed by sea planes operating from Malta, saw it off, chasing the Marina Militaire to within twenty-five miles of the Italian coast. Breaking off temporarily from its relentless attacks on Malta, the Regia Aeronautica concentrated its energies on attacking Cunningham's ships. Inspired by Cunningham's aggression and by Malta's resistance, Churchill ordered that the island's defences be strengthened to enable it to hold out to become a more painful thorn in the enemy's side.

Although no one could travel far, breaks of leave came round occasionally. In mid-July, the Dorsets' diarist Private Coogan enjoyed three days' leave at Ghajn Tuffieh in the north-west of the island, where he was able to swim and enjoy the sun on a sandy beach, and visit St Paul's Bay and Mosta. Back on duty, on the 28th from his observation post Jack Coogan saw an RAF Sunderland attack a submerged German U-boat and mentioned it in his diary. The next day he recorded the hundredth air raid alert in the six weeks since the war had reached Malta and, a few days later, the welcome arrival of the Battalion's first mail since June.

And so the precarious early days of the siege continued. On 31st July 1940 the 1st Battalion's war diary recorded its strength as 774 augmented by the arrival of sixty men of the 8th Manchesters attached temporarily to the Battalion. The diarist also reported the loss of one of the Gladiators, whose pilot was rescued from the sea. By the end of July the RAF's fighter strength was reduced to one Hurricane and two Gladiators, but three days later twelve more Hurricanes flew in from the aircraft carrier HMS *Argus*.

On 7th August the Malta Infantry Brigade was split into two – a Northern Infantry Brigade and a Southern Infantry Brigade, which the 1st Dorsets now joined. Throughout August and September the Italians kept up their attacks but, early in September, a small convoy reached Malta with fuel, guns and ammunition. Reinforcements for the RAF and for the army arrived at the end of September. An extra 2,000 troops were now on the island, including 116 Dorsets who arrived on the 30th and were added to the Battalion's strength.

On 8th October Private Eric Green, with a batch of reinforcements fresh from England via the Cape and the Suez Canal, was aboard the light cruiser *Liverpool* steaming for Malta. He had been enjoying a swim in Alexandria when abruptly *all military ranks were hastily called out of the water and hustled aboard...* Once at sea, all around he could see the *grand sight* of the Mediterranean Fleet, which included the carriers *Illustrious* and *Eagle* and battleships *Malaya*, *Ramillies* and *Warspite*, five cruisers and eight destroyers.

Over the tannoy we heard that the Italian fleet was coming to do us mischief. Soon bombs were dropping around us and all military ranks were ordered below decks, not before I saw a Caproni bomber come spiralling down hitting the water some hundred yards off our starboard bow... Luckily for us, the enemy did not do us any harm and the next day we arrived in the Grand Harbour, Valletta.

In mid-October the Dorsets were visited by the Colonel of the Regiment, Major-General Hubert Huddleston, and the Secretary of State for War, Anthony Eden. During that month their war diary recorded 130 air raids to date. At the end of October the Italians invaded Greece, diverting their attention from their attack on Malta. Two weeks later, a force of Fairey Swordfish, flying from the carrier *Illustrious*, sank half the Italian fleet at Taranto, forcing Mussolini to withdraw his ships to Naples. An Italian seaborne invasion of Malta suddenly seemed less likely.

Still the bombing continued and the Dorsets' war diary for 28th November recounted an attack on a convoy entering Grand Harbour in which one Italian bomber and two of their fighters were destroyed.

Jack Coogan described the scene more colourfully.

Once again the Royal Navy swept in and out of Malta's harbour bringing another convoy safely in. A brilliant sunny morning made the harbour look its best. Overhead were to be seen our own aircraft. As the fleet left harbour, each ship was trimmed as in the days of peace and the ships' bands lined up on the decks. The people of Senglea and all around the bastions cheered "Long live the Royal Navy".

Despite a grand total of 153 air raids since 11th June, the year closed with a degree of optimism. But events in North Africa now transformed Malta's fortunes. General Dick O'Connor's lightning advance into Libya and the crushing defeat his tiny force inflicted on the massive Italian army stung Hitler into action. Despatching Rommel and what would become the Afrika Korps to reinforce the Italians in Libya, he transferred 200 aircraft, Junkers 88 twin-engined bombers and Junkers 87 Stuka dive bombers, from Norway to Sicily as a preliminary to a German invasion of Malta in the spring.

1941

The Luftwaffe struck first on 10th January 1941, when the Mediterranean fleet had met a convoy from Gibraltar and were escorting it to Malta. Having been hit six times by their Stukas, the desperately damaged aircraft carrier *Illustrious* limped into Grand Harbour for repair. Thus began what would be remembered as the *Illustrious Blitz*, when, throughout her repairs, the German bombers pressed home their attacks on the docks while Malta's anti-aircraft gunners did their utmost to maintain a protective barrage.

The Dorsets encountered the Stukas on 16th January, when they were first employed on attacks on the island. Coogan assessed the day's experience as Malta's greatest air raid. *Three formations of enemy planes flew over the island. Diving from a great height, over the dockyard, dropped bombs. Damage done very little. Malta had a great victory that day, bringing down twenty-one planes. Most of these were German dive bombers, Junkers 88s and 87s.*

Three days later a German bomber crashed near the Battalion's rear HQ at Corradino. On 31st January the Battalion lost twenty-seven-year-old Second Lieutenant Guy Follett from Bournemouth, who died of appendicitis in Imtarfa Hospital and was buried in the nearby cemetery.

During February the island suffered sixty-three raids with the Luftwaffe pressing home their attacks with far greater determination and efficiency than their Italian allies had displayed. On the night of the 8th/9th, the Dorset war diarist recorded two raids lasting from before 2100 until 0015 and from 0120 until 0320. Five nights later Private John Wellman was wounded by a bomb, suffering a fractured skull from which he died in Imtarfa Hospital on the 16th.

The Dorsets' war diary for March painted a life of peculiar contrasts. On the 2nd it recorded the commissioning of no fewer than six warrant officers: RQMS Eaton and CSMs Durden, Norton, Treadwell, Bray and Vincent. (RSM Goodson, CSMs Woodrow and Lovering and CQMS Hubbard were also commissioned around this time, bringing the remarkable total to ten.) At 1200 on the 23rd the diary described twenty Stukas attacking naval vessels in the docks and a heavy bomb falling near the Battalion's rear HQ. At 1500 hours it sadly recorded the Battalion's defeat 3–0 by the Royal Engineers in the Final of the Malta Army Cup (1940). At 1600 it noted another twenty-five Stukas bombing the docks.

And so it went on. In April two Dorsets were wounded by bombs, one in Valletta and one at Corradino. On 4th May another was wounded and four other ranks were repatriated to the UK. May's total was fifty-three raids. Private

Coogan's diary entries for Sunday 11th May described what he had witnessed the previous day.

A raid materialised late yesterday and a dog-fight took place high up in a clear blue sky. With wild cheers from distant onlookers an enemy fighter was seen to crash. The noise of diving aircraft and the rattle of machine gun fire were clearly heard and occasionally a plane was caught sight of as its wings glistened in the sun. There was some anti-aircraft fire. Saturday afternoon – enemy fighters came over the island. One Me109 made a machine gun attack on one of our seaplane bases, where one of our aircraft was set on fire.

June, which began with an anti-personnel mine killing two 1st Battalion men and wounding four more, brought another thirty-one attacks. On 12th July Second Lieutenant Peter Dale was killed on board an aircraft destined for the Middle East that crashed at Safi. It was his 21st birthday.

Although by this stage Malta's fighters and anti-aircraft gunners were reducing the bombing, it was four months since the last convoy had arrived and the island was running dangerously short of supplies. While Cunningham's fleet distracted the Luftwaffe and Regia Aeronautica by sailing north from Alexandria, a convoy was able to sneak through to Malta, arriving on 24th July. The troopships in the convoy brought the Dorsets a draft of sixty reinforcements. Since Hitler's eyes had turned east to invade Russia in June, the Luftwaffe's attacks on Malta had eased. But the Italians meanwhile maintained their offensive and, at 0445 hours on 26th July, George Beadle of the 1st Battalion, at his observation post overlooking Grand Harbour, found himself witnessing perhaps the most dramatic event of the three-year siege.

We had just stood to when there was a considerable explosion from the direction of the Grand Harbour; simultaneously the 6-pounder guns of the Anti-Motor Torpedo Boat batteries at the harbour came into action. It was the start of the one major Italian sea assault on Malta...

... the Italians used two 2-man submarines and nine 1-man launches together with three carriers and two escorting and rescue launches... The details of the plan were that the net at the viaduct on the shoreward end of the mole was to be destroyed by the submarines. This done, the launches were to enter the harbour and sink what shipping they could... An air raid on Valletta was to be put in to coincide with the sea attack...

But several things went wrong. First the Italian air force made an unfortunate mistake. They missed Valletta and bombed a small harbour some eight miles to the north. Next the submarines in some way lost contact and failed to make the second rendezvous. The result was that the commander of the flotilla of launches found himself off Valletta Harbour with daylight fast approaching and the operation as planned very badly handicapped.

With considerable resolution he decided to use his launch instead of the submarines to destroy the net at the viaduct. The explosion which I heard was the explosion of the charge in his launch against the central pier of the St Elmo viaduct.

In fact, the alarm had been given a few seconds before then. At 0444 hrs the lookout at St Elmo had spotted the launch. He sounded the alarm, the lights lit up the illuminated area and a launch coming in about 200 yards out was sunk with the first three rounds fired. Five of the remaining launches were seen about 1,000 yards out moving in and making for the Grand Harbour entrance. They were engaged at once... Within five minutes from the alarm, that is by 0450 hrs, the 6-pounders had sunk three of the launches and disabled the others.

We all awaited first light for some more excitement. As it became lighter two of the launches were seen about 3,000 yards out, motionless. At 0540 hrs they started to move, were at once engaged and, despite their avoiding action, both were sunk. At 0600 hrs some wreckage much further out was seen to move, and this was engaged. It turned out to be two motor boats which turned away at great speed. One subsequently sank, presumably from the effects of the fire. Meanwhile, RAF fighters had taken off to see what was in the offing. They caught up with the remnants of the attacking force on their way back to Sicily, attacked them... and sank the lot, save one, which was brought to a standstill. This was afterwards towed in. One of the fighter pilots, who had been shot down during the encounter, had managed to reach the launch and found the crew dead except for one man who was seriously wounded. This man died shortly after the boat was towed in. The fighter pilot was OK.

So ended Mussolini's one and only attack against Malta with 100 per cent casualties on his side and on our side one Hurricane fighter plane.

In August Colonel Grimley was appointed CO, succeeding Colonel de la Bere, who had been promoted Brigadier and appointed to command the new Central Infantry Brigade. Ivan de la Bere would spend the entire war on Malta and as Commander of Troops would reach the rank of Acting-Major-General. Arthur Grimley had been commissioned in 1917 and had distinguished himself as a subaltern in the Malabar campaign in 1922. Now, under his command, the Dorsets found themselves brigaded with the two battalions with whom they would develop a unique partnership throughout the rest of their long war: the 1st Hampshires and the 2nd Devons.

Private Eric Green, who by now had spent some ten months on the island, remembered that as *the war in North Africa swayed back and forth and Malta suffered accordingly, rations were cut to a minimum. All the local buses were taken off the roads and everywhere we went we had to walk; they only ran in the morning and in the evening to get the workers to and from their work.*

Early in September even water had to be carefully husbanded because there had been so little rain during the summer. The air raids continued sporadically and, on 29th September, Coogan's diary reported the arrival of a large convoy bringing reinforcements for the RAF.

For the Dorsets the end of 1941 brought a temporary respite from the bombing when they spent November training on Gozo, rehearsing repelling a German invasion which looked ever more imminent. They returned on 5th December, having lost one man – Private Francis Talbot – in a road accident in the tiny Gozitan port of Mgarr. But now the air raids became more frequent. In the next fortnight the Dorsets' light machine guns engaged a Messerschmitt 109 heading for RAF Luqa at 300 feet and a Junkers 88 attacking the dockyards. Around Christmas the Battalion's positions were bombed several times, their communications between posts were damaged and, on 29th December, three men were wounded at Marsascala. Their war diary closed 1941 by recording 135 raids during December.

During the summer and autumn of 1941, with the Luftwaffe's attentions directed towards Russia, Malta had turned increasingly to the offensive. Her submarines, based at Manoel Island in Marsamxett Harbour, were achieving real success attacking German and Italian shipping supplying their armies in Libya. Her photographic reconnaissance aircraft were invaluable in this and in identifying suitable targets for attack by Malta's Blenheim and Wellington bombers and Beaufort torpedo bombers. In November nearly 80% of all Rommel's supplies had been sunk just as the Eighth Army launched Operation *Crusader*. Enraged by these losses, Hitler transferred Luftflotte II from the Russian Front to Sicily and gave command in the Mediterranean to Marshal Kesselring with orders to neutralise Malta. Meanwhile, half the U-boat fleet in the Atlantic was moved to the Mediterranean. Malta and her defiant people and defenders were to be destroyed, once and for all. The year 1942 would bring Armageddon.

1942

On Sunday 4th January the Battalion were put on a higher level of readiness and Second Lieutenant Luff was wounded in the bombing. Later that day, Private Coogan recorded in his diary that *German Stukas have been carrying out a non-stop attack on Malta's aerodromes during the last 36 hours. Between breakfast and teatime there were five alerts. The attacks lasted several hours. But the Nazis have failed to keep our aircraft on the ground while their Junkers and protecting Messerschmitts have been severely dealt with by our fighters and guns... During the night the alerts were sounded for enemy aircraft had crossed the coast. Bombs were dropped but there is nothing to report.*

Next day he recorded six alerts during the morning and a retaliatory raid by Malta's small bomber force, which *attacked the aerodrome of Castel Vetrano near the south-east coast of Sicily. Two raids were carried out after a large number of heavy German aircraft had been observed on this aerodrome. The first attack was made by our aircraft flying at deck-height and bombs smashed home among assembled aircraft. Flying at anything between 25 to 100 feet off the ground, our bombers created havoc and then returned to create further chaos with their machine guns. When darkness had fallen we put another attack in, this raid lasted for nine hours.*

The war diary for January recorded more than 200 raids during the month. On the 6th the Dorsets' Reserve Company was moved to the airfield at Safi to supplement the anti-aircraft gunners based there. The danger from the skies was intensifying – as two Military Medals won by Dorsets around this time demonstrate. Both were earned in engagements with aircraft and the first, perhaps uniquely, was won at sea.

On 23rd January Private Ken Leach of Parkstone and twenty-four-year-old Private Francis Smith from Lyme Regis were manning a Bren gun aboard the launch *Lord Plumer*. Their role was to provide anti-aircraft defence during a short trip from Marfa along the coast to Grand Harbour. When the launch was strafed by a low-flying Messerschmitt, Smith opened fire. Leach was passing a fresh magazine to Smith when German cannon shells raked the boat, killing Smith and sending Leach sprawling. Undeterred, he quickly rallied, took over the gun and continued to engage the German fighter.

The Dorsets' second MM was won by a 4th Battalion man, Private John Wynne, who had somehow found himself on Malta attached to the Queen's Own Royal West Kents. His citation read:

For the past sixteen months Private Wynne has been employed in various capacities on aerodromes. During this period he has frequently manned anti-aircraft light machine guns during air raids and has on numerous occasions engaged enemy aircraft. On one particular occasion he was Number 2 of a gun sited in a disused Bofors pit. An air raid developed and fifteen Junkers 88s bombed the aerodrome, and a bomb landed on the side of the sangar knocking down Private Wynne and wounding him. He immediately picked himself up and got the gun into action in time to engage some Messerschmitt 109s which were carrying out a low-flying attack on the drome.

After the raid Private Wynne went to the Advanced Dressing Station for treatment, returning soon after and carrying on normal duty for the remainder of the day. Private Wynne's steadiness and devotion to duty under hazardous conditions, on one occasion although wounded, has been an excellent example to the remainder of the battalion.

RAF Hal Far being bombed

John Snook, serving with the Royal Air Force at Luqa, received a letter from his father in Bridport describing how he had shared his Royal Observer Corps watch for German aircraft with another officer whose son was on Malta. The picture of the two fathers thinking of their distant and endangered sons prompted him to write a touching poem entitled *The Dorsets at War*.

When mail from home reached Malta days ago
My father wrote of plotting German planes;
Observing from his Corps post deep in snow
Above the Chesil Beach and Dorset lanes.

Dad also wondered if my ears had burned
When last his duty watch was jointly spent
With Captain Tucker, whose son Bob he learned
Is based here with the Dorset Regiment.

I tracked down Robert at a Bren gun post
Despite a bombing raid in fading light,
And there, we raised two cocoa mugs to toast
Two dads, who watch the Dorset skies by night.

At sixty plus and near retirement age,
Both fathers, fearing for their sons at war,
Share qualms paternal, each time planes rampage
Across the island dropping bombs galore.

Meanwhile the Dorsets based at Luqa strain
At building aircraft pens and manning guns,
Whilst driving bowsers filled with high octane
Is just another chore for Dorset sons.

They strive as German air attacks increase
To keep the runway free for planes to land
And, barely waiting for a raid to cease,
The Dorsets sally forth with stone and sand.

As 'bungers up' of bomb-blast crater holes,
The lads from Wessex toil for planes to fly,
And we on Malta praise the many roles
Accomplished by the Dorset PBI.[4]

---

4   PBI was coined in the Great War and stood for *Poor Bloody Infantry.*

Brigadier Charles Woodhouse OBE MC DL JP by Juliet Pannett

Major-General George Wood CB CBE DSO MC by Edward Seago

Brigadier Sir Ivan de la Bere KCVO CB CBE by Leslie Cole

(Imperial War Museum LD 3545)

Brigadier Speedy Bredin DSO MC by Ken Howard

*Sergeant William Evans MM and Bar, and Lance-Corporal Denis Bounsall DCM
by Anthony Gross*
(Imperial War Museum LD 3939)

Sergeant Ginger Pearce by Francess Richardson

The Bungalow, Kohima by Jock Murrills

The Battle of the Tennis Court, Kohima by Jock Murrills

1st Battalion Colours

4th Battalion Colours

4th Battalion Airborne Pennant

Scroll marking the Liberation of Hengelo

Around this time two important changes took place in the chain of command above the Dorsets. A new Brigadier – Kenneth Pearce Smith – replaced Brigadier O'Donovan in command of the Brigade. A veteran of the Battle of Arras and the March Retreat, Pearce Smith had served between the wars in Ireland, North Russia, Africa and India. He came to the Brigade from Northern Ireland, where he had been commanding and training a battalion of his own Regiment, the Royal Berkshires. A keen trainer of troops and a believer in mobility in defence, he was shocked by the dispositions of his new Brigade's defences.

The ground defence policy was purely static. Around the coast and aerodromes in some depth were situated concrete pillboxes, about 300-400 yards apart, supplemented by a continuous belt of wire and landmines. Each pillbox was garrisoned by a section of eight or so men with Bren guns and other weapons. Undoubtedly they would have presented considerable opposition and inflicted many casualties but smoke and modern weapons would have defeated them, so I gave orders that slit trenches were to be dug outside every pillbox. The troops had even made little gardens and some even kept hens! One day my Brigade Major, Paul Atkins, and I visited seven unoccupied pillboxes and collected seven Bren guns.

Presciently, Pearce Smith thought that his Brigade's next job would be to invade Sicily and he duly briefed the three COs and began a programme of training entitled *Exercise Cecilia.* Still more remarkably, the stretch of coast on the fictional island of Cecilia (which was an exact reproduction of Sicily) would be the site of the Brigade's actual landing in July 1943. He concentrated on developing his soldiers' toughness and fitness, and marches around the island became commonplace. Private Lambert Old, a native of Affpuddle who had served in the 2nd Battalion in Palestine, remembered marching with full pack the length of the island from his post in Marsaxlokk to Golden Bay beyond Ghajn Tuffieh. But even these strenuous route marches across its rocky terrain did not put him off Malta. In 1941 he had married a Maltese girl, and he would return after the war to spend the rest of his life on the island.

Lambert Old was far from alone in this. Albert Mockridge also married a local girl on Malta in 1941 and returned to settle there for most of his life. In the late 1940s a branch of the Regimental Association would be formed on Malta with more than thirty members.

The second change in command was the appointment, above Pearce Smith, of Major-General Beak. Daniel Beak was an outstandingly brave man. Serving in the Royal Naval Division during the First World War, he had won a VC, a DSO and

Private Lambert Old

two MCs. Pearce Smith saw him as *a difficult man but a terrific fire-eater* who supported his emphasis on mobility. He also shared Pearce Smith's enthusiasm for physical fitness, as the Brigade Intelligence Officer remembered:

Shortly after his arrival, General Beak gave a lecture to all officers in the command... 'You will do PT every morning before breakfast,' said the General. 'You will cycle in full equipment for twenty miles.' 'You will run and walk alternately for fifteen miles in full equipment.' 'You're lazy and some of you are too fat,' he said, fixing his eye on one major renowned for his high standard of living.

Pearce Smith recalled this lecture as *a most inspiring talk, warning us of the probability of an invasion in the near future and reminding us how much we owed to our own beloved country. There would be no surrenders and no prisoners. Dulce et decorum est pro patria mori.*

The combination of the intense bombing and the arrival of Pearce Smith and Beak created a more purposeful atmosphere. General Beak, who seems to have been a real-life version of Evelyn Waugh's Brigadier Ritchie Hook, may have overdone it. Within a few months Gort sacked him and he joined the Eighth Army as a brigadier in North Africa, where Monty sacked him again after the Battle of Mareth. Pearce Smith, however, was remembered for the enormous professional effort he devoted to bringing his three battalions up to a high level of efficiency, fitness and battle-readiness, which later – in the Sicily invasion he so accurately foresaw – would save lives.

While Beak and Pearce Smith were sharpening up the island's defence, the Germans and Italians were finalising Operation *Hercules*, their invasion plan. Instead of invading (as most of the defenders expected) in the north-west at Mellieha, the Germans were going to land gliders around Qrendi and parachute troops from Dingli to north of Takali, and from Takali to Kirkop. Their task would be to put the airfields at Takali and Luqa out of action. The Italian seaborne assault would then come in on the south coast between Dingli and Zurrieq and would be supplied through the port of Marsaxlokk. Had the invasion come, the Dorsets would have found themselves in the front of the battle.

Meanwhile, at the foot of the military hierarchy, Private Jack Coogan continued to maintain the daily diary he had kept meticulously since June 1940. By January 1942 he was routinely recording three, four, five or six air raids each day and the combined efforts of the RAF and anti-aircraft gunners to counter them. In the entry for 11th February he sang the praises of fighter protection, which had enabled a handful of warships, laden with supplies, to break through and dock in Grand Harbour. But such windfalls, however welcome, were not enough. Malta was being starved of the food, ammunition, equipment and aviation fuel essential for her survival.

Twice in February German fighters attacked British seaplanes in Kalafrana Bay. On the 5th their attack was successful and the aircraft was destroyed. On the 21st the Dorsets' machine guns engaged the 109s, and the Sunderland survived the attack.

Suddenly, on Sunday 22nd February, having written and underlined the date preparatory to writing his entry, the Dorsets' unofficial diarist stopped recording his experiences. Why should a man, who has kept a fairly detailed diary for more than twenty months, abruptly stop recording events just as they reached their crescendo? Happily Jack Coogan was not killed, wounded or taken ill. His illicit diary-keeping had been discovered and his diary confiscated. Sadly, the Dorsets' diarist would not be available to record the cataclysmic spring and summer when Malta's ordeal would reach its dramatic climax.

Brigadier Pearce Smith recalled that, during *the first few days of March, raids by Ju88s, escorted by Me109s, became more intensive: Kesselring obviously feeling his way, and on the evening of March 21st, standing on the roof of our mess, we watched wave after wave of enemy planes attacking Ta Kali aerodrome which was north-west of my area. The next day Paul [the Brigade Major] and I went to Ta Kali aerodrome to see the damage done. As we approached the air raid warning sounded and shortly after squadron after squadron of Ju88s came over, destroying more of our aircraft and the landing strips were pitted with craters. One or two bombs fell perilously close to us and for the first time, I think, they were dropping some land-mines, causing enormous craters and blast effects.*

In late March two merchantmen had reached Malta from Alexandria but they were not unloaded before they were sunk by the Germans' relentless bombing of the docks. Less than 5,000 tons of precious cargo were salvaged.

Pearce Smith and his Brigade Major saw the ships being bombed in the harbour.

... apparently the SS Breconshire had been badly damaged; she was a very fast ship that had run the gauntlet many times with vital cargoes... she was still afloat and one of the bombers, flying at roof-top height, fired its rear machine guns at Paul and me.

Then another tragedy: approaching from the east were several squadrons of Ju88s and Stukas (dive bombers) and we watched Hal Far, probably the most modern aero-drome in Europe, and the base of four RAF and Fleet Air Arm squadrons, completely destroyed.

Malta's Governor reported to the Chiefs of Staff that there was enough flour to last until the end of May and that supplies of most other food would be exhausted by the end of June. Stocks of light anti-aircraft shells would also be spent by the end of June, and heavy anti-aircraft shells by the end of July. Aviation fuel would be exhausted by mid-August. Malta was fighting desperately for her life against a ferocious, determined enemy. Supplies were running low and time was running out.

Pearce Smith recalled that in March and April 1942 *over 2,000 tons of bombs fell on the Brigade area. About 150 officers and other ranks had been killed or wounded, chiefly from the Hampshires and Devons.* Each soldier's rations *were reduced from the normal 3200 calories a day to about 1250. We had all lost a stone or more in weight.*

The events recorded in the Dorsets' war diary in April reveal the intensity of the German offensive. On 1st April Corporal William Foote, Lance-Corporal Charles Pearce and Private Ernest French were killed when the bombs aboard a crashed Stuka exploded. Two other men, Lance-Corporal John Bell and Private Garrett, were wounded; sadly, Corporal Bell would die of his wounds three months later. On 4th April the Dorsets had to deal with an unexploded bomb on one of their positions while other bombs on the dockyard caused the RAOC magazine to explode. On the 7th Private Cecil Peace was wounded at Corradino and died the next day. Two days later Corporal Edgar Evans was wounded at Floriana and died on the 10th. On the 11th D Company and Battalion HQ engaged a low-flying Junkers 88 with their light machine guns. It crashed nearby. A week later a stick of bombs at Zejtun wounded Captain Norman Golding and Lieutenant Treadwell, who died two days later. George Treadwell had many years' service in the Regiment and was one of the CSMs who had been commissioned a year before. On the 19th Lance-Corporal Alfred James and Private Donald Macpherson were killed by a bomb at Gzira. And every day the war diary listed between four and six separate air raids. At their base at Manoel Island in Marsamxett Harbour the submarines had to remain submerged to survive the bombing.

Repairing Malta's bomb damage

In April the island was awarded the George Cross in recognition of her people's bravery during the long siege. Equally inspiriting but of more practical use, forty-seven Spitfires flew in from the carrier USS *Wasp* to help protect the island from the merciless bombing. Eighty more would arrive from *Wasp* and HMS *Eagle* a month later and, on each of Malta's airfields, troops and RAF groundcrew formed teams to meet each aircraft, refuel and re-arm it in ten to twenty minutes, and get it back into the air to intercept the inevitable bombers sent to destroy the Spitfires on the ground. The Spitfires could and did regain air superiority over the island. But they would be of use only for so long as the fuel supply held out, and there was no prospect of another convoy breaking through to provide that or any of the other things that Malta needed so desperately. Meanwhile the relentless, tightening grip of the Axis blockade brought starvation.

When it was discovered that Private Eric Green had once attended some regimental nursing orderly courses, he found himself appointed Company Medical Orderly. He remembered that, around this time, it was *decided as a precautionary measure to put a company of the 1st Dorsets on the neighbouring island of Gozo. A small boat which had up till then not been sunk took us across... to the island where we took up defensive positions. The small room I took over was part of the adjacent school and had nothing to commend it but a few empty bottles and fracture splints, so I set to make it look like a medical inspection room. There being no hospital or medical officer available, I had to improvise by purchasing from the local village a bottle of Ambeet, the local wine which tastes like ink. This I shared out into the bottles and some water. For antiseptic I used a shell dressing which all ranks carried – by soaking it in water it produced a fine bottle of amber looking fluid for dabbing on wounds, providing they were not extensive, plus some Calamine lotion I picked up somewhere. I managed to look fairly professional; fortunately no dire need occurred, the enemy left us alone... In due course we had a visit from Malta – one Medical Officer who, on inspecting my MO room, asked what was in the bottles. When I explained, he thought it very funny.*

On Malta, in May the Dorsets recovered the dead body of a German airman washed ashore and a guard from B Company captured a live German, who had baled out of his Me109. Meanwhile, they manned the defences, repaired the airfields and roads, stood ready to supplement the Maltese stevedores unloading ships in the dockyards, and even strengthened the gunners' anti-aircraft batteries. May saw the appointment of a new Governor of Malta. Lord Gort's arrival at this, the darkest hour of the island's ordeal, signalled a renewed, single-minded determination never to submit. A dazzlingly brave man, Gort would provide inspirational, selfless leadership throughout the climax of the siege.

In June two convoys set out, one from Gibraltar, the other from Alexandria, but, after severe losses, most of the ships were forced to turn back before reaching the seventy-mile radius from Malta protected by the island's fighters. Only two of the seventeen ships reached Grand Harbour. Lessons had been learnt. After the tragic debacle of the March convoy, the unloading of the surviving merchantmen from the June convoy of seventeen ships was carefully planned and the Dorsets were involved in its swift execution.

Willie Hayes later recalled being ordered, as a very junior officer, to supervise the unloading. *The whole of the last convoy had been sunk in the Grand Harbour because the civilians could not work during an air raid and indeed all the lights went out. So the next convoy we would unload working through all the air raids and the lights would remain on. Each battalion would have a ship, which of course meant an inter-battalion competition. The next convoy arrived. I was in the hold with my chaps all stripped to the waist. We were unloading cigarettes and drink – very dangerous with nicotine- and alcohol-starved soldiers. The air raid siren went and all the lights were extinguished. What should an ignorant second-lieutenant do? I should have got all my men on deck and thus away from temptation. This didn't cross my mind. Our place of duty was in the hold and there we would stay, sober or drunk. I got each soldier to light two cigarettes and keep them moving one in each hand. It worked. At the end of the raid we carried on working as usual with all the lights on again.*

Private Bill Chutter remembered his twenty-four-hour stints at the docks, working eight-hour shifts unloading merchant ships. Supplies for the island were so precious, he recalled, that pilfering from convoys led to certain court martial. He also described the frequent task, after big raids, of searching through bombed buildings to salvage anything – particularly cooking oil and food of any kind – which could be redistributed, summarising his three years on the island as *4,000 air raids, little food, plenty of work, filling up bomb craters on runways, unloading ships as fast as you could go...*

In four and a half days the Dorsets and other troops unloaded between 3,000 and 3,500 tons of supplies. It was a stay of execution, but not a reprieve, as Lord Gort made clear in his candid but bleak broadcast on 16th June to the people and garrison of Malta. Apart from promising that *every effort* would be made to replenish stocks when a favourable opportunity arose, Gort could offer little comfort beyond *faith in Almighty God*. Short of a miracle, Malta would either be starved into submission or forced to surrender because its aircraft had run out of fuel. Meanwhile, to the south the desert war had reached a new low for the Eighth Army, who had retreated far into Egypt to an unheard of halt on the railway at a place called El Alamein. A new general, Bernard Montgomery, had taken command on 13th August.

On 20th July men of C Company helped rescue a Spitfire pilot who had baled out over the sea. At the end of the month a Junkers 88, shot down by a Spitfire, crashed on Wolseley Camp, destroying a light van, a carrier, the sergeants' billet and 4 Platoon's stores. The body of one of the crew, whose parachute had failed to open, was buried at sea on the 29th. Meanwhile, the RAF, under the inspiring leadership of Air Vice-Marshal Keith Park, applied interception tactics which he had employed to great effect in the Battle of Britain and which, with the larger supply of Spitfires, transformed its results. Wresting command of the skies from the enemy, the Spitfires greatly reduced the daylight bombing raids.

Welcome though this respite was, it could do nothing to ease the pressure on food and fuel supplies. By July the daily ration on Malta had been cut to half that provided in Britain. The population – including Lord Gort, who characteristically insisted on sharing their rations and travelling only by bicycle – were slowly starving. But in London the Chiefs of Staff had ambitious plans that might relieve the pressure on besieged Malta. Operation *Pedestal* was a convoy of unprecedented size sent from Britain via Gibraltar with fourteen merchant ships escorted by two battleships, four aircraft carriers, seven cruisers and twenty-seven destroyers. Passing Gibraltar on 10th August and refuelling at sea, the convoy came under sustained, concentrated and determined attacks from German and Italian submarines, e-boats, bombers, torpedo bombers and dive bombers. The cost, like the scale of the convoy and the ferocity of the enemy assault, was without precedent. Four of the escorts were sunk, including the aircraft carrier *Eagle*, and five were so damaged that they were out of action for a long time. Nine of the merchant ships were sunk and, of the five still afloat, four were severely damaged.

The first of the five to reach Malta, at 1825 hours on 13th August, was *Rochester Castle*, bomb-scarred and with a hole twenty-five feet long ripped in her side by a torpedo. Next came *Melbourne Star* and *Port Chalmers*. The arrival of these war-torn survivors brought the Dorsets to the docks, where, with the rest of the Brigade, they worked shifts to complete the task of unloading *Melbourne Star*'s vital cargo as rapidly as possible. This time there was no mistake. The Maltese dockers and the troops of her garrison unloaded the battered ships in record time, and the vital fresh supplies were rapidly dispersed to be stored around the island to avoid any bombing.

Next day the Dorsets' observation posts sighted *Brisbane Star* as she approached Malta under cover of a protective formation of Spitfires. Torpedoed by an Italian bomber and separated from the convoy, she had hugged the Tunisian coast, bluffing her way through Vichy French coastal defences before making a final successful sprint for Malta.

Around 0800 on the 15th the same posts reported the scarred, blackened hulk of the tanker *Ohio*, lashed between two destroyers and steered by a third, making her painful way into Grand Harbour while tiny tugs bustled solicitously around her battered hull. Bombed, torpedoed and burning, with two crashed bombers on her decks, she had been first abandoned then reboarded and, with her fires extinguished, towed slowly towards Malta. The fuel still in her tanks, and the food and ammunition aboard the other merchantmen, were Malta's salvation. The waving, cheering crowds cramming the ancient fortifications around the harbour sensed this, greeting *Ohio*'s arrival on Santa Marija, the greatest of Malta's feast days, as a miracle. Perhaps it was.

The *Pedestal* convoy, which had cost 350 sailors' lives and delivered 32,000 tons of cargo, marked the beginning of the end of the siege. Three weeks later the tide in North Africa, which had been flowing strongly for Rommel, ebbed abruptly when his tanks confronted Montgomery's unyielding defensive positions at Alam Halfa. Badly mauled, Rommel's army backed off. By early November, their crushing defeat at Alamein presented the Germans and Italians with a grim choice: withdrawal or total destruction. Malta-based aircraft, ships and submarines played a major part in the victory, sinking a great number of tankers and merchant ships on their way to supply the Axis armies in North Africa.

With a victorious Eighth Army advancing rapidly westwards through Libya, and two Anglo-American armies advancing east into Tunisia, the desert war was nearing its end and, with it, Malta's long struggle. Meanwhile, hard times and hard work continued. Although *Ohio*'s scarred tanks had replenished the island's stocks of aviation fuel and starvation had been averted, food remained pitifully short and the bombing continued.

Colonel Broke Ray – sometimes known as Bill – now took command of the 1st Dorsets. Forty-two years old, he was the eldest of three brothers from Wimborne, all of whom were Regular soldiers. One, a major in the Worcesters, was killed in Eritrea in 1941; another, a Royal Fusilier, would die of wounds received in Normandy where he commanded the 7th Hampshires in the same brigade as the 4th and 5th Dorsets. Broke Ray had been commissioned in April 1918 and survived

Colonel Broke Ray DSO

just over three weeks as a subaltern with the 6th Battalion in France before being wounded. Between the wars he had served in the Malabar operations with the 2nd Battalion and, having been on Malta from the outset of the siege, was well known throughout the 1st Battalion.

In September the Dorsets' war diary reported a bomber crashing in the docks. In October CQMS Rampling was wounded in Tarxien. In November some Dorsets formed fire fighting teams on ships in the docks while one section, near Zejtun, found themselves administering first aid to a civilian whose leg had been blown off by an anti-personnel mine. In December they were back in the docks unloading ships from convoys which at last were reaching Malta in comparative safety and increasing numbers.

1943

In the New Year the garrison found time to repair, rebuild and consolidate, and to train for operations elsewhere. The Dorset Commando Platoon was prominent in this training and, in late March, Sergeant Francis Norman won a very well deserved British Empire Medal for his bravery on a Commando exercise in the north of the island that went awry. In the evening of 25th March, the Dorset and the Royal West Kent Commando Platoons set out on a two-day exercise to test the endurance of the men and the seaworthiness of their assault boats. During the night they paddled from Manoel Island in Marsamxett Harbour to Mellieha Bay and then carried their boats across the island to launch them again in Anchor Bay. At 2030 next evening they set out in six assault boats to land at Ghajn Tuffieha. Encountering rough seas and a strengthening wind, the boats were separated and forced out to sea. Five managed to reach shore after paddling for four hours, but two of these were wrecked. On the sixth was Sergeant Norman and his crew of six.

Sergeant Norman lost contact with the leaders but kept trying to drive his boat around the point and in so doing got blown out to sea. The waves were breaking aboard constantly and it soon became obvious that no headway was being made. Sergeant Norman then decided to turn back, the crew paddled for five hours as hard as possible but were blown further and further from land. All this time it was necessary to bail almost continually to keep the craft afloat. By about 0200 hours some of the crew began to despair of reaching safety but Sergeant Norman encouraged them and kept up their spirits by telling them stories of tougher spots from which he had escaped. The Corporal was the first man to give in but he was soon followed by the others who from sheer exhaustion and cramp could paddle no more. From then on Sergeant Norman alone, or with the help of one other man, kept the boat head to sea, at the same time baling out each time she became dangerously full of water.

Once the engine of a launch was heard nearby and the Sergeant with great presence of mind ordered the men to fire their tommy guns all together at his word of command. Signal cartridges had been rendered unserviceable long before.

When dawn came the boat was found to be near Gozo. Sergeant Norman managed to rally the men with an attempt to reach Xlendi but they had not enough strength left to make any headway. At about 0800 hours the boat was close under a line of sheer cliffs when a large wave swept down on her and, before Sergeant Norman could turn her bow-on, the boat swamped and turned over. One of the men grabbed hold of Sergeant Norman so tightly that both were carried under. Sergeant Norman managed to break the grip of the drowning man and pulled him over to the upturned boat. He also caught hold of the Corporal and secured him a handhold on the bottom of the boat. He then arranged the men three a side so that their weight was balanced but the Corporal tried to climb on the boat and in so doing slipped, and sank under the water and drowned. Sergeant Norman swam under the boat looking for him but to no avail. Soon afterwards the remaining five were rescued by a fishing boat.

It is typical of Norman that, although so weak from continuous exposure and strain that on being landed he could not use his legs for several hours, he yet felt it his duty while swimming in the water to salvage a pistol he found hanging from the upturned boat.

All the men are certain that they owe their lives to Sergeant Norman, and the boat would have foundered during the night and all hands have been lost had not Sergeant Norman, by his own labour and leadership, kept the crew together.

This recommendation for a George Medal was reduced by the Admiralty and the Ministry of War Transport to a BEM. Anyone reading the citation with any knowledge of the nature of the southern coasts of Malta and Gozo, and of the treacherous currents in the channel between the two islands, would find this decision unfathomable.

Four days later – on 30th March 1943 – with a degree of pomp and celebration which would have been unimaginable a few months earlier, the Governor and people said their formal thanks and farewells to the Dorsets, Devons and Hampshires in what by then was known as the 1st Malta Brigade. They had defended the island, protected her people, withstood the longest and bitterest siege in modern history and emerged victorious. The experience had not been without cost. Some thirty men had been killed, and a similar number wounded. Among the deaths were a handful caused by self-inflicted wounds: evidence of the mental stress that accompanied the long-term physical demands and sustained poor nutrition the siege had brought.

Meanwhile, the world beyond Malta had changed dramatically. When the siege had begun, Britain, like Malta, had been alone, on the defensive and vulnerable to invasion; although few countenanced the thought of defeat, it was impossible realistically to predict victory. In 1941 the German invasion of Russia and the Japanese attack on the American fleet at Pearl Harbour had forced first Russia and then the United States into the war. Since then, the British victories in Egypt, Libya and Tunisia, the Anglo-American capture of Tunis and the crushing Russian victory at Stalingrad had made an ultimate Allied victory inevitable: it was now only a matter of how long it would take.

The immediate question facing the British and Americans was where, when and how to begin the liberation of Europe. In 1942, concluding that an invasion of France would be impossible that year, the Allies agreed to start with Operation *Torch*, the invasion of North Africa from the west. Committing to that operation entailed abandoning the prospect of being able to assemble sufficient forces in England for a cross-Channel invasion in 1943. Churchill and Roosevelt agreed at Casablanca in January 1943 that the next step should therefore be to knock Italy out of the war, to neutralise the Italian fleet, and to open the Mediterranean to Allied shipping. The provisional

Memorial to the 1st Dorsets, Valletta

date for a landing in France was put off until the spring of 1944 and it was agreed that, once the campaigns in North Africa were won, Sicily, whose south coast lay within sixty or seventy miles of Malta, should be invaded.

Events would move fast. Malta and even Gozo would turn entirely to the offensive and both islands would become a base for the invasion of Sicily. Before the short campaign in Sicily was over, Mussolini would be forced from power and, a few days after the Allied landings on the Italian mainland, Italy would be knocked once and for all out of the Axis. The rest of the war would take the 1st Dorsets and their sister battalions in 231 (Malta) Brigade further and further from Malta. Following the plans made at Casablanca, they would land on the beaches of Sicily, then Calabria and then Normandy, and finally the 1st Battalion would be the first British infantry to penetrate the German frontier. But, wherever the long, costly liberation of Europe took them, they would carry with them the symbol of the unique bond they had formed with the island between 1940 and 1943. On their sleeves they wore their Brigade badge – the red and white cross of Malta.[5]

---

5 Sometimes history can demonstrate a sense of symmetry. When, thirty years later, the British forces were finally withdrawing from Malta, the last infantry battalion to leave was the 1st Battalion of the Devon and Dorset Regiment.

Landing in Sicily by John Worsley

3

THE 1ST BATTALION, SICILY AND ITALY 1943

A TOEHOLD IN EUROPE

ASSAULT LANDING ON SICILY

At 0245 hours on 10th July 1943 the 1st Dorsets landed in darkness on the south-east coast of Sicily. Captain Charles Martin's lightly equipped C Company made a scramble landing on the rocks north-west of the tiny fishing port of Marzamemi. Encountering an Italian pillbox, the Company suffered their first casualty when Private Arthur Smith, who had married a Maltese girl during the siege, was killed. Martin personally led a platoon against the pillbox and dealt with its occupants. In the course of this brief fire-fight four men of Lieutenant Lawson's 14 Platoon were wounded. One of them, Corporal Bertie Butel, was later awarded the Battalion's first MM in the campaign for carrying on with the attack despite his wounds.

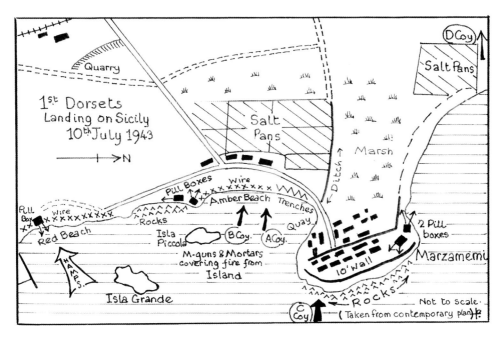

1st Dorsets' Landing on Sicily 10th July 1943

Having scaled a sea wall ten feet high, the Company turned right towards the village. When 13 Platoon's commander, Lieutenant David Ruttledge of the Duke of Cornwall's Light Infantry, was wounded, his platoon sergeant took command. With fire support from a Bren gun, Sergeant George Wilson led a bayonet charge that penetrated the defensive wire and captured his platoon's objective on the right of the Company's advance.

In this first, successful fight on a strange, darkened shore 13 and 14 Platoons lost one man killed and six wounded. Martin re-organised the company and cleared and secured the beach on which the rest of the Battalion was to land. Now he was able to signal the landing craft containing the mine gapping parties who would check the beach for mines and clear paths through them for the companies to follow. Meanwhile, Captain Richard Harris, a pre-war Territorial now acting as the Unit Landing Officer, set off up the beach to find a track that would be the Battalion's axis of advance.

Charles Martin, who came from Rampisham, was later awarded a DSO – partly for leading this assault and partly for his bravery later in the short campaign. His citation noted that: *It was to a large extent due to his action that the main landings were carried out so rapidly and successfully.*

Major Charles Martin DSO

Having disembarked from the *Strathnaver* some seven miles from the shore at about 0030, the other companies, waiting in their pitching landing craft, saw the night sky lit by explosions inland as the RAF bombed targets ashore. Reassuring though it was to have air support capable of inflicting such violence, most of the Dorsets were beyond caring. B Company's Corporal George Beadle recalled that *the first man to be sick was the Assistant Beachmaster who was in our craft. It looked bad for a sailor to be sick. But, before we had been on the water half an hour, we were all sick. I felt that even if there had been a machine gun on every yard of beach I would have landed. I felt that ill... As our landing craft approached the shore, Italian mortar shells were dropping all along the beach, and once a [searchlight] switched on and flashed on the boats. Whoever was operating the light must have been blind for we were not picked up. About fifty yards from the beach the Italian mortar fire was lifted. Mortar bombs were flying over our heads and into the sea doing no damage. At 0400 hours we linked up with C Company.*

Winding their way through the saltpans, the companies crossed the coastal road and railway and dug in on a hill, where they remained until 0600 watching some Italian artillery exchanging fire with the ships off shore. Although some German Messerschmitt 109s strafed the beach, the Dorsets met little resistance. They had – literally – caught the Italians napping. Indeed, Captain Willie Hayes, commanding the Carrier Platoon, remembered capturing one senior Italian officer in his pyjamas, who spoke good English.

"What the hell are you doing here? Don't you know from the wireless that it is too rough for an invasion?"

My first prisoner and a bollocking from him too! My soldiers then brought to me a young Italian chap in his early twenties dressed as a civilian. He was also cross – "I know I am a soldier but I am on leave so you cannot capture me." Much to his disappointment my soldiers wouldn't take that as an excuse.

Opposition had been slight and the beaches were found to be clear of mines, but, like any operation, the landing had not gone without its share of hitches. The landing craft transporting the Dorsets' Second-in-Command, Major Bobby Nicoll, found itself far to the south and, in the words of the Brigade history, *had a long voyage before reaching the correct beaches.* Landing on the Dorsets' left, the Hampshires had shared in both the success and the confusion: one of their platoons was landed far to the north and had to pick its way through the Dorsets' area to find its own battalion. Now both battalions were ashore, the plan was for the Devons, supported by Sherman tanks, to pass straight through to capture a German coastal defence battery two miles inland.

Unwilling to risk losing the momentum of the advance, Broke Ray allowed his own B Company to press ahead and capture the battery position, which had already been engaged by the 3.7 Howitzers of 165th Field Regiment. One gun had taken a direct hit and the broken bodies of its crew lay all around, but everyone else had gone. The three other guns stood silent; their crews had fled. The accuracy of the Royal Artillery field gunners and the Dorsets' rapid advance against melting opposition had left the newly arrived Devons less to do. Their supporting Shermans, however, proved their worth when six French light tanks crewed by Italians put in a sudden counter-attack and were all knocked out. This gallant but futile gesture was the only Italian attack the Brigade sustained throughout the campaign. Any enthusiasm the Italian army might once have had for war had ebbed away.

By noon on 10th July the Brigade had achieved all its objectives and captured nearly 800 prisoners, most of whom seemed unnervingly anxious to surrender. Having grabbed one of the first bits of the now rapidly expanding bridgehead, the 1st Battalion were back in Europe three years after the 2nd Battalion's evacuation from Dunkirk.

231 Malta Brigade had left Malta on 30th March 1943, with bands ashore playing the regimental marches of the three regiments. As their ship pulled out of Grand Harbour they were cheered by the crowds and saluted by the Governor, Lord Gort, from his launch. After a short rest in Alexandria, they were sent to the Suez Canal training camp for training in amphibious assault landings. Meanwhile, the Brigadier, Kenneth Pearce Smith, and the three COs – Broke Ray of the Dorsets, Bill Valentine of the Devons and Bill Spencer of the Hampshires – were sent to the Eighth Army in Tunisia. Attached to experienced units, they were given the chance to observe and absorb in a couple of weeks some of the lessons Monty's army had learnt in its long advance from Alamein. Others, including Charles Martin, also took the opportunity to see some of those final battles in North Africa.

Back in Cairo, Brigadier Pearce Smith was told which part of the coast of Sicily would be his Brigade's objective and began working out his plan with the supporting arms and services and with the Royal Navy, who would protect and land the troops. He was devastated, after all his hard work with the Brigade on Malta and now in Egypt, when at a conference of senior officers Monty announced with characteristic high-handedness that in the invasion of Sicily 231 Malta Brigade would be commanded by Roy Urquhart. Battle had taught Monty the value of battle-experienced commanders and there was considerable force in his argument: men might die and units fail while a new commander learned his trade. Although Pearce Smith had injected new life and professionalism into the Malta Brigade, he had never commanded anything above a company in battle. Nevertheless, Montgomery could be ruthless and unkind in dismissing senior officers, especially those he thought too old or who were not 'one of his chaps'. At forty-six, Pearce Smith probably failed on both these counts, but his Brigade, which had profited from the training he gave them on Malta, greatly missed him. He was sent home and later trained and commanded another brigade on D-Day.

Brigadier Roy Urquhart, who would later command 1st Airborne Division at Arnhem, was five years younger than Pearce Smith and one of Monty's protégés. After service in India, he had commanded a battalion in North Africa before holding a staff appointment in 51st Highland Division. He now took command of the Malta Brigade in the run up to the Sicily operation.

Although they did not know it, the Brigade had good reason to be glad of Monty's sometimes ruthless professionalism. While his army was still fighting back at Mareth in Tunisia, he had got hold of the Anglo-American plans for invading Sicily, and pronounced in a signal to Alexander that *the operation planned in London breaks every common sense rule of practical battle fighting and is completely theoretical. It has no hope of success and should be completely recast.* Instead of landing troops in penny packets at seven points on the north, south, west and east coasts, Monty's revised plan concentrated the assault in the south-east of the island and transformed Operation *Husky* into a workable proposition. His was the plan towards which the Brigade now directed their training effort. Their task, operating independently of any division, would be to create a bridgehead south of Syracuse containing an airfield that could rapidly be turned to good use by the Desert Air Force. Each division then had to drive inland to a line between ten and thirty miles from the coast to ensure that the newly captured airfields were no longer within range of the enemy artillery.

The Dorsets were joined on the Suez Canal by experienced officers from 51st Highland Division and 4th Indian Division who were attached to help with their training. Under its new commander the Brigade carried out a three-day desert exercise beneath the blazing sun, preparing themselves for the day-to-day requirements of infantry warfare. They were then taken, aboard the Landing Ship *Strathnaver* which would take them to Sicily, to the Gulf of Aqaba, where they took part in a dress rehearsal daylight assault landing.

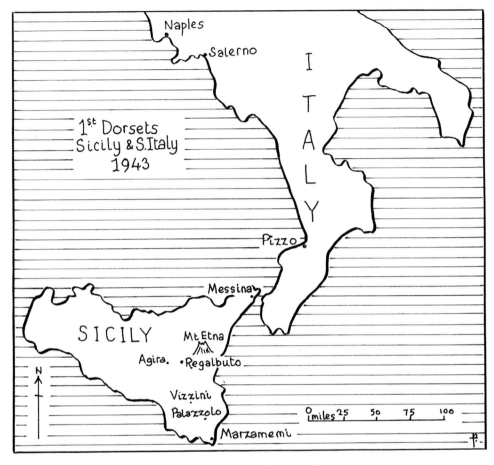

Sicily and Southern Italy

At the end of June the company commanders were told that their objective was Sicily and, after a couple of days' leave, the Dorsets embarked aboard *Strathnaver* at Suez on 1st July. Willie Hayes remembered the voyage to Sicily.

... the naval officer commanding our ship asked our commanding officer to please post sentries all round the ship to look out for torpedoes. This of course we did, posting sentries in pairs for the usual military two hours. In no time they were all asleep. Our Commanding Officer was furious. Eventually officers were posted just to show the soldiers how to do their job. They lasted no longer. Thus the poor Commanding Officer had to break a well-established military tradition and drastically reduce the time spent on duty. No one, it seemed, could watch the sea really carefully for more than about twenty minutes without going to sleep.

Malta had not forgotten them. On 8th July Lord Gort signalled:

The Service Commanders, the Lieutenant Governor and myself send you our heartfelt good wishes. The 1st Malta Brigade, the title by which we shall always remember you, is very much in our thoughts on the eve of battles to come which are sure to discomfit the enemy on his own soil. Never shall good fortune desert the men of Devonshire, Hampshire and Dorsetshire. This constitutes our fervent prayer. May victory be yours.

Corporal George Beadle later recalled the troops being let in on the secret.

... on the morning of the 8th July we were all called to the Officers' Ward Room, and there in front of us was a large map of Sicily. Our Commanding Officer was standing there, baton in hand, ready, as it were, to conquer Sicily without even landing. We were lectured for an hour and after looking at an exact scale model of the island, and many aerial plots, we were dismissed...

The weather at sea was appalling and Eisenhower had nearly postponed the operation. As the invasion fleet neared Malta, a summer storm blew up with thirty-seven-knot winds and twelve-foot waves in which the heavily laden ships pitched and tossed. Above decks the wind howled around the superstructures. Below decks, as the fleet crashed, lurched and juddered its way through the hurricane, thousands of American and British troops, packed claustrophobically and inhaling the stench from overflowing lavatories, were distracted from their fear by the agonies of seasickness.

George Beadle remembered, by the evening of the 9th, that *both below decks and above there were hives of industry. Arms and grenades were cleaned and made ready for action. All ammunition was checked; we couldn't afford any slip-ups. At last everything was ready, equipment and rifles ready at hand. A big supper was served at ten o'clock and tea at eleven. At half past eleven I went up on top deck and watched an air raid taking place on Sicily. Flak was very heavy, but many bombs were dropped. At last it was time to take to our landing craft. These we boarded and were lowered to the sea at 0045 hours on the morning of the 10th July, seven miles from the coast of Sicily. The sea was very rough and our landing craft were thrown around like corks. We each received a tot of rum before we boarded...*

And now, twelve hours later, the Malta Brigade had completed their initial task rapidly, with much less opposition than expected and with relatively light casualties. Under the baking Sicilian afternoon sun, some men trying to draw water from the wells were repeatedly fired on by enemy snipers. The Dorsets' war diary remarks that this *caused a great amount of bitterness, particularly as the snipers gave themselves up when they found that their positions had been discovered.*

In the evening the Battalion were ordered to concentrate and prepare to move north next morning but, while they assembled on the beach, they were bombed by enemy aircraft. Major Speedy Bredin,[6] commanding HQ Company, recalled *some remarks that we might as well still be in Malta!* Although a number of bombs landed around them, no one was wounded: a rich reward for the tiring effort of digging in.

THE ADVANCE INLAND

With the beach-head in Allied hands, the Italian forces in front of 50th and 51st Divisions and the Germans concentrating their counter-attack on the American forces on the left, Monty decided to launch a rapid thrust northwards. On 11th July, while 1st Parachute Brigade dropped to seize Primasole Bridge south of Catania ahead of XIII Corps' advance on the right, XXX Corps' 51st Highland Division and 231 Malta Brigade were sent north-west towards Enna, centre of Sicily's road network. The Dorsets now lent most of C Company, under Charles Martin, to help form a new composite mobile armoured brigade which would lead the advance north-west. *Harpoon Force,* as it was called, was commanded by Brigadier Richards and included 23rd Armoured Brigade, the Devons, a Vickers machine gun company from the 1/7th Middlesex Regiment, some self-propelled guns and some anti-tank guns. By the evening of the 12th, Martin's company, accompanied by two squadrons of tanks from the 46th and 50th Royal Tank Regiments and the gunners of the Honourable Artillery Company, had reached the outskirts of Vizzini.

Transport was scarce in the beach-head: 50th Division's transport had been sunk by bombing before it had even landed. The "lorried infantry" – the Devons and Martin's C Company – had only one lorry per company. In his book *We Landed in Sicily and Italy* Colonel Bill Valentine of the Devons later recalled the difficulties posed by the lack of motorised transport.

That day we learned a lot about ferrying troops in MT. We used every form of transport we had. The Anti-Tank Platoon portees did noble work and their drivers deserve

---

6   Major (later Brigadier) A E C Bredin earned his nickname by often being slightly late and therefore arriving on parade in a rush.

1st Dorsets' Campaign on Sicily July–August 1943

special mention for their noble efforts. The designer of the portee would probably have had a shock if he had seen them carrying complete platoons with all their arms and equipment. This they frequently did, often towing the guns as well. Both Bren and mortar carriers carried as many as ten men. Lorries captured later in the day proved a godsend.

   The rest of the Battalion experienced similar difficulties and resorted to requisitioning horses and carts to follow the Hampshires in their march to Noto, where they relieved units of the 50th Division. During the move a tank ran over a two-inch mortar bomb, wounding four men in A Company.

Next day they again scraped together whatever forms of transport they could to provide a shuttle service to move the Battalion forward towards Palazzolo, where they assembled five miles short of the town, with A Company well forward forming a road block ahead of the rest of the Battalion. Late that evening they were alerted about some German Mark IV tanks heading their way, and a troop of six-pounder anti-tank guns was rapidly sent up to reinforce A Company, but the tanks failed to materialise.

As the Brigade pressed north-west towards Enna, the country and the going changed. While the main roads near the coast had been metalled, the roads inland were rough and unmade. The country became rocky and precipitate with tiny villages perched on high, forbidding promontories approached by steep climbs and usually a single, unmade-up road. In the summer heat the roads were dry, and the vehicles and marching troops kicked up white dust as they advanced in the glare of the July sun. George Beadle remembered a welcome ride on a lorry after a thirty mile march across mostly cultivated soil. On the way they passed columns of prisoners and many wrecked vehicles. Here he heard of the capture at Palazzolo of thirty officers and 300 other ranks, bringing the Brigade's bag of prisoners to more than a thousand.

On the 13th the advance continued and the over-stretched shuttle service took most of the day to move the Battalion to Vizzini, where they concentrated on an open hillside north-west of Buccheri. Beadle recorded:

Here we were held up, this time by the Germans, and we all realised that we would have to fight and fight hard. The Germans had very strong dug in positions all around the town of Vizzini and in the surrounding mountains. It was almost impossible to pass down the road as the Germans had it covered with mortars and machine guns... We moved about 500 yards off the right of the road and dug in... Our artillery came into action and the Germans answered with their 88mm artillery. Exchanges took place all night and we didn't have much sleep. A 4.5 Howitzer battery was in rear of my position and as they kept firing it became impossible to sleep.

Orders were received to push through Vizzini at speed (with two Dorset companies attached to Harpoon Force) but these had to be cancelled when intelligence reports revealed how heavily the town was defended. Instead, next day, Captain Pat Chilton's B Company was ordered, without becoming too involved, to send a substantial fighting patrol to test the strength of the enemy's defences while two battalions of 51st Highland Division attacked from right and left.

In front of B Company lay two small features – known as *Straggly Hill* and *the Pimple*. Chilton sent two of his platoons forward: 10 Platoon commanded by Lieutenant Muriel and 11 Platoon led by Nigel Stickland, a twenty-four-year-old lieutenant attached from the Leicestershire Regiment. While Muriel's 10 Platoon attracted heavy fire from the Germans holding Straggly Hill, 11 Platoon under Stickland crossed the open ground towards the Pimple, which remained ominously silent. A wireless malfunction prevented Chilton recalling Stickland, who pressed on unchecked to the crest of the Pimple. George Beadle takes up the story:

At 0930 hours we moved across country so as to skirt the road and not come under fire, but as we reached the open country we were spotted and once again we were mortared. The shells were soon falling short, but we moved behind cover again and dug in. We were then in a position about four kilometres from Vizzini... The German had certainly got his mortars concealed for we couldn't spot them, neither could we spot his OP. Probably it was on the ridge in front. At 1155 hours we put in an attack.

At the bottom of the hill was a monastery. My Company jumped into three lorries and tore hell for leather down the hill towards the monastery. We were machine-gunned but made the monastery without receiving any casualties. Once at the monastery we deployed and kept cover. The object was for us to draw the enemy's fire while two battalions from another division... attacked from the rear... trapping the Germans in a pincer movement. Something went wrong... the battalions didn't show up so we were ordered to put in an attack. It appeared suicide to me at the time but orders are orders so we attacked.

We reached the top of the hill, supported by No 10 Platoon giving us covering fire, and inflicted casualties on the enemy. On [our] reaching the top, the Germans immediately counter-attacked and we were driven off, suffering seven casualties... No 11 Platoon Commander was killed and an NCO and a Private. The wounded included three NCOs. Several of us had grazes. I was pretty fortunate. A bullet struck me a glancing blow above my left eye and went straight through my steel helmet. I thought I had been kicked by a mule. I am positive that the Germans try to pick off officers and NCOs first.

As we withdrew, bringing our wounded with us, our artillery put down a barrage on Vizzini Ridge; this assisted us greatly in getting back. Just as we got back two Me 109s flew over strafing but there were no casualties on our side. One Me was shot down in flames by a Bofors gun.

When Nigel Stickland was killed on the crest of the hill, his platoon sergeant, Arthur Skingley, took command. A thirty-one-year-old Regular soldier from Canning Town, Skingley had already fought with the 1st Northamptons in the invasion of Madagascar. He later recalled the action at Vizzini.

I took command of the Platoon and carried on with the attack. Zig-zagging, I got to the top of the hill, the enemy machine-gunning from all sides. At this stage my Platoon was completely disrupted. I was by myself and looking over the ridge I saw what seemed to be a section of the enemy lying on the ground about five yards away. I fired into the enemy but they did not move. I was attracted by a movement to my left, and at about four yards distance an enemy soldier was kneeling beside a tree – I can see him now. He was covered by a camouflage net – it looked like one of ours! I swung my gun towards him and aimed. We seemed to be aiming at one another for hours, yet it was only seconds. I next felt as if a ton weight had fallen on my left shoulder. I immediately turned and jumped for cover under the ridges of the grape vine and sat down.

I stayed under cover a while as I had lost my gun. I felt very shaken and frightened. I thought I was going to die but I tried to keep my senses. I felt my shoulder. I was not bleeding. I got hold of my water bottle, took a drop and poured the rest over my head. I had also messed myself. Laying low for a while, I decided to move and got away under cover of the grape vines. Being on my own, I started on my way back. I must have been anything between three or four thousand yards in front of my own Company HQ. God knows how far back I went when I came upon some stretcher-bearers. The wound I had received had put my left arm out of action, my collar bone was broken, my scapula was fractured, my arm was hanging useless. I was now starting to feel pain. As I approached the stretcher-bearers I saw that one of them had a Sten gun and supposed he had picked it up. I immediately went for him, took the Sten gun from him and went back to resume the attack. The stretcher-bearers came after me, overpowered me and tied me onto a stretcher.

I was taken to Battalion HQ still on the stretcher. The first man to greet me was my Commanding Officer. His words were: "Who have we here?"

Someone remarked "Sergeant Skingley, Sir."

He shook me by the hand and said "Well done."

I was given morphine tablets and sent back to the Forward Casualty Clearing Station.

For his gallantry Arthur Skingley was later awarded the Distinguished Conduct Medal. When the position was finally captured by a battalion of 154 Brigade, it was discovered that the Dorsets' opponents at Vizzini had been part of the Hermann Goering Division.

Next day 231 Malta Brigade left 51st Highland Division to join the Canadian Division and, on 16th July, they moved to Caltagirone. After a fraught journey much delayed by road blocks and traffic hold-ups, they settled into their positions north-west of the town, sending out Lieutenant Eric Hannah's 18 Platoon to clear the road of mines and to reconnoitre the route for the next day's advance. Hannah's platoon excelled, clearing the road for fifteen miles before reaching a blown bridge over a dried river bed. Early next morning a team of Sappers, supported by B Company, was sent to repair the bridge and make the road passable but when, by 1400, it was still impassable, the Battalion took a long detour to bypass the bridge. Rejoining the road above the bridge, two miles on they found the road blocked again. A day of frustrations and improvisation ended with the Dorsets astride the road two miles south of Raddusa, which was held by the enemy.

Next morning A Company, clearing the road to Raddusa, found the town to be deserted – the opposition had melted away in the night, withdrawing quietly to their next defensive position. But two miles north of Raddusa the Company were mortared from a high feature overlooking the road. They dug in and took some casualties before the Devons took the feature and silenced the mortars. The Germans were giving a textbook demonstration of how to conduct a tactical retreat.

THE BATTLE FOR AGIRA

In the face of fierce German defence, casualties were mounting. On 19th July the Dorsets followed the Devons across the river Dittaino towards the hill town of Agira. When the Devons' advance was checked south of Agira, the lorries carrying the Dorsets' A and C Companies got too close to the action and took some more casualties from the German mortars. Once again the Battalion hastily dug in while the stretcher-bearers, Lance-Corporal Denis Bounsall and Private William Burt, scurried about under fire administering first aid to the wounded. Among those killed were Lieutenant John Venning, an attached officer from the Duke of Cornwall's Light Infantry, Corporal Walter Baxter from the Isle of Wight and twenty-year-old Private Denis McPhee.

Among the dead, the stretcher-bearers came across the very badly wounded commander of A Company, Major *Top* Knapp. As they put him on the stretcher one of them said: "He's finished. Let's dump him."

But a commanding voice from the stretcher replied: "No I'm not. You carry me, you... "

Despite having lost a leg, Top Knapp survived to complete a long army career, retiring as a lieutenant-colonel. He was replaced in command of A Company by Captain Arnold Jones.

Back at B Echelon a rations lorry disintegrated in a huge explosion having run over an anti-tank mine. Three men were wounded and among the thirteen dead was Lieutenant Hubbard, the thirty-eight-year-old Quartermaster. A stalwart of the Battalion, Harry Hubbard had been commissioned from CQMS early in the siege of Malta. Meanwhile, the anti-tank gunners lost a seventeen pounder gun and 64 Battery of 165th Field Regiment its two senior officers when a mortar bomb hit their scout car.

On the 20th the Dorsets despatched two patrols to gauge the strength of the enemy around Point 462, a ridge south of Agira. Lieutenant Royle of A Company took his patrol to the left while Lieutenant Browne of B took the right. Although Leonard Browne's patrol achieved its objective without being detected, Royle's patrol bumped into trouble. Under mortar and machine gun fire, Denis Bounsall once more distinguished himself, again tending the wounded and carrying one wounded man to the cover of an empty house. When he saw what had happened, Lieutenant Lawson took some men of C Company to help the wounded Royle and his men withdraw. Meanwhile Bounsall had remained with his casualty until after dark, when he carried him to the Devons' regimental aid post before returning to his own unit to find he had been reported missing. He later received the DCM for his bravery, while both the subalterns who had led the patrols received Roy Urquhart's congratulations.

The Dorsets remained in these positions for the next two days, exposed during the day to the unrelenting ferocity of the Sicilian sun and at all hours to intermittent shell and mortar fire. All around them fires blazed in the fields and columns of smoke rose to the blue sky as the Sicilian farmers, having gathered in the harvest, burned the stalks. George Beadle described his experience in this area.

Have encountered fleas ever since I came onto the island. Fleas have certainly been enemy number 3, with Jerry enemy number 1 and the Italians number 2. A few shells have dropped about twenty yards from here. No casualties but plenty of dust everywhere. Only occasional shells are coming over... Twenty-four Fortresses escorted by Lightnings have just been bombing his position also American Mustangs have been dive-bombing him. The rumble of Allied artillery can be heard in the distance. The time now is 2340 hours and as I am not on duty section I am going to try and have a couple of hours sleep. Stand-to will be 0430 hours in the morning, so I will be able to get a couple of hours. I could do with it.

The time is now 0755 hours and no rations have arrived. It is rumoured that the rations lorry received a direct hit from an 88mm shell. There are many sad faces and all are feeling hungry, but I still guess we will get some rations up shortly.

Finally, at 1630 on 22nd July orders were given for a night attack on the ridge at Point 462. After an artillery stonk on the ridge, B Company led off and captured the first objective. At 0440 George Beadle, promoted sergeant the day before, was sent out on a patrol led by Sergeant William Evans.

We came upon an Italian machine gun position and found two sentries asleep. They shouldn't go to sleep on sentry duty. They were killed by bayonet. We walked into this position and took two officers and twenty-six other prisoners. We also had six machine guns, several thousand rounds of ammunition and dozens of grenades. I sent the prisoners back to HQ with a couple of men, and continued the patrol, and finished up by rounding up one more officer and fifty-six other ranks... We were eight all told, so that was odds of over ten to one, yet they surrendered. They didn't want to fight for, when they were brought to HQ, they tore off all their badges and threw them away, muttering something about Mussolini, and they all seemed pleased that the war, at least for them, was finished.

B Company's success allowed C and D Companies to pass through and take either end of the ridge. On that moonless night the two companies had somehow crossed each other's paths and ended up taking each other's objectives!

Leading C Company was Charles Martin, whose DSO citation later described the action.

The position was an entrenched one on commanding ground and covered by medium machine-guns, mortars and light automatics. As the enemy's position was being approached and after the artillery covering fire had ceased, an enemy machine-gun post opened fire, pinning one of Captain Martin's platoons to the ground. Captain Martin, having observed this, stalked the enemy post himself over a distance of some 60 yards. He shot one member of the machine-gun crew and then rushed in, picked up a rifle and disposed of the remainder of the crew by using the butt of the rifle. By this action the company was enabled to continue its advance and subsequently to secure its objective.

In a letter home Martin wrote of this action: *The pistol actually behaved very well but in the heat of the battle I had forgotten how many bullets there were left and got the most awful shock when the thing went 'click' in the middle of the fracas. Still – 'all's well that ends well'!* According to the Brigade's Intelligence Officer, who later wrote the history of 231 Malta Brigade, Martin *was eventually found at the bottom of a slit trench grappling with the fourth occupant.*

Martin's citation, which earned him a Distinguished Service Order, described his seminal part in both this action and the landings two weeks earlier. In the Second World War it was unusual for a subaltern or captain to win a DSO and, when they did, the award was often seen as a near-miss for a VC.

Sergeant George Wilson of C Company, who alongside Martin had played such an important part in the landing on Sicily, was killed in this battle. One of C Company's section commanders, Lance-Corporal Len Bunning from Kentish Town, was awarded a Military Medal for his leadership, while the Brigade's histo-rian mentioned particularly the inspiring leadership of Sidney Stoy, a South Staffordshire subaltern commanding 17 Platoon in D Company, who also played a major part in the successful capture of Point 462. Beadle recalled:

Have just heard that the Yanks took Palermo and without a fight, so now three quar-ters of the island is in Allied hands... We are remaining here tonight and we may be here all day tomorrow as well. Of course it all depends on the situation. All the ridges to the east, west and south of the town have been captured and there is very little fire coming from the town itself.

But Agira was proving a tough nut for the Canadian Division to crack. Beadle remembered the next day, Saturday 24th July.

The Germans have established several strong positions on the outskirts of the town and the Canadians are hammering these positions with their 25-pounders. Mustangs have dive-bombed him, but failed to shift him. Fortresses are going to have a go at him this afternoon. The Canadians have captured one objective and are pushing on. This Canadian Division has only just arrived from England and several men have gone down with the heat stroke, and quite a lot are suffering from fatigue. It is quite possible the Brigade will have to go in to assist them but that won't be before tomorrow so that gives us one more night here. Jerry has two lines of retreat from Agira. One is the mountain road and the other is a second class road, but the second class road is being looked after by our artillery. Their FOOs have got this road under

Agira, Sicily by John Worsley

observation and so we are alright... Fortresses are now blasting his positions but a lot of the bombs are missing their marks. Only light AA is being thrown against the Forts and there are no signs of the Luftwaffe.

Over the next three days the Brigade edged up as far as it could towards Agira and sent out fighting and standing patrols to fire on any enemy evacuating Agira along the mountainous road east towards Regalbuto. To keep the road clear the Germans launched a fierce attack on A Company's standing patrol who were occupying some high ground overlooking the road. Sergeant Edward Kenny won a Military Medal for covering the patrol's withdrawal under heavy fire, he himself killing several enemy including a German officer who had demanded his surrender.

The Canadians finally took Agira on the night of 27th/28th July, freeing the Malta Brigade to advance due east, skirting the southern slopes of Mount Etna, towards Catania. Their first stop would be Regalbuto. Meanwhile on the 25th Mussolini had been ejected from power and the new government under Marshal Badoglio was preparing to make overtures of peace. Two weeks on, the invasion had already achieved its primary strategic aim: it had knocked Italy out of the war.

THE BATTLE FOR REGALBUTO

On 28th July, with his C Company held up at an open stretch of ground which the Germans had well covered by machine guns, Charles Martin spotted the Brigade commander's jeep just across the valley. Roy Urquhart had driven out to see what was happening. Having picked his way across the valley, Martin explained the problem to Urquhart, who ordered two flanking attacks to support C Company's advance. On the left a company of the Devons, supported by tanks in hull-down positions, attacked and took one feature while, on the right, D Company of the 1st Dorsets put in another attack.

Despite suffering eleven casualties as a result of mortaring, heavy sniping by Italian troops hidden in the thick undergrowth, and being fired on by their own artillery, D Company took their objective. During the sniping and mortaring both the Company's stretcher-bearers were everywhere, tending the wounded and trying to protect them from the enemy fire. One – Bandsman James Maloney – was killed and the other, William Down from Sherborne, was awarded a Military Medal. D Company took about eighty Italian prisoners that day.

Passing through D Company's position, B Company continued the advance for another two miles. George Beadle remembered:

Enemy artillery was engaging us, but we suffered no casualties. REs who were with us had two lorries and a jeep destroyed with several killed and wounded. We attacked and captured a small hill feature about seven and a half kilos from Regalbuto. We were supported in the attack by our own 3 inch mortars. We had a bit of a battle at the crest of the hill but captured it with only minor casualties. Several machine gun posts were destroyed by the 3 inch mortars' shooting and many German dead and wounded were lying around. As we are going to hold this position we had to dig in, so here I am reclining in my slit trench and I am hoping for a spot of sleep tonight.

The Dorsets' advance had now brought them to another dominant feature, Point 608, which would have to be taken. Beadle takes up B Company's part in this action, on the right.

Had a few hours' sleep last night but it was restless as it was so cold. Kept dozing off and then waking up to get warm. We pushed on a further 3 kilos and occupied a high feature overlooking Regalbuto. Opposition on this feature was somewhat stiffer but we made the tip with five killed and eight wounded. One of our own platoons opened up on us once, but luckily they didn't hit anybody. I had two killed and three wounded in my section but we found twenty dead Germans on the top and twelve wounded. The wounded were badly shaken up by the artillery. Most of them were only boys of about eighteen years of age. We were supported in the attack by a field regiment of Canadian Artillery and these boys are sure enthusiastic. They kept blazing away until we were nearly on the top before they lifted their barrage, and several times we were nearly caught. We are occupying slit trenches which the Germans had previously occupied. We are lying on the forward slopes and Jerry is mortaring and machine gunning from across the way.

Meanwhile, on the left, D Company encountered more difficult terrain and stiffer resistance. Lieutenant Sidney Stoy led his 17 Platoon across open ground, finding and crossing a deep ravine that did not appear on the maps. In the approach to the attack Private Thompson's platoon lost two of its section commanders. He immediately took command of one of the sections, rallied the men and attacked the enemy position from a flank, enabling his platoon to press home the attack. D Company's commander, Captain Desmond Wakely, had clinched victory on the ridge by leading a section of 16 Platoon against the enemy positions and hurling grenades into them. Sadly, Lieutenant Stoy was wounded in the head during the closing stage of the battle, and he died the next day. He and Desmond Wakely won the Military Cross that day.

In his short history of the Brigade's time on Malta and Sicily, Major Gilchrist quoted from the diary he kept as Brigade Intelligence Officer. This entry describes his perspective of B and D Companies' capture of Point 608.

An action is in progress. The Dorsets are attacking a large hill on the right of the road. On the map this is called Stupari. At the same time the Hampshires are attacking the lower ground to the left of the road. Nothing can be seen of the troops of either battalion as the ground is far too broken and wooded.

There is a tremendous noise as, from time to time, the tanks come out of the cutting and fire at the ground in front of the Hampshires with everything they have got. I can see their tracer fire searching the area.

Battles are usually disappointing spectacles, but this scene might have been set by Hollywood. The tanks have no cover – they are in full view. Their tracer fire is like a firework display and in the noise it is almost impossible to hear oneself speak.

Also on the road and in full view of the enemy is the Brigade Commander and round him the COs of the three battalions and Lieut-Colonel Awdry of the 165th Field Regiment. They are in a magnificent position to direct operations, but one enemy shell would wipe out the lot.

... a shout comes from the higher ground on the left. 'We've captured our objective!'
It is Colonel Ray.

'Well done, Dorsets,' replies the Brigade Commander.

Gilchrist's later account stressed the importance of the capture of this feature, mentioning particularly the part played by B Company's commander, Pat Chilton, who later received a Military Cross.

The Dorsets had done well to capture their objective, which was a huge hill with a commanding view over the whole Regalbuto area. Captain Chilton of B Company had particularly distinguished himself. As his company struggled up the lower slopes of the steep hill they came under intense machine-gun and mortar fire which caused many casualties. Captain Chilton, having got his company under cover, went forward himself to make a reconnaissance. He then put in his attack, leading his company with great dash and determination. He was the first man into the enemy positions

Captain Pat Chilton MC

and by the use of his revolver and hand grenades he personally accounted for several of the German defenders.

The Battalion were now in some of the most inhospitable country they had encountered: steep rocky slopes punctuated by sheer ravines. The tank crews and anti-tank-gunners did remarkably well to keep up with them as much as they did, but the environment was one in which the advance depended principally on the infantry. Confronting a mixed enemy of usually despondent Italians and consummately efficient Germans, and chastened by rumours based on hard experience of the firepower and armour of the Germans' new Tiger tank, the infantry faced advances across a terrain that strongly favoured the defenders. Every rock or stretch of scrub could hide a sniper or a Spandau team. Round every corner could be an anti-tank gun or an enemy position. The Italians might be dispirited and close to surrender and the Germans outnumbered and on the retreat, but the latter would continue to exact a high price in Allied blood to the very end.

Willie Hayes, commanding the Dorsets' Carrier Platoon, remembered:

Near Mount Etna, surrounded by lava, the Commanding Officer said, 'German tanks are reported to be moving towards us, so take your carrier platoon and drive them off.'

Thirteen Bren guns – I ask you! Across all this lava – in a few hundred yards we will lose every track.

'Go – or I will have you court martialled for cowardice.'

All thirteen tracks were off within a few hundred yards. The noise made in hammering them on again was enough to waken the dead, let alone the Germans, though of course we were covered with our thirteen Bren guns! Off next day leading the advance.

The notion of confronting German tanks with a handful of Bren gun carriers seems as absurd as the threat of court-martialling for cowardice the only officer in the 1st Battalion to win two MCs. But the pressures on a CO trying to maintain the momentum of the advance day after day must have been enormous.

Only Regalbuto Ridge now remained before the town itself could be taken, but it was heavily defended. On the night of 29th July the Hampshires put in an unsuccessful night attack and on the following night the Devons, well supported by field and medium artillery, finally took it. In between these two attacks, Sergeant William Evans won a Military Medal. During a daylight patrol on the 30th, he stayed behind with a Bren gun, allowing the enemy to close to within 150 yards of his position while his platoon withdrew safely. After dark he then guided his company to a forward assembly area from which a successful attack could be made on the enemy positions.

Early on the morning of 31st July the Germans counter-attacked the Devons' positions on the ridge with parachutists and an assault engineer company supported by tanks. During the Devons' gallant defence of the Ridge, the Dorsets stood by, waiting to help.

When the Dorsets were able to push forward, A Company captured the railway station and then C Company took some high ground beyond, killing and capturing some forty-five enemy in the process. C Company's own casualties amounted to one killed and two wounded. Relieved by a Canadian battalion, A, B and C Companies moved to some high ground and prepared for the attack on Regalbuto itself.

D Company had been detached from the Battalion and had launched a night attack on the Castle feature, south-east of the town. Again Private Sam Thompson inspired his section to greater efforts, killing fifteen Germans and capturing an enemy machine gun position and an anti-tank gun. Sadly, enemy tanks denied them their objective, which next day repelled a full battalion attack by Canadian troops. Meanwhile, for his bravery in this action and on 29th July, Thompson was recommended for a Distinguished Conduct Medal. Although General Oliver Leese, the Corps Commander, reduced the award to a Military Medal, Sam Thompson would win a DCM on D-Day before losing his life during the fighting in the Normandy bocage. He was the only Dorset throughout the war to win both the DCM and MM.

At 0600 on 1st August, with fire support from gunners and a squadron of tanks, A and B Companies attacked the rear of Regalbuto. On their way in, Lance-Corporal Sam Ennis, from Northern Ireland, realised his section had become separated from the rest of his platoon. The section found itself immediately below an enemy position which included a 20mm gun and was on a ledge about thirty feet above, commanding all the intervening ground. Spotting Ennis's section, the Germans started to hurl hand grenades down on them and the Platoon Sergeant was wounded. Ennis immediately took command and, under heavy fire from an enemy who was very close at hand, he moved his section to the left flank and attacked the strongpoint, which he captured. Ennis's tactical nous and bravery won him a Military Medal and also helped win his platoon entry to the town of Regalbuto.

The two companies fought their way into the town and grabbed the marketplace, where they took up defensive positions against counter-attack. George Beadle takes up the story:

Proceeding with caution we moved up the first street we came to. We had moved about 200 yards up this street when we came under heavy gunfire. Luckily this fire was high so we immediately took to cover. It was impossible to get on the rooftops as they were all slanting and not too safe in any case. However, we crawled round to a flank, driving the machine-gunners out and killing them. We pushed on for about another hundred yards when we were fired on from at least eighteen different positions. Here we had to remain. 10 Platoon came up on our right and 11 Platoon on our left. These two platoons were also held up. Tiger tanks came up and machine-gunned and shelled us, but we suffered no casualties.

But, because the Castle feature remained in German hands, launching an attack from the nearside of the town to reach A and B Companies was impossible. They therefore found themselves in imminent danger of being surrounded and annihilated by the tanks Beadle had encountered.

The order to withdraw was given so we pulled out using fire and movement and withdrew to the edge of the town. We took up our position on the right flank and covered 10 and 11 Platoons...

We lined up and Jerry attacked again with great force. We were once more pushed back. A Company on the left withdrew and as they went back one of the sergeants shouted 'B Company, you're on your own.' And on our own we certainly were...

10 and 11 Platoons raced back and took up positions to cover us. One of our sections was forward and we had a devil of a job to get them out. Jerry was in sight in all directions. We got this section out and I remained with my section behind a small building. The other two sections from my platoon moved back and then covered my withdrawal. When I joined the remainder of the Company they were stretched out in line. We let Jerry get to within about two hundred yards of us and then opened fire with everything we had.

11 Platoon was commanded by Sergeant Charles Edwards, who was ordered to cover the withdrawal of the remainder of B Company. His DCM citation amplifies Beadle's account.

Although surrounded by three German tanks and approximately fifty German infantry, Sergeant Edwards held his position and was himself last to leave having successfully covered the withdrawal of the Company and beaten off at least two attacks on his position... Twice the enemy supported by tanks and mortars attacked the Platoon and on one occasion hand-to-hand fighting took place. On both occasions the enemy were driven back and the position was held. During the course of this action Sergeant Edwards was wounded but he fought on and encouraged his men to hold the position. Later in the action he was again wounded but still refused to be evacuated until the final attack was beaten off.

B Company withdrew, next to A and C Companies, to a position beside a cemetery about a thousand yards from the town. Beadle remembered: *There was a horrible smell as some of the bodies had been blown from the earth. There were also five bodies in the mortuary – a German officer, three women and a man. It appeared the women had been raped, then shot.*

That night the Canadians took the Castle feature and on 2nd August Regalbuto itself fell. While many of the Germans slipped silently away, some remained and B Company took part in some vicious street-fighting against a few last-ditch defenders. Beadle describes his last battle experience on Sicily:

At 1100 hours seven regiments of artillery battered the town and then we went in. He was still occupying the town and we had plenty of street fighting to do. I posted one chap watching a window while I went round the back. No sooner had I got round the back than there was an explosion and a groan. I ran round to the front again and found the chap I had posted badly cut about the face, neck and back. He had received a grenade all to himself. He must have been at fault of course or he would have seen it. The grenade appeared to come out of a small alley just where it turned. I could hear the Germans talking and they were in a kind of cul de sac. The chap I was with tripped over a stone and down came two grenades. One didn't go off and the blast from the other picked me up and threw me to the ground...

Before I got clear one of the Germans came from the cul de sac and took a quick shot at us. I felt the draught of the bullet... As soon as I got my wind back I took off my boots and crawled forward again to the corner. Withdrawing the pin from the grenade I released the lever and counted to two, then threw the grenade. I was a bit scared as it was a four second fuse. I heard it strike the wall and explode. After this I heard groans and a weak voice shouting 'Kamerad. Kamerad.'

Along with the other chap we went stealthily into the alley and found one German dead, literally blown to pieces, and his mate bleeding from a badly shattered thigh which he was trying to bandage.

In a number of similarly vicious little encounters, the battle of Regalbuto was won and the Dorsets' part in the capture of Sicily completed. Since 10th July they had spent twenty-four days on the advance, marching 140 miles on foot and travelling considerably further by lorry. Since the successful assault landing they had fought two major actions – Agira and Regalbuto – and countless smaller ones.

They had earned three new battle honours and fifteen decorations. And they had seen sixty-three of their strength killed and twice that number wounded – a figure that was nearly increased on 4th August when a formation of USAAF Mitchells bombed Regalbuto by mistake. Happily no Dorsets were killed or wounded.

Now that their campaign was over, time was spent on reorganisation, maintenance and training, but on 12th August they held a gymkhana with displays by a light anti-aircraft regiment and a field ambulance detachment. The next day found them upping sticks and moving to Giarre on the north-east coast. Five days later it was announced that all organised resistance on Sicily had ceased: the island was in Allied hands.

While the Dorsets trained and rested, in Quebec Churchill and Roosevelt and their advisers were making decisions which would dictate the 1st Battalion's destiny for the next eighteen months. Prompted by the rapid conquest of Sicily, the dismissal of Mussolini and the new Italian government's peace overtures, the British case for an early invasion of Italy was hard to resist. The Americans reluctantly agreed, but insisted that the invasion of Northern France should be set in hand, and General Sir Frederick Morgan's plans for those landings were approved. By the end of the Quebec Conference on 24th August the stage was set for two more assault landings in which the 1st Dorsets would lead. The first – on the toe of Italy – would follow in a little over a fortnight.

ASSAULT LANDING IN ITALY

The Italian mainland lay only a few miles across the Straits of Messina. The Italian government had sued for peace – their surrender was finally agreed on 3rd September – and within a few days the entire Italian fleet would lie at anchor under the guns of Malta. Sicily offered a springboard onto a vulnerable, defeated Italy. But where to land?

Having saved the invasion of Sicily from disaster by entirely recasting the plans, Monty might have been regarded as the obvious choice to plan the invasion. But political considerations, growing American self-confidence and personal antipathies developed in North Africa and Sicily (partly as a result of Monty's inability to hide his contempt for what he regarded as American incompetence) saw him effectively excluded from the planning. Instead, the task was given to the unblooded American General Mark Clark, who lacked the confidence or experience to stand up to senior quasi-political interference in the planning process. The Eighth Army, less General Brian Horrocks's Corps which was placed under Clark's command, was relegated to a minor, arguably unnecessary yet demanding role on the toe, sole and heel of Italy while Clark's Fifth Army invaded below Naples on the beaches of Salerno.

The 5th Division would cross the straits of Messina and land in Calabria and 231 Malta Brigade was to follow afterwards and seize a beachhead ahead of 5th Division to speed and facilitate their advance north. The last few days of August and the first few of September were therefore spent training hard and practising boarding and disembarking from landing craft.

On 31st August the Battalion said farewell to a draft of twenty-eight men who had served in their ranks since their time in India. These men had not been home for eight years, had served on the North West Frontier, suffered and starved on Malta and fought and won a bitter campaign in Sicily. They were due a break. Among those who had endured all these wartime hardships was Sergeant William Townsend, who had previously served with the 2nd Battalion in Palestine, where he had won the Military Medal.

On the day of Italy's surrender the Battalion were briefed about the landing and received sixty reinforcements for the task that lay ahead. By 1800 their kit was packed and they were ready to go.

On 5th September they moved to Messina ready to embark the next day, but the operation was postponed because of rough weather. Because of the postponement and 5th Division's rapid advance up the toe of Calabria, the Brigade's planned landing beach had to be moved further north. They embarked on the afternoon of 7th September with the intention of landing that night near Pizzo, but the delay and change of plan came at a price.

Commandos were supposed to land at 0230 followed at 0300 by the forward companies of the Hampshires on the left and the Dorsets on the right. At 0330 the Devons would follow. But the preparation time and hasty briefing given to the sailors commanding the landing craft had been inadequate. The flotillas of landing craft dispersed and were lost in the darkness. Thus the first troops ashore were not Commandos but the Hampshires' Tactical Headquarters, who found themselves landed on the wrong beach at the wrong time. The first Dorset ashore was the Second-in-Command, Major Bobby Nicoll, of Rear HQ, carrying a sack of mail for the Battalion.

By the time vehicles and troops in any number were landing on the beach it was nearly 0600 and daylight. The German coastal batteries and 88mm guns began

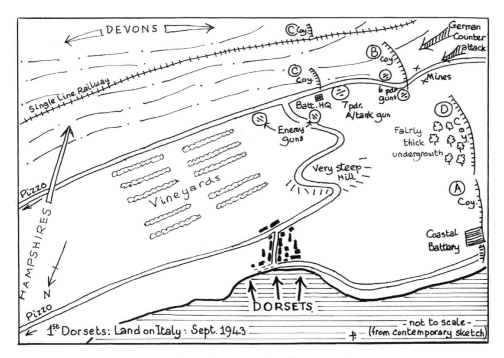

1st Dorsets' Landing in Italy 8th September 1943

to shell the beaches. Happily, the beaches were not mined, and the Brigade had rehearsed a plan for assembling the battalions and sorting out a tangle of this kind. Disaster was thus averted although the battalions were shelled as they assembled and concentrated.

Major Gilchrist describes the terrain facing the Brigade.

The ground was level for about 500 yards from the beach. After that it rose sharply for about a mile up to a height of about 1500 feet. A railway line crossed the sector in a series of cuttings and tunnels near where the ground commenced to rise. Two main roads ran right through the sector. One was a coast road and the other ran along the side of a hill at a height of about 1,000 feet. Only one lateral road connected the two main roads. This was in the Dorsets' sector and it ascended the steep hill in a series of hairpin bends. It will be seen therefore from this description that the Devons' sector, which was farthest away from the beaches and in the centre, consisted of hilltops. The Dorsets and the Hampshires who faced the flanks had part of their battalions up the hill and the other part in the low ground.

While the Hampshires engaged enemy vehicles on the main road and a Devon company came under fire from tanks as it climbed the steep hill, A Company of the 1st Dorsets took their objective on the right flank, capturing sixty Italian prisoners and a coastal defence battery of eight 155mm guns.

Meanwhile, B Company took the lateral road up the hill accompanied by Broke Ray and Roy Urquhart. According to Gilchrist's account: *Gunfire was still falling all over the area and the Brigade Commander's Tam o'Shanter bonnet was blown off his head by a near miss. The Dorsets were meeting German opposition on this road and were coming under fire of guns on half-tracked self-propelled vehicles and tanks. Sergeant E Brown of the Dorsets materially assisted this advance by quickly placing his 6-pounder anti-tank gun into position and putting two of the half tracked vehicles out of commission. He was wounded, but refused all medical assistance until he had seen the advance continue.*

A troop of armoured cars, together with a Mark IV tank, attacked the left flank of B Company. While Sergeant Ernest Brown's six-pounder anti-tank gun knocked out the tank, a stalwart of B Company, Sergeant William Evans, threw a grenade into the leading car and shot the German troop commander. George Beadle witnessed this incident and described Evans's grenade dropping into the hull of the armoured car, which then went straight over the edge of the hill. The armoured car crew were unlucky to have encountered Evans who, according to Willie Hayes, was one of the Battalion's fast bowlers. Brown was later awarded the 1st Battalion's only Military Medal won on the Italian mainland while Evans was given a Bar to the MM he had won on Sicily.

By noon the Dorsets and Hampshires had taken all their objectives but, half an hour later, the Germans counter-attacked the Dorsets on the inland road. Lieutenant Leonard Browne, commanding a platoon in B Company, found his platoon facing the main thrust of an attack by 100 troops supported by tanks. The citation for Browne's Military Cross describes the incident.

Owing to the closeness of the country, German infantry were able to get to close quarters and hand-to-hand fighting took place. Lieutenant Browne, with total disregard for his own personal safety throughout this action, went from one section to another, giving orders and words of encouragement to his men to hold on and fight back. It was to a large extent due to this officer's action that sufficient time was gained to allow troops from the reserve company to be brought up on the flank... and the enemy to be driven off with heavy loss.

Shortly afterwards the Brigadier called down air support on some enemy positions, but the flight of Kittyhawk fighter-bombers strafed and bombed the Brigade's positions in error.

Sergeant Evans winning the Bar to his MM by Bryan de Grineau

Although the Hampshires were also counter-attacked and the Devons had a tough fight to gain all their objectives, the Brigade had emerged from the initial confusion and completed their task by the time the leading units of 5th Division reached them that evening. The next morning the Devons led the Brigade and 5th Division's advance north. After a gruelling twenty mile advance, late in the afternoon Roy Urquhart's jeep was characteristically well up with the leading companies when it encountered a German armoured car. A shell miraculously missed Broke Ray, who was sitting on the bonnet of the jeep, but burst in the back, killing the wireless operator, seriously wounding the new Brigade Intelligence Officer and slightly wounding Urquhart.

The 1st Dorsets' Commanding Officer, who was awarded an immediate DSO for his leadership in Calabria, would be one of the last – if not the last – of his Battalion to be shot at in the Italian campaign. Although they did not know it at the time, the Dorsets would see no more action in Italy. Their experience had been short, sharp and muddled – in conception and in execution – but they had emerged from the muddle triumphantly, completing their task rapidly and effectively with the loss of only eight men.

On 10th September, while Monty's army moved north to help Clark's who were in trouble at Salerno, 231 Brigade were stood down. After a brief move to Sapri, they heard that they were to be returned home.

Charles Martin left the Battalion, having been appointed Second-in-Command of the 1st Hampshires. He wrote in a letter home: *It is a bit of a wrench leaving the old Dorsets after all these years, but as the Brig himself picked me from all those eligible in the Brigade one feels rather pleased and prepared to do something in return.* We will meet him again on the D-Day beaches.

The Dorsets left for Sicily on 23rd September and, a month later, embarked for Britain, from where they would play a part in opening the second front in France. The 1st Battalion's next, and third, assault landing would be a very different proposition in scale, effect and – sadly – casualties.

A NORTH AFRICAN AND MEDITERRANEAN POSTSCRIPT

The 1st Battalion's was not the Dorset Regiment's only contribution to the campaigns in North Africa and the Mediterranean. Three awards of the Distinguished Service Order and two of Military Crosses tell part of the story.

Lieutenant-Colonel James Gifford, who had first been commissioned in the Dorsets in 1924, had been seconded to the Sudan Defence Force since 1934. Serving under General Noel Beresford-Pierse, he fought in the Sudan and Abyssinia, commanding the Blue Nile Force, a composite battalion and the Sudan Column in a series of operations between November 1941 and April 1942. At Chelga, when his troops were in close contact with the Italian enemy during an advance, he accounted for twelve of the enemy himself with a rifle. The citation for his DSO, awarded in September 1942, describes this incident as *typical of his conduct throughout and of the consistent gallantry which he displayed in leading his troops.* He would remain in the Middle East for most of the war, be thrice mentioned in Despatches and achieve the local rank of major-general.

In the eastern Mediterranean, an officer of the Dorsets who had been commissioned on the same day in 1936 as Charles Martin, was playing a major role in the ill-fated attempt to seize the islands of Cos and Leros after the Italian surrender. Still shown in the Army List as a captain in the Dorsetshire Regiment, Kit Forsyth was an acting squadron-leader commanding a flight in 216 Squadron. When he joined the Squadron in October 1942, he had already commanded a fighter squadron in the Middle East and flown two tours of fighter operations – one in Britain and the second in North Africa. As a fighter pilot he had shot down three enemy aircraft, scored one "probable" victory and damaged four more. On the night of 13th September 1943, he led a formation of six Dakota aircraft to drop parachute troops on Cos. The Commanding Officer of 11th Parachute Regiment described Forsyth's crews' performance as *without parallel in the history of British parachute operations*. After this first operation, Forsyth made several more sorties to Cos and Leros and was awarded a DSO. Kit Forsyth would formally cease to be a Dorset only in March 1946, when he was given a permanent commission in the Royal Air Force.

After the 1st Dorsets had returned to England, at least four more Dorsets would continue the army's hard slog up Italy. One was Donald Price who, as Brigade Major of 139 Infantry Brigade, was awarded the American Bronze Star for having been *a constant inspiration to all ranks* during the operations on the Garigliano and Gothic Line. After the war he commanded the 2/5th Leicesters in Greece, Italy and Austria but sadly died of his injuries after a riding accident.

Another was Jock Woodhouse, a twenty-year-old lieutenant commanding the Battle Platoon of the 1st East Surreys. The son of one distinguished Dorset and

Lieutenant Jock Woodhouse MC with the East Surreys in Italy

the cousin of two more, Woodhouse had fought with the East Surreys in First Army's battles in Tunisia before making a name for himself – and winning an MC – leading daring patrols on the Italian mainland. On his last patrol, in March 1944, he was captured and spent the rest of the war in countless escape attempts from prison camps. After the war, Jock Woodhouse returned to his own Regiment and served with the 1st Dorsets in Austria. We shall meet him again later in our story.

A third was Bill Heald, who served with the Hampshire Brigade, commanding first a platoon, then a company and finally a battalion. In September 1943, while commanding a platoon of the 2/4th Hampshires, his position was over-run by German armoured cars. He was awarded a Military Cross for extricating his platoon and then restoring the situation by counter-attacking and seeing off the attackers, forcing one armoured car into a minefield. A year later he was commanding D Company of the 5th Hampshires at Montescudo and led them in an attack. When enemy machine guns opened up, he ran from platoon to platoon, directing their fire against the machine gun positions. When a troop of tanks appeared he also ran to direct the troop commander's fire. When all his platoon commanders were wounded, Heald rallied the Company and led it forward to clear his objective. Finally, when his CO was called away, he took command of the Battalion and co-ordinated the whole defence of the captured ground. He was awarded a DSO and temporarily took command of the 5th Hampshires in September 1944. He later served as ADC to General Eisenhower, was appointed MBE and rejoined the 1st Dorsets in Austria. After leaving the army, Bill Heald helped to establish the Duke of Edinburgh's Award Scheme and was appointed Commander of the Royal Victorian Order.

The fourth Dorset was Major Mike Sanders, who as a subaltern had escaped with the 2nd Dorsets from Dunkirk before fighting in Tunisia, Sicily and Italy with the Royal Armoured Corps. During the lull after Dunkirk he had joined the newly formed Reconnaissance Corps and landed in Algiers with the 56th Reconnaissance Regiment in First Army. Later he fought at Monte Cassino and in the vicious battles in the spring of 1945, earning a mention in Despatches and an American Silver Star. In the post-war period, despite a number of extra-regimental postings, he served with both the 1st and 4th Dorsets and was appointed MBE for his service in Nigeria. In the 1960s Mike Sanders helped tell the army's story of the Second World War by working as a researcher for the popular television documentaries presented by Sir Brian Horrocks.

4

The Regiment at Home, United Kingdom
1940–45

Defeat to Victory

The Battle of Britain

On their return from Dunkirk, the 2nd Dorsets were packed off up to Pudsey in Yorkshire but their gallant Colonel, suffering from double pneumonia, was admitted to hospital. What he had seen during the retreat to Dunkirk – the collapse of the French army, the defeat and evacuation of the BEF and the bodies of women and children who had been bombed and machine-gunned by the Luftwaffe – now persuaded him that invasion was imminent. He and his wife decided to send their four-year-old son, Christopher, across the perilous Atlantic to the safety of Canada. After his exertions in France Colonel Steve never fully recovered his health, although he would soldier on in England and in the Middle East throughout the war.

Meanwhile, another 2nd Battalion man, Private Alf Finch (who had escaped on the last boat from St Malo), returned later than the rest of the Battalion. Sent via Aldershot to Southampton, he joined a mixed platoon (including Devons and Dorsets) forming the military guard for 1,200 enemy aliens who had been interned and were to be transported to Canada. The internees and their guards sailed from Liverpool on 1st July 1940 aboard the SS *Arandora Star*. At 0705 hours next morning, seventy-five miles west of the coast of Donegal, the ship was torpedoed by the German U-boat U47. A boiler exploded and *Arandora Star* broke in two. She sank thirty-five minutes later. Alf Finch found himself locked in his cabin and had to break down the door to get out. With everywhere below decks flooded, he was unable to reach the boat deck but finally jumped into the sea. Covered in oil, he hauled himself onto a life raft, where he stayed for nine hours before being rescued by the *St Laurent*. Here he was reunited with a handful of fellow Dorsets who had also survived the sinking. In total, 743 of those aboard *Arandora Star* had died, among them nineteen men of the Devons and four Dorsets: Private Frederick Kellaway of the 2nd Battalion[7] and Privates William Chick, Robert Godfree and Ronald Terrell of the 4th. Alf Finch was a very lucky man to survive first shot and shell in France and then a torpedo in the Atlantic. Within a few days, he returned to his young bride in Sherborne. Happily, he would survive the war, serving in Africa and rising to Colour Sergeant before returning to Sherborne to work at the Coldharbour Hospital.

As Colonel Steve had recognised, the country now faced the greatest threat to its survival since Duke William of Normandy had landed at Pevensey in the autumn of 1066. Not the Kaiser, nor Napoleon Bonaparte nor Philip II of Spain had represented such a formidable enemy. Poland had been crushed, Denmark, Norway, the Netherlands and Belgium overwhelmed and now France, a staunch ally a generation before, had fallen without much fight. To the south, Mussolini's Italy rapidly allied itself with the victorious Germany and it seemed likely that Fascist Spain would follow suit. Across the Mediterranean, the colonies of France and Italy would now be in hostile hands, leaving the whole of North Africa, from Morocco in the west to the Egyptian border in the east, under Axis control. Hitler's ally, Stalin, having grabbed eastern Poland in September 1939, tightened his grip on the Baltic states. Across the Atlantic, the United States of America had yet to awaken from its isolationist dream. Although the Empire – India, Canada, Australia, New Zealand and South Africa – mobilised to help, there was little they could do at this stage to help defend the British Isles against the imminent danger of a German invasion.

In Yorkshire the 2nd Dorsets were rebuilt, receiving and training reinforcements. After Dunkirk the home army was severely under-strength and very short of equipment. The 43rd Wessex Division, which included the 4th and 5th Dorsets, was now the only fully equipped infantry division in England. From the West Country, where they had been since the outbreak of war, they were sent to Hertfordshire to form a mobile reserve to be used to repel any invasion. Len Sharpe, then a twenty-year-old soldier in the 4th Battalion, remembered the entire Division being *on standby to move in coaches to anywhere on the east or south coast in the event of invasion.*

Churchill's speech to the House of Commons on the evening of 16th June acknowledged that, now that the Battle of France was over, the Battle of Britain was

---

7   The Commonwealth War Graves Commission list Frederick Kellaway, a Sherborne man, as a Sapper with a Dorset number. It seems likely that he was attached to the Royal Engineers at the time of his death.

about to begin. The Prime Minister made plain that nothing less than the survival of western civilisation depended upon victory in the coming battle to defend Great Britain. The army, licking its wounds after its escape at Dunkirk, could play only a supporting role in preventing an invasion. The country's fate lay in the hands of the Royal Navy and the Royal Air Force, whose task was to dominate the sea and air approaches to deter any attempted landings.

While the Royal Navy guarded the Channel, North Sea and Atlantic approaches, the heavily outnumbered Hurricanes and Spitfires of RAF Fighter Command tangled with Goering's Heinkels, Dorniers and Messerschmitts over the southern counties. Meanwhile RAF Bomber Command attacked the German barges assembling in the Channel ports. These were desperate times and the stakes were high. If the Germans won control of the air and sea, they would invade. If that invasion succeeded, Hitler would be free to look east and turn on Soviet Russia. Whoever – Hitler or Stalin – emerged victorious from that titanic encounter would dominate the whole of Europe and beyond for decades to come. For the British, the Battle of Britain was an entirely defensive battle, the first ever fought in the air. It could not bring victory. At best it would prevent immediate defeat and at worst it would end in subjugation.

On 30th June the first British territory was occupied when the Channel Islands were invaded. In July the battle proper began. It would continue throughout the summer and into the early autumn and, in Wellington's words, it would be a close-run thing.

Recognising Air Chief Marshal Stuffy Dowding's Fighter Command as his principal opponent, Marshal Goering set out to destroy their fighter airfields. It was during this phase of the Battle (when Goering's repeated attacks on the airfields were achieving solid success) that, on 18th August, Sergeant James Cowell of the Dorset Regiment was able to play a minor but gallant part. Cowell was commanding a guard at a post on Skid Hill in Kent, between West Wickham and the fighter airfield at Biggin Hill. Spotting an enemy bomber approaching at a height of fifteen feet, he ran to a Bren gun, which was mounted in the open some twenty-five feet from the nearest trench, and opened fire. Meanwhile his men engaged the aircraft with their rifles. Despite return fire from the bomber's machine guns, Cowell maintained his fire and the aircraft crashed just beyond his guard's position. James Cowell was credited as having been largely responsible for bringing it down. He was later mentioned in Despatches, a rare soldier and probably the only Dorset to be decorated for bravery in the Battle of Britain.

Within days, Hitler misguidedly switched the Luftwaffe's attention to London, relieving the pressure on Britain's fighter airfields. Dowding's Command made good use of the respite gained at the expense of the people of London, and by September had conclusively denied Goering's aircrew control of the skies over Britain. On 12th October Hitler cancelled his plans to invade Britain in 1940.

At around this time 43rd Wessex Division were given responsibility for guarding the straits at Dover. The 4th Dorsets were based for a time in Dover Castle while the 5th were at Grand Shaft Barracks. Known to the navy as *Hellfire Corner*, this stretch of coast was the front line in the defence of England. For the British, throughout that icy winter and well into 1941, invasion remained a strong possibility, with frequent alarums and excursions. During the 4th and 5th Dorsets' first two years of war, Rupert Wheatley served as Adjutant of each Battalion. One of the brightest stars among the young Dorset officers, Wheatley had been mentioned in Despatches in Palestine with the 2nd Battalion and had served as their Intelligence Officer until April 1940. Later he would be talent-spotted by Monty and given a staff job in XII Corps. We will meet him again – back on the European mainland – in 1944.

In November 1940 one Dorset earned distinction afloat. Private John Madle was serving aboard the converted fishing vessel MV *Chesapeake* off the Lizard when she was bombed and strafed by an enemy aircraft. His King's Commendation appeared in a list of Merchant Navy awards.

On 24th February 1941 an explosion in a minefield at Hythe killed several NCOs and soldiers. Four wounded survivors were marooned in the minefield, surrounded by unexploded mines and mutilated bodies. The field was enclosed by barbed wire entanglements, which made rescuing the survivors more difficult – not least because it was known that some mines were buried under the wire. Major Gerrard Blandford Matthews, a pre-war TA officer of the 4th Dorsets, decided that the only way to reach the wounded men was to place planks over the wire. Fully aware of the unexploded mines below him, he walked over the planks (within six inches of a mine) into the minefield and helped the four men to safety. Blandford Matthews added a George Medal to the Military Cross he had won as a Sapper officer in the First World War and survived his second world war to become a stalwart of the Regimental Association.

Serving with the 14th Queen's, RSM Legg confronted a similar incident in July when some of his men strayed into a minefield and several were killed. When their CO walked into the minefield to rescue a wounded man, Legg assisted before helping the Sappers clear the mines. The Colonel, a Sapper officer and sergeant, and Ernest Legg from Dorchester, all later received the George Medal.

Churchill visits the 2nd Dorsets

The 2nd Battalion meanwhile found themselves guarding a nine-mile stretch of the Yorkshire coast near Hornsea, where they remained until the spring of 1941. In March one of their men, who had been wounded on 26th May 1940 during the retreat to Dunkirk, arrived at Gibraltar. Private Graham, a pre-war merchant seaman, had been captured and treated at a German Casualty Clearing Station before being admitted to hospital in Lille. He remained in hospital until 6th October when, his stomach wound having healed, he escaped into the town, where he lay hidden until late January 1941. Crossing the Somme near Abbeville, he moved south to Moulins and then jumped trains to Mâcon, Lyons and finally to Marseilles, from where he was repatriated to Gibraltar by the French Vichy authorities. On his journey he had stolen, and was able to hand the intelligence services, a map of German coastal defences in Northern France. Graham, whose ship docked at Greenock on 17th March 1941, was mentioned in Despatches for his courage and initiative. A year later another wounded 2nd Battalion man, Private Knight, was also mentioned in Despatches for a similarly brave escape from hospital through Occupied France.

During their time on the Yorkshire coast the 2nd Dorsets were visited by King George VI and by Winston Churchill. Some familiar faces – Tom Molloy, Bob Goff and Peter Brind – all moved to new appointments. Three of their brightest stars – Oner Bray, John Peebles and Chips Heron – also left, having volunteered to join Number 5 Commando. Later, John Peebles was fatally wounded by a grenade during training on the Isle of Wight, but happily Bray and Heron would return and will rejoin our story later. Colonel Steve moved on at the end of his period of command and was succeeded by Lieutenant-Colonel *Peggy* Boon, whose tenure proved short-lived. George Wood arrived during the summer and the pace of training accelerated as the Battalion were warned to prepare to move overseas.

Internationally, 1941 saw two seismic shifts in the course of the war. In late June Hitler made another strategic blunder by invading Russia, ending the uneasy pact of non-aggression which until then had left him a free hand in western Europe. And in early December the United States of America were hurled into war when Japanese aircraft bombed the American Fleet at Pearl Harbour. Two giants, one of whom had been cynically profiting from the war and the other trying to avoid it, were now pushed into it as formidable enemies of Nazi Germany. Great Britain and her Empire were no longer alone, and Britain's position was transformed. From 1942, although many dangers remained and new ones such as Hitler's V-weapons would arise, the balance of power had shifted dramatically and permanently. The army at home, which until now had been braced to repel invasion, now steadily adapted, grew and prepared to return to France to liberate Continental Europe.

Meanwhile, one Dorset officer won a Military Cross fighting the French. Commissioned into the Regiment aged twenty in 1939, David Shireff volunteered a year later for the King's African Rifles. Having been mentioned in Despatches for his bravery fighting the Italians in Abyssinia, he took part in the bloodless liberation of the nearby island of Mayotte, during which he surprised the French Chief of Police in bed with his mistress. In the six-month campaign that followed on Madagascar the resistance of the Vichy French proved much fiercer. Near the end of the campaign Shireff was decorated for his gallantry and leadership in an attack when his platoon captured their objective in the face of heavy machine gun fire. Later he commanded a company of the 5th King's African Rifles in Burma.

Although wounded, he survived to serve as a District Officer in Kenya before becoming a solicitor. He later wrote *Bare Feet and Bandoliers*, an account of the campaign in Abyssinia in 1941.

Tony Lewis, commissioned into the Dorsets in July 1939, had scraped into the last stages of the campaign in France in 1940, escaping from Cherbourg before volunteering for the Commandos. In 1941 he had taken part in the raid on the Lofoten Islands, in which the Commandos brought home with them more than 200 German prisoners and 300 Norwegians. Later Lewis served in North Africa with 105th Light Anti-Aircraft Regiment (previously the 8th Dorsets) before rejoining the Commandos. We will meet him again on D-Day.

THE DORSET HOME GUARD

In May 1940 the War Office gave instructions that six battalions were to be formed of Local Defence Volunteers to defend Dorset against invasion. Quickly renamed the Home Guard, these units wore battledress, the Dorset Regiment cap badge and Home Guard flashes on their shoulders. They recruited men ineligible for military service because of their youth, age or reserved occupation. Many, including most of their officers, were veterans of the First World War. Later, the six battalions became seven and a motor transport company was formed within the Home Guard's Hampshire and Dorset Transport Column.

With hindsight (and especially when viewed through the television camera lens of *Dad's Army*) the Home Guard's activities seem faintly comical and touchingly ineffectual. In 1940 and 1941, however, with invasion imminent, the need was pressing and the cause noble. Throughout those years the Home Guard trained, prepared and waited for the call that happily never came. It is unlikely, had the Germans landed, that the Home Guard would have delayed them long, but many elderly men and teenage boys would have fought and died bravely in the process.

A handful were killed. Early on Whit Monday   25th May 1942 – the Luftwaffe bombed Poole. A defensive decoy system diverted the bombers onto Brownsea Island, where most of the bombs fell without causing casualties. One, however, hit a company headquarters of the 3rd Dorset (Poole) Battalion of the Home Guard. Private William Griffiths, a Monmouthshire man, was killed at his post in Lindsay Road. Fifty-eight years old, Griffiths had been well in his thirties when he had served in the First World War. Now he lost his life defending Dorset in the Second. He is buried in Poole (Branksome) Cemetery.

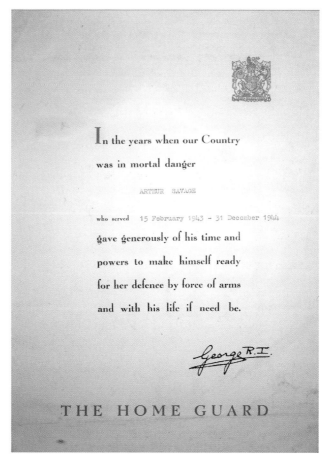

Home Guard Certificate of Service

Some were injured. On 25th November 1942, during battle practice with phosphorous grenades, one accidentally burst close to a soldier of the 5th Dorset (Weymouth) Battalion. CQMS Marsh and Sergeant Andrew saved the man's life by promptly – and bravely – tearing off his burning uniform.

Nine were decorated. Their awards – two OBEs, five MBEs and three BEMs – are included, as they should be, in the appendix to this book which records the Dorset Regiment's honours and awards.

By late 1944 the tide had turned and, on 3rd December, the Home Guard were stood down. A year later, on 31st December 1945, they were finally disbanded. In Dorset, their commander, General Sir Henry Jackson, said of them: *The spirit of comradeship and service which was brought to life by service to the Dorset Home Guard must never be allowed to die.*

THE UNKNOWN DORSET BATTALIONS

Separately from the Home Guard, since 1936 National Defence Companies had been forming throughout the country. Often based close to TA units, they attracted volunteers who, like many of the Home Guard, were really past the age of military service. In 1939 the 81st Defence Group had formed in Dorset, Hampshire and Wiltshire, and had been employed guarding airfields and other sites that were liable to be attacked. During 1940 the Group had metamorphosised into the 6th (Home Defence) Battalion of the Dorset Regiment, which now began attracting volunteers who were too young for full military service. The Battalion's three rifle companies were scattered around Wiltshire and Hampshire while Battalion Headquarters was at the Drill Hall in Salisbury; the youngsters were based at Bemerton and were later redesignated the 70th (Young Soldiers') Battalion.

The 70th were initially under the command of Cobby Spencer until Rex Steel, a Green Howards officer, took over. Sadly, Steel died in August 1941 and was replaced by Bill Ryding of the Border Regiment. In September Battalion HQ moved to Bournemouth with companies guarding RAF Ibsley, RAF Hurn, RAF Warmwell and the cliffs at Canford. Among their soldiers was Private (later Corporal) Grice, who had lied about his age to enlist in June 1940 *at the ripe old age of fifteen years and nine months*. During the closing phase of the Battle of Britain he remembered an incident when his B Company were guarding RAF Warmwell.

The 70th Dorsets in Gosport

The day in question was dull, overcast and I feel sure that it was either misty or was a light drizzle. It was so bad that the usual RAF fighter patrol had not gone up. Having had our midday meal everyone, including RAF and WAAF, were dispersing to our various locations, myself in a group of three or four mates, when we spotted three planes flying low on a direct line up the main road. Visibility was so bad that we could not identify them and were more or less arguing amongst ourselves as to whether they were Blenheims or not. We soon found out. They were so low that we actually saw the bombs released and fall. This was where luck played a great part. They were obviously after the hangers and buildings so the bombs dropped way behind us. Even now I shudder to think what might have been if they had been five minutes earlier when the majority of RAF, WAAF and Dorsets were still among the main building area. Even so the RAF personnel did have casualties including dead, but how many I don't know.

... one night raid... was particularly severe. It was so bad that RAF and WAAF personnel were evacuated and the only ones left were the RAF fire-fighters and guess who? Yes, the Dorsets! Imagine our horror when daylight broke and we saw a number of unexploded bombs that we had been 'guarding' all night. These were removed (very gently) to the Quarry itself to await the Bomb Disposal experts.

The following spring, still not seventeen, Grice was *appointed Lance-Corporal, and was duly sent to Bn HQ at Southampton for my NCOs Cadre. It must have been March/April as it was during the course that I received the sad news that my brother, a Regular soldier and Lance-Bombardier with the Royal Horse Artillery, had been killed during the fighting in Libya. That was 25th April 1941, fifteen days after his 24th birthday.*

After the completion of the course, I rejoined my Company at Gosport. Battalion HQ must also have moved as I remember them being in Fort Brockhurst whilst the company had once more been deployed around the Fleet Air Arm Station... Being so close to Portsmouth, we again had our share of night raids but even more disturbing was the damn great big gun which appeared at night on the railway lines some 100 yards or so from where we were. When that opened up to assist the rest of the ack ack guns the noise was deafening. Around this time the experiment of firing wires with small grenades like bombs attached was being carried out and we had been warned "not to touch" if we came across any of them. One of my sentries must have been a little careless, as he kicked or tripped over one of the wires and his back was peppered with tiny shrapnel fragments. I remember picking some of them out of his back until the ambulance and first aid arrived, but the wounds were only superficial and he was soon back with us. Nevertheless, a lucky escape.

Upon reaching the age of twenty, it was the 'done thing' to transfer to an active battalion. As far as I recall, there was no coercion, but it was expected. I had now passed my 'official' 20th birthday [he was actually just eighteen] and so followed suit. Like other lads from the Midlands, I opted for Warwicks, Staffords or Worcesters, in that order. There couldn't have been too much choice really as the majority, if not all, went to the 8th Worcesters, a training battalion at Market Rasen in Lincolnshire. It meant, of course, that NCOs reverted to private, and when my time came, instead of going direct from Christchurch, I went via D Company who carried out the duties of Transit Company at, of all places, Warmwell. Perhaps it was fitting that my last few days as a Dorset were spent there. I eventually departed on or around 1st September 1942.

Upon arriving at Market Rasen I met up with quite a few ex-Dorsets. Of all things that we were expected to learn was the Vickers Medium Machine Gun. As we had been using this gun for two years, and most of our duties were at night, we had literally been taught to strip and assemble the gun, including the lock, when blindfolded. We were obviously so far ahead that any ex-Dorset was excused future Vickers training. After three or four months, I was again appointed Lance-Corporal and attended a Battalion Weapons Cadre in which I achieved top marks. Because of this I was promoted straight to Corporal and nominated for a course at Northern Command Weapon Training School at Catterick. I must have impressed, as the Chief Instructor interviewed me and later contacted 8th Worcesters requesting that I be sent back as an instructor. By June 1943, therefore, I was a Sergeant instructor at Command School and taught not only weapon training but later mines, explosives and booby traps. None of this could have happened without the initial ground work done by the Dorset instructors during my two years.

Without wishing to appear disloyal in any way to a Regiment with whom I spent 20 years, I still and always will feel that none of this could have happened without the period June 1940–September 1942. I make no apology for using the cliché 'Once a Dorset, always a Dorset'.

At around this time the 70th Dorsets were redesignated the 9th Battalion and moved to Colchester, where they were joined by newly commissioned Second Lieutenant Len Sharpe. Sharpe had just emerged from an Officer Cadet Training Unit at Morecambe commanded by Bob Goff, who had so distinguished himself with the 2nd Battalion in France. Shortly after Sharpe's arrival at the 9th Battalion, he heard that a new CO had arrived and was astonished to find it was Goff, who seemed to be following him about. Indeed, senior Dorsets seemed to dog his footsteps. When he was later sent out to India to join a battalion of the South

Second Lieutenant Len Sharpe, 9th Dorsets

Lancashire Regiment, he discovered that a fellow passenger as far as Egypt was none other than Colonel Steve. Sharpe would spend the rest of the war in India, reaching the rank of major before returning to work for his old Colonel, Donald Baxter, at the brewery in Sherborne.

Meanwhile, the 6th Battalion (which had become the 30th Dorsets and moved to Portland under the command of Lieutenant-Colonel Robinson) supplied a draft of men for the 9th before they left for Antrim.

Two other Dorset battalions – the 7th and 8th – were formed in 1940 and a year later converted to gunners to become, respectively, the 110th and 105th Light Anti-Aircraft Regiments of the Royal Artillery. The 105th later fought in North Africa and Italy while the 110th would land in Normandy with the 43rd Wessex Division and fight throughout the campaign in North West Europe in close proximity to the 4th and 5th Dorsets.

After the Allied invasion of French North Africa in November 1942, the 30th Battalion were despatched to Algiers and Tunisia and then, via Philippeville, to Sicily, where they remained as garrison troops for six months. Organising these various moves while a company commander and Adjutant of the 30th Battalion,

D Company, 30th Dorsets, in Sicily 1944

Captain Howard Jefcoate earned an MBE. Born in 1904, Jefcoate had been Chief Clerk in the 1st and 2nd Battalions before being commissioned in 1940. While in Sicily the Battalion provided the Guard of Honour for Lord Gort when he visited the island from Malta. After six months they were posted to garrison Gibraltar, where they spent the rest of the war.

In Northern Ireland the 9th Dorsets had become a very efficient and well trained battalion and, in early 1944, returned to England to be the Demonstration Battalion at the School of Infantry at Barnard Castle in Yorkshire. Later they moved to Sheringham in Norfolk, where for the rest of the war they continued to help train infantry recruits to the Dorset and Royal Norfolk Regiments. A fine battalion, they were never used in battle. One of their officers, Bob Powell, later became a long-serving headmaster of Sherborne School. Another, who joined the 9th Battalion in Norfolk, made good use of his army experience in his later career as a BBC producer and comedy writer. Having served in North Africa as a Gunner, David Croft was commissioned into the Dorset Regiment in 1944. Later, with Jimmy Perry, he wrote both *Dad's Army* (which was *not* based on the Dorset Home Guard but was filmed in the Norfolk countryside where Croft served with the 9th Dorsets) and *It Ain't Half Hot, Mum*.

King Peter of Yugoslavia visits the 5th Dorsets

FAIR STOOD THE WIND

50th Division's return from Italy in November 1943 saw three Dorset battalions – the 1st, 4th and 5th – in England preparing for the long-awaited invasion of France. Meanwhile, the Depot in Dorchester was occupied by American troops. Having come thousands of miles to play the larger part in the cross-Channel invasion, they were welcome guests even if their style of drill might have made any Dorset warrant officer wince.

The 1st Dorsets, based at Halstead in Essex, were visited in February 1944 by their King, who watched a demonstration company attack on a strongpoint supported by the Battalion's assault pioneers. After their selection as part of one of the Assault Brigades on D-Day, they began to receive intensive training for the task that lay ahead. Colonel Broke Ray, who had recently received the DSO he won in Italy, left the Battalion and was succeeded by Colonel Evelyn Norie of the King's Own Royal Lancaster Regiment. Major Speedy Bredin arrived as Second-in-Command. From

March they were in Hampshire, where they were visited three weeks before D-Day by the Supreme Allied Commander, General Eisenhower.

The south of England had become an enormous armed camp, containing a British group of armies and an American one, all of them waiting for the off. The beaches had been mined and fenced off for four years. Even off duty, officers carried side arms and behaved as though in a theatre of operations. In May all leave was cancelled and the whole area down to the coast was sealed off.

On 28th May, awaiting D-Day in Hampshire, Major Charles Martin (now Second-in-Command of the 1st Hampshires) wrote a letter home.

It is incredibly lovely here today... it is very hard to realise that the world is in just about as bloody a mess as it can possibly be. Very often I feel that existence is quite pointless and then I reflect how really interesting life is and what tremendous hope there is for the future.

Not far away, also waiting to land on D-Day, was the poet Keith Douglas, a veteran of Alamein and Tunisia, whose Sherwood Rangers Yeomanry would support all three Dorset battalions in the coming campaign. The last verse of the last poem the twenty-four-year-old Captain Douglas ever completed captured the powerful blend of anxiety and anticipation shared by – literally – an army of young men.

> *The next month, then, is a window*
> *and with a crash I'll split the glass.*
> *Behind it sits one I must kiss,*
> *person of love or death*
> *a person or a wraith,*
> *I fear what I shall find.*

The 4th and 5th Dorsets were in Sussex, having spent nearly five years training for the eleven-month campaign that for them would begin on 23rd June 1944. When D-Day dawned and Douglas's Regiment and the 1st Dorsets were landing on the Normandy beaches, Private Cliff Lloyd of the 4th Dorsets remembered the sky above Bexhill *black with planes flying to Europe.* That day his Battalion took a train from Bexhill to Eastleigh, from where they marched to Southampton to embark for Normandy. If, as Churchill had asserted, El Alamein had been the end of the beginning, D-Day was the beginning of the end.

5

The 2nd Battalion, India and Burma 1942–45

Almost Primus ex Indis[8]

The Road to Kohima

Among the many major engagements fought by the British Army in the two world wars, a handful stand out for their sheer horror. The mention, for example, of *Passchendaele* or *Monte Cassino* brings a reverent awe to any discussion. That awe is founded primarily on a deep respect for anyone who was there and who somehow continued to do his duty in such ghastly conditions. A combination of circumstances – often terrain, weather and the fierceness of the fighting – conspired to create for the soldiers who fought there a unique reputation. The siege of Kohima is one such battle, its name evoking images of close, savage fighting against a relentlessly ferocious enemy in unremitting rain amid the stench of rotting corpses and the cacophony of mortaring, shelling and machine gun fire. Kohima would be the 2nd Dorsets' first taste of the war against Japan.

The Battalion reached Kohima on 26th April 1944, after a long journey which had begun more than two years earlier when, at Liverpool on 10th April 1942, they had boarded HT *Reina del Pacifico*. In England their Colonel, George Wood, had twice turned down command of a brigade in order to lead a battalion of his Regiment in battle. Now, with the veteran Major Tom Molloy (who had helped Colonel Steve navigate the Battalion's route from Festubert to Dunkirk) as Wood's Second-in-Command, they were on their way. With the campaign in Libya dominating the headlines, many had assumed they were destined to join the Eighth Army but, after their ship had rounded the Cape, they were told that their Division was bound for India. In his history of the Battalion Knocker White, then commanding A Company, remembered George Wood mastering his own disappointment at the 2nd Battalion being sent to India and announcing bracingly: "Gentlemen, you *will* like India." He then started teaching them Urdu.

---

8   *Primus in Indis* means "First in India", a title earned by the 39th Foot under Clive of India at the Battle of Plassey in 1757.

Japanese dead in the jungle by Jock Murrills

The 2nd Dorsets would not, however, be the first members of the Regiment to meet the Japanese in battle. On 29th January 1942 Major John Reid had landed at Singapore with the 1/5th Sherwood Foresters. Undefended in the air, Singapore was being heavily bombed and, as they landed, the Foresters' troopship was bombed. The Battalion lost their machine guns and, as the troops were transported in lorries to their billets at the Chinese High School, Australian soldiers shouted "Hallo, prisoners of war!" Thrown into the colony's inadequate defence against the Japanese invasion, the Sherwood Foresters and the rest of their Brigade were engaged in several days' fierce fighting. After heavy bombing and sniping, the Sherwood Foresters were attacked by Japanese tanks and an ammunition lorry was hit and exploded, killing many of their soldiers. They were finally ordered to surrender and passed into a savage captivity: 450 of their number would die during three and a half years of beatings, disease, overwork, starvation, torture and murder. John Reid was spared this. He died in battle on 12th or 13th February, leaving a widow and two young children in Canada. He is buried in Kranji Cemetery.[9]

---

9   John Reid was forty-two and had been commissioned in the Dorset Regiment in 1920. His son, Jeremy, would later serve in the Dorset Regiment alongside his lifelong friend, Colonel Steve's son, Christopher Stephenson.

Practising an assault landing by Jock Murrills

George Wood's private ambition to command the 2nd Battalion in battle was thwarted when he was soon promoted to command a brigade. During his period of command his professionalism and influence had permeated the 2nd Battalion and helped them to regain their fighting efficiency for whatever lay ahead. Meanwhile, Tom Molloy succeeded him as Colonel and, in turn, Knocker White became Second-in-Command.

Based at first in some comfort at Secunderabad, they spent a fortnight training as an assault battalion on the lake at Kharakvasla near Poona, before moving to Ahmednagar, whose limited facilities proved entirely inadequate to accommodate two infantry brigades. Here, though, they renewed their friendship with the 2nd Royal Norfolks. Both battalions visited the Mahratta Training Centre at Belgaum and presented them with a specially commissioned Norsets' flag in memory of the Mahratta battalions who had served in Mesopotamia alongside the previous generation of Norfolks and Dorsets.

In December the Battalion were sent to Ahmedabad, where – as in other parts of India at that time – there were fears of civil unrest. But either the fears were unjustified or the Dorsets' presence discouraged any rioting; they were able to spend a pleasant Christmas far from home.

The first three months of 1943 were spent on the coast above Bombay, starting the combined operations training which was to last until November.

Norman Havers, then commanding 8 Platoon, remembered:

We were well sited for not only were we camped on the beach, but adjacent to a creek, on the far side of which we were to do our training. At low tide we could wade across, but at all other times it was anything between two and three hundred yards in width and with a fair current. Thus when crossing we had rafts for our weapons and for the support of the non-swimmers. With every encouragement and from sheer necessity those who could not swim learned to do so, apart from a resolute five, who preferred to keep their feet on the ground.

To be under canvas within a grove of palm trees on the shore of the Arabian Sea, that ocean seen across a wide beach of golden sand, the water blue on which sailed the traditional craft of the local fishermen and the beach uncluttered by civilians – what a paradise!

... Ours was a remote world, for the houses lining the shore behind us were empty and, but for the native fishermen, casting their nets on the surface of the creek, we had the place to ourselves.

Two days of lectures on combined operations were followed by a night exercise, when we swam the creek and crossed the mud flats beyond, into which we sank to our knees and then did battle, or whatever, within a tongue of semi-wilderness.

Major Tiger Havers MBE

When Tom Molloy was promoted to be Second-in-Command of 5 Infantry Brigade, Knocker White succeeded him. Pleasant stations alternated with unpleasant ones throughout these months of training, which took them first to Bhiwandi below the Western Ghats and then into the mountains at Mahableshwar for their first experience of the jungle.

Sergeant Tom Cattle

Tom Cattle, then a private soldier in D Company, remembered *one large exercise when we travelled to Bombay and boarded the trooper 'Dilwara', put to sea and scrambled down nets into landing crafts... making landings on a beach at Juhn.*

We also spent weeks at a time in the jungle at Belgaum, sleeping rough, digging trenches, living with the 10–12 foot long snakes, gibbons with their loud shrieking calls, large spiders and those little horrors, scorpions. We also found out that nothing could be left on the ground as numerous white ants would appear from nowhere and start to eat everything left lying about. I can remember one lesson learnt in the jungle and that was on a Field Firing exercise firing live ammunition when mortars were set up and the first bombs to be fired struck tree branches and were deflected to fall and detonate amongst the mortar crew and officers who were watching this exercise, caused a number of serious wounds.[10] We also carried out a lot of night excursions

10   Colonel White's history lists two officers – Lieutenant Harold *Jonah* Jones and Captain Jock Wilson – seriously wounded and one – Captain Dick Purser – slightly wounded. Wilson, commanding the Carrier Platoon, never returned to the Battalion.

having to use a compass and maps, most difficult trying to force your way through thick jungle at night making as little noise as possible. Elephants and tigers were also to be found but caused us no trouble.

During this time Colonel Robert Linklater, who had been wounded before the war as a subaltern with the 2nd Battalion in Palestine, arrived from England to take command. His stay was not long: towards the end of their second spell of jungle training in March 1944 he was posted to a staff job. His successor was Colonel Jock McNaught, an officer of the Royal Scots Fusiliers, who also arrived fresh from England.

The Supreme Commander, Admiral Lord Louis Mountbatten, visited the 2nd Division and told them that, because they were an amphibious unit and because the war in Europe had priority for landing craft, it was likely that they would not see action until early 1945. Events decreed otherwise. Jock McNaught would have little time to acclimatise or to get to know his new Battalion before, at the end of their six months' jungle training, he received the order: *Move Ahmednagar immediately and mobilise for active service.*

The Japanese had invaded Southern Burma on 14th December 1941, a week after their attack on Pearl Harbour. By May 1942 the British had retreated more than 1,000 miles and withdrawn into Assam behind the River Chindwin in North West Burma. Here the Japanese had stopped. 1942 and 1943 had seen two British offensives in the Arakan (the western coastal region of Burma) and the first of Orde Wingate's controversial Chindit expeditions, which attacked the Japanese far behind their front lines. But, in the north-west on the border between India and Burma, for nearly two years the British and Japanese had faced each other across the River Chindwin. Now, in March 1944, three Japanese divisions of General Mutaguchi's Fifteenth Army crossed the Chindwin. Mutaguchi's immediate object was to capture the British bases at Kohima and Imphal, and to prevent the British using the airfields in Assam to supply the Chinese forces fighting the Japanese further east. But he may also have had in mind the possibility of breaking through Assam and, with the help of Indians sympathetic to the Japanese cause, seizing India from the British.

Unruffled by the attack, General Bill Slim realised that the Japanese had over-stretched themselves, gambling on feeding from British stores captured at Imphal, and had left themselves vulnerable. His plan was to deny them Imphal and then to fight them on the Imphal Plain and to rout and destroy them there. With characteristic candour he later acknowledged that he had dangerously under-estimated the scale of Mutaguchi's threat to Dimapur and Kohima, where, as a consequence,

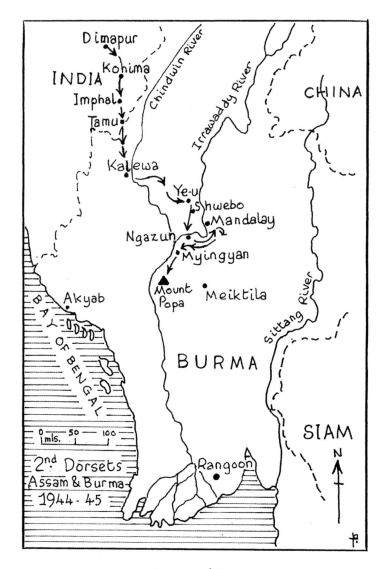

Assam and Burma

a tiny garrison now seemed likely to be overwhelmed by an entire Japanese division. Commanding the pass into Assam, Kohima was of considerable strategic importance and its loss would open the door for the Japanese into India. Realising his error, Slim flew 5th Indian Division up from the Arakan front and asked General Gifford to send him the 2nd Division. Thus Major-General John Grover's 2nd Division, including the 2nd Dorsets, were sent at short notice to reinforce the Kohima garrison and to prevent Kohima and Dimapur falling to the Japanese.

While the Dorsets and the rest of the 2nd Division were on their way, the newly formed Assam Regiment fought doggedly to delay the Japanese advance towards Kohima. At the end of March, the leading units of 5th Indian Division arrived and 161 Brigade was despatched to reinforce Kohima Ridge. The 4th Queen's Own Royal West Kents joined the Kohima garrison on 4th April, just after the first Japanese night attack on its defences. By the morning of 6th April the Japanese had surrounded Kohima and cut it off. A garrison of 1,500 fighting soldiers faced a continuous assault by 15,000 Japanese troops. The 2nd Division were on their way, but the question now was whether the garrison could hold out until a strong enough force was assembled to relieve them.

2nd Division's 6 Brigade flew in from Bangalore while 4 and 5 Brigades moved north by train. Tom Cattle, however, realised that the Battalion Transport would be going by road and managed to team up with Leo Orchard, a fellow native of Corfe Castle, to drive the 2,000 miles from Belgaum in a 15cwt truck.

... as far as I can remember we travelled all day, stopping at night for rest for about 10 days, covering about 2000 miles. The only thing that happened out of the ordinary was at a place called Nowgong in North India, where we arrived to stop for the night. On arrival each vehicle had to be refuelled. At Nowgong a huge arms and fuel dump was situated; we had started to refuel when there was a huge explosion and a large cloud of flame and smoke went skywards. We were at once ordered to remove stores, ie petrol, oil and ammunition, not threatened by the fire; explosions continued throughout the night. In the far distance to the north we could see the towering mountains of the Himalayan Range but we knew our destiny lay to the north-west, where as we drew near we could see the hills here were quite high and covered in thick jungle. We reached Gauhati where all our vehicles were taken from us and we were told from now on we would be 'flamping' (travelling on foot). We were pushed forward quite rapidly to join up with the rest of the Regiment, who had arrived earlier and were now moving into action against the Japanese.

The Dorsets would soon become connoisseurs of jungles. Knocker White wrote later: *Of the many jungles we have encountered I would say unhesitatingly that the Bokajan species was the worst. It was wet and prickly, dank and gloomy, and it was not only rank but stank.*

Cattle remembered their first experience of the jungle around Kohima.

... I had learned at school that Cherapungi in Assam was the wettest place in the world with an annual average rainfall of about 700 inches...

Manipur State where we were heading within Assam contains numerous ranges of steep sided hills covered in thick jungle with the tops continually covered in rain and mist and cloud and during the monsoon the rain is heavy and continuous... Kohima lies within the Naga Hills of which Pulebange Mountain rises steeply to some 10,000 feet above sea level. The road, there is only one, follows the valleys along the sides of the hills; the road was not like ours with a smooth tarmac surface but a single track carved from the side of the hill consisting of rock and soil, which was only really a muddy track. We arrived in this place at the beginning of the monsoon; remember we had no vehicles, everything had to be carried on our backs, food and water and ammunition had to be dropped by parachute by allied air forces, mainly Dakotas piloted by Americans. The 'front line' was mainly astride the road; the steep jungle-clad hills washed with heavy monsoon rains made it very difficult to advance against a well dug in enemy; flanking movements up the hills were treacherous and hard work cutting a way through the thick jungle. In these circumstances there is little comfort for the poor infantryman in battle, wet through to the skin with only a water-proof groundsheet over your shoulders to serve as a cape to try and keep off the rain. The streams off the hills would become torrents, sweeping away large chunks of the road; weeks at a time we slept with our boots on; rather than sleep it was more of 'shut eye' for short periods.

At 0900 on 11th April the Dorsets followed the 7th Worcesters and 1st Camerons up the road from Dimapur to Kohima, which the Japanese had cut. They encountered no enemy until the evening, when B Company were checking that the village of Kiruphema was clear of the enemy. Here the leading column bumped into a Japanese patrol and a section commander was killed. Twenty-two-year-old Lance-Corporal Guy Nursaw, from York, was the Dorsets' first battle casualty in the Far East. A couple of hours later, a night patrol led by Lieutenant Mayer of C Company moved up to make contact with the Worcesters and had a lucky escape when a shower of grenades was hurled at them.

On the road the Dorsets were strafed by Japanese Zeros. They also encountered Naga tribesmen, who were *very stocky and friendly*. Each was covered in blood and carried the severed head of a Japanese soldier. Captain David Harris, like most Dorsets, developed a great respect for the tribesmen.

Throughout the campaign we got tremendous help... they are a remarkably fine race and 100% loyal to us. They carried terrific weights up places where the mules could not go; they carried our wounded; they fought the Japs with spears and with bows and arrows... They would not take money from us. One Headman told the CO of one unit to give the money to the Red Cross. They never begged for food, even though the Japs had taken their rice, but they were always willing to accept it if offered. The women were not frightened of us and even looked after us in the villages (insisting on fetching water etc). They let our doctors heal their illnesses. Our troops respected them and behaved very well. That is one of the reasons they liked us so much because the Japs raped them. Several hundred Naga women were found in bunkers captured from the Japs.

The advance stalled as the leading troops encountered Japanese positions astride the road. For D Company 13th April was a difficult day. 17 Platoon, commanded by the very experienced Sergeant Yorky Seale, repulsed three enemy attacks, inflicting several casualties. But four men were killed, including three stretcher-bearers who ran out under fire to fetch a wounded man. When Lance-Corporal Alan Critchley went out to help, he too was wounded and trapped in the open until he could be helped back to cover. The Company Commander, Major Paget Fretts, was severely wounded while on patrol and Captain David Harris, his popular Second-in-Command, took his place. Paj Fretts would carry the piece of shrapnel in his spine for the rest of his life but nonetheless returned to the Battalion twice more during the campaign. He was mentioned in Despatches.

Up ahead, the Worcesters were under pressure from the Japanese, who launched a strong attack at dawn on the 14th. That afternoon, supported by heavy and accurate artillery fire, the Camerons finally cleared the enemy bunker that had held up the Brigade's advance. David Harris later wrote home: *The Artillery killed an enormous number of Japs here.* But the Dorsets' advance was slowed by a burning bridge, which had to be repaired by Sappers, and a road block formed by two civilian buses, which had to be removed by their supporting tanks. David Harris described the going, which was hard and dangerous.

The Japs held every height along the road, and we had to get him off every one of them, sometimes going up to 5,000 or 6,000 feet with heavy packs (80 pounds) and usually a pick or shovel, as well as our weapons. While this was going on we managed to get carriers up to Garrison Hill, where the Royal West Kents... were holding on by the skin of their teeth.

Broken trees at Kohima by Jock Murrills

By now the Kohima garrison were on their uppers. The 4th Queen's Own Royal West Kents had been besieged for a week in a tiny perimeter on Garrison and Hospital Hills. The Japanese had cut the water supply and, since 7th April, the garrison had relied on water dropped by transport aircraft. In the hospital wounded men suffered thirst as well as pain and the noise and danger of the constant attacks by the huge Japanese force surrounding them.

On the 19th an attack by the 2nd Durham Light Infantry finally made possible the relief of Garrison Hill and, next day, the Dorsets' Carrier Platoon escorted the convoy of ambulances that evacuated the wounded. That day the 2nd Dorsets were lent to 6 Brigade under Brigadier John Shapland, who had been ordered to make the attack on the centre of the Japanese defences.

THE BATTLE ON THE TENNIS COURT

On 20th April the 4th Royal West Kents holding Hospital Hill were finally relieved by the 1st Royal Berkshires. Their fifteen-day ordeal was over. It had cost them more than half their strength in killed and wounded, but they had held on and, by doing so, had saved the Kohima position and blocked the Japanese route to India.

Six days later, leaving B and D Companies under Knocker White on Picquet Hill, the remainder of the Battalion moved up Garrison Hill to relieve the Berkshires. The relief did not start well. In the approach they were heavily mortared and sniped. By the time they reached their new positions they had taken sixteen casualties, who were tended by their heroic doctor, Joe Chamberlin, and equally courageous padre, Gus Claxton.

While sending 6 Brigade (including the Dorsets) forward into the heart of the Japanese defences, General Grover had despatched 4 and 5 Brigades to work their arduous way round the right and left flanks of Kohima. On the left 5 Brigade had been held up and, to support their advance with tanks, the Manipur Road would have to be cleared. Colonel White described the geography.

On the top of the pass over the Kohima Ridge, where the Manipur Road swung right in a hairpin bend for Imphal, a side-road led left-handed up the side of Treasury Hill towards the Naga village. This road junction was dominated by a spur on which was situated the District Commissioner's bungalow. This spur rose roughly due west in four steeply terraced ridges to Garrison Hill, on the extreme top of which stood the Summerhouse...

The spur was divided into four main terraces, each separated by a steep bank varying in height from ten to forty feet. Starting from the top, there was the club square on which in happier days the members had played badminton. Ten feet below the club lay the tennis court. On the south side the tennis court was bounded by a large iron water tank and a long tin building which appeared to be servants' quarters. These themselves were sunk so that only the roofs appeared level with the tennis court.

The next drop was a very steep and deep one of about thirty to forty feet to the terrace, on which was situated the bungalow itself in its own compound.

Finally, below the bungalow, there was another drop which brought us to the lower garden, which overlooked the important road junction twenty feet below.

Viewed from the eastern side of Garrison Hill, the north, or to the Dorsets attacking, the face of the spur was extremely steep with a fall from the club square to the road of nearly a hundred feet in all.

On the south side of the club (topmost terrace) rose a small 'pimple' about thirty yards long, fifteen broad and twenty feet high.

A bungalow, in a peaceful hill station reminiscent of Simla, with landscaped garden, terraces and tennis court, was an incongruous place for a battle. The topography required the Dorsets to hold a ridge and attack downhill on the various terraces that formed the garden and grounds of the bungalow. It was extremely difficult terrain, as Knocker White explained.

An extraordinary feature of this whole spur was the impossibility of being able to see what was happening on the terrace next below. Owing to the thickness of the trees and the conformity of the ground, reconnaissance from a flank was practically impossible. Intelligence about this feature was almost nil.

Throughout the battle this lack of intelligence about the terrain – and especially about the siting of enemy positions – would create untold difficulties. David Harris remembered his time at Kohima as *the most unpleasant three weeks of my life. Sitting for the first two weeks twenty-five yards from the Japs, who sniped us every time we moved. We had to crawl everywhere, and dared not go to sleep at night, nor did sleep come easily in the daytime. By day he just sniped, but most nights he put in some sort of an attack, which was always abortive. During this period we were supplied by parachute – marvellous rations, and enough water for drinking.*

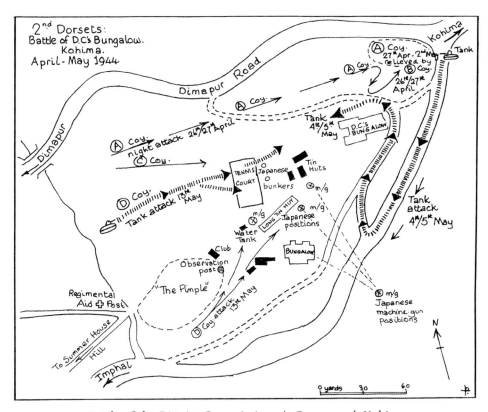

Battle of the District Commissioner's Compound, Kohima
26th April–13th May 1944

Late on 26th April A and C Companies received orders for a two-company night attack on the bungalow. At 0300 hours next morning C Company reached the crest of a slope, where 14 and 15 Platoons met withering small arms fire. The defenders also fired grenades at them from grenade dischargers, and the Company was forced to pause to try to locate the Japanese positions. At this point Captain Dick Castle led a number of men over the crest and managed to throw grenades into several Japanese bunkers before being wounded. Lieutenant Mayer led 13 Platoon forward in support but he and his Platoon Sergeant, William Perrett, were both killed. Humphrey Mayer, a Staffordshire man attached from the Royal Warwickshire Regiment, was twenty-four. Lance-Sergeant Perrett was ten years older; his death left another Dorset Regiment widow, back in Wyke Regis.

When Dick Castle was evacuated, Company Sergeant-Major Paddy Keegan assumed command of C Company until Captain Michael Morice, who had been left out of the battle to take over if required, was able to reach them and take command. Having re-organised the survivors of the Company in two platoons, Morice led another attack before Colonel Jock McNaught recalled them and asked for tank support. But the bank from the road proved too steep for the tanks and, by last light, a working party had still not managed to reduce it sufficiently to enable the tanks to get forward. The day had cost C Company four killed, three missing and thirty-four wounded. But they had destroyed a large bunker on the north-east corner of the tennis court and eliminated one of the Japanese forward positions.

Major John Bowles's A Company had got below the level of the tennis court and reached the bungalow, in which they managed to set up a position. But at first light the enemy turned a very heavy fire on these hard-won positions, and the forward platoons were forced to withdraw. In the withdrawal Corporal Harry Softley, a long-serving Regular who had boxed for the 1st Battalion before the war, was killed trying to rescue some wounded men of his platoon. Meanwhile, Bowles and the rest of his Company, under ferocious attack, held fast to their positions on the lowest slope below the tennis court and above the road junction.

Late that night the Japanese mortared Battalion Headquarters on Summerhouse Hill before launching an assault. Although the main attack was repulsed, a small party got through and even began digging in. The Dorsets' Guerrilla Platoon, under Lieutenant O'Driscoll, saw them off.

During the next day a Sapper bulldozer, covered by two tanks, was brought up to clear the southern slope and to drag a tank up it to engage the enemy on the tennis court. Sadly, the alarming steepness and the weight of the tank pulled the bulldozer down on top of it, damaging the tank beyond repair.

On 29th April Jock McNaught called Knocker White forward. White was horrified by what he found. ... *heavy fighting had been taking place on these slopes, in intense heat, for nearly a month. So close had been and still was the fighting, and so heavy was the sniping, that it had been quite impossible to collect the dead even though, as in many cases, they lay just beyond a section post. Indeed, in some places where the Jap had put in a 'Banzai' attack his dead lay piled deep where they had fallen... In a steep gully not forty yards from the club square, at the top of which lay one of our posts, were piled high the bodies of about one hundred and fifty of the enemy who had perished as they made one of their suicidal attacks against the Royal Berks.*

... Our first greeting was from the outstretched hand of a long-dead Jap, who had been slaughtered in an attempt to reach the hospital and get in among the wounded of the garrison in the earlier days.

... I found Battalion Headquarters pretty tired. They had had a rather rough two or three nights... The smell on the hill and the flies were simply awful... Three battalions, plus a mixed collection of the old garrison, Assam Rifles, who had not been evacuated and a battery of mountain gunners were all herded together round the steep slopes of this conical hill. Washing and shaving were out of the question. There had been no rain for some days... the garrison was rationed to three pints of water a day... Jock McNaught was trying to figure out whether to finish his half-cup of weak 'compo' tea or save the half-inch at the bottom to clean his teeth.

During the day a Japanese 75mm gun augmented the snipers' fire on A Company's positions but, because their own supporting gunners were short of ammunition, no effective counter-fire could be brought to bear: the troops just had to live with it and keep their heads down. A second attempt to get a tank into action failed when first its wireless failed and then it ran out of fuel.

During the night some minor attacks were repulsed, but next day several men were wounded by the 75mm gun's shelling. At one point, during the early evening of 1st May, the gun fired over open sights to destroy ten pits on the north face of A Company's positions, killing and wounding a large number of men. Meanwhile B and D Companies had followed Major White and now arrived to reinforce their comrades on the spur above the Bungalow.

The war diary recorded that during this period Lieutenant *Highett*[11] *had visited the Company daily during the hours of daylight in an armoured car, bringing water,*

---

11   Lintorn Highett's father, Cecil, had fought with the 2nd Dorsets in Mesopotamia in the First World War.

food and ammunition, and occasionally cans of hot tea, it being impossible... to light a fire. Excellent service was rendered by an armoured ambulance and crew, who arrived at first light each morning to evacuate wounded, and also coming up on call at any time during daylight.

Great assistance was rendered by close and accurate 3" mortar and 25-pounder artillery fire, the latter as close as 25 yards. Total Jap dead 35, but the majority were taken away by the enemy during the night. The policy at night was to use grenades in preference to Small Arms.

Just before midnight Major Bowles sent Corporal Mansfield, Lance Corporal Breely and Private Morgan back to report his Company's state to Battalion Headquarters. They arrived safely, having picked their way through the Japanese positions. Liberally dosed with rum, Mansfield then returned to A Company with the good news that they would be relieved next morning. For his bravery here, and on two other occasions, William Mansfield was awarded the Military Medal.

On 2nd May, after five days, A Company were relieved by B under cover of smoke. The Battalion war diary recorded that, from their original strength of about 100, the Company *marched out with a total of 3 officers and 29 other ranks.* Among the dead was their Company Sergeant-Major, the redoubtable Herbert Downton of Sherborne. Major John Bowles, who had been mentioned in Despatches as a Platoon Sergeant-Major in the retreat to Dunkirk, would be mentioned again for his work as a major in the campaign in Burma.

After the relief on 2nd May the Japanese 75mm gun fired six rounds, three of which hit B Company's new positions. The last scored a direct hit on Company Headquarters, killing seven men and wounding another eight. One of B Company's fatal casualties was another stalwart, CSM George Draper. Meanwhile, a third attempt to get a tank on to the tennis court failed when it was hit by an anti-tank gun and, although its crew survived, was put out of action.

In the early morning darkness of 3rd May, Sergeant Yorky Seale led a section of 17 Platoon forward to try to infiltrate the Japanese bunker position on the north-west corner of the tennis court. One of the patrol, Tom Cattle, remembered... *the slightest noise could be heard miles away. We went down over the hill through the Regimental Aid Post and C Company lines; we knew then we were in 'no man's land'. We also knew we must be getting close to the Japs' forward position as we could hear voices as we climbed upwards. Suddenly all hell was let loose, machine guns, rifle fire, grenades and mortars were falling all around us. Yorky shouted 'Duck and get down.' We slithered back down, I got down into a shell hole where a grenade landed near my head and I had got my head down into the soil as it went off, blasting and deafening me. I was surprised that I had not suffered any injury; we lay still for what seemed to be hours but could only have been half an hour or so. The barrage of grenades and machine gun fire became less intensive and we were able to retire back to our trenches to thank God that we had been able to do so.*

Nine Japanese were killed by Seale's patrol and by the covering fire provided by B Company. It was a busy night. Lieutenant John O'Driscoll and a section of his Guerrilla Platoon attacked a Japanese sniper position and killed four Japanese. C Company repulsed a Japanese attack on their positions while American dive bombers attacked some of the Japanese positions on B Company's front, killing several more.

Throughout 4th May C Company were heavily shelled by Japanese mortars and their 75mm gun. A second attempt failed to get beyond the bunker position attacked by Sergeant Seale's patrol. Under cover of a smoke screen laid by the Dorsets' supporting gunners and guided by Captain Jock Murrills, a tank managed to climb up to the bungalow, where it shot up a Japanese bunker. Despite enemy machine gun fire from their flank and rear, a section of 10 Platoon managed to reach the tank, losing two men in the process. Captain Dick Purser then led the rest of the platoon into the bungalow, hurling grenades into the Japanese fox-holes, killing several enemy and setting fire to the bungalow before being forced to withdraw. The bungalow blazed for several hours, ammunition exploding in the fire, until only its iron walls remained standing.

The Japanese 75mm gun retaliated, wounding Major Alan Watts, who had served with the 2nd Battalion in France, England and India. Dick Purser now took command of B Company.

Next day a Grant tank reached the bungalow and Dick Purser led a second attack, this time with 11 Platoon. Having hit ten of the enemy, they were forced by machine gun fire to withdraw once again. That evening B Company's two-inch mortars engaged some Japanese who were heard digging – either new positions or laying mines – in the track leading to the bungalow. Later that night heavy rain caused some of the trenches to subside, and two men in C Company were killed.

So, day after day, night after night, these intense, highly localised battles of attrition continued. On 6th May another Grant tank climbed up to the bungalow and attacked Japanese bunkers. On the 7th a B Company sniper found and shot a Japanese sniper in the roof of an outhouse. On the night of the 8th increased enemy activity on D Company's front provoked a shower of grenades. On the 9th Norman Havers's 'I' Section established and maintained for four days an observation post on the top of Summerhouse Hill, overlooking the bungalow. A machine gun set up here to fire on fixed lines managed to kill six Japanese.

Captain Snagger Highett MC

On the 10th Lieutenant Snagger Highett took three men beyond the perimeter 400 yards east of the bungalow and returned with some useful information about the Japanese supply line to their troops in the area of the bungalow.

A fresh battalion of Rajput infantry arrived and Knocker White noticed that, in clearing some of the trees in front of their position, the Rajputs had also provided – for the first time – a clear view of the Japanese positions beyond. He called Jock McNaught up to admire the view, and together White and McNaught considered the possibilities for a fresh attack.

On the morning of the 11th a six-pounder anti-tank gun, which had been agonisingly manhandled into position, fired five rounds rapid into the bunker on the north-east corner of the tennis court. This was the signal for C Company to attack and try to snatch control of the bunker. But the flanking movement by one of the sections took longer than planned, the attack lost momentum, the enemy recovered and the commander of C Company's leading platoon was wounded. The attack was abandoned, although some useful intelligence had been gained about Japanese positions.

That night Snagger Highett returned to the area he had patrolled. This time he brought with him Sergeant Spiller and twelve Dorsets, and a Royal Engineers officer and five Sappers, who would lay mines along the tracks used by the Japanese. Norman Havers takes up the story.

Venturing into enemy territory at night was always a suicidal and nerve-racking undertaking and this patrol was more than usually chancy, the territory into which they were going being the Japs' only remaining approach to their positions on the spur. Snagger would have found that it was not possible to negotiate the steep slopes in the silence needed to maintain surprise. On halting near their objective, they found that their presence had been discovered by some Japanese who were following them – a dicey moment. Most leaders would have decided that they had had enough; however their extra numbers disappeared, and Snagger took his patrol down into the low ground, a place where the road was thirty feet above them. Then... a strong force of Japs appeared, and ran down onto them. With surprise lost and any hope of laying the mines gone, they scrambled out and by some miracle were all in our lines by 0200 hours.

Later that day Lieutenant David *Dixie* Dean from Dorchester, the Motor Transport Officer who had just arrived from India with all the battalion transport, was killed by a sniper. Meanwhile, the Sappers were bulldozing a track up the hill to see if a tank could be brought up a slope that seemed impossibly steep. By midnight gravity had been defied, the dream had been realised and the tank was standing, ready to move. The Mountain Gunners had also managed to lift a 3.7-inch gun into a position where it could fire into the Japanese positions from the other side. D Company, commanded by Captain Clive Chettle, was prepared and ready. The scene was set for battle.

Snagger Highett later described his arrival on the tennis court aboard the tank.

I was not the commander of the tank. One of the unsung heroes of Kohima was Sergeant Waterhouse [of 149th Regiment, Royal Armoured Corps]... He had to go down a vertical drop of six feet on the tennis court. If the tank had been out of action on the tennis court it would have been a disaster. We were firing point-blank at the Jap positions from about twenty to thirty yards. I was firing one of the machine guns.

Knocker White continued the story of the attack.

Sergeant Waterhouse just let the Nip have it with his 75-mm, firing straight into their bunkers at a range of the length of a standard tennis court. On the first round of the 75-mm gun the infantry moved forward and the 3.7 opened up and let the enemy have fifty rounds fire, at point-blank range, up their sterns. With great skill Sergeant Given manoeuvred his platoon round to the north-east corner, where he deployed

Lieutenant Jock Given MM (when a Corporal)

and started setting about any opposition he could find. On the right Sergeant Cook waited until the gun fire had switched and then got in among the shell-happy Nips.

Out in the open, Sergeant Jock Given moved around with apparent unconcern talking to Snagger Highett on his tank telephone and directing the tank's fire onto the most stubborn enemy positions.

Sergeant William Cook, commanding 18 Platoon, remembered: *My objective was a black water tank. I took one section with me, when I came under fire. I dropped off a Bren to cover the enemy, came under fire again, and dropped off another Bren. This left me with one Bren, another man and myself to take the black water tank. The tank had fired a few rounds into the black water tank, it was shot to pieces and there was no water in it. The Japs had dug trenches all round the tank, which was about twelve feet square, and underneath it I had a pole charge, an eight-foot length of bamboo with gun-cotton tied on the end with a fuse attached. When I jumped down into the enemy trench and looked round the corner, there were three or four Japs. There shouldn't have been any left alive – the tank was supposed to have killed the lot. So I had no option but to put the pole charge in. We had been told that if you pushed the charge in before pulling the fuse, it would be pushed out by the Japs onto you, so I pulled the fuse, counted five and put the charge in, and it must have blown the Japs to bits. Unfortunately I forgot to close my eyes and I was temporarily blinded by debris...*

Sergeant Henry Cook later reflected: *People behave differently in action from their normal behaviour. One chap, Corporal Day, normally a mild-mannered man who wouldn't hurt a fly, stood on the top of a little trench at Kohima, shouting and cursing the Japanese – he was in another world.*

Suddenly, Private Tom Cattle of 17 Platoon later wrote, *some of the Japs started running. And we knew we had done it. We mowed them down as they ran. There were bodies that had been there weeks, covered in flies and maggots; the stench was terrific.*

Captain David Harris remembered Sergeant Waterhouse's tank as *magnificent. It crushed the bunkers and the Japs inside them, while we bunged grenades and pole charges in... A few ran away straight into our machine guns... all the rest were killed in their bunkers. We then quickly finished off the DC's bungalow (only a chimney was left) and joined up with our other Company at the road junction, where it had held out magnificently under fire for a week.*

By 1115 hours, Norman Havers recalled, *we had obtained the occupation of all the enemy territory on the spur, but the blasting of bunkers continued... Thanks to Sergeant Waterhouse and his crew, our casualties had been one dead and four wounded, a fraction of what had been dreaded.*

Tom Cattle recalled that at this stage they *could now walk about without being fired on by snipers. But we were still being shelled by Japs on the high hills overlooking Kohima. I was filthy, unshaven, covered in impetigo, covered in lice, with boils on my arms. My feet were in a terrible condition. We were thin, hungry, thirsty and tired.*

Richard Sharp, a BBC war correspondent who spent a great deal of time with the Dorsets, described his impressions of the battle in a recording broadcast on the BBC *9 O'Clock News* a few nights later.

... I know we've taken the tennis court... because I've seen it this afternoon. The men who took it came from a battalion of a West Country regiment. They've been plugging away at that tennis court for sixteen days, and when I got there at noon they were on it at last. In these sixteen days they'd become personal enemies of the Japs there, who used to taunt them at dusk, calling across the tennis court: 'Have you stood to yet?' Today they're on top and they walked on their toes, laughing, among the bulges in the earth of dug-out roofs, their muscles limber, ready to swivel this way or that in an instant. There was a company commander [Clive Chettle] – a robust man with a square, black jaw covered with stubble. The skin between his battle-dress

trousers and his tunic was bloody, and he swayed as he stood with his legs straddled. But his brain was working at full speed, and he laughed and shouted to his men as they went eagerly from fox-hole to fox-hole with hand grenades and pole charges...

... and now all that's left is the litter of war – piles of biscuits, dead Japs black with flies, heaps of Jap ammunition, broken rifles, silver from the District Commissioner's Bungalow. And among it, most incongruous of all, there's a man cleaning a pair of boots, another boiling tea, and an official photographer, who used to photograph Mayfair lovelies, saying: 'Move a little to the left, please.' And there's another chap reading a story headed 'Edgar Wallace Thriller' in a Sunday newspaper.

There was clearing up to be done. Norman Havers remembered *all who could went to see the place for which so many had suffered, or had given their lives. Everywhere there was the debris of war, bodies of friend and foe, shattered and unrecognisable buildings, bunkers and trenches, discarded weapons and equipment, and crumpled corrugated iron. The ground, where not dug up for defences, was broken by shell bursts, so that few natural or original features remained unchanged. We found one or two steps where there had been a flight to a terrace. As everywhere, trees were reduced to little more than torn and broken stumps. There was no life, it was a place of desolation and very horrible. By the pile of wreckage that was the bungalow, out of which rose a stone chimney stack and a piece or two of walling, there were bodies, some much as they fell in that first attack, a long seventeen days ago. Now Gus was to have the grim task of identification and the removal of one of the two identity discs worn by all of us, on a cord around the neck. And the Pioneer Platoon began the burials.*

The Padre and the MO, Gus Claxton and Joe Chamberlin, had been inspirational throughout the battle, appearing fearlessly, often with the stretcher-bearers, wherever the fighting was heaviest. Many men owed their survival to their courage, determination and professionalism.

The casualties did not stop. On 14th May two men were killed by Japanese shelling. Next day two men were killed and several injured when one of the three-ton trucks carrying them back to rest slid over a steep hill and crashed. That day Lieutenant Lionel Halahan took the Dorsets' only Japanese prisoner throughout the battle when he grabbed a wounded soldier captive before he had had time to kill himself.

Their part in this uniquely ghastly battle had lasted nearly three weeks and had cost the Dorsets seventy-five killed and several times that number wounded. Among the many wounded was twenty-eight-year-old Private Sid Avery, who lost a leg. His connection with the Dorset Regiment, however, was far from over. From 1957 until his retirement in 1981 he worked at the Keep Museum as Attendant and Assistant Curator.

After the survivors were relieved, Norman Havers took a last look at Garrison Hill.

I pause to think of Corporal Softley and the many like him. Of Lieutenant Mayer, leading his platoon, of the sapper who drove the bulldozer and of Sergeant Waterhouse, whose bravery in driving his tank over the ten-foot drop made that final day possible. I think of the decimated A Company and of the incomparable 8 Platoon. Of Jock Murrills, John Bowles and Preb [Captain Prebble, the Adjutant]. *I remember Lance-Corporal* [William] *Smart of the 'I' Section, who on the 27th had picked up a Bren gun and fired it without regard to his own safety, until he was shot down and killed. Also buried there among his pals is Private* [Philip] *Dudman who, a little over a year before, got lost on the night exercise at Juhu.*

THE MANIPUR ROAD

Tom Cattle described the Battalion's extensive cleaning-up process back at Zubza: *we had the luxury of hot baths out in the open. 50-gallon petrol drums had been cut in half and filled with disinfected water, all our clothes and boots were discarded, all the hair on my body was shaved off and after relaxing in the bath we were treated with 'powder' and jungle sores covered with gentian violet liquid. We had new clothing and boots, after a medical check and* [being] *treated for our various ailments. My feet were blistered and septic, the boils on my arms treated and my arm put in a sling.*

The numbers of killed and wounded were swollen by cases of malaria, dysentery and other diseases. Jock McNaught was forced to disband A Company and to reduce his Battalion to three severely under-strength companies. Back at Dimapur, on 18th May they were visited by their Corps Commander, Lieutenant-General Monty Stopford, who described the bungalow as *the key to Kohima* and its capture as *a turning point in the operations of XXXIII Corps.* With Stopford was his Brigadier General Staff, George Wood, who came to enquire solicitously after his old Battalion and to offer his congratulations. Writing home, he concluded his description of the Dorsets' part in the battle with the words: *They couldn't have done better.* That evening Gus Claxton held a memorial service for the dead.

But for the survivors this respite did not last long. They were needed to help speed the advance south towards Imphal, whose British and Indian defenders were forcing the Japanese north towards them. By 1900 hours on 23rd May they were near Kohima, in position on Two Tree Hill, and Dick Purser had just set out on patrol with the Guerrilla Platoon to gather intelligence for a forthcoming attack. Four days later his men guided C Company to their new positions and, by 28th May, the whole Battalion was in position. That afternoon Captain Morice was killed by what today would be called *friendly fire*. Accompanied by Company Sergeant-Major Keegan, he was examining enemy positions from a reverse slope when a burst of machine gun fire came from another friendly unit behind. Having survived the bloodbath at Kohima, Michael Morice's loss seemed a tragic waste. He was thirty and left a young wife in Hampstead.

David Harris recalled this arduous advance. *For the first ten miles or so they left strong rear guards on every spur. It meant very often climbing about 2,000 feet of almost perpendicular mountainside in dense jungle, with the Japs firing down on us from well prepared positions... They blew nearly every bridge as they retreated but our Sappers did the necessary in record time.*

Having been temporarily withdrawn, on 3rd June the Dorsets found themselves on a pouring wet day leading 5 Brigade along the Kohima-Imphal road towards Dyer Hill. A five-hour daylight patrol led by Snagger Highett confirmed that the hill was clear of enemy but that it was under fire from Japanese guns on nearby Big Tree Hill. After a miserably wet and hungry night, next morning Clive Chettle led his Company onto Dyer Hill, where they realised that, to hold Dyer, they needed to capture Big Tree Hill, and to capture Big Tree Hill they needed first to take a smaller hill known as the Pimple.

C Company, led by Dave Davies, and the Guerrilla Platoon, led by Dick Purser, began their attack on the Pimple at 0905 hours. Meeting machine gun fire, both units were temporarily checked and took cover. After a firefight in which four Japanese were killed, Davies decided to withdraw but, during the withdrawal, a number of men were wounded. Davies was killed as he knelt beside Private Collis, a stretcher-bearer, who had been shot in the stomach. At about the same time and a small distance away, Dick Purser was giving an order when he was shot in the head by a Japanese soldier, who was then shot by Sergeant Maule.

Hearing that one wounded man was still lying out in front of a Japanese bunker, Joe Chamberlin, the Battalion's redoubtable doctor, set out with a small party to the rescue. The citation for his hard-earned Military Cross described how *Captain Chamberlin himself went forward with a small party and, under fire from the enemy light machine gun, personally brought back the wounded man. His courage so inspired the forward troops that a deliberate and orderly withdrawal was effected without further loss, and the wounded brought to safety.*

With the Padre as usual well to the fore, the wounded were brought safely back to the Regimental Aid Post, among them Private Collis and Captain Purser. Sadly, John Collis died of his wounds later that day and Dick Purser followed him three days later. The Battalion was hit hard by these losses, which came so suddenly and to such little purpose so soon after their success at Kohima. But the losses did not end there. Seven others died that day, among them Laurence Hobby, one of three brothers from Lytchett Minster who all served in C Company. Snagger Highett now assumed command of a sadder C Company, becoming their fourth commander in as many weeks.

For the men of Bill Slim's Fourteenth Army, that cataclysmic day for Europe, 6th June 1944, was just another unpleasant, unremarkable day in the jungle. The Dorsets spent it at Pfuchana, patrolling ahead of the advance to retrieve documents and identification from the blood-soaked pockets of Japanese corpses. But things were going well. The various parts of Slim's plan to halt the Japanese advance and destroy their army were succeeding. The enemy had been ejected from Kohima, the advance on the Kohima-Imphal road was making progress, and the British and Indian forces besieged at Imphal were giving better than they were getting, pushing the Japanese back. After two depressing years on the ebb, the tide in Burma was turning. But, although Slim could sense this, for those more directly absorbed in the daily turmoil, danger and discomfort, this change in their fortunes may not – yet – have become clear.

For one man among the 2nd Dorsets, 8th June 1944 was probably the best day of his life. That day Major Geoffrey – Knocker – White, the Battalion's fearless and ebullient Second-in-Command, achieved his life's ambition. A son of the Regiment, White had absorbed its ethos and traditions with his mother's milk and in the cigar smoke in the Officers' Mess. He was a traditionalist: his pride, loyalty and sense of belonging took little account of even the army reforms of 1881. For him, the 54th Regiment of Foot still existed and the 2nd Battalion of the Dorset Regiment was its living embodiment. But he was also fiercely protective of his officers and men, whom he took great trouble to get to know, and of whom he spoke (and later wrote) with proprietorial affection. Now Jock McNaught's promotion to command 4 Brigade gave White command of his preferred Battalion of his own Regiment in action. McNaught had led and fought the Battalion throughout the nightmare of Kohima. A Royal Scots Fusilier, he had soon won the respect and

Colonel Knocker White DSO

loyalty of the Dorsets, whom he had led and commanded in battle with determination, courage and great success. Now it would fall to Knocker White to command the 2nd Battalion as they pursued and harried their defeated enemy south through Burma.

The Battalion which White took over could muster only six weak platoons. In round numbers, of the 830 officers and men who had assembled at Ahemdnagar in April, only 360 remained.

Temporarily placed in 4 Brigade under the command of Jock McNaught, they were ordered to send a company down the Manipur Road to reinforce the 2nd Royal Norfolks around the village of Viswema. White sent Captain Peter Feeney with B Company, accompanied by the Guerrilla Platoon, now commanded by a newly arrived New Zealander, Captain Andrew Mackenzie. Reaching the Norfolks after a steep climb through jungle after dark, B Company were absorbed within the Norfolks' own defences while Mackenzie's Platoon were sent to carry out a detailed reconnaissance of the Japanese positions on a ridge above them.

Andrew Mackenzie remembered Colonel Carroll of the Norfolks *ordered me to establish whether or not the Japs were above him in strength – they were. We fired at them to draw their fire, during which one of the Platoon was hit. I crawled out with my batman to pull him back and we did so while shielded by artillery fire. Somehow this wounded man was evacuated and... recovered. The following day a combined patrol (Norfolks and the Guerrillas) under a Norfolk major drove down the ridge to dislodge the Japs, but there were several ridges – all wired. We found that we were on the wrong one with the result that we then had to attack the correct one from below. We did not know where the Japs were until they fired at us from directly above. Luckily I was shielded by a dip in the ground, but was as near damned killed... We rolled down the hill to safety shielded by the undergrowth. One of my men had been hit and a stretcher party sent to bring him down was able to do so. This was the only time the Japs were to show this sort of chivalry.*

Mac Mackenzie omitted two facts from this later account: that, in drawing the enemy's fire to establish their strength and whereabouts, his platoon took four casualties, and that the Colonel of the Royal Norfolks wrote to Knocker White to thank Mackenzie and his platoon for the valuable work they had done. Ever-conscious of regimental history, White realised that this action was the first time since Mesopotamia nearly three decades earlier that a force of Norsets had seen action.

In Tiger Havers's book, Joe Chamberlin later recounted his memories of this action.

It was the most unpleasant, dense jungle we had been in... Mac made an impressive first appearance, locating the Japs by drawing their fire with calm deliberation. The mortaring was such that even Sergeant-Major 'Gary' Cooper found it necessary to throw himself into someone's trench, regardless of who was underneath him. And such was the warm respect that everyone had for him that he was credited with having deliberately protected the occupants. He said that nothing was further from his thoughts. He was hit by a fragment and consented to have a dressing on it. I have a very distressing memory of something that happened during this mortaring. Someone who had been hit – invisible in the dense scrub and trees – was crying for help. The cries went on for so very long and we couldn't even begin to try and find him. By the time someone got to him he was dead. He was one of the recently joined and very young soldiers, who looked as if they should all be at school.

The dead soldier's name was Private Leslie Willimott. From Halesworth in Suffolk, he had just passed his twentieth birthday.

Meanwhile the rest of the Battalion received a visit from their Corps and Division commanders, Generals Monty Stopford and John Grover. In front of them, despite some pockets of fierce resistance, the Japanese seemed to be disintegrating. A three-battalion attack by the Camerons, Royal Scots and Worcesters had finally cleared the enemy from Viswema. Now columns, led by a troop of armoured cars followed by tanks and motorised infantry with their Gunner Forward Observation Officers, forced their way down the road towards Mao Songsang. Here, a heavy artillery bombardment and the threat of encirclement persuaded the Japanese to withdraw again. The column was to continue down the road and, this time, the Dorsets, now back with 5 Brigade, would be in the lead.

Through the driving monsoon rain the column pressed on, White conscious of General Grover's order: "Crack on, Geoffrey." At a landslide the Worcesters took over the lead. That day – 18th June – the Brigade had advanced sixteen miles: a record in this campaign.

At 1700 hours on 19th June the Dorsets were sent with great despatch to secure the next position – known as the Maramei feature – where the Japanese might make a stand. Here they came under intense machine gun fire and were very lucky to emerge with only one casualty when Snagger Highett was hit in the hand. They paid the price of being so far below strength. With all their companies committed, they were unable to complete the task without help from the Royal Scots. Nonetheless, a position which the Japanese had hoped to hold for ten days had been captured within twenty-four hours.

In *Defeat into Victory* Field Marshal Lord Slim later wrote:

By the 18th June, the spearheads of my two corps were some forty miles apart on the Kohima road, the 2nd Division approaching Maram and the 5th nearing Kangpokpi. Although he had given up the much stronger defences of Mao Songsang, the enemy attempted to hold against the 2nd Division another rearguard position at Maram, about eight miles further south... This was the last serious attempt the enemy made to delay the advance of XXXIII Corps. It was now evident that the 31st Japanese Division was disintegrating and the enemy higher command no longer controlled the battle.

On the night of 20th/21st June, working its way in darkness around the base of the Maramei feature, one of the Dorsets' patrols encountered and exchanged shots with what turned out to be a sentry post of 149th Regiment, Royal Armoured Corps. The patrol's leader, twenty-nine-year-old Corporal Stanley Robinson of B Company, was killed.

Three days later, deep in the jungle, they celebrated Plassey Day.[12] While, 5,000 miles to their west, the 4th and 5th Dorsets joined the 1st in the Normandy

---

12   Plassey was an important battle honour for the Dorsets. The 39th Foot fought in this Battle under Clive of India on 23rd June 1757.

beach-head, the 2nd Battalion completed their part in clearing the Manipur road. With the opening of the road, the Battalion's arduous, costly part in the war against the Japanese came to a much-needed pause. They – and the rest of the Division – were withdrawn to Imphal to rest and recuperate. The cost of the past ten weeks had been 330 of their number killed or evacuated wounded or seriously ill. The prize had been the defeat of the Japanese at Kohima and the sight of a long victorious, confident army plunged into headlong, disorganised retreat. Slim's strategy had succeeded. As he later put it: *The Imphal-Kohima battle, the most decisive battle of the Burma campaign, was not yet over, but it was won.*

REPAIR AND RECONSTRUCTION

Soon after their move to Imphal, the Battalion received two visitors and some bad news. The visitors were their Corps Commander, General Monty Stopford, and Admiral Lord Louis Mountbatten, the Supreme Allied Commander, who inspired 5 Brigade with a speech recounting tales of Japanese defeat and confusion.

The bad news was the loss of their Divisional Commander, John Grover, who it seems had clashed with the different attitudes of the British commanders of the Indian Army. Commanding a largely Indian Army force, Slim – who had served in both the British and Indian Armies and usually towered magnanimously above such pettiness – could not afford factions. Grover returned to the UK and, sadly, did not command again. From the Dorsets' perspective, his departure was a personal loss. He had built and trained the 2nd Division before commanding it throughout the protracted horror of Kohima. They would resent what they saw as his *shabby treatment* and miss him greatly, despite the obvious abilities and popularity of his successor, Major General Cameron Nicholson, a veteran of the campaign in Tunisia.

The Brigade held a Memorial Service for their dead. The gaps in the ranks extended to the padres, who had lost one of their number, Father O'Callaghan, early in the campaign.

Knocker White described how, although in the Imphal perimeter there *didn't seem to be much of a war on,* outside... *a fierce and stern battle was still being fought down three of the four roads that led to Imphal... It was when we visited our sick and wounded... in hospital that we saw the latest battle casualties and really appreciated what a dour conflict was still being fought around us.*

When the 23rd Indian Division needed strengthening in its advance towards the border of Burma near Tamu, 5 Brigade was sent to help. The terrain was demanding and spectacular. Tiger Havers remembered *the distance from Palel to Tamu is about forty miles but, as the road rises 2,300 feet from Palel and then drops 4,200 feet to Tamu and throughout its length it undulates over ridges and hollows, the road distance must be nearer fifty...*

After a few days at Palel the time came for us to start up the road and we covered the ten miles to Recce Hill, on the apex of Shenam Ridge, the highest point on the road. There, when not enveloped in cloud, as it was for us other than one evening and the following morning, the view extended in every direction over jungle clad mountains to distant horizons. We had actually been there some days seeing nothing, when suddenly the mist had gone and we found ourselves on top of the world, and chaps who had never bothered with a view before stood agape at the immensity of a land of mountains that seemed to have no end.

Here the still severely under-strength Dorsets were mainly supporting the advance, but some energetic patrolling was undertaken, especially by Mackenzie and his Guerrilla Platoon, who brought back evidence of the continuing Japanese retreat.

On 5th August as they advanced from Bulldozer Ridge and neared the border with Burma, the opportunity did not escape the notice of Knocker White. Never one to miss a chance to publicise his Regiment's history and achievements, he drove ahead down the road to claim for his Battalion the distinction of being *Primus ex Indis* and *Primus in Burma*. Sadly, though, the demands of the rapid advance meant that the Worcesters got there first. But the Colonel could comfort himself with the thought that the Dorsets, if not quite the first, were among the first troops back into Burma.

Five days later the 2nd Battalion were relieved by an East African battalion and withdrawn to Maram to reorganise and refit. Here they received welcome reinforcements, who came mainly from Royal Artillery light anti-aircraft regiments which had been disbanded because the Allied air forces controlled the skies. Old friends, wounded or taken ill at or soon after Kohima, found their way home to help rebuild their shattered Battalion. New friends arrived, including Major Mervyn Jones of the Monmouth Regiment, who joined the Dorsets from a staff job in the Arakan. He was appointed Second-in-Command, releasing Major Tommy Tucker, a recently arrived Hampshire officer, to command a rifle company.

On 31st August General Bill Slim addressed a Special Order of the Day to the 2nd Division.

In my last order of the day I told you you had defeated the Jap Armies opposing you and that it remained to destroy them. The extent to which you have done that is shown by the fifty thousand Japanese left dead on the soil of India and Northern Burma, the great quantities of guns and equipment you have captured, the prisoners you have taken, the advances you have made, and the flight of the remnants you are still pursuing...

The 2nd Division, one of the oldest divisions in the British Army, with a history going back to the Peninsular War, has shown itself worthy of its magnificent traditions. In the bitter fighting around Kohima you showed every quality – courage, stubbornness, cheerfulness – that has distinguished British soldiers throughout history. The offensive contribution of your Division was unsurpassed.

To the Officers and men of the 2nd Division I send my congratulations. The Fourteenth Army has inflicted on the Japanese the greatest defeat his Army has yet suffered. He is busily trying to build up again and reinforce his broken divisions. He will fight again and viciously, but we have paid him something of what we owe. There still remains the interest. He will get it.

In October Slim visited the 2nd Dorsets and, later in the month, the Battalion were entertained by the 2nd Royal Norfolks, who held a Norset Day at Kigwema.

Although removed from the battle, the Battalion continued to suffer a number of casualties, mainly to scrub typhus, which was painful, debilitating and, sometimes, fatal. A batch of new officers arrived, together with a detachment of fifty men from the 1st Glosters, commanded by Major James Heath, who were joining the Dorsets to gain battle experience.

On 15th December 1944 at Imphal, in a unique investiture in the field, Field Marshal Lord Wavell, the Viceroy of India, dubbed Bill Slim and his three corps commanders knights. Lieutenant-General Monty Stopford's knighthood recognised his leadership and XXXIII Corps' magnificent performance at Kohima and Imphal. Six months later, Major-General John Grover would be made a Companion of the Order of the Bath for his leadership of the 2nd Division at Kohima.

It was fitting that the generals should be honoured for the decisive, horrific battle of Kohima but a dispassionate observer, seventy years later, cannot fail to be struck by how few gallantry awards were given to the junior officers and men who fought and won the battle. Colonel Jock McNaught was awarded a DSO for his leadership and determination. Lieutenant Snagger Highett and Captain Clive Chettle each received a Military Cross, while Sergeant Jock Given was awarded a Military Medal and an immediate commission in the field. In other campaigns one can imagine John Bowles, whose Company seized and held a decisive position

Gus Claxton MC consecrating the Dorsets' Memorial at Kohima

Memorial to the Dorset Regiment, Kohima by Jock Murrills

during the very worst of the protracted battle, receiving a DSO or certainly an MC. His mention in Despatches was in keeping with what seems a parsimoniously short list of awards given to the Dorsets for their part in winning what was one of the most fiercely contested, relentlessly savage battles in the history of British infantry warfare.

During their rest from the battle, many Dorsets returned one last time to Kohima to attend the service and witness the unveiling of the 2nd Division's Memorial there. Sixteen feet high and donated by the Naga community, the obelisk bore words that still echo powerfully down the years:

> *When you go home*
> *Tell them of us and say,*
> *For your tomorrow*
> *We gave our today.*

THE ROAD TO MANDALAY

After relieving the Dorsets near Tamu in August, the 11th East African Division made good progress, crossing the Chindwin and establishing a bridgehead on the east bank. In December the 2nd Division were recalled to resume the advance and General Nicholson, their new commander, visited the Dorsets and described the operation that lay ahead. Slim's ultimate objective, Rangoon, lay 600 miles to the south. XXXIII Corps' intermediate objectives were Shwebo and Mandalay. The Division's objective was Shwebo and the likeliest places the Japanese might stand and fight were Pyingain (renamed inevitably as *Pink Gin*) and, thirty miles further east, Ye-U on the River Mu. The advancing forces would be supplied by air.

En route to the front, the Dorsets were able to celebrate Christmas traditionally, the officers serving the men's dinners. The only break with tradition was the date: 18th December. Two days later they marched or drove across the Royal Engineers' 1,100-foot Bailey bridge over the River Chindwin.

Tom Cattle remembered: *As we advanced we saw evidence of the retreat of the British Army through Burma in 1942. Hundreds of trucks, guns and some tanks which had been abandoned and destroyed by our retreating troops... We were now relying more and more on the mules to carry essential stores; all we had in the way of Company trucks was one 15cwt Dodge and altogether the Battalion had about fifteen vehicles...*

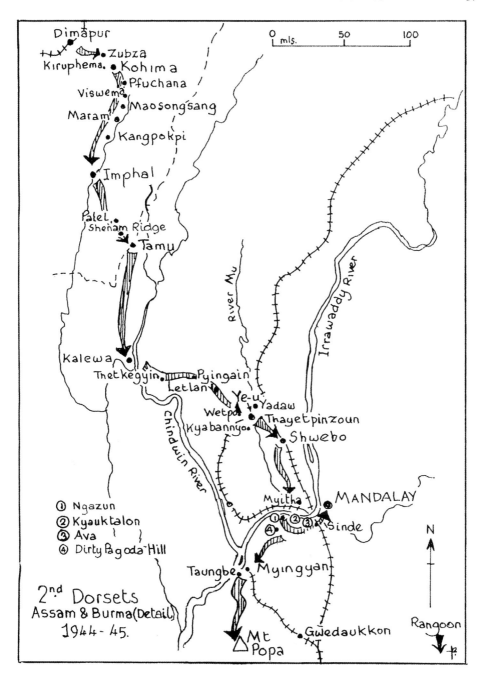

2nd Dorsets' Campaign in Assam and Burma April 1944–March 1945

Christmas Day 1944 was spent, between night marches, at Thetkegyin, where
their stay was enlivened by RAF Transport Command, whose Douglas Dakotas

demonstrated the Allies' total command of the air by flying over, trailing a streamer wishing the advancing troops *A Merry Christmas from the RAF*. It was reassuring that the all-important task of resupplying the 2nd Division was in such capable and friendly hands.

Early on 27th December the Dorsets arrived at Pink Gin, which the Japanese had decided not to defend. So peaceful was the place that Knocker White and Mervyn Jones went for a ride in the hills. On New Year's Eve the Dorsets took the lead in the advance. After a few miles, they finally emerged blinking from the dense jungle that had been their home since India and on to the startlingly bright, open Burmese plain.

But things on the plain, as Tom Cattle described, *were almost as bad, having to contend with banana groves, usually cover for a Jap defensive position. The tall elephant grass, some over six feet in height, made it very difficult to advance with any speed... Although our general line of advance is along the so-called road, it is not possible to keep to road sections. Platoons and companies have to extend to cover wider areas. We could not always rely on information from the locals as to the whereabouts of the Japs; although we had interpreters, they were not up with the leading section, but more often back with Battalion Headquarters. The Burmese language was difficult, the 'squaddie' could get by using a smattering of words but* [it was] *almost impossible to carry on any kind of intelligent conversation.*

By New Year's Day 1945, John Bowles's A Company had reached the canal at Letlan to find that the bridge there had been blown. Planning to establish a bridge-head over the river at Ye-U, White ordered another company to resume the advance to establish if the railway bridge beyond Wetpo was still intact. Scenting an opportunity, White was in his element and waxed enthusiastically biblical in his orders. He despatched Snagger Highett and his Guerrilla Platoon even unto Ye-U on a long reconnaissance and they returned, having found no Japanese anywhere. Ye-U appeared to be unoccupied and open for the taking.

Early on 2nd January the Battalion set out for Ye-U and were joined by Bowles's A Company, who had found their way across the canal. At the railway crossing east of the town, White sent A Company along the railway to protect the Battalion's left flank, clear the north of the town and to block any Japanese attempt to enter Ye-U from the north. Although Tommy Tucker's C Company encountered some enemy snipers, the Dorsets found Ye-U as Highett's patrol had described it: deserted.

The bridge over the river had been destroyed and the enemy could be seen on the far bank. White asked his supporting machine-gunners from the 2nd Manchesters to engage them. Immediately the Japanese artillery retaliated to defend what was clearly a strong position in the 2,000 yard-wide salient formed by a bend in the River Mu. Across the river the Dorsets could see the villages of Yadaw on the left and Thayetpinzuon the right. Between them and closer to the river were two copses, which they called Pagoda Copse and Gun Copse.

That night, while the Japanese continued to shell the rest of the Battalion, Snagger Highett was sent across the river on reconnaissance. He returned, having shot up a Japanese vehicle, with valuable intelligence including the fact that Yadaw itself was occupied by the enemy. Meanwhile, Knocker White laid his plans. Rather than attack the Japanese defences head-on, he would try to cross the river to the west near Kyabannyo, establish a bridgehead at Yadaw and (in his words) *descend on the Nip from the north and roll him up from his right flank to his main position at Thayetpinzuon.*

In the morning of 3rd January, leading a battle group consisting of A and D Companies, the Pioneer Platoon, a mortar detachment, a troop of Grant tanks from the 3rd Dragoon Guards, some gunner forward observation officers in their armoured vehicles, and his own Tactical Headquarters, Knocker White set off towards Kyabannyo. Behind him he left Mervyn Jones and the rest of the Battalion holding Ye-U. By 1400 hours his troops were in position in a deserted Kyabannyo, ready to attack across the river behind smoke, but the RAF was unable to provide an air strike that day. White champed impatiently at the bit until late afternoon, when the fighter bombers appeared and rocketed the Japanese positions, enabling Clive Chettle to get D Company across and occupy Yadaw. John Bowles and A Company followed at 0400 next day but the supporting tanks became bogged in the sand by the river and had to be left behind.

As the Dorsets emerged from Yadaw they encountered a force of sixty Japanese coming the other way. Both sides deployed, but the Royal Artillery were able to bring down a heavy and accurate concentration on the Japanese positions, enabling D Company to clear the way. Without tank support and with only two companies with limited ammunition and dwindling rations, White paused and asked Mervyn Jones back at Ye-U to send up Tommy Tucker and C Company with as much ammunition as they could carry.

Early on 5th January a patrol reported that Pagoda Copse was clear and White decided to occupy it and to use it as the starting point for his attack on Gun Copse. As Tucker arrived in mid-afternoon, he ordered him to hand over the ammunition his Company had brought and then to lead the attack with A and D Companies. At 1700 hours, after a thunderclap barrage on the Japanese positions, A and C Companies advanced under cover of smoke.

Evacuating casualties by night across the River Mu by Jock Murrills

C Company, which contained the Gloster Platoon, met strong resistance. Private Harry Newcombe of 13 Platoon remembered:

We emerged into open ground beyond which was Gun Copse, a long thickly wooded area... As our double line passed the half-way point the woods suddenly erupted with machine gun fire and everybody dropped to the ground and as there was no cover all we could do was hug the ground...

Tommy Thomas lay next to me and I could see the shock on his face and read his thoughts... I heard a cry behind and turned to see the chap flip over on his back, obviously hit, one hand weakly waving; but no one could move under the intense fire. I heard Lieutenant Jock Given's voice calling for smoke, and then the sound of our 2-inch mortars beginning to fire and the first smoke bombs falling in front of the line of trees. Then Major Tucker and Jock Given began shouting as they stood above us – telling us to get up and attack. Both were taking a great risk, standing there, as they exhorted us to action.

Sergeant Alec Nott recalled:

It was so sudden, one minute deathly silence, then all hell breaking loose. It was like a hail storm with bullets cracking overhead in a continuous stream and bouncing off the ground ahead. I heard them shout, jumped to my feet, bayonet out and feeling very alone began to charge. I was struck a sudden blow on my left hip and the machine gun bullet passed through and exited from my buttock, before I fell.

Harry Newcombe described the momentum created by Tucker and Given being taken up by the Company in a wave of cries:

Up the Dorsets! and Up the Glosters! were heard above the shooting and soon were echoing through the wood as we entered and the battle became close combat. I saw one of our chaps and a Jap fighting with bayonets and, through the smoke, fired twice at two Japs carrying something between them. But I lost them in the smoke and it is difficult to shoot accurately on the run with a bayoneted rifle. Just ahead was a covered trench with a slope cut in the ground to a small doorway and, as I was almost on top of it, I caught a glimpse of a steel helmet and the bottom half of a face. I lunged at it with my bayonet and as I did a voice shouted almost in my ear: 'Grenade! Cover!' and I glimpsed a 36 grenade whizzing down the slope and the chap who threw it nearly fell on me. As we went down I felt pain in both ears as the grenade lifted the dug-out roof six inches and smoke and dust poured out of the doorway. The chap was on his hands and knees, holding up two fingers and shouting. I could hear only bells. He gesticulated that there had been two Japs, but I had seen only one. As I carried on I passed a dead Jap in a praying position; he keeled over when my boot touched him. And then we were converging on the far side of the wood, with more shouting than gunfire, and were just in time to see the Jap survivors running for the village of Thayetpinzuon. Someone was calling out that we were not to continue in pursuit.

A Company, on C Company's left, met less opposition but at one point ran into some heavy grenades fired from dischargers. One of the grenades killed John Bowles, who was advancing with one of his platoons. White immediately asked Captain Thom, the Gunner Forward Observation Officer, if he could take command of the rear of A Company and was told that he would have "a bloody good try". Jimmy Thom then proceeded to reorganise the reserve platoon, direct his battery's fire, and send Company Sergeant-Major Bedlow back to report to White because the wireless was malfunctioning, enabling Bowles's Second-in-Command, Lieutenant Roger Johnson, to lead the other two platoons of A Company on to gain their objective.

The Japanese defenders had again been routed and fifty of them killed, at a cost of six killed and fourteen wounded. Several of those killed were recent Gunner reinforcements. The loss of John Bowles was a severe one. The son of an Indian Army officer, he had enlisted in the Dorsets in the mid-1930s and had fought as a warrant officer with the Battalion at Dunkirk before being commissioned and excelling as a company commander at Kohima. Such experience, such men, were irreplaceable. John Bowles left a widow at home in Cosham.

As usual, Joe Chamberlin, Gus Claxton and the stretcher-bearers worked tirelessly to evacuate the wounded under fire. Lance-Corporal Henry Jesty from Christchurch organised the medical orderlies who tended C Company's casualties; we will meet him again later in our story. Jimmy Thom, the Gunner officer who took command of part of A Company, was later awarded the Military Cross for his part in this victory, which cleared the way to Shwebo.

As, covered in dust from their three-week, 125-mile journey, the Dorsets marched into Shwebo, they watched a fleet of Dakotas flying in supplies. Despite the Allies' superiority in the air, some Japanese Zeros managed to get in amongst the transport aircraft and shot two down in smoke and flames.

While the 2nd Dorsets had been fighting their way across and beyond the River Mu, one of their previous colonels had distinguished himself in the Arakan campaign. Now a major-general and commanding 25th Indian Division, George Wood had won a reputation for rapid action, pushing his division through and past the enemy, leaving them disorientated and far in the rear. At Akyab he mounted an amphibious assault involving a Commando brigade and five infantry battalions within thirty-six hours of receiving the order. The town was captured six weeks ahead of schedule and Wood added a DSO to the MC he had won in 1920 as a junior officer in South Russia.

The last natural and defendable barrier before Mandalay was the broad, swift-flowing River Irrawaddy. Private Tom Cattle of D Company later recalled his first sight of the river.

The Irrawaddy is a mile wide. I was a bit apprehensive: I couldn't swim. We could see the Japs on the other side and knew it would not be an easy crossing. We were at a village on the west bank and dug in. We were patrolling across the river and so were they. One night the Japs managed to get in amongst us. It was hand-to-hand fighting, and hope for the best. We were so close to each other you couldn't even use grenades, just bayonets. Eventually they left. There were not many of them.

By the time it was 5 Brigade's turn, three Indian divisions were already across. The 19th, under General Pete Rees, had crossed to the north, the 20th to the

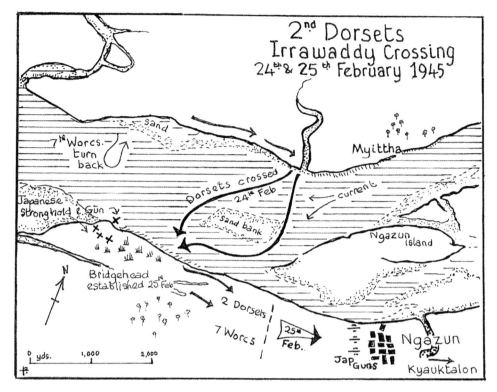

2nd Dorsets' Crossing of the Irrawaddy 24th–25th February 1945

south and then, suddenly, the 7th burst across the river and turned south towards Meiktila. Supplemented by the 1st Royal Welch Fusiliers, 5 Brigade were to lead 2nd Division's crossing and the Dorsets were to follow the 7th Worcesters on the right. The assault crossing, with very inadequate and unreliable boats, began at 2230 hours on 24th February. Knocker White takes up the story.

The Worcesters got into mid-stream and soon found themselves in difficulties. Some of the boats began to fill and as they approached the south shore they came under small-arms fire which holed the surviving boats. The Commanding Officer [Colonel Tom Irvine] found himself swimming about in the water and by his own personal gallantry saved a number of lives. The opposition on the far side being stronger than had been expected, and the difficulties of navigating... obdurate craft by paddle in the four-knot current proving much greater than had been anticipated, the Worcesters were back again on the north bank by midnight.

In the centre, also, things had not gone well. The Camerons came up against strong opposition and could get only about a company and a quarter across, with

*the Commanding Officer and a very small tactical headquarters. They had to land
and assault a cliff, but had gained a precarious foothold in the thick jungle grass on
the top. When, however, they tried to get their assault craft back again they failed
completely. The current was much too strong and the Nip was picking off the boatmen
at his leisure. On the extreme left the Royal Welch Fusiliers were... across but with only
two platoons.*

Faced next day by this situation, Brigadier Michael West was forced to change
his plan. Ordering some DUKWs[13] forward along bulldozed tracks, he decided
to use the Dorsets to reinforce the Camerons' tenuous bridgehead in the centre.
This involved the 2nd Battalion moving 5,000 yards across country to Myitha
before sending their leading troops – B Company and White's Tactical HQ –
across, bouncing from sandbank to sandbank, in a flotilla of DUKWs and boats.
Tom Cattle recalled the *fold-up canvas boats operated by Royal Engineers with an
outboard engine... These boats weren't very stable and the engines were not reli-
able. Some people had to paddle to get across... It was a steep bank on the other
side, and immediately we were into high elephant grass. We were being shelled and
machine-gunned...*

The Intelligence Officer, Norman Havers, remembered his own landing... *on a
tiny beach below a high bank, under conditions resembling a medieval hell. Above us
on that bank was a raging fire, the flame and billowing black smoke of which masked
all else, but for Camerons issuing from it carrying their blood-covered dead to the
safety of the beach, out of reach of the flames. On climbing the bank we found the
Camerons not fighting Japs but the flames, which threatened to sweep across their
bridgehead. The elephant grass... was burning, the fire having started a quarter of
a mile downstream, where we had been shelling a Jap position, and the flames had
come downwind to us. Those Japs had a bunker... inside the face of the river bank. It
contained a machine gun with which they shot at our DUKWs. From first light it had
been subjected to all the bombing and artillery fire that we could muster. It operated
spasmodically and irrationally; we were amazed that it operated at all and, while
cursing them for the casualties they inflicted, we had to admire the courage of those
who manned it.*

The DUKW containing Joe Chamberlin, Gus Claxton and the Dorsets' Regimental
Aid Post arrived unscathed to find the Camerons' redoubtable Glaswegian medical
sergeant, Jock McEvoy, acting as Medical Officer. Their own doctor, Peter Barkley,

---

13   The DUKW was an amphibious troop-carrying truck. (Today yellow ones take tourists
on the Thames.)

The Dorsets cross the Irrawaddy

Dorset carriers cross the Irrawaddy by Jock Murrills

had been killed crossing the river. Gus Claxton assumed responsibility for ferrying the wounded and dead back across the river while Joe Chamberlin took over as MO for both battalions.

By dusk, with all but the Battalion's tail across, Knocker White had agreed with Colonel Angus McAlester of the Camerons that the Dorsets would try to develop the bridgehead to the left while the Camerons did the same on the right. Despite the best efforts of the very determined Japanese machine-gunners, the crossing had cost the Dorsets only four killed and nine wounded. Most of these casualties were from the Mortar and Gloster Platoons in the last craft across.

Tiger Havers recalled hearing the commander of the Mortar Platoon, Captain Michael Newte – *he with the ready smile and wit, who had the keenest brain* – shouting for stretcher-bearers. He also remembered a corporal, a veteran of Kohima and every battle since, becoming *bomb happy* and going out sniping *while shouting his head off. His pals were able to bring him in and he was eased away for rest and recuperation.* When a shell-burst caused a trench to collapse, twenty-six-year-old Channel Islander Corporal Alfred Reynel was buried and suffocated.

With the bridgehead secured, Brigadier West now ordered the Dorsets and the Worcesters to capture the town of Ngazun, twenty miles east on the south bank of the Irrawaddy. At 1300 hours, in a copybook assault, Ngazun was first heavily attacked by RAF Hurricane fighter-bombers and then shelled by the Royal Artillery. At 1350 the Dorsets advanced, with the Worcesters on the right and supported by a troop of tanks and the machine guns of the Manchester Regiment, into Ngazun.

Knocker White remembered their advance, with fixed bayonets, as *reminiscent of a peace-time Army Cup match as A and C Companies closed on the town with cries of 'Up, the Five and Fours!' and 'On, on, Do Dorset!' answered by 'Up, the Twenty-Eighth' from the Gloster Platoon in the van of A Company.*

Paget Fretts and Tommy Tucker, with their companies, swept through the village, and any sign of movement from a basha or hut called for a No 77 grenade, which promptly ignited the building. The going was quite thick and the fire started by the air strike slowed up our advance considerably, and it was not until close on three o'clock that I could report to the Brigadier that our section of the village had been cleared.

The Dorsets lost not a single man in this attack, although six were wounded, among them Lieutenant Jock Given MM and Private Harry Newcombe. Later a captured Japanese soldier revealed that the garrison had withstood both the air and artillery bombardment but had been persuaded to withdraw (leaving only a token, suicidal defence behind) by the sight of the Worcesters and the Dorsets deploying for the attack.

The 2nd Dorsets capturing Ngazun

After ten days around Ngazun, on 7th March 5 Brigade continued their advance, with the Camerons and Worcesters leading and the Dorsets in reserve. Five miles from Ngazun the Worcesters encountered strong Japanese defences in the hills towards Kyauktalon. The Dorsets were ordered forward to make a night attack on what – because of the small, battered, black pagoda on its summit – became known as Dirty Pagoda Hill.

At 0045 hours on 10th March, the Dorsets quietly slipped through the Worcesters' positions and scrambled up the hill in darkness. Meeting no opposition but finding warm embers of fires on which the enemy had cooked their supper, B and C Companies pressed on and occupied the ring contour 1,200 yards beyond the Dirty Pagoda. Paget Fretts's A Company meanwhile dug in around the Pagoda and Clive Chettle's D Company veered left to deploy on another rise there.

Knocker White ordered Chettle to send a patrol down to the main road to check if it was clear of Japanese. Around 0500, at first light, the patrol stirred up a hornets' nest, disturbing a Japanese medium machine gun post, which opened fire on the men of D Company who were digging in. For Tom Cattle *it was hell,*

Dirty Pagoda Hill by Jock Murrills

men were being hit and shouting and screaming, we were being attacked by quite a strong number of Japs. C Company who were stuck out in front in the most exposed position suffered the worst and had the most casualties. The medical staff including the stretcher-bearers were kept busy and there were many heroes that went unknown and unrecognised that morning.

Norman Havers *was awakened by the screams of those of Clive's Company whose positions were on the north and east facing slope, a few feet away... I can still see myself and those I was with, lying across the track facing east, our heads and shoulders in the gutter. To our front the ground fell steeply before levelling out in the saddle; not so far to our right stood the forlorn pagoda. A few final members of D were coming up that steep slope, having evacuated their most forward positions. I heard one of the last say, 'Bill is still down there.' Whereupon, someone behind got up and ran back down the slope and out of sight; soon to reappear with Bill on his back and, as he passed, I could see that the man making the rescue was a sergeant.*

Yorky Seale of D Company insisted on carrying on fighting despite his own wounds. Dr Joe Chamberlin later referred to those *like the indestructible Sergeant Seale who picked bits of mortar bomb out of themselves and soldiered on.* Seale's courage in this battle – and in a later one – led to the much deserved award of a Distinguished Conduct Medal as well as a mention in Despatches.

Major Paget Fretts and A Company fairly rapidly brought the Japanese attack on their front to a standstill. Beyond the Pagoda on the ring contour, B and C Companies had a tougher fight. Lieutenant Harold *Jonah* Jones, leading 11 Platoon, had a humorous reputation for speculating aloud about the abilities of senior officers. He now managed to fight his way back to the Pagoda and to consolidate there. Major Tommy Tucker, commanding C Company in their exposed position, had to remain under heavy fire for some hours. Here Corporal Warren earned an MM for tending the wounded while surrounded and under heavy fire. When the wireless set was hit, Tucker made his way back across 1,000 yards to report the situation to Knocker White before returning to his Company. He was later awarded a Military Cross for his bravery in this battle.

Several spoke of the sang-froid of Major Barney Brook Fox, commanding the supporting battery of the 10th Field Regiment, Royal Artillery. Throughout the battle he was well forward in exposed places, directing the fire of his guns to support the Dorsets in their vicious battle. Joe Chamberlin remembered that, despite the Japanese mortar fire falling around him, Brook Fox remained *sitting on a shooting-stick in a very unsheltered place, observing the Japs through his field glasses as if he were at a point-to-point. That he had a bad limp from an old injury did not seem to interfere with his cross-country walks.*

Finally the Camerons and seven Grant tanks reached the Dorsets and the enemy were forced to withdraw. The battle of Dirty Pagoda Hill was over.

Among the fifteen Dorsets killed was twenty-four-year-old Private Ronnie Easter, the stretcher-bearer, from Eltham in Kent. Twenty-five-year-old Lieutenant Robin Cuthbertson of 13 Platoon also died. Under heavy fire, he made every effort to extricate one of his sections who had been pinned down, returning to check every dead body to make sure no wounded were left behind. Finally he fell to a burst of machine gun fire. Knocker White later wrote that *his deeds that day certainly placed him in a very high position among those famous men who throughout the long history of the Regiment have distinguished themselves by their personal valour in action and have laid down their lives that their men may live.* Sadly, Cuthbertson's extraordinary bravery went unrewarded. Tom Cattle's friend, twenty-year-old Private Jim Peavoy from Sutton Poyntz, and thirty-nine-year-old Victor *Old Man* Cole, one of the recent gunner reinforcements, were both among C Company's dead.

The fifty-two wounded included Percy Basham, who had been seriously wounded at Kohima and had recently returned to the Battalion; now he was paralysed by a spinal wound. Lieutenant Roger Johnson, who had led the forward platoons of his

Company so bravely onto their objective at Gun Copse, suffered a bullet wound in the head from which he never recovered. He died later in England.

In such an engagement many had lucky escapes, but none luckier than Joe Chamberlin and Gus Claxton when a twenty-five-pounder shell, falling short, landed beside them while they were brewing tea for the wounded but failed to explode. Now, as the battle ended, Claxton began his grim task of retrieving and burying the dead.

By 14th March the Dorsets reached the village of Sinde, just sixteen miles from Mandalay. On the way they had advanced fourteen miles across country, on the right flank of the Brigade's advance, clearing that flank of pockets of Japanese defenders. Snagger Highett's Guerrilla Platoon, aboard the Battalion's carriers, did spectacular work during this rapid advance. On taking Sinde, Knocker White uncharacteristically resisted the temptation to emulate General Napier's famous message from the Indian Mutiny, *Peccavi*.[14] Instead, he pushed the Dorsets beyond the village where they aroused and then despatched another Japanese defensive position.

At 0830 hours next morning the leading Companies, B and C, hit another, more formidable and better prepared, enemy position half a mile west of Kadozeik. Two of the Dorsets' three supporting tanks were disabled by anti-tank grenades fired from rifles. The first tank simply exploded in flames, its crew incinerated in an instant. Eight Dorsets were killed and another twelve wounded. Among those killed was thirty-five-year-old Private Charles Hampton. The indestructible Sergeant Yorky Seale had taken a burst of shrapnel in the foot and this time had to be evacuated. Grievously wounded in the lung, Lieutenant Jonah Jones, who had done so well on Dirty Pagoda Hill, seemed close to death. His stretcher-bearers and Gus Claxton were greatly relieved when they accidentally banged his arm and he swore with his usual force. It was a welcome portent of his full recovery.

The Battalion's carriers again went to work, rounding up several Japanese, while a new subaltern, John Joslin of D Company, brought back from a very hazardous daylight patrol some valuable intelligence about the extent and nature of the enemy positions. Colonel White called for air support, but the RAF's Hurricane fighter-bombers were not immediately available. When they did arrive, they began to attack the Dorsets' own positions but were called off just in time. In the end the

---

14   In Latin Peccavi means *I have sinned.*

Knocker White and his gunman by Jock Murrills

Dorsets did not attack the enemy but poured fire into their positions throughout the night. By the morning only dead Japanese remained: the live ones had withdrawn.

If the name of Sinde had brought a faint echo of the Indian Mutiny, the name of Ava rang louder in regimental history. It was a battle honour of the 54th Foot, earned for their part in the Burma War of 1824–26. In fact, like many awarded the honour, the 54th had not reached Ava itself but now, 120 years later, their most direct descendants – the 2nd Dorsets – crossed the River Myitinge there. The Colonel's carrier, named *Ava* after the battle honour, was photographed on the bridge.

They were now ten miles by road from Mandalay and despite their heavy casualties in the actions on 10th and 15th March – seventeen killed and sixty-seven wounded – their tails were up. Save for pockets of fierce resistance, the Japanese were beaten and locked into an increasingly disorderly retreat. Knocker White recalled their arrival, on 19th March, at Mandalay.

D Company... were certainly determined to waste no time in getting to the city. On arrival at the north wall of the ruined Hmandan Fort, where the road actually pierces the ancient defences, the leading platoon came under fire from a pagoda compound ahead.

Clive Chettle quickly deployed and within a very short time he had attacked this pagoda, crossed the garden wall, and the Dorsets were fighting within the municipal boundary of Mandalay. Having brushed aside this opposition, we were all for pushing on and trying to link up with the 19th Division, which was fighting hard for Fort Dufferin in the middle of the city, a couple of miles farther on. However, the Brigadier called a halt. We had not got all our guns up, our supply line across the Myitinge was tenuous in the extreme, and we were not in a position on this day to become embroiled in street fighting.

The next day brought a distinguished visitor. General Sir Oliver Leese, who had succeeded Monty commanding Eighth Army, was the new Commander-in-Chief of the Allied Land Forces in South East Asia – Bill Slim's new boss. Leese visited the Dorsets, stood on a Jeep and impressed all ranks with a talk about the state of the campaign. They did not see him again. His wrong-headed attempt to remove Bill Slim from command of Fourteenth Army ended with Slim replacing him instead.

That day, after a protracted and savage battle, Mandalay fell to General Rees's 19th Indian Division amid great relief and some celebration. But in the small hours of the following morning, suddenly and unexpectedly, a heavy barrage of shells fell around Hmandan Fort. Two men – Private George Burden from Shaftesbury and Gunner Jack Howe of Romford – were killed and three others wounded.

Attending 19th Division's parade at Government House, where Slim raised the Union Flag once more over Mandalay, Knocker White met a friendly face from the past. Colonel Sam Symes, who had won an OBE for his skill as a company commander in the retreat to Dunkirk, now showed White some of the destruction wrought in Fort Dufferin. Since leaving the 2nd Dorsets, Symes had commanded the 2nd Worcesters with distinction. He would twice be mentioned in Despatches and win a DSO.

With the monsoon six or so weeks away, the race was now on to reach Rangoon. In oppressive heat on 27th March the Dorsets drove eighty miles south along dusty roads to Taungbe, south of Myingyan. White described the terrain as *bare, rocky and sparsely populated. A desert in an otherwise fertile land.* In this area 4 and 5 Brigades met from east and west, and the Japanese caught in between were squeezed further southwards in their endless retreat. Here too they heard that the 2nd Division would be returned to India for a rest, reinforcement and retraining. The Dorsets' last operation would be the twenty-five mile advance to and capture of Mount Popa, where the Japanese had decided to mount the next substantial line of defence.

As they advanced, 5 Brigade encountered pro-Japanese Indian National Army troops who were anxious to surrender. According to White, most of them were ex-prisoners of war who had been ordered by their officers to volunteer for the INA and then to surrender to the Allies at the first opportunity. But they also encountered some stubborn Japanese defenders. While the Worcesters forced the Japanese back down the road, the Dorsets moved further south to block their escape. Here they set up a road block and ambushed the retreating Japanese column. Some of the Japanese ran into the rough country beside the road and, supported by some more dedicated members of the INA, launched attack after attack on the Dorsets' positions. Later the Japanese managed to bring their 75mms into action and shelled them as well.

In the advances of this last fortnight of their campaign the Dorsets suffered relatively few casualties, losing only three men killed. A fighting patrol, led by Lieutenant Gerry Overman, caught a Japanese company eating their breakfast near Gwedaukkon and killed and wounded a great many at no loss to themselves. Overman was later mentioned in Despatches. On 12th April the Battalion took Kyauktaga after *a short but brisk fight* with the INA. Knowing their Japanese enemy, they anticipated a longer, tougher battle for Mount Popa. But, at the last, after an air strike on the enemy's positions on and around Popa, the Japanese withdrew without a fight. The 2nd Dorsets' long campaign was over.

It had been a hard-fought, savage campaign in inhospitable terrain against an implacable, brutal and skilful enemy. The Dorsets had lost many friends, suffered heavy casualties and endured hunger, thirst and almost incessant sickness. Several had died from disease. They had faced up to a ruthless enemy who, holding his own life and other lives cheap, gave no quarter and accepted none. But they had won through, earning new honours and adding a new chapter to the story of the Dorset Regiment in one of the most horrific campaigns in British military history.

At the end of the campaign, Colonel White was awarded a long-overdue DSO for his skill and courage in leading the Dorsets through most of their ordeal in Burma. His stalwart Quartermaster, Freddy Edwards, and gallant Intelligence Officer, Norman Havers, were each appointed MBE. But, as is often the case, more earned decorations than received them. John Bowles and Robin Cuthbertson are two of many examples. Another longstanding omission from the Battalion's list of honours was the Padre, Gus Claxton, but happily Knocker White was able to correct this oversight. Back in India, he would sit and write a three-page citation for the man who had been the 2nd Dorsets' padre since October 1939, who had been with them throughout the battles in France and in India and Burma, who had tended the wounded, comforted the living, buried the dead and never spared a thought for his own comfort or safety. In due course White's epic recommendation – seldom can there have been a longer one – brought Claxton a much deserved Military Cross.

Gus Claxton composed the Dorset Regimental Collect, which (with suitable amendments) survived the amalgamation with the Devons and is still used by the Rifles.

O Christ, our Redeemer, the sure stronghold of each succeeding age; grant that we, who bear arms in The Dorset Regiment may endure as our fathers did before us, with steadfast courage. Lead us in every quarter of the earth; that we may not only honour and proclaim Thy Name, but also serve to open a highway for Thy Salvation for all mankind, through the same Jesus Christ, who liveth and reigneth with the Father and the Holy Spirit, one God, world without end. Amen.

It seems fitting to end this chapter with Knocker White's description of most of the survivors' last memory of the campaign, which was a service conducted by Gus Claxton on their last day in Burma.

Our last act at Popa was to hold a memorial service in the banana grove to all those who had given their lives in this last campaign. It was a sad moment when I read the list of the thirty-nine officers and men who would not return with us; but we left the battle at a time when we knew that our task was well on the way to completion, and we knew that their sacrifice had not been in vain.

6

THE 1ST BATTALION, NORTH WEST EUROPE 1944

PRIMUS IN GERMANIA

ASSAULT LANDING ON D-DAY

Seventy years on, here in Britain, our abiding image of our part in the D-Day landings is the black and white newsreel footage taken from a landing craft over the shoulders of its passengers, steel-helmeted infantrymen, as it approaches the beach. The time is 0730 on 6th June 1944. Among the assault brigades are 231 (Malta) Brigade, and in their first fleet of landing craft to reach the beach are two companies of the 1st Hampshires on the right, and A and B Companies of the 1st Dorsets on the left. For both battalions this was the third time in eleven months they had been ordered to land on a hostile shore. Many of them must have had a strong sense of déjà vu.

D-Day Landings by Juliet Pannett

The sea wall at Asnelles

Their plan was to land on a width of beach of 900 yards. The Hampshires would overcome the beach defences at Le Hamel and turn west to seize Asnelles, a gun position at Cabane, Arromanches and the strongpoints at Tracy-sur-Mer and Manvieux. The Dorsets, landing east of the Hampshires, would seize Strongpoint 886866 on the beach and another at Les Roquettes. They would then advance south-west and capture Point 54 and the strongpoints 500 yards to the north and west, including a 155mm battery position. The Dorsets would then move south and take over Ryes from the 2nd Devons, who were to land after the Hampshires and Dorsets and capture that village.

The plan provided tank support from the Sherwood Rangers Yeomanry and close artillery support from self-propelled guns. B and C Squadrons of the Sherwood Rangers were equipped with Duplex-Drive amphibious tanks, which would be launched from ships four miles from the shore and then propel themselves the rest of the way. They would land at 0725, five minutes ahead of the leading companies of the assault battalions, and deal with any immediate opposition ashore. Tank crews and Gunners had long practised firing their guns afloat as their landing craft ran into the shore. The more powerful guns of the Royal Navy would also provide support by shelling targets ashore.

The gods of war decreed otherwise. For this, their third assault landing in eleven months, 231 Brigade yet again faced freakishly foul weather. The landing craft pitched and tossed in the churning grey seas, causing many of the troops to throw up, and preventing the tanks and self-propelled guns from firing during the run in. The amphibious DD tanks also failed. Although launched only 700 yards from the shore, eight were lost at sea and the survivors were unable to play much of a part in the landings. By the time they were ashore, the leading infantry had landed and the flail tanks (crewed by Sappers and specially adapted to clear mines) had already dealt with the immediate defences.

The driver of one flail tank, Private Joseph Minogue, remembered 231 Brigade landing.

I could see that the three tanks in front of us were not doing too well. The first tank had stopped because its commander had been killed, the second tank had been a bit too close to him and had slewed to the right and hit a clay patch on the beach, and the tank behind him had taken a hit in the side, which had set it on fire. I saw the crew busily scrambling out. This didn't do a great deal for our confidence.

Fortunately at that moment the tank commander hit me on the head with his microphone, which was his famous signal to do a 360 degree traverse in the gun turret to break the waterproofing round the turret ring. This gave me an absolutely fantastic view of the whole thing. There was absolutely nothing one could see on the beach in the way of opposition; I mean there weren't thousands of people waiting to fight us off, which is the kind of thing we vaguely expected.

As I began to traverse to the left I saw an odd pillbox here and there, but I wasn't quite sure whether anything was coming from it or not. Then as the turret came back towards the sea I could see the infantry just beginning to come ashore. It was all a bit like a cartoon, a bit unreal. I suppose there must have been a couple of machine guns raking across the beach. You could see infantrymen getting into the water from the small landing craft, some chest deep, some waist deep, and they would begin to run across the beach and suddenly you'd see the odd figure fall here and there.

It wasn't a matter of a whole line of men going down, it seemed as though just one in five, or a small group, might go down. A chap would be lying doubled up on the beach and some people would run past him and then a couple of his mates might get hold of the epaulettes on his battledress and drag him forward to the shelter of the sand dunes.

As the Dorsets and Hampshires landed they discovered that the weather conditions had also thrown out the Royal Navy's navigation. Both battalions had been

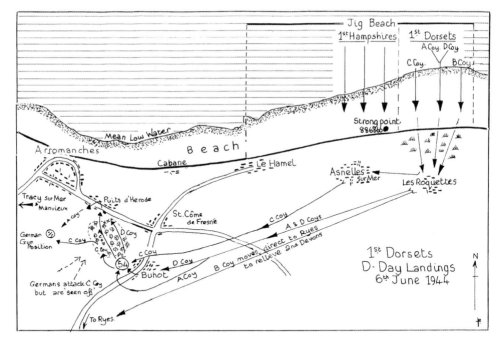

1st Dorsets' Landing in France 6th June 1944

put ashore about 800 yards too far east. Thus, the Hampshires' left-hand company landed opposite the Dorsets' first objective, the strongpoint on the beach at 886866. Applying the same flexibility that had retrieved the Brigade's chaotic landing in Italy, the Hampshires immediately captured the strongpoint. Meanwhile, on their left, A and B Companies of the Dorsets (under Majors Arnold Jones and Patrick Chilton) landed and fought their way ashore and up the beach.

Landing fifteen minutes behind A and B Companies, C and D followed, led by Majors Bobby Nicoll and Willie Hayes.

Sub-Lieutenant Bernard Sullivan of the Royal Navy Volunteer Reserve commanded five of the landing craft which delivered C Company of the 1st Dorsets to the beaches. He had previously been warned that, because Gold Beach would be the first to be invaded, he could expect 50% casualties. A motor launch equipped with the latest radar would guide them to the beach aided by a midget submarine, X20, which would be positioned a mile offshore in an accurately identified position. The landing craft were to land the troops just to port of a wreck on the beach.

So... we arrived off the Normandy coast. It was rougher than we'd ever known for landing craft manoeuvring (Gold Beach had the worst weather of all five beaches), but, after a few nightmares during the lowering process (one of my men had two

Major Bobby Nicoll MC

fingers torn off), we formed up and started to follow the Motor Launch. This was it – and the more imaginative among us began to wonder if this was to be our last journey.

My craft carried the Senior Major in charge of the 330 very highly trained soldiers that we were taking in. We were very glad to have him aboard. He was everyone's idea of a hero: tall, broad, handsome and icy calm – just the sort of chap you need when you're beginning to get a bit excited yourself. He [Bobby Nicoll] won the Military Cross about an hour later.

We passed the tiny submarine and sped on, to applause from a lonely figure in its conning tower. Then the Motor Launch turned away. Half a mile to go...

Soon we were near enough to discern the shapes of fortified houses and concrete pillboxes on shore. It was getting very exciting. Rockets were being fired, four hundred a time, over our heads from the landing crafts. Rockets, just astern of us, and heavy shells were whistling over like express trains.

Planes were zooming in from the East, the North and the West and on our left in line with us, roaring in like a wave of surf, were the landing craft from the other ships in Force G.

At about this point, the soldiers in my boat asked my permission to smoke. What discipline! For all they knew we were all within minutes of death...

'The old wreck should be out there on the left,' said the Major, pointing slightly to port. 'Can you see it?'

'No, I can't, Sir,' I replied. 'But it might have been blown up.'

'I'd feel more comfortable if I could see some part of it,' he grunted.

We continued to scan the beach – he from his six-foot odd, me from about four-foot two (I had less pluck than he, but perhaps more sense, and was crouching!) and then we both gasped 'It's over there', pointing to the right.

The blasted wreck was well over to starboard! All the pinpointing by the midget submarine, all the state of the art radaring by the Motor Launch, and we were a quarter of a mile to the east of where we should have been! It was the weather of course.

I looked at the Major and he looked at me. He knew I had absolutely rigid instructions to go straight in after the Motor Launch peeled off and I now strongly suspected that, if we did so, we would land his men some 400 yards to the left of the strongpoint they were supposed to wipe out.

Strict naval training had reinforced my innate respect for authority and then, as now, I did not lightly disobey orders...

'Can we be sure, Sir?' I asked him.

In reply he showed me his picture of the wreck, taken by the RAF a few days earlier. There was no doubt. That was our wreck, well over to starboard instead of slightly to port.

A few moments of absolute torment, with visions of very brave men being needlessly mined, sniped at or even set alight as they ran along the four hundred yards of exposed, mined beach, and then I shouted to my signalman, 'Signal a ninety-degree turn to starboard!'

'We can't do that, Sir, we've... !'

'DO IT!!' I roared at the poor nineteen-year-old.

He raised a green flag on a short stick and we waited impatiently for the coxswains of the other nine craft to acknowledge that they understood the order by raising their right hands. Eventually, after a lot of shouting and cursing across the water, they did.

'Execute!' I screamed.

Down came the flag and all my ten boats turned to the right, crashing into waves that had been previously, and more comfortably, on our starboard quarter, and heading, it seemed, towards the Atlantic rather than France!

The Major grunted approval and he and I listened sardonically to shouts like, 'What's the silly bastard doing now?' or more kindly 'Going home, chums?' coming faintly across the wind and water.

I said to him 'We'll keep our eye on that wreck, Sir, and when we are level, I'll turn. That's if we can get level!'

'Thanks,' he replied – and I felt calmer and more prepared to explain to the Court of Inquiry which I was now sure I'd have to face.

After what felt like hours but was probably about five minutes, we seemed about level with the wreck. 'Say when' I said 'and I'll give the order.'

He waited another eternity (perhaps thirty seconds) and then said 'Now will do, I think, old boy.'

'Ninety degrees to port,' I roared to the signalman.

Up went his hand with a red flag; up went the hands of the other nine coxswains. 'Execute!'

Down went the flag and we all turned for France, increasing to 1900 revs to try to arrive on the beach at the same time as the other groups, none of which had altered course. Shells and mortar bombs exploded in the water about ten yards directly ahead of us and again about ten yards astern, but that was all apart from some small arms fire and then we were through, straight to the beach.

The Major and his men, these strangers we'd never seen before and would probably never meet again, dashed (or if seasick we[re] carried) ashore at exactly the place they needed to be, and we headed back to sea to pick up more soldiers.

D Company's commander, Willie Hayes, remembered his own landing:

Hitler's much vaunted and so-called impregnable sea defences of mines and bombs on stakes stuck in the seabed were, in the event, quite third form for the Navy to deal with. By careful judgement the tide was such that all these horrid things were showing above the sea. Thus by going at a steady pace we zig-zagged round all the hazards. In the event only one battalion assault craft was hit, and that above the water line. Thus the entire battalion touched down on French soil without a single casualty – it was now up to us.

... Our well-liked and respected commanding officer, Lieutenant-Colonel Norie, was in my craft. Of course he leapt out too soon to lead the battalion onward. He was tall but his feet were nowhere near the bottom. Of course he couldn't swim, carrying all that extra kit. So I leant over the side and kept him up. This was simply super for me – all my secret and so important 'bumph' was a sodden mess. I knew one couldn't fight the Germans eyeball to eyeball if all the time one was to stop and consult some

The 1st Dorsets landing on D-Day

code or essential report – what wasn't now in my brain was quite useless to me and my soldiers.

To enable his company to negotiate the minefields on the beach, Nicoll directed two German prisoners of war to lead the way. Hayes, following B Company, spoke to Patrick Chilton about the mines and they *decided just to walk in single file through this minefield, rather than wait on the beach as a super target for the Germans. So our two companies, 250 men, went off – due to experience every man knew this was far better than staying put to be killed for certain.*

Once ashore, C and D Companies crossed the coast road and stepped down into the marsh beyond towards Les Roquettes. Their experience landing in Sicily and Italy had taught them not only flexibility but also the vital importance of establishing and maintaining the momentum of advance from the moment they hit the sand.

Private Minogue in his flail tank encountered them again as they crossed the road.

... we were trying to negotiate a bomb crater right in the centre of the road and suddenly the tank began to slide into the crater. We obviously couldn't move and so we got out and by this time the infantry – I think it was the Hampshires and Dorset Regiments – had got off the beach and were breaking through onto the road. Their officers were most impatient about the fact that we were holding up their advance and they cursed and swore in those fancy voices that ordinary soldiers learned to imitate so well: things like, 'I say, old chaps, can't you move that damn thing out of the way?'

On the road Hayes met *a German soldier with his horse and cart no doubt taking rations round – we left him completely alone. We were through – only one man in Pat's company of our two companies was blown to bits. I believe one odd bullet hit the Thomkins Anti-tank mine in his pack.*

Beyond the road, passage through the marsh was possible only for infantry or tracked vehicles and, in the face of shell, mortar and machine gun fire, the advance of the leading Dorset companies came at a cost. In A Company, Major Jones, Lieutenant Ellis and CSM Howell were all wounded by shell and mortar fire. In B Company twenty-one-year-old Lieutenant John Whitebrook was killed along-side his remarkable platoon sergeant, William Evans, who had won the Military Medal in Sicily and a Bar in Italy.

Realising that B Company had been held up short of its objective, the strong-point at Les Roquettes, Nicoll led C Company forward and by about 0900 had captured it, handing it over to B Company to defend.

At about this time the Brigade Commander, Brigadier Sir Alex Stanier, made a dramatic arrival when his landing craft was blown up by a mine or shell. Establishing his tactical headquarters near Strongpoint 886866, he now had to assess and get a grip on what his three battalions were doing. The Dorsets were concentrated around Les Roquettes. The right hand companies of the Hampshires and the Devons were still involved in heavy fighting on the right around Le Hamel. The Hampshires' CO, Colonel Nelson-Smith, had been wounded and the Second-in-Command, Major Charles Martin (the distinguished Dorset who had led the landing in Sicily) had taken command. Stanier now ordered Martin to capture the pillbox at Le Hamel that was blocking the Hampshires' advance. Sadly, a few moments later Martin was killed by a sniper, and a delay ensued while the commander of the Hampshires' C Company was summoned to take over the Battalion.

Defences near Les Roquettes – the Dorsets' second objective

Meanwhile a collaborative effort between Nicoll's C Company and B Company of the Hampshires successfully captured Asnelles, allowing Major David Warren, now commanding the 1st Hampshires, to change his plan of attack on Le Hamel. Le Hamel was proving a costly objective. When Brigadier Stanier ordered the Sherwood Rangers forward in support, their Commanding Officer, Colonel Anderson, was wounded twice by a sniper after dismounting from his Sherman tank to examine the situation on foot. The Devons, on their way to capture Ryes, found themselves drawn into the fighting in Le Hamel and, when finally extricated, had to alter their route, moving through the marsh via Les Roquettes.

Throughout, each of the battalions faced varying weights of fire from their front and from the high ground just behind them. They also encountered frequent *Achtung Minen* signs, which slowed the advance.

Whatever difficulties they faced inland, the rifle companies had been wise to crack on towards their objectives. Behind them, the beaches were still far from clear, and the going on the beach was harder than had been anticipated. Clay strips across the sand proved troublesome for vehicles while German fire – shell, mortar and machine gun – still hammered the whole area. Captain Charles Whittington, commanding HQ Company and for this operation acting as Unit Landing Officer, had painted his steel helmet in rainbow colours to make himself stand out as he directed the landings through the hail of fire. A Queen's officer attached to the Dorsets, he had been wounded early on but was still at work. So, as usual, were the Battalion's stretcher-bearers, who stayed in the beach area under constant attack to tend the wounded. One of them, Sergeant Albert Talbot, later received a Military Medal, which was published in the same *London Gazette* as Whittington's Military Cross.

Corporal Eric Green (whom we last met masquerading with strange potions as a medical orderly on Gozo), recalled his landing with the Carrier Platoon:

There were thousands of planes buzzing about my bonce as we chugged across the Channel. Just as we got to the beach a Dutch destroyer fired a 4.7 gun right in my ear. I thought I'd gone deaf. At that very moment the bows of the landing craft struck an 88m shell, one of the hundreds that the Germans had lashed to supports sticking out of the water. One of our blokes up front with me was hit. His body was thrown something like twelve feet in the air, twirling over and over, and it came crashing down on the deck. I never found out whether he lived or died.

Then the ramp, with the hole blown in it, went down and our Bren carrier rolled down into the sea. We were heading for the beach with German shells bursting around us when our driver, a lad called Barnes, said the carrier was stuck and couldn't go any further.

I went along the beach and asked the driver of a bulldozer to help us. We were under shell fire at the time and he told me to clear off, which I did.

A Royal Marines captain told me to get the carrier out of the way or he would have it sunk out at sea. I couldn't let him do that – I had all my rations, food and baccy on board. When I got back to the carrier I saw it was on the move again.

Then along came our sergeant. He told me our officer had been hit in the chest and he'd had his fingers blown off. He was frightened and told us to stay where we were. I told him no fear, I'm going forward to make my rendezvous at the convent. So we went up a lane from the beach. A beautiful, shady lane it was, just like a lane in Sussex. The weather was good, the sun was out and the birds were singing. We got to the convent and found we were the first there. We hadn't seen a soul.

Further inland, between 1300 and 1400 C and D Company of the 1st Dorsets approached the Battalion's three final objectives: Point 54 and the two strong-points – the infantry position at Les Puits d'Herode and the 105mm gun positions nearby. En route Hayes's D Company had captured Buhot, to the left of their advance, where they took prisoner an entire German pioneer company together with its lorries.

Meanwhile, Nicoll's C Company crossed the main road between Buhot and St Côme de Fresné and attacked Point 54, advancing under cover provided by trees and brick walls. Corporal Sam Thompson of C Company – whose DCM recommendation in Sicily had been downgraded by General Leese – again showed his courage and powers of leadership as his section led the Company's rapid advance up and onto Point 54. The capture of this feature and of seventeen prisoners brought them close to the next objective: the infantry strongpoint at Les Puits d'Herode.

Having taken Buhot, D Company moved to the south of Point 54. Supported by Shermans from C Squadron of the Sherwood Rangers and the Vickers machine guns of 11 Platoon, C Company of the 2nd Cheshires, they launched their attack on Les Puits d'Herode. Willie Hayes takes up the story.

... my commanding officer said, 'Willie, you see your objective. Here is your squadron of tanks rumbling along, so get on with it – I will watch and help if needed.'

... Our objective was a German position on high ground on the far side of a corn-field. So we set off in correct School of Infantry formation through the corn. Platoon of infantry with troop of tanks, platoon of infantry with troop of tanks, company headquarters and squadron headquarters, reserve platoon with troop of tanks. All

fine and Aldershot to a tee! I was chatting away with the squadron leader, who of course had his turret open. Suddenly the naughty Germans opened fire on us with 88mm anti-tank guns and machine guns. All turrets of our tanks closed at once and they were firing back and moving all over the place to present a difficult target. It was like having sixteen very cross and charging elephants in our midst. Needless to say, the telephone on the back of each tank was quite useless. My soldiers were down in the corn, and I was afraid that they would get run over. Again we broke all the military school teaching. There was a lone tree on our left flank, obvious to see and a good target. However, I went round shouting to each soldier, the noise was terrific, to get to the lone tree. When about forty of my soldiers were there, I did not count them, off we went to take the German position from their right rear. Never did we attack again with tanks like that.

Moving through the wood short of the objective, 17 and 18 Platoons encountered strong resistance. Despite casualties, they pressed on, capturing a mortar position and anti-tank gun and machine gun post. Among those killed were 18 Platoon's commander, Lieutenant Turloch Lancaster, and his platoon sergeant. One of the section commanders, Corporal William Hawkins, took over and led 18 Platoon throughout the battle, winning a Military Medal. The same award went to 17 Platoon's Lance-Corporal Joe Miller, whose leadership and courage enabled his section to lead the way through the wood short of the objective. But their advance was checked when they tried to break out of the wood across the open ground towards Les Puits d'Herode.

The citation for Willie Hayes's Military Cross describes his part in the attack.

The position proved to be very much stronger than was anticipated and the company was brought to a standstill by heavy and accurate fire. Major Hayes immediately and without regard to his own safety reorganised his company and restarted the assault, continuing to press on until the company was again brought to a halt by heavy casualties.

Because the enemy position at Les Puits d'Herode had been heavily reinforced, Colonel Evelyn Norie now decided greatly to increase his attacking force. Captain Royle's A Company advanced further north through the wood and renewed the attack from a new angle, supported by covering fire from C and D Companies, and with the help of the Sherwood Rangers and Cheshires. 90th Field Regiment, who had managed to get their self-propelled guns forward to support the Dorsets, now shelled the enemy position. This attack carried the position, and A Company captured forty more prisoners of war. A simultaneous determined counter-attack on C Company was repelled by Captain Robert Tucker, enthusiastically supported by Corporal Thompson. Again Sam Thompson had earned a Distinguished Conduct Medal and this time the recommendation was successful, adding a DCM to the MM he had won at Regalbuto.

A and C Companies now moved swiftly to capture the Battalion's final objective of D-Day – the 155mm battery position 500 yards west of Point 54 – but the action proved a welcome anti-climax. The German gunners had gone, abandoning their four guns and a large quantity of equipment. The story was the same for the Hampshires and the Devons. After a ferocious struggle throughout the day, the German defenders seemed to lose heart and withdraw. (A German commander interviewed after the war maintained that, by late afternoon, the German infantry and artillery were running out of ammunition.)

Now there was tidying up to do. Positions had to be secured, patrols were sent out and B Company moved to occupy Ryes, which, after a hard fight, the 2nd Devons had taken before advancing towards Longues. At a cost of 182 casualties, the Hampshires had finally overcome the fierce resistance in Le Hamel. 231 (Malta) Brigade's task was done and by last light on 6th June 56 Brigade passed through them to continue the advance to within 1½ miles of Bayeux.

Early on D-Day morning Major Tony Lewis, now of 6 Commando in Lord Lovat's Special Service Brigade, had landed on Sword Beach. A few days later, when Lovat was wounded, Lewis was appointed to lead 6 Commando aged just twenty-four. He was the youngest lieutenant-colonel to command a fighting unit in the British Army.

Another Dorset officer, normally on the staff of 231 Brigade, had landed that day on Omaha Beach with the Americans. Lieutenant Hugh Payne was leading the British liaison party attached to the US army's 16th Infantry Regiment. His party had landed shortly after the first wave and walked into the shelling, mortaring and machine gun fire that had characterised the Americans' experience. Despite this, Payne had continually exposed himself to enemy fire to observe and report important information about the enemy positions. Nearly five years later he was awarded the American Bronze Star for his bravery on D-Day.

June 6th 1944 is a day that will always stand out not only in regimental or military history, but in the history of the modern world. It cost the 1st Dorsets 128 casualties, thirty-four of whom were killed. Fourteen of their forty-one officers were casualties and four had died: Lieutenant Turloch John Lancaster (18 Platoon) and three subalterns attached from other regiments – Lieutenants Joseph Bradbury (16 Platoon) of the Hampshires, John Whitebrook (12 Platoon) of the King's Shropshire

Light Infantry and Donald Youngs (the Battalion Intelligence Officer) of the Royal Norfolks. Sadly, among the dead were some stalwarts from Malta, Sicily and Italy, including Sergeant William Evans MM and Bar, Lance-Sergeant Len Bunning MM and Major Charles Martin DSO.

They had won high honours. Colonel Norie had won a DSO for his leadership and courage throughout the day. Three company commanders – Bobby Nicoll, Willie Hayes and Charles Whittington – had won the Military Cross. In all, the Battalion had won a DSO, three MCs, one DCM and three MMs in this single, long-awaited, protracted, cataclysmic day on which so much had depended.

The whole Brigade had shone, and the 1st Dorsets had achieved every one of their objectives. As one of the handful of assault battalions, theirs had been a leading role in the largest amphibious assault landing in history. They had begun and made possible the liberation of the North European mainland and, once again, they had shown themselves more than a match for an expert and determined enemy in strong defensive positions. Four years after the 2nd Battalion had left Dunkirk after a shattering defeat, the Dorset Regiment was back, firmly entrenched in French soil.

ENLARGING THE BEACH-HEAD

After the drama, tragedy and triumph of D-Day, D+1 brought the Dorsets comedy and adventure.

Incongruously, the comedy centred around a burial party led that morning by the Dorsets' padre, Captain The Reverend Robert Watt of the Royal Army Chaplains' Department. While he and a handful of men were engaged in digging graves, they were suddenly surrounded by thirty to forty Germans. Thinking he had better surrender, Watt approached the German officer who promptly surrendered to him. Having disarmed his captives, Watt marched them back, reappearing at Battalion Headquarters with two platoons of German prisoners under guard. Thus it came about that the unarmed, non-combatant Padre practically single-handedly captured more prisoners than any other Dorset officer in Normandy. A twenty-seven-year-old Scot from Helensburgh, Robert Watt remained the 1st Battalion's Padre throughout the campaign and later served with the Cameronians during the Malayan emergency.

The adventure began a couple of hours later while the Battalion were still occupying Ryes. Just before lunch it was reported that Brigadier Senior, the commander

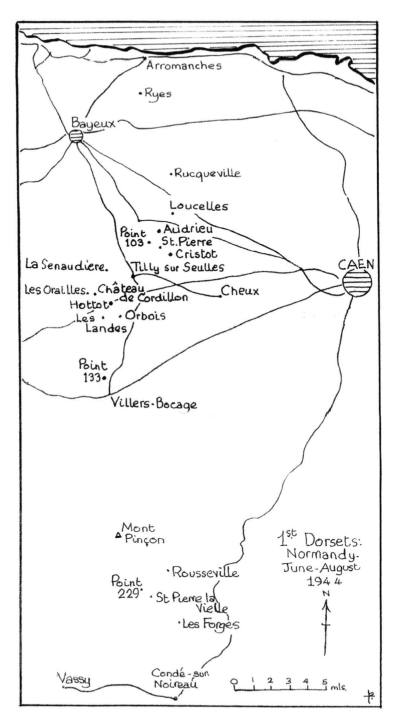

1st Dorsets' Campaign in Normandy June–August 1944

of 151 Brigade, had been captured. A sizeable group of Germans who had somehow avoided the advancing units of 50th Division now held him prisoner. Patrick Chilton's B Company were sent to the rescue, together with a mortar detachment, Captain Eric Hannah's carriers and a supporting troop of Sherwood Rangers' tanks. They were entirely successful. The Brigadier escaped during their attack, which killed forty enemy and captured seventy more. The Dorsets had only two fatal casualties in the shoot-out – one officer and one private soldier. The officer was twenty-seven-year-old Lieutenant Ernest Mayes, who had been a London solicitor until the lottery of war brought him command of 10 Platoon. The soldier was Private Leonard Hann from Bristol who, at eighteen, had hardly been allowed to reach adulthood before losing his young life near Ryes. Today, Mayes and Hann are buried in the small cemetery there with Charles Martin.

Montgomery's invasion plan had succeeded with fewer casualties than anticipated. On D+1 his main concerns were the difficulties faced by the Americans on Omaha beach and a number of strongpoints which had been bypassed by the invading troops and which were still holding out. His immediate aim was to eliminate those strongpoints and thus to merge the various beach-heads into a single fifty-mile-wide bridgehead. A key and oft-expressed principle of his approach was to maintain the initiative – to make the enemy dance to his tune. Instead of allowing the enemy time to regroup and to respond to the invasion strategically, he would make continual thrusts to which the Germans would be forced to respond piecemeal. One such thrust, whose purpose was to get his armour established on commanding ground inland, would be made by 8 Armoured Brigade east of 231 Brigade's axis of advance, southwards towards Tilly-sur-Seulles and Villers Bocage.

THE BATTLE FOR POINT 103

Because 8 Armoured's motor battalion, the 12th King's Royal Rifle Corps, had not yet landed, on 8th June the 1st Dorsets were sent to take this role in the advance. Without the vehicles required by a motor battalion, Colonel Norie found himself in precisely the same position described by Colonel Valentine when, after the Sicily landings, the lorryless 2nd Devons had been asked to provide the lorried infantry for Harpoon Force's advance. As the Dorsets' Second-in-Command, Speedy Bredin, put it, the Dorsets now became a motor battalion *without the motors*.

Their objective was the commanding feature, Point 103, north-east of Tilly. At 1600 hours, the Battalion, transported in Royal Army Service Corps lorries, moved to Rucqueville and, through the leading troops near St Leger, towards Loucelles, which they captured relatively easily. But, beyond Loucelles, B Company ran into tougher opposition and were held up first by a machine gun at the railway crossing on the line towards Bas d'Audrieu. This was dealt with by 11 Platoon, but fire from the station and from the village itself stalled the Company's advance.

C and D Companies outflanked the enemy position to the right and, because of the urgency of the advance, had to clear Audrieu in darkness. C Company's Second-in-Command, Captain Tucker from Bridport, was killed leading an attack on an enemy position near the church. Robert Tucker had won a Military Cross serving as a brigade liaison officer in Sicily and had already shone in this campaign, leading a fierce counter-attack against a German attack at Les Puits d'Herode.[15] His loss deprived the Dorsets of yet another gallant and able young officer. Suffering similar losses among some of their best NCOs, the Dorsets were already running out of experienced leaders.

Early the next morning another stalwart, A Company's Second-in-Command Captain Royle, who had also distinguished himself in Sicily and on D-Day, was wounded when the Company moved through Le Haut d'Audrieu to link up with C and D Companies in Audrieu itself. In one of the villages the Dorsets found the rows of bodies of twenty-four Canadian and two British soldiers murdered the previous afternoon by the retreating SS: a stark and tragic reminder of the evil they were fighting.

While the Dorsets cleared and occupied Audrieu and its surrounding three villages, their supporting armour bypassed the village and by 0230 had occupied Point 103, encountering no opposition. Over the two days 8th and 9th June, the Brigade's first objective en route to Tilly had been secured at a cost to the 1st Dorsets of six killed and twenty wounded. At this point the Brigade's southward thrust had put them well ahead of the main bridgehead with open flanks either side. The whole Brigade was in a very vulnerable position.

Before the Dorsets had cleared the villages the 12th SS Panzer Division, realising the tactical importance of the feature, attacked Point 103 with Tiger tanks. Major Peter Martin of the 2nd Cheshires remembered:

At first light, German tanks approached from the south and engaged the forward tanks of the Sherwood Rangers, knocking some of them out. The remainder withdrew to the reverse slope of Point 103, leaving my two platoons totally isolated.

The enemy stood off about 120 yards away, hull down, and began shelling our bank with high explosive, causing casualties. On several occasions, when the Tigers

---

15   Robert Tucker was mentioned in John Snook's poem *The Dorsets at War*.

cruised too far forward with turrets open, our machine-gunners fired at them to make them close down. The situation was precarious, because if the enemy put in a determined attack from the south, he would be right on top of us before encountering our tanks or anti-tank guns. So we were very cheered when, soon after midday, recce parties from the 1st Dorsets arrived to say that Audrieu was being cleared and the Battalion would soon come up to join us.

By dusk the Dorsets had dug in around Point 103, forming a defensive box around the entire Brigade.

Overnight some of 8th Durham Light Infantry, who had withdrawn to Point 103 from St Pierre, joined the box and at 1000 next morning a squadron of tanks reinforced each of the Dorset companies guarding it. This was timely because within twenty minutes the Germans brought down a heavy concentration of shelling on D Company's position. Among the casualties was Willie Hayes.

In the morning I took a small piece of shell in my right eye. I must have looked terrible because my soldiers were so concerned. That evening, after dark, the medical officer arrived and told me that I would be blind in my right eye and that he thought I was bound to lose the sight in my left eye.

Flown home to hospital in Southampton, Hayes was back with the Battalion in three weeks. Meanwhile, Captain Richard Harris (who had been the Dorsets' Unit Landing Officer in Sicily) replaced him as Company Commander.

At 1142 hours German infantry and tanks emerged from the woods towards Cristot and attacked B Company who, with the aid of their supporting squadron of 4/7th Dragoon Guards, saw them off.

Eleven hours later, B Company called for artillery and three-inch mortar support to beat off another counter-attack.

With the 1st Dorsets providing a defensive perimeter, 8 Armoured Brigade remained on Point 103 until the late afternoon of 11th June, when the 6th Green Howards passed through the position on their way to attack Cristot. Three hours later German tanks – without supporting infantry because the Green Howards had already dealt with them – launched an attack on C Company and Battalion HQ. Colonel Norie and Bobby Nicoll led the defence against the heavily gunned and armoured Tigers while A Company moved behind C and D Companies to add depth to the defence. Another stretcher-bearer, Private Goddard, and Lance-Corporal Hockley of the regimental provost each earned the Military Medal during the attacks. Reg Goddard from Bridport tended the wounded in and around Battalion HQ while George Hockley from Surrey delivered messages and ammunition under heavy fire. Meanwhile, the energetic Second-in-Command, Major Bredin, ran between the five headquarters of the Battalion, Brigade, armoured regiments and Gunner Regiment trying to co-ordinate the defence.

Peter Martin recalled:

For two days, the battle for Point 103 raged on. I was hailed by the CO of 24th Lancers, sitting on the ground with his arm in a sling. He handed me a rifle, saying, 'Put a round in the breech; at least I'll take one of them with me.' I thought, 'Good God, it's as bad as that.' Shortly afterwards, all firing ceased. It was the final attempt by the enemy before pulling out and leaving St Pierre.

At 2200, unable to take Cristot, the Green Howards withdrew through Point 103 and half an hour later the German attack subsided. However, the planned relief of the Dorsets by the 5th East Yorkshires had become impossible. Instead, the East Yorkshires dug in to cover the Dorsets' left flank. The German shelling and attacks on 11th June had killed ten Dorsets and wounded twenty-six others. Among those killed was yet another junior officer, twenty-two-year-old Lieutenant Maurice Markham, a Royal Berkshire officer who had joined the Battalion as a reinforcement only the day before. Another loss was thirty-two-year-old Private Edward Broom from Lyme Regis, whose grave is in the cemetery at Tilly-sur-Seulles surrounded by a thousand comrades. On his right lies the poet Keith Douglas. The question posed in his last poem before D-Day had been answered.[16]

At noon on 12th June the East Yorkshires relieved the Dorsets, who now returned west to 231 (Malta) Brigade in the woods at Vechy behind the Hampshires and Devons. The Brigade's objective was some high ground to the south at Les Landes but, when the Devons were held up at Les Orailles, Sir Alex Stanier decided that they must first clear the area around La Senaudière.

After some patrol work on 13th June and a quiet night, at 1000 next morning the Dorsets watched Typhoon fighter-bombers attacking the woods in the area they were about to assault. At 1200 A and B Companies moved off with the Hampshires on their left and at 1201 the supporting barrage, which was meant to fall on the enemy positions, fell instead on the advancing troops. Pat Chilton's B Company was especially badly hit and took several casualties. Chilton himself was wounded and Captain Arthur Harris replaced him in command. At 1215 the advance was resumed. On the right A Company met no opposition while B Company, advancing

---

16 Douglas, who was posthumously mentioned in Despatches, is now regarded (with Alun Lewis) as one of the two finest poets of the Second World War. His sharply observed prose memoir, *Alamein to Zem Zem*, is a tiny classic.

through the woods beside the Hampshires, mopped up some machine gun posts and snipers.

By 1600 B Company had reached the east-west road through La Senaudière, and C and D Companies passed through to clear the crossroads while A Company continued on the right. An hour later, C and D Companies came under heavy fire around the crossroads from three Panther tanks and supporting infantry. The Dorsets surrounded one of the Panthers and killed its crew while one of Captain Hebden's six-pounder anti-tank guns damaged another, which was later abandoned. Within an hour the crossroads was in Dorset hands and the Germans had been beaten off, but both companies had taken heavy casualties. Among them was CSM Nick O'Connell, who was killed while rallying part of D Company to repel a German counter-attack. A Dorchester man, O'Connell was a popular and respected figure, having served in India, Malta, Sicily and Italy with the Battalion. Wounded a few days before on Point 103, he had refused to be evacuated and continued his work. He was mentioned in Despatches. Lance-Corporal Henry Barnes, acting as despatch rider throughout the battle, proved as valuable to the Colonel as he was courageous, earning a Military Medal.

The day had cost the Dorsets five killed, five missing and forty wounded. During the night at 0230 the Vickers guns of the 2nd Cheshires beat off an attempted infiltration but, by the morning of 15th June, the Germans had slipped away, allowing the Dorsets to consolidate. Two patrols that night established that the Germans were still in Longraye and Les Orailles. Second Lieutenant Dibben of 9 Platoon, leading one of the patrols, was one of two wounded; two soldiers were missing. One of Dibben's patrol, Corporal John Mannion from Leeds, stayed behind to look after one of the wounded men and was captured. After being locked up in a small room with three other soldiers, Mannion led the way out through a window. Two days later, while hiding in a farmhouse, the group were fired on by German troops. Mannion was wounded and his three friends killed. Taken to hospital in Rennes, John Mannion was freed in early August by American troops and later mentioned in Despatches for his bravery and enterprise.

In the afternoon of the 17th two more stalwarts were lost when the Adjutant, Leonard Browne, and the Signal Officer, Lieutenant Stade, were wounded when Battalion HQ was shelled. A third was lost when Major Richard Harris was struck down by a recurrence of malaria, but during the day nine new officers arrived, most from the 9th Battalion in England. Another old hand, Captain Eric Hannah, took over as Adjutant on top of his other duties. That day three Messerschmitt 109s flew low over Battalion HQ: the first enemy aircraft the Dorsets had seen since D-Day.

THE BATTLE FOR HOTTOT

At 0400 on 19th June B Company took over a position from the 6th Green Howards to form a firm base prior to a battalion attack through the woods upon Château de Cordillon. The purpose of the attack was to protect the right flank of the rest of the Brigade who would attack Hottot. After a brief reconnaissance, the other companies moved forward with A Company on the right, D on the left and C following A to protect the right flank. As they advanced, some enemy mortar bombs fell around B Company. After a fifteen minute barrage from the supporting field regiment, the companies attacked through pouring rain and increasingly heavy German mortaring. Colonel Norie was one of the first to be wounded by the mortaring, and Major Bredin took over command. Captain Hebden, the Anti-Tank Platoon commander, and Lieutenant Shambrook, commanding the Mortar Platoon, were also wounded. Communication broke down as wireless sets were damaged by the mortaring, and line parties were sent out to lay lines to the companies. Meanwhile, Spandau light machine guns towards La Taille engaged A and C Companies, A Company suffering particularly severe casualties.

Meeting less resistance, D Company pressed on to the outskirts of the orchard north of the Château, where they were attacked by two or three Panther tanks. Speedy Bredin ordered them to hold their positions and to provide supporting fire for an attack on the Château by B Company. But at this moment B Company were themselves attacked by six or seven tanks supported by infantry. Their commander, Major Martin, who had arrived from England two days earlier, was wounded while attacking one of the tanks with a 77 grenade. Sergeant Stevenson somehow managed to knock out a Panther with a PIAT. He was later awarded a Croix de Guerre for this and other exploits.

Moving between his companies under the relentless rain and heavy fire, the acting Commanding Officer saw many other acts of courage. In A Company Sergeant Norman Elgie (who later won a Military Medal) and Corporal Fred Noble both proved to be valuable leaders in a battle that cost the Battalion eighty-six casualties all told. Four of the nine reinforcement officers who had arrived two days earlier were wounded. Worst of all, the battle cost the Dorsets' Colonel his life. Evelyn Norie died of his wounds five weeks later. Among the missing was Private Jonathan Reeves from Weymouth, a Regular who had served in Palestine and France with the 2nd Battalion. He had been severely wounded and taken prisoner, and he died in enemy hands two days later.

The 1st Dorsets' mortars near Hottot

Realising that further progress was impossible while the machine guns towards La Taille were still firing, Major Bredin ordered the Battalion to consolidate and hold the ground they had won. Lieutenant Foster of D Company found himself and some of his men cut off during the afternoon but managed, after a gruelling, wet night, to return with information that the Germans had more tanks and defensive positions in the south of the wood. Meanwhile, the Hampshires and Devons had each fought their way into Hottot before being forced to withdraw. It was clear that the Germans intended to defend the area around Hottot at any cost. For his leadership and courage on 19th June Major Bredin was recommended for a DSO but instead received an immediate Military Cross.

The Malta Brigade remained in this area until 7th July, holding their ground and enduring shelling and mortaring. Speedy Bredin later recalled:

On the 20th June and the succeeding days we continued with our reorganisation and the improvement of our (temporary) defences. The enemy on our front, who at this time included the 130th Panzer Lehr Division, were extremely watchful and prepared to resist any further advance on our part. Every day brought its toll of casualties (for example, on the 20th there were 13 killed and 17 wounded from shelling and mortaring). Casualties in a static position are always more maddening than those incurred in an attack, and it is often the leaders who go – the various commanders visiting positions, and others whose duty takes them into the open (signallers, runners and ration parties).

... We carried out as much patrolling as possible to dominate No Man's Land.

During the afternoon of the 21st, two more officers – Lieutenant Windebank and Major Jones – were killed in the shelling. Colin Windebank, aged twenty-four from Bournemouth, had commanded 13 Platoon since the landing. Arnold Jones had fought away from the Regiment in North Africa and with the 1st Battalion in Sicily and Italy. Wounded on D-Day, he had returned immediately to resume command of A Company. He was posthumously mentioned in Despatches. These were still more losses of experienced leaders who would be hard to replace. Eleven new officers arrived on 22nd June, including three Canadian officers whose arrival doubled the Dorsets' Canadian officer contingent to six. One of them, twenty-seven-year-old Lieutenant Ivor Baldwin from Toronto, survived only two days before being disintegrated by a shell.

The losses continued. On the 23rd four men were killed and twelve, including Lieutenant Mortley, were wounded. The 24th saw the deaths of the unblooded Ivor Baldwin and the veteran Corporal Sam Thompson DCM MM; six other men were wounded. On the 25th two salvoes from a Nebelwerfer fell across the Battalion's positions and twenty-four men were wounded. On the 26th RSM Dorey was wounded by a mortar bomb and another soldier was killed.

On 27th June Captain Tony Babington – who, like Sergeant Stevenson, would win the Croix de Guerre – was wounded, and Lieutenant Vernon Robinson, a twenty-five-year-old Buffs officer who lived with his young wife in Lewisham, was killed.

A new CO arrived. Colonel Willoughby was a Middlesex Regiment officer who had served with Montgomery's 3rd Division in France in 1940. He had been unwell for some time and unsurprisingly was evacuated to hospital on 6th July. Speedy

Bredin resumed command of the Battalion and miraculously would survive to the very end.

On 30th June the Dorsets saw the sky filled with 150 Lancasters and 100 Halifaxes on their way to bomb the German positions at Villers Bocage. The Germans loosed off continuous bursts of unaimed machine gun fire as the bombers flew over, providing a visible demonstration of the Allied air forces' unchallenged domination of the skies above the battle.

A comparison of the 1st Dorsets' complement of officers on 1st June 1944 with the list prepared a month later is telling. Of the thirty-seven officers listed in June, after three weeks' fighting in Normandy only nine remained. Twelve of the missing twenty-nine were dead. Only one officer – Captain Arthur Harris – survived the whole three weeks in a rifle company.

The casualties continued. On the 6th another 1st Battalion veteran of Malta and Sicily, Captain Edmund Lushington, was reported missing. A search revealed that he had been killed by mortar fire while making his way between A Company's positions.

This proved to be the Dorsets' last day in these positions above Hottot. On 7th July they were relieved by the 6th Durham Light Infantry, and next day they moved north-east of the Château to relieve the 1st Hampshires, who were withdrawn from the line to prepare for the Malta Brigade's next attack. On the 8th Speedy Bredin was promoted lieutenant-colonel and confirmed as commanding officer of the 1st Battalion, whose gruelling three weeks in defence were now coming to an end.

During those three weeks the nature of the campaign in Normandy had changed, casualties had increased and the opposition had intensified. The essence of Monty's plan, often overlooked by the American high command and misrepresented by their press, had been to draw the bulk of the German armour onto the British and Canadian front to allow the Americans to break out of their much more lightly defended end of the bridgehead, to liberate Cherbourg and to break out southwards and eastwards into northern France. By the end of June, eighty per cent of the German armour in Normandy faced the British and Canadian armies, who in consequence fought a grindingly slow, costly campaign of attrition through the Normandy bocage.

The country might have been designed with infantry defence in mind. Its small fields and ubiquitous, dense hedgerows provided ideal places to hide an infantry section, a couple of Spandaus or an 88, while its tiny, overgrown, often sunken lanes were impassable for tanks. This was country in which the infantry had to lead, despite the heavy toll exacted by the hidden defenders. The question facing every battlefield commander from Monty down to the newly-appointed Colonel Bredin was: how long would the supply of infantry – and especially of competent junior officers and NCOs – hold out in such savage fighting with such fearsome losses?

By 0110 hours on 9th July the Battalion were in position but still under intermittent mortaring, which had cost them two casualties – one killed and one wounded – during the relief. Another man was wounded later in the day. Meanwhile, patrols were sent out to establish the enemy's positions in advance of the attack on Hottot, which was scheduled to start at 0700 on the 11th. One of the most experienced and keenest leaders of patrols was Sergeant Stevenson who, not content with having knocked out a Panther with a PIAT beside the Château, now on patrol dismantled a German booby trap and killed two of the enemy with a 36 Grenade. These patrols gained some useful intelligence. For example, at 1600 on 10th July a D Company patrol returned with two men missing, having drawn enemy machine gun fire from an area that had previously been believed unoccupied. Another patrol sent out late that night to find the missing men located their bodies. Both had been killed.

Forty-five minutes before the barrage began, yet another patrol discovered that the enemy had re-occupied an area south of what was known as *Brigadier's Farm*, which B Company had cleared. Then, at 0700 as the Gunners began their barrage, the Sherwood Rangers' tanks moved into position up a track specially cleared by the Dorsets' pioneers and an assault detachment of Sappers, who had blown up the close hedgerows.

At 0730 the 1st Hampshires cleared the orchard south of *Brigadier's Farm* and, an hour later, the second phase of the attack began with a further artillery barrage and D Company, under Major Bill Meredith, moving forward to guard the Hampshires' right flank. At 0845 a squadron of Crocodiles – Churchill tanks carrying flame throwers – moved up ready for the attack on Hottot village itself. As the Churchills creaked up the tank track, the enemy brought down a heavy concentration of mortar fire around them. Colonel Bredin later paid tribute to one of the Dorsets' stretcher-bearers, Private Lewis, who maintained his calling's proud tradition by braving the mortaring to tend the wounded.

Meanwhile two enemy tanks were reported in the Hottot area and C Company sent a party with a Bren and a PIAT to the south end of the orchard. Although the 90th Field Regiment brought down a stonk[17] on the area where the enemy mortars were located and air reconnaissance reported that they had hit it, mortaring continued from other localities. On the left the 2nd Devons had made good progress and were almost in Hottot. Because small arms and mortar fire was holding up the Hampshires' advance, Brigade ordered Meredith's D Company not to move forward.

At 1132 the Sherwood Rangers engaged and destroyed two enemy tanks and, half an hour later, a prisoner sent back by the Hampshires revealed that the Germans had about twelve tanks along the front. By 1300 the Hampshires and Devons had re-organised and made more progress, enabling D Company to get into position on the Hampshires' right. Moving slowly forward under heavy mortar fire, the Hampshires reached the western end of Hottot. At 1400 they reported a counter-attack brewing on their right flank near the Dorsets' D Company, south of Château de Cordillon. As the Château area was still occupied by the Germans, this placed Meredith and his men in a very exposed position.

When infantry and enemy tanks assembled south and west of D Company, the gunners and three-inch mortars brought down a heavy barrage on them, breaking up a counter-attack. But the 90th Field Regiment's Forward Observation Officer, Captain Vine, who was well up with the forward companies directing his battery's fire, was wounded. His Battery Commander, Major Wells, had already been wounded earlier in the morning.

Soon after 1500 the 6th Durham Light Infantry, to the Dorsets' right, reported little progress on their front and, an hour later, a section of Typhoons rocketed the area. Although some of their rockets fell among D Company, happily they caused no casualties. The Sherwood Rangers reported seven or eight enemy tanks destroyed for the loss of a single Sherman.

In the late afternoon the Dorsets' A and B Companies each sent out patrols, who returned reporting several knocked out German tanks and that the enemy had withdrawn from a number of positions. But at 1705 D Company were heavily attacked. Their forward platoon, 16 Platoon, was over-run. Major Meredith was killed and a Canadian officer, Lieutenant Hal Foster, took command. Helped by Company Sergeant-Major Northam, Foster rallied the rest of the Company, who held their ground. CSM Northam also took on a German tank with a PIAT and disabled it until it could later be destroyed by a Dorset patrol. Leslie Northam, from Street in Somerset, would survive to receive a Military Medal while Foster was promoted Captain a few days later.

---

17   A stonk was a sudden, heavy concentration of shell or mortar fire.

At 2230 the Brigadier withdrew the badly mauled 1st Hampshires into reserve and the Dorsets assumed responsibility for the western half of the Brigade's sector. Bredin was able to reinforce his heavily depleted D Company with two Sherman tanks that had been supporting the Hampshires. Nevertheless, the German counter-attacks continued into the following day and, when the CO visited them during the morning of 12th July, he found D Company successfully repelling another. Throughout the day B and D Companies would remain in close contact, exchanging fire with a watchful, aggressive enemy.

The two-day action – mainly in a supporting role – had cost thirteen Dorsets their lives. Seventy-six more were wounded. Major Bill Meredith, who left a young widow in Exmouth, had arrived on 17th June and had survived just three weeks and three days as a company commander in Normandy. The Devons had lost more but the Hampshires had lost most, including their Colonel, who was killed. Two days later, the Devons would lose their own CO when Colonel Nevill was wounded.

Although the Brigade was once again within an ace of taking Hottot, the centre of the village still evaded their grasp. After a day spent consolidating their gains, on 14th July the Dorsets were relieved by the 9th Durhams and spent the next few days in brigade reserve or in the line near Hottot relieving one of the other battalions. They still faced a determined enemy, who they found had booby-trapped his positions before being prised from them. The Luftwaffe also attacked the Brigade's positions at night, dropping flares and bombs. The German mortaring continued and on the 17th Lieutenant William Coll, a Canadian officer from Winnipeg, was killed. Two days later Lieutenant Paul Luffman, attached from the Border Regiment, was killed by shelling. That night patrols reported that at last the enemy had abandoned Hottot.

During this period General Montgomery visited the Brigade and presented ribbons to those who had won decorations in June. Of the forty-two awards won by the Brigade, the Dorsets had been awarded fourteen, but only six recipients remained with the Battalion to be honoured. Of those six, two had recently returned from hospital. Willie Hayes was one of them, having miraculously recovered his eyesight and discharged himself from hospital in Southampton. Bobby Nicoll was the other, but he had returned too soon: his malaria would recur again in the next fortnight. Peter Brind, whom we last met in Yorkshire with the 2nd Battalion, took over as Speedy Bredin's Second-in-Command while Captain Ronald Macnamara, a South Wales Borderer from Hereford, took over A Company.

Another loss was the MO, Captain Lassman, who was posted to a Field Ambulance and succeeded by Captain Neil. Laurance Lassman had survived since

Normandy and would be mentioned in Despatches for his courage and service in the campaign. Happily for the Dorsets, Neil proved a worthy successor.

In reserve for the next two days, the Brigade were visited by their Divisional Commander, Major-General Douglas Graham, and by a face from the past – their Brigadier from the days of Sicily and Italy. Roy Urquhart was now a major-general and commanding the 1st Airborne Division. In a few weeks' time he and the Dorsets would be involved in one of the most audacious airborne operations in history.

THE DRIVE SOUTH

In the evening of 27th July the 1st Dorsets relieved the 6th Green Howards near Les Croix des Landes in preparation for a divisional attack southwards. This attack was part of a Second Army offensive to support the American break-out in the west, which had begun on the 25th. While the Americans broke through and turned south and east, the British would drive south towards Vire, Condé and Falaise. 50th Division's first objective was to secure the high ground west and north-west of Villers Bocage.

On the 29th 231 Brigade received orders to attack the following day. Their objectives were a succession of ridges, the last of which, known as Point 133, overlooked Villers Bocage. The Dorsets would attack on the left with the Hampshires on the right and the Devons in reserve ready to pass through and exploit success. Support included a squadron of the 13/18th Hussars' Shermans, two troops of Crocodiles, a troop of flail tanks to tackle any mines, a regiment of field Gunners, another of anti-tank Gunners from the Northumberland Hussars, a Sapper field company and a company of the 2nd Cheshires' medium machine guns. D and A Companies (under Willie Hayes and Ronald Macnamara) would lead the first phase of the Dorsets' attack with a troop of tanks from the 13/18th, another of Crocodiles and a section of the Battalion's Bren gun carriers.

The preliminary artillery barrage began at 0515 and, forty-five minutes later, A and D Companies led off. D Company passed through Les Landes. Although the Cheshires' Vickers guns seemed to be keeping the enemy's heads down, as they advanced Willie Hayes's men were heavily mortared. At 0740 a huge formation of Bomber Command's Halifaxes and Stirlings roared over very low on their way to bomb Villers Bocage.

On D Company's left, A Company hit more determined opposition and at 0805 reported being held up by machine gun fire. Having overcome this, they pressed on in the face of stiffening resistance. At 0845 Lieutenant Bernard Mitchell was killed and A Company's advance was halted. Macnamara realised at once that the enemy position – a house and a surrounding slit trench – must be taken if the Brigade's advance was to continue. Collecting eight men from his reserve platoon, he led them in a bayonet charge across the open ground towards the hidden enemy machine guns. Only three of the nine Dorsets reached the German guns. The first in was Macnamara who shot two of the machine-gunners and, with his two survivors, cleared the enemy from their positions, killing and capturing most of them. Fifteen, however, escaped from the back of the house and got into a slit trench in a hedge at the edge of the field. Macnamara followed them up so rapidly that they surrendered immediately. He then led his Company to their final objective, taking heavy casualties as they advanced down a forward slope in full view of the enemy.

By 0920 hours A and D Companies had sent back seventeen prisoners and, ten minutes later, C Company was ordered to move up to join them. By 1020 the Regimental Aid Post had received thirty-seven casualties. Many more would follow.

At 1100 D Company captured some buildings enclosing an 81mm mortar position. And, at 1125, the Brigadier ordered the forward companies of both the Hampshires and Dorsets to dig in on their present line. More casualties were sustained from heavy mortaring, and Arthur Harris, commanding B Company, and his batman were wounded by a mine.

That evening, Major Leslie Thomas's C Company, sent to make contact with the 9th Durham Light Infantry at Orbois Château, ran into some enemy machine gun positions but managed to capture two of them, taking four prisoners.

At 2000 the Germans counter-attacked. On A Company's front, Captain Macnamara walked from position to position under heavy mortar and Spandau fire, encouraging his men to stand firm. The counter-attack was driven off although Macnamara himself was severely wounded in the leg. He stayed with his men, cheering on their efforts, until the stretcher-bearers removed him from the battlefield supervised by Company Sergeant-Major Perriment. On D Company's front, their forward platoon under Second Lieutenant Willis was over-run and forced to withdraw. But B Company, supported by some Devons who were passing through, held the attack.

At 2030 C Company, supported by flail tanks, attacked and saw off some enemy machine-gunners. Half an hour later their 13 Platoon suffered some casualties from Schu-mines in an area in which the flails could not operate.

After the battle Speedy Bredin recommended Ronald Macnamara for the Victoria Cross most would say he fully deserved. The award, however, was reduced to an immediate Distinguished Service Order. Most importantly, though, Macnamara survived to receive his medal from the King on 16th March 1945. Others at Les Landes were less fortunate. Three officers, including Bernard Mitchell from Ramsgate, had been killed together with nine soldiers. The other two 1st Battalion officers killed were Lieutenant Douglas Bird of the Wiltshire Regiment and Second Lieutenant Angus Fraser who, like Bernard Mitchell, was an officer of the Buffs. In addition to Major Harris, Lieutenants Scott and Cass and seventy men were wounded.

The rifle companies spent the next morning under heavy mortar fire, consolidating and adjusting their positions while the Battalion's pioneers cleared an array of mines from paths, woods, hedges and houses. Patrols sent out during the morning reported that the enemy had withdrawn from various localities but at 1800 hours B and C Companies reported an enemy position. Leslie Thomas, the youthful Gloster Regiment officer commanding C Company, was fired on while carrying out a reconnaissance near some houses and an orchard. At 1950 three-inch mortars attacked the area and ten minutes later Thomas led his Company into the attack. Four machine gun posts and enemy mortar fire wounded twenty men of C Company and Thomas himself was wounded while rescuing his batman. Another officer, Lieutenant Hack, was wounded. Despite his wounds, Major Thomas carried on and, deciding that it was impossible to take the orchard, withdrew his Company to B Company's positions overnight. When the set-piece attack on the area went in next morning, the advancing troops found that, characteristically, the Germans had withdrawn.

Early on 2nd August the Dorsets reached the last of the ridges, Point 133, overlooking Villers Bocage. Ordered to halt there, over the next couple of days the Battalion's patrols strongly suggested that the enemy in this area were finally beaten and on the retreat. They would not fight to defend Villers Bocage. Their prolonged barrage on the Dorsets' area on the morning of 4th August confirmed this theory. They were withdrawing. The first Allied patrol into what remained of Villers Bocage was from the 1st Dorsets and was led by Sergeant Moss.

Sixty days after landing at Le Hamel, the 50th Division were pulled out of the line for training and a brief rest. Lieutenant-General Brian Horrocks, who had just succeeded General Bucknall in command of XXX Corps, visited 231 Malta Brigade and gave a talk to all its leaders from corporal to colonel. His praise for members of what he described as "the finest fighting division in Normandy" was timely and appropriate. The Division had pretty much given its all. But there was to be no rest. Monty now ordered his divisional commanders in Second Army to drive south towards Falaise. They were to put their heads down and go like hell. Two great prizes were at stake: the completion of the American break-out in the west and the destruction of the German army in Normandy. In his diary of 4th August Monty presciently noted: *There is a good chance that by D+90 we may be on the line of the Seine.*[18]

50th Division were now ordered to continue the advance south towards the strategically important Condé sur Noireau, which lay at the confluence of two rivers and a road junction. On 6th August at considerable cost 43rd Wessex Division had taken Mont Pinçon, which dominated the route between Villers Bocage and Condé. Beyond Mont Pinçon, 231 Brigade were ordered to capture Point 229, St Pierre-la-Vieille, Rousseville and the ridges beyond.

The attack began at 0800 on 11th August with the Hampshires on the right, the Devons on the left and the Dorsets in reserve, but the Hampshires met fierce opposition and it became clear that they could not take Point 229. The 5th East Yorkshires of 69 Brigade had already tried to capture the feature but it had also eluded their grasp. At 1845 the barrage fell on the objective and the 1st Dorsets began their attack, led by B Company under Major Robert Jackson, a West Yorkshire officer, and C Company under Major Leslie Thomas. Each company was supported by a troop of tanks from 4/7th Dragoon Guards.

On the right B Company came under fire from enemy positions on the flank, but successfully cleared some of these before being brought to a halt by a strongpoint at a road junction south-east of St Pierre. Major Jackson was mortally wounded leading a bayonet charge against the position and Company Sergeant-Major Meakin was wounded. B Company took the position after a hard fight, killing or taking prisoner several Germans and capturing a field gun. Corporal Albert Lewis won a Military Medal for his courage and leadership commanding a rifle section in this battle.

When the Colonel set out in search of his forward companies he found B Company, now under Lieutenant Tom Bradley, on the road junction, and C Company even further ahead, having taken four enemy posts and forty-five prisoners. He ordered A and D Companies, who until now had been in reserve being heavily shelled, to close up to consolidate the ground won. During the night anti-tank guns were brought up to strengthen the defence. In the darkness D Company captured a Wehrmacht colonel in his staff car who had got lost looking for his own companies. The day's fighting had cost the Dorsets five killed

---

18   Monty over-estimated by a week. 43rd Wessex Division crossed the Seine at Vernon on 28th August: D+83.

and twenty-nine wounded, including yet another platoon commander, Second Lieutenant Forster.

Early on 12th August the Dorsets and Devons attacked again and this time sensed the enemy's resistance slackening. The two battalions made good progress during the morning and occupied the final objective: the ridges south of Les Forges. The Germans retaliated with heavy shelling and, around lunchtime, attempted to infiltrate on the right flank. These attempts were repelled by D and C Companies. At 1500 a section of Bren gun carriers fired on some more Germans attempting to get into some houses.

In the late afternoon and early evening the forward companies reported a great deal of activity in front of them. Combined small arms and mortar fire and a shoot by 4/7th Dragoon Guards inflicted heavy casualties. At dusk the 4/7th withdrew but a troop of Cromwell tanks appeared unexpectedly in their place.

But the Germans had not finished yet. At 2145, supported by a tank, they put in a battalion attack on the Dorsets' position, reaching within thirty yards of Speedy Bredin's command post before being beaten off by the combined efforts of B and D Companies and members of Battalion Headquarters. In the chaotic battle that ensued around the command post Private Winn and Corporal Harris, both of the Carrier Platoon, employed a Bren gun and a PIAT to great effect, while Captain Grimsdell made good use of a two-inch mortar. In the fighting on their front, Sergeant William Blundell of B Company and Private Eric Dawes of D Company each won a Military Medal for their part in beating off the German attack, which was finally broken off after the supporting Gunners brought down a heavy stonk on the rear elements of the German battalion. Around the Dorsets' position a blackened Cromwell tank stood abandoned and smoking not far from one of the Dorsets' brewed-up carriers. Both had been knocked out by a German bazooka.

At the end of the day the Battalion war diary recorded five Dorsets killed and another twenty-two wounded. Between 11th and 13th August the Dorsets captured 162 prisoners, eighteen machine guns, one 88mm gun, one 105mm gun, one 81mm mortar and a truck. Their final advance had taken them deep into the rear areas occupied by the Germans' artillery. Their casualties on 13th August were five killed, four wounded and two missing.

These proved to be the 1st Battalion's last casualties inflicted by the enemy in Normandy. 43rd Wessex Division, including the 4th and 5th Dorsets, now passed through them towards Condé, while the 1st Dorsets remained for five more days in the positions south of Les Forges which had cost the Malta Brigade so dearly. Sadly, their last casualties in Normandy were the result of a mistaken attack by a flight of American Thunderbolt fighter-bombers.

But even these losses were not quite the Regiment's last in Normandy. Nor had the 1st Battalion been the first Dorsets to land in Normandy on 6th June. The experience of one Dorset officer – Major Reginald Tarrant – spanned the 1st Battalion's entire Normandy campaign. Commissioned into the Dorset Regiment in 1933, by 1944 Tarrant was attached to the 13th Parachute Regiment, who had landed in the very early hours of D-Day. On 19th August he led B Company in a fiercely contested attack near the village of Putot en Auge. Severely wounded in the stomach and in great pain, he continued to direct his company until he was evacuated. He was recommended for, and later awarded, a Military Cross but died nine days later in hospital. He was thirty-one and married. His MC citation described his leadership and dash as *an inspiration and encouragement to his men and in the finest traditions of the Parachute Regiment*. They were also in the finest traditions of the Dorset Regiment.

The invasion of Normandy – the largest amphibious invasion in the history of warfare – had been a triumph of arms in which every service could take pride. Despite bad weather and the immensity of the operation, the Royal Navy had got the assault troops there and had provided essential and very effective fire support for the battalions ashore. They had then continued, still in unpredictable conditions, to land reinforcements and equipment as the bridgehead was expanded. The RAF's strategic and tactical bombers had helped clear the way for the invasion and for later advances. Their fighter-bombers, operating a cab-rank system, waited overhead, enabling the forward army units to call down accurate, devastating attacks by bombs and rockets on targets just ahead of the leading infantry companies. Meanwhile, their fighters dominated the skies above, ensuring that the armies moved unhindered by the Luftwaffe.

The Sappers, whether in their flail tanks or on their bellies feeling their way through minefields or blowing paths through the tangle of trees and hedges of the bocage, had been indispensable. The Gunners, equipped with their magnificent twenty-five-pounders and with heavily armoured self-propelled guns, and especially their Forward Observation Officers eternally up with the leading infantry platoons in the liveliest places, had been superb. And the armoured units, usually out-gunned and invariably out-armoured by their opponents, had managed, despite the close and inhospitable terrain, to provide the support their infantry colleagues so desperately needed.

The United States army, after a difficult and bloody landing on Omaha beach, had excelled in their rapid advance south and east to link up with the more heavily opposed British advance southwards.

The close nature of the country in which the campaign had been fought, combined with Montgomery's plan to hold almost all the German armour on the British and Canadian front, had resulted in unprecedented losses among the infantry of 21st Army Group. The results vindicated the plan, but the cost had been high. The infantryman never knew what was dug in below the next hedgerow or hidden behind that barn or in that fold in the ground. Anywhere might hide a sniper, a section of infantry, a Spandau or even a Tiger tank. Every advance to contact was nerve-wracking as they waited for the burst of fire or mortar bomb that would almost certainly kill or wound several of the leading riflemen and their platoon or section commander. In this environment the 1st Dorsets alone had lost 184 killed (including twenty officers) and around three times that number wounded. As we shall see in the next chapter, the 4th and 5th Dorsets in 43rd Wessex Division also lost heavily. The American breakout and the final bloody destruction of the German armies in Normandy had been bought to a large extent with the blood of British and Canadian infantrymen.

Given the immense contribution made by the fighting and support services of all the Allied forces, it is infinitely sad that the American high command would later denigrate the British and Canadian part in this triumph of arms. From Marshall and Eisenhower down, they seemed incapable of grasping and retaining the nature of Montgomery's plan, which they had endorsed. Despite the disparity in the strength of the enemy forces facing them, they seemed instead to expect equal advances across the front. This was not, and never had been, the plan to which they all had agreed. More worrying, though, was the politicking back in England in late July when Eisenhower expressed to Churchill his dissatisfaction with progress on the British and Canadian front. Sadder still, two British air marshals were involved in this politicking, among them a former Dorset – Eisenhower's deputy, Air Chief Marshal Tedder. Tedder, like many and with a degree of justification, found Monty's bombast deeply unattractive. His own diffident, reserved style was a complete contrast. But the fact that, just as hard-won victory was within reach, he allowed a personal antipathy to spill into intriguing to get the architect of that victory sacked casts a cloud on the otherwise brilliant career of a very distinguished airman.

The Allied victory in Normandy was Montgomery's triumph, both in design and execution. The German army had been shattered and the front now lay open. The

Allies could advance as far and as fast as their supply chain would permit. But in Normandy three seeds had germinated in the hothouse of the Allied command whose roots would grow, entangling and tripping up the future conduct of the war in North West Europe.

The first was mistrust. Eisenhower's doubts about Montgomery, which he expressed in England but never directly to Montgomery himself, struck at the roots of what should have been a candid relationship between the theatre commander and his land forces commander. The second was professional jealousy on the American generals' side and contempt for the Americans' lack of professionalism on Monty's side. No American general at this stage had the experience or professional ability to have achieved what Monty had achieved in Normandy. He knew it and made no real attempt to hide it. They knew it and some of them resented it. Patton's remark, on his advance being halted at Argentan – "Let me go on to Falaise and we'll drive the British back into the sea for another Dunkirk" – was symptomatic of that resentment. As the number of American troops began greatly to exceed the number of British and Canadians, the American politicians, generals, press and public became ever less willing for them to serve under British command. The third seed was a difference in strategy. Montgomery wanted to combine the British, Canadian and most of the American forces into one huge thrust towards the Ruhr and on into northern Germany. (Undoubtedly he wanted to command this force, but he offered nonetheless to serve under Bradley if an American general was required.) Eisenhower, lacking experience of command and strategically naive, favoured a slower, broad front strategy, which four months later would leave the Allies vulnerable to the German counter-attack in the Ardennes.

As the campaign continued, these three seeds – mistrust, jealousy and differences in strategy – would together distort and disrupt future operations. Had Eisenhower shared Monty's strategy, the war might have been won in late 1944. The Allied advance might have reached further east, to the great advantage of the people of Central Europe and of the post-war balance of power. As it was, *amour propre*, disagreement and lack of determined, professional direction after Normandy led to missed opportunities. They led also, via Monty's frustration with the American command, to the ill-chosen, mistimed and unsuccessful airborne operation at Arnhem, in which three battalions of Dorsets would be heavily involved. Their road north-east into Germany would be long, hard, frustrating and bloody.

THE ADVANCE THROUGH BELGIUM

For the moment the Allies could enjoy the fruits of the crushing defeat they had inflicted upon the German army in Normandy. The enemy in front had evaporated and, once across the Seine, the road ahead – into Belgium and the Netherlands – lay open. While 43rd Wessex Division crossed the Seine at Vernon, 50th Division advanced behind them, clearing towns and woods and capturing often bewildered German stragglers. The severely under-strength 1st Dorsets received welcome rein-forcements in the form of a complete company of Durham Light Infantrymen transferred from the 11th Durhams in 49th Division. In Italy, ineptly managed cross-regimental postings had led to mutiny. Here they were handled more sensi-tively. Speedy Bredin ordered that they be kept together as platoons, each platoon joining one of the Battalion's rifle companies. The addition of a Durham platoon to a Dorset rifle company was another example of the peculiar flexibility based on fierce regimental pride that had enabled the Dorsets, Devons and Hampshires to shine among the brightest stars of a Northumbrian Division.

The first part of their advance passed towns familiar to their fathers who had fought there thirty years before: Amiens, where they received a warm welcome from the French inhabitants, Albert and Arras, where the Dorsets and Hampshires took over the defence from Guards Armoured Division. Again, Dorsets allowed to *walk out* in Arras met an enthusiastic welcome in the streets, bars and cafes. And now the Malta Brigade was ordered to forsake its Geordie friends and temporarily join the Guards Armoured Division for the advance to Brussels.

Near Bersée, the Dorsets' mortar and anti-tank platoons and their supporting self-propelled field gunners from the 90th Field Regiment, some firing over open sights, engaged and greatly depleted a motorised German column moving south. Later the 2nd Devons, leading the advance with the Grenadiers' tanks, handed fifty German prisoners of war to the Dorsets' carrier platoon. At dusk on 3rd September – the fifth anniversary of the British declaration of war - the Dorsets followed the 2nd Grenadier Guards' Shermans across the border into Belgium.

The advance, in which units of the Guards moved seventy-five miles in one day, met token resistance and the 1st Dorsets spent the night near Tournai, which the 2nd Dorsets had last seen ablaze from German bombing during the BEF's retreat in May 1940. Next morning they received reports of a large number of German troops near Lessines, and a fighting patrol from A Company, supported by a troop of Shermans, reported many enemy in the town. The rest of A Company, strengthened

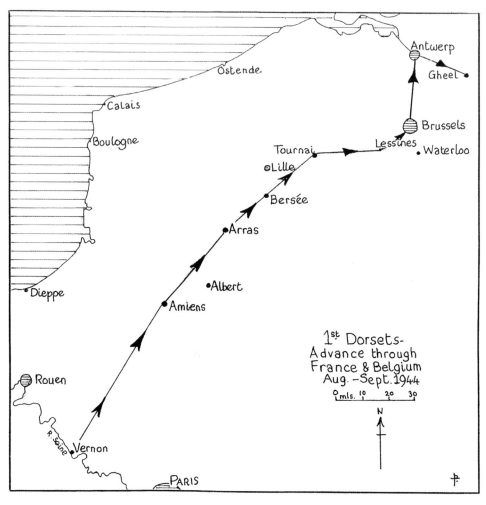

The Advance through France and Belgium August–September 1944

by a platoon of B Company and a section of the Cheshires' Vickers guns, put in an attack and took more than a hundred prisoners. The remaining enemy scattered into the surrounding woods and fields. Here Corporal John Newland, a thirty-two-year-old man from Hertfordshire, was killed beside a member of the Belgian resistance. Today a memorial marks the spot where both men died.

The advance was renewed and, after lunch, an enemy machine gun fired on the leading vehicles of their column, but a few belts fired by the Cheshires silenced it. The advance continued. At 1710 hours on 4th September the Malta Brigade entered Brussels, and the Dorsets heard another, more distant, echo from history when they were ordered to guard the city's southern approaches from Waterloo. Their war diary recorded the Battalion taking up their defensive positions and moving *across the city amid tumultuous enthusiasm.*

After some chopping and changing of orders on the 5th, the Brigade rejoined 50th Northumbrian Division and moved on at 0800 on 6th September. At 1400 hours they were ordered to move into Antwerp and cover the south-west of the city along the eastern bank of the Scheldt. After some sniping from the Germans on the west bank, the next day B Company saw the enemy strengthening their positions and, at some 500 yards which was the maximum range for the weapon, brought down a two-inch mortar stonk on their positions.

On the 7th three men of C Company were reported missing from a patrol sent over the river to capture a prisoner. Two later found their way back to the Battalion having hidden in the rushes and then with a Belgian family until they were able to make contact with British troops. Next day C Company engaged an enemy patrol of about ten men, killing five of them. Meanwhile A Company's area on the only bridge over the Albert Canal, and the approach to the bridge, were repeatedly shelled, mortared and sniped. Overnight the Battalion were relieved and, early on 9th September, they moved along the Albert Canal towards Gheel, where the Green Howards had established a small bridgehead. But, when it was decided that a similar bridgehead won by the Guards at Beeringen might prove easier to exploit, the Malta Brigade were returned to the Guards Armoured Division to support their advance.

Operation Market Garden

After two days spent guarding two bridges over the canal and on the receiving end of two attacks by German fighter bombers, the Dorsets moved up behind the Guards towards the Escaut Canal and the Dutch border. By 15th September they were guarding Joe's Bridge, recently named in honour of Colonel J O E (*Joe*) Vandeleur, whose Irish Guards Group had captured it. On the next day General Brian Horrocks, commanding XXX Corps, called his commanders together at Bourg Léopold to explain their role in the forthcoming Operation *Market Garden*. He began with characteristically humorous showmanship: *Gentlemen, I'm now going to tell you about an operation you will be able to tell your grandchildren about. And mightily bored they'll be...*

Speedy Bredin was among the battalion commanders packed tightly into the cinema, hearing how American and British airborne forces were to be dropped to capture the canal and river crossings ahead of XXX Corps' axis of advance. The

Corps would then drive rapidly up the path cleared by the airborne troops, across the Maas at Grave, the Waal at Nijmegen and finally the Neder Rijn at Arnhem, before wheeling to encircle and isolate the Ruhr. With its centre of arms production eliminated, Germany would collapse and the war would be won in 1944. This was heady stuff but, after their lightning advance through Belgium, it seemed possible. The Germans were in disarray. The sad reality, however, was that the opportunity to end the war rapidly had already been missed. Having assumed direct command of the land forces in North West Europe, Eisenhower had remained too long too remote from the battle to be able to control and direct it. Nor had he the skills or experience to do it. A politician rather than a fighting soldier by nature, he was a man of diplomacy and compromise. His compromise between Monty's urgent and repeated pressure to reinforce his northern thrust and Patton's demands to support his advance in the south now meant that Monty's already over-ambitious *Market Garden* was doomed before it began. Even had the Second Army reached and crossed the final bridge at Arnhem, they would not have had sufficient strength to achieve the strategic objective of encircling the Ruhr.

There were also tactical weaknesses in the *Market Garden* plan, some of which were pointed out during the planning stage by Major Brian Urquhart, a Dorset Regiment officer who, after airborne service in North Africa, was now on the staff of General Boy Browning's Airborne Corps. Later Brian Urquhart remembered:

My job as chief intelligence officer was to try to evaluate what the enemy reactions were going to be and how our troops ought to deal with them. The British airborne troops were going to be dropped at the far end of the operation at Arnhem – it was across the third bridge, so there were three bridges that had to be captured before you got to the British airborne troops. I became increasingly alarmed, first of all at the German preparations, because there were intelligence reports that there were two SS Panzer divisions right next to where the British troops were to be dropped. These were the star troops of the German army, the 10th and the 9th SS Panzer divisions. They had been very badly mauled in Normandy and were refitting in this area. These were the best fighting troops in the German army and they had heavy tanks. Airborne troops in those days had absolutely nothing. They could carry their personal weapons, and a few Jeeps could be landed by glider, but that was about it. They had no heavy weapons, no supplies, very limited supplies of ammunition, and they could not fight heavy armour because they didn't have the weapons to do it.

I was also worried about the state of mind of the senior officers in my outfit, who were all extremely gung-ho and were talking about Christmas in Berlin, and this kind of thing. Somebody said they were going to take their golf clubs because it

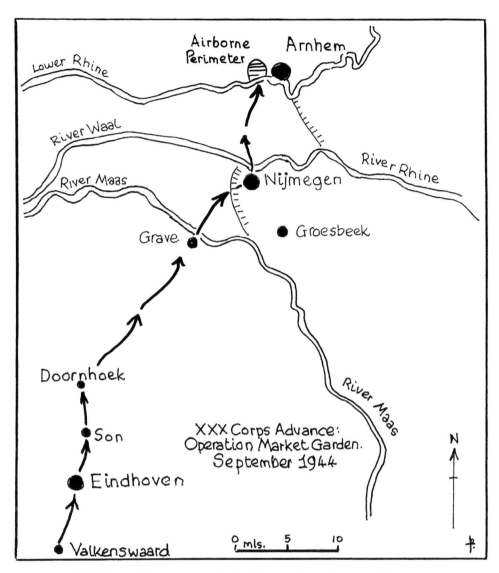

XXX Corps Advance towards Arnhem 17th–25th September 1944

was going to be a pushover. This seemed to me to be extremely dangerous, because the German army, in fact, is not an army to surrender without being told to do it. And furthermore, these were the best troops in the German army. I tried to get this point of view across and pointed out that, if we were going to do it properly, we were going to have to drop the troops in a different place so that they could immediately capture the bridge, and that there was a big question as to whether the relieving troops could get up from near Brussels in time. They were stuck on the Albert Canal, which was sixty miles away, and the country there is flat, dyke country. The roads are all causeways. These are perfect roads for an armoured force to stop another force from advancing. All you've got to do is to disable one tank, and that blocks the whole thing. Well, I didn't get anywhere with this. Everyone thought that I was hysterical, nervous, and so on, and I finally got sent away, I think, for a remark which turned out to be oddly prophetic. Our general, who was a very dashing figure called Boy Browning, said to Prince Bernard of the Netherlands that the Allied forces were going to advance into Germany over a carpet of airborne troops. And I said to our chief of staff, "I wonder if they're going to be alive or dead airborne troops." This didn't go well at all, and everybody decided that they'd had enough, and I got sent away. I asked if I could stay just as an ordinary officer in the operation. They said, "No, you'll be court-martialled if you disobey orders." Everybody had enough on their hands by that time, so I went.

In 1945 Brian Urquhart was mentioned in Despatches and appointed MBE. The MBE citation praised his work as a staff officer at Second Army Headquarters and the long hours he worked and difficult journeys he undertook despite suffering constant pain from a parachuting injury earlier in the war. After a distinguished post-war career as a senior official in the United Nations, Sir Brian Urquhart chivalrously offered his help when General Browning's widow, Daphne du Maurier, was deeply upset by the savage portrayal of her late husband in Richard Attenborough's film, *A Bridge Too Far*.

The Dorset Regiment's part in this fateful operation would not end with Brian Urquhart's unsuccessful dissent. The 1st, 4th and 5th Battalions would each be intimately involved in its various phases and the 4th Battalion would play a heroic part in helping to evacuate the survivors of 1st Airborne Division across the Neder Rijn. We will hear more of the gallant part played by the 4th and 5th Dorsets in the next chapter.

The 1st Battalion's involvement began at the operation's outset when, at 1200 hours on 17th September, RAF Typhoons and USAAF Lightnings rocketed and bombed the German positions in the line of the advance ahead of the start positions on the Escaut Canal. An hour later an aerial armada of aircraft and gliders headed northeast towards the dropping zones. At 1420 their own supporting artillery opened up and, at 1435, standing up in his Dingo scout car, Colonel Joe Vandeleur gave the order for the leading squadron of his Irish Guards Group to advance. Behind them on that first day came 231 Malta Brigade with the 2nd Devons and 1st Dorsets tasked with clearing the woods either side of the road.

They encountered their first opposition at a road junction south of Hoek and, at 1500, Bredin went forward to discuss the situation with Sir John Carew-Pole of the Devons and Joe Vandeleur. Despite losing several tanks of their leading squadron, which were shot up by RAF Typhoons, the Irish Guards continued through Hoek to Valkenswaard, pushing aside the slackening opposition. Meanwhile, the Devons cleared the woods around Hoek and the Dorsets stood ready to support the Irish Guards on the road towards Valkenswaard.

By 1800 hours another defect in the plan was slowing progress. The single road up which they were advancing was choked with traffic, and units could not move forward as rapidly as they were needed. Having ordered his companies and Tactical HQ forward at 1700, Bredin found that the move took Tac HQ an hour and the companies an hour and a half or more. Ahead of him it was the same, with tanks and lorried transport double- and triple-banked across the road. Having picked his way up the road to meet Vandeleur and agreed to help the Irish Guards hold Valkenswaard, Bredin found his way back to his HQ to find that orders had been received for the Dorsets to dig in where they were. By now, their war diary tells us, it was *raining and pitch-dark, the enemy is all round us, and mortaring commences along the line of the road.*

Speedy Bredin was champing at his bit and, up ahead, the Irish Guards were keen to leave Valkenswaard and advance to Eindhoven. But Brigade stood firm: the Dorsets needed to stay put partly to protect their supporting gunners coming up behind them and partly because the enemy situation ahead remained obscure. Instead of advancing at once, Bredin therefore pressed Brigade to let him advance at first light.

At 0445 Speedy Bredin went ahead to meet Vandeleur and at 0500 A Company of the Dorsets on Cromwell tanks of the 15/19th Hussars moved up the road to Valkenswaard. C Company followed in lorries while, on foot, B and D Companies swept the woods either side of the road. By 1000 the whole Battalion was installed in Valkenswaard, where Bredin made what had been the German headquarters his own.

The 1st Dorsets' role was now to defend Valkenswaard – principally from attack from the open flanks as the thread of XXX Corps' narrow advance unravelled further and further ahead of them. They stayed for five days, dividing their time between patrolling, strengthening the defences and working with the local population, who were thrilled to have been liberated so unexpectedly. Old friends passed

Valkenswaard during Operation Market Garden

through on their way to livelier places. Among them were more than 1,000 Dorsets from the 4th and 5th Battalions in 130 Brigade and a single Dorset visitor, Rupert Wheatley, who dropped in for a cup of tea. Major Wheatley was serving in a Wiltshire battalion in 129 Brigade with whom he would later win a DSO before being badly wounded.

While Guards Armoured and 43rd Wessex Divisions fought their way up to Nijmegen and beyond to reach the airborne troops, 50th Division protected the road which was their only connection with the rest of Second Army. This entailed 50th Division's units moving from place to place to counter one actual or potential German assault on the road after another. Thus, in the next few days, while battle raged further up the road and in the 1st Airborne perimeter north of the Neder Rijn around Oosterbeek, the 1st Dorsets found themselves at Son (captured by the US 101st Airborne Division), Doornhoek, Veghel, Keldonk, Volkel and Langenboom.

Finally, conclusive news of the battle filtered through. All the crossings had been seized, although the bridge at Son had been blown up and had had to be replaced by the Royal Engineers. Nijmegen, the last crossing before Arnhem, had been taken late by the joint courageous efforts of US 82nd Airborne and Guards Armoured Divisions. Only one battalion – Colonel John Frost's 2nd Parachute Regiment – had reached Arnhem bridge. The rest of 1st Airborne Division were trapped north of the Neder Rijn in the Oosterbeek perimeter, which was being squeezed and steadily destroyed by the German armour surrounding it. Despite opposition, XXX Corps had managed to advance at considerable speed, but they crossed Nijmegen bridge behind schedule and, by the time they were across, Frost's gallant Battalion on Arnhem bridge had been overwhelmed. Monty, Dempsey, Browning and Horrocks had agreed that the survivors of 1st Airborne should be withdrawn across the river. While the 4th Dorsets had crossed to aid the evacuation, the 5th Battalion helped from the opposite bank. Meanwhile, the leading troops of 43rd Division had reached the town of Elst, just south of Arnhem and, from the church tower, they could see the bridge Frost's men had held. Success had been tantalisingly close, but a combination of factors had resulted in strategic failure.

The operation had, however, liberated large swathes of the Netherlands, right up to the German border, which now needed to be occupied and defended. The 1st Dorsets thus found themselves on the River Maas near Mook. A patrol sent downstream towards Cujik crossed the Maas by boat and made contact with the US 82nd Airborne Division, who had landed in that area – around Groesbeek – twelve days earlier. Groesbeek stood very near the German border: a fact that did not escape Speedy Bredin. The Colonel of the 1st Battalion of a regiment whose motto was *First in India* was unlikely to pass up an opportunity of this kind and, on 29th September, he despatched a patrol under Lieutenant Walsh with orders to cross the border and return safely. Thus it was that, at 1635 hours that day, Walsh, Sergeant Pinfold and Lance Corporal Davis (all of the Carrier Platoon) became the first British infantry to penetrate Germany. They returned bearing proof: two German flags and an armband. One of the flags – an SS banner – is still displayed proudly at the Keep Museum in Dorchester.

ON THE ISLAND

Two days later the Battalion moved into the low-lying country, known as *the Island*, between Nijmegen and Arnhem. Here, the 43rd Wessex Division and Guards Armoured Division were dug in among flat fields, criss-crossed by dykes, facing the defending Germans. Up near the front it was reminiscent of the First World War. The German artillery could bring down accurate shelling on any movement while their machine guns could scythe low across the polderland and bring down anyone who broke cover. As in the Flanders trenches, the infantry kept their heads down, feeding and conducting reliefs only after dark and avoiding particular spots – crossroads or railway crossings – on which the Germans had fixed their artillery. At this stage the British expected a German attack towards Nijmegen bridge.

It was into this environment that the 1st Dorsets entered in the late afternoon of 1st October. At first they came under command of 69 Brigade, who had just been attacked north of Bemmel. Because one of the Brigade's battalions had been partly over-run, the Dorsets' job was to bolster the defence by holding the railway line south-west of Bemmel. After a night in which the artillery of both sides competed to keep everyone awake, 69 Brigade were withdrawn and the rest of 231 Brigade – the Hampshires and Devons – joined the Dorsets at Bemmel. Deciding that attack was the best form of defence, Brian Horrocks was resolved upon counter-attacking the Germans to eliminate any chance of their breaking out of the island.

After some unsuccessful attempts by the Devons and Hampshires to drive the Germans back with fighting patrols, on 3rd October orders were received for an attack next day by the Dorsets with two Hampshire companies on their right. The aim was to force the Germans back to the line of the canal north of Elst, and the attack would start at 1200. A and B Companies would lead the Battalion attack, with A on the right and B on the left. A Company's objective was a large orchard,

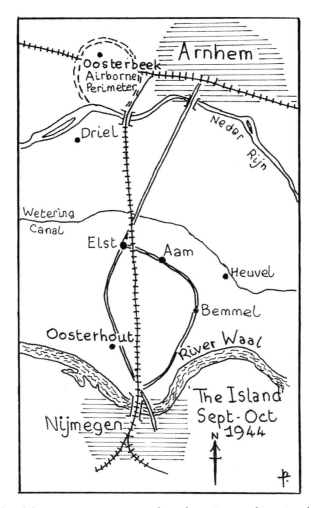

The Island *between Nijmegen and Arnhem September–October 1944*

and B's the hamlet of Heuvel and its surrounding orchards. A Company was commanded by Major Francis Laugher, universally known as *Skinny*. A contemporary of Speedy Bredin's who had been away from the Regiment with the First Army in Tunisia, he had now returned, via the Staff College and a staff job in another division. B Company was led by the veteran Major Richard Harris.

During the night the Battalion had been heavily shelled and one shell had fallen in a slit trench, killing two men in B Company. Next morning at 1030, after the CO's Orders Group, the companies moved to the assembly area. At noon the mortars, Gunners and medium machine-gunners opened up as A and B Companies moved off. Immediately the Germans brought down a heavy barrage on the attacking

Lieutenant Frank Shackell

Lance-Corporal Reg Cook

troops. At Bredin's Tactical HQ Major Wells, commanding 465 Battery of the 90th Field Regiment, was wounded but insisted on carrying on. Shells also fell on the other companies' assembly areas.

Lieutenant Frank Shackell, a Royal Berkshire officer who had joined the 1st Dorsets in the early stages of Operation *Market Garden*, was commanding 14 Platoon. In his late twenties, he had been surprised by the extreme youth of his new Company Commander, twenty-three-year-old Leslie Thomas from the Glosters. But he had quickly recognised his qualities, writing home about having acquired a *young Major – a grand fellow with a level head – a fine Sergeant and a first rate batman named Cook.* But now a salvo of shells changed everything in an instant.

… no sooner had our Company Commander, the young Major, gone off to receive orders from the CO – Lieutenant-Colonel Speedy Bredin – than the shelling began and then followed the greatest traumatic experience in my Army career. A runner came back through the shellfire to tell us that our very young Company Commander was killed and that Colonel Bredin requested the company of the C Company platoon commanders PDQ. Lieutenant Gilhooly, our Canadian, Sergeant Rowe MM (Acting Platoon Commander) and I, for we had no 2iC, advanced through shot and shell towards Speedy Bredin. Near him we saw the body of our Company Commander – one arm stretched out as if in sleep. Speedy Bredin (who with my batman runner Reg Cook, were the two bravest men I had ever met) said: "Find yourselves cover and wait till I send you orders."

He stood, calmly brushing his tooth brush moustache as we three dived into the first unoccupied slit-trench we could find. I couldn't get down far enough so I took off my small pack and placed it at the base of an apple tree just above my head. I settled down.

Suddenly there was a terrific bang; my tin hat blew onto the bridge of my nose, and I found myself completely deaf and numb down my left side. I was soaked with rum.

I opened my eyes and pushed Sergeant Rowe from me to find him dead, with two great holes in his back. Lieutenant Gilhooly was in a bad way, groaning with two wounds in his stomach but still alive.[19] *Pushing Sergeant Rowe's body forward, I scrambled out of the trench to find the nose cap of an 88mm shell embedded in my small pack. The water bottle containing the Platoon's rum ration, my shaving kit and personal belongings were destroyed and my moustache scissors were ruined.*

---

19   Sgt Cyril Rowe had won his MM with the Durham Light Infantry in Normandy before joining the 1st Dorsets. Happily Graham Gilhooly, a Canadian subaltern, survived.

I can so vividly remember the next few minutes going up to Speedy Bredin, giving him an excellent salute, saying: "Sir, the rum is external not internal – my small pack bears witness. Stretcher-bearers required urgently. I have to report that I am the only officer remaining in C Company, your orders please!"

He gave a rare smile saying: "We have radioed for stretcher bearers. We will look after Gilhooly and Rowe. Return to C Company, take command and hold them in reserve until further orders."

I made my way back to C Company by a different route via a large ditch, gave the CSM the orders and returned to my Platoon to give my Sergeant his orders.

Reg Cook said: "Sir, we thought you'd had it – there was a Spandau fixed line of fire along that ditch!" I hadn't noticed – I must have been still in shock.

With no Second-in-Command, I had toured the other platoons and arranged Company HQ near the ditch, scraping out a hole for myself away from the apple tree roots. My neighbours were three lads who had found some sheets of corrugated iron, placed it over the ditch out of any fixed line of fire, and, to make more room for themselves, had dug out underneath putting about four inches of soil on top. To give themselves still more room, two had removed their webbing equipment, which contained their 36 grenades, and placed them on top of the earth and iron.

During the dark watches of the night we were subjected to frequent mortar attacks and one scored a direct hit on their shelter. Brocks benefit followed – their grenades exploded and we kept our heads down until all became fairly peaceful again. We thought they must have perished in the explosions, but the miracle happened – they crawled out from their shelter unharmed but chastened, wondering what had happened to them. The four inches of earth had saved them.

Meanwhile, Skinny Laugher had led A Company across the ground swept by Spandau fire, suffering heavy casualties in the advance. Once the Dorsets had grabbed the orchard, a troop of Coldstream tanks rolled forward to support them. In the battle for the orchard, Sergeant John Collins won a DCM and Company Sergeant-Major Norman Elgie an MM. Laugher, who miraculously survived the attack, was awarded a Military Cross.

B Company under Richard Harris was equally successful but at a similar cost. In taking Heuvel two of their platoon commanders, Lieutenant Quigley and Sergeant Robinson, were wounded and their Company Commander was killed by a shell. Richard Harris had served with the 1st Battalion on Malta and had been unit landing officer on the beach in Sicily. A gentle man who made an order sound like a suggestion, he would leave an unfillable gap. Back in Bournemouth, he left a young widow who was expecting their first child. The third platoon commander, Tom Bradley, took command of the survivors in the forward platoons, and consolidated the position.

Bredin now ordered Willie Hayes's D Company forward into Heuvel. This entailed crossing an area covered by Spandaus. Once on the objective D Company cleared the hamlet of enemy, winning two Military Medals – one each for Sergeant Charles Scott and Sergeant Wilfred Else. They too were heavily shelled, and Hayes and his Company HQ were buried. Shaken but not noticeably stirred, the redoubtable Hayes continued to reorganise the position under intense fire. His bravery at Heuvel, combined with his gallantry at Les Landes on 30th July and his leadership throughout the campaign, earned him a Bar to the Military Cross he had won on D-Day.

As B and D Companies went to ground, darkness fell and the shooting died away. The menacing silence was broken only by the persistent, pathetic cries of a badly wounded German soldier stranded in front of the ditches occupied by Tom Bradley's men. Some men from 10 Platoon scuttled out and dragged him back on a makeshift stretcher made from a ladder, which broke when they were halfway home. Rations could not reach them and the pangs of hunger made them think longingly of some long containers, dropped by Dakotas trying vainly to resupply 1st Airborne, which now lay 150 yards from their positions. Hunger finally defeated caution. A scrounging party retrieved some badly dented ration packs including tinned meat, which were enthusiastically opened with bayonets.

Speedy Bredin had done it again. Despite heavy casualties, including two company commanders killed and three other officers wounded, under intense artillery and machine gun fire, Bredin had moved from company to company, directing the advance. At one point he had even taken over one of the companies and led them to their objective. After the battle he was once again recommended for a DSO and this time – most deservedly – he got it.

Now the Cheshires' Vickers guns and 4.2-inch mortars came up to help strengthen the defences, together with a troop of M10 tank destroyers, a squadron of tanks and a troop of six-pounder anti-tank guns. A sweep of the road east of Heuvel by a section of the Dorsets' Bren gun carriers and a section of Pioneers engaged and overcame a group of enemy who had been causing the Devons some trouble. They returned with eleven prisoners while another twenty gave themselves up to the Devons. Among other prisoners were a Pole, press-ganged into the SS, and a member of the crew of a Tiger tank, which had been disabled in front of the Dorsets' forward companies.

The 1st Dorsets had done well, as Brigadier Sir Alex Stanier's congratulations confirmed. Ordered not to push on, they dug in for the night. Their success had seen off the SS and won them a DSO, two MCs, a DCM and three MMs. But it had cost them fifteen lives, seventy-one wounded and three missing. Among D Company's dead was twenty-year-old Private Eric Dawes, who had won an MM in Normandy.

Taken out of the line on 7th October, the Battalion lost nine men wounded from shelling in the so-called rest area in Malden before being returned to the line next day. This time they were further north, at Elst, in reserve behind the Hampshires and Devons. Their role was to counter-attack any enemy attempting to break through towards Nijmegen. The Germans shelled the town sporadically and, on 9th October, hit Bredin's Battalion Headquarters. Happily, only two men were wounded, neither badly. One was Peter Brind's batman, the other Major Wells commanding the supporting field battery who had only just returned, having been wounded five days earlier.

After a few days spent guarding the bridge at Nijmegen (which the Germans had unsuccessfully tried to attack with frogmen), late on 17th October the Dorsets found themselves back at Bemmel. They were again rejoined by the doughty Major Wells, who had already decided he had recovered from his second wound. Here the Battalion received an exotic mix of visitors, including: a Romanian prisoner of war who had deserted from the SS (who had shot at him as he ran away); a Dutch interpreter, Mr Kruisinge, who was attached to the Battalion and later proved a valuable acquisition; two elderly Austrian conscripts from the Wehrmacht; three rowing boats full of Dutch civilians who had escaped from further upstream; and a corps commander, Lieutenant-General Brian Horrocks, who had tea with the Malta Brigade's three commanding officers. Shelling throughout was intermittent – except on the 21st, when the German artillery shelled the area of Bemmel church very intensively and provoked an equally fruitless British retaliation. The war diary recorded that the Gunners fired over 4,000 shells on the Brigade front.

Patrolling was constant. On the 23rd Lance-Sergeant Lovering led a patrol from A Company across the Wetering canal and heard a great deal of noise from an orchard. Deciding that his patrol was not strong enough to attack a position of this strength, Lovering silently withdrew. On the 25th an SS patrol threw hand grenades at the house held by the left forward platoon of B Company. Corporal Brandon's section replied with a burst from a Bren, killing one of the Germans.

At 0630 on 1st November the Germans raided a forward section of 14 Platoon, capturing two men. The raid had been carefully planned and included support

Wartime cemetery at Bemmel

from 50mm mortars, Spandaus and an artillery concentration on the platoon on
14 Platoon's right. Happily, Sergeant Moss, commanding 15 Platoon on the left, was
able to drive off the enemy. Next day, Captain Babington – who had been wounded
in Normandy and won a Croix de Guerre – was wounded again when a shell burst
in his room, showering him with splinters. Tony Babington[20] had recently replaced
Skinny Laugher in command of A Company when Laugher had injured his leg.
Captain Darts Dartnall now replaced Babington just as the Battalion was withdrawn for a rest in Nijmegen.

On 8th November the Dorsets returned to the island, this time to take positions
north of Elst. Here a network of dykes and canals crossed east-west both the road
and railway running north-south. The low-lying ground was waterlogged. Winter
was approaching. The Germans opposite shelled the Battalion's positions frequently
and sporadic bursts of Spandau fire ripped low over the flat fields. Three times the

---

20   Severely wounded in the head, Tony Babington was lucky to survive. He became a
Circuit Judge and wrote several books, including the first analytical but compassionate
study of the soldiers executed in the First World War.

enemy also attacked the standing patrol kept by the Dorsets' forward company north of the Wetering canal. On the 18th Corporal George Golder, a Londoner from Walthamstow, led the entirely successful defence and beat the Germans off, winning a Military Medal.

George Golder's proved to be the last decoration won by the 1st Battalion in the Second World War because, on 29th November, they were withdrawn from the island. 50th Division had spent its strength and was to be returned to Britain to become a training division at home. Some stayed, transferring to other units in Second Army. Old faces left. Peter Brind replaced Sir John Carew-Pole as Colonel of the 2nd Devons and went on to win a DSO. Bobby Nicoll, who had spent recent months at XXX Corps HQ gaining experience for Staff College, left for Camberley.

The 1st Battalion investiture at Buckingham Palace March 1945
Standing l to r: *CQMS Collins DCM, CSM Elgie MM, Sgt Blundell MM,*
CSM Northam MM, Capt MacNamara DSO, Cpl Brandon MM,
Lt-Col Bredin DSO MC, Capt Whittington MC, Sgt Talbot MM,
Maj Hayes MC and Bar, Major Holdsworth MC, Capt Dartnall MC,
Cpl Wright MM, Sgt Scott MM and Cpl Barnes MM.
Kneeling l to r: *Cpl Carter MM, Pte Goddard MM, Sgt Redpath MM,*
L/Cpl Bounsall DCM and Cpl Golder MM.

The Division concentrated at Ypres, surrounded by the familiar names of their fathers' battlefields, and prepared for their new role back in England.

Pat Chilton had recovered from the wounds he received on D+8 and was despatched on a lecture tour to the United States of America, where – in Dorset uniform – he told American audiences about his Battalion's experience on Malta and Sicily and in the D-Day landings.

The 1st Dorsets' long war was finally over. They had withstood a three-year siege on Malta, fought a bitter campaign in Sicily, landed in Italy, led the D-Day landings and fought their tragically costly way from the Normandy shore to the polder-land of the Netherlands. From a unit whose strength should have been about 880 officers and men, they had lost 327 killed and 1,029 wounded or missing. In Sicily, Normandy and finally on the island, they had met, matched and beaten often crack German troops. Their bravery had won five DSOs, eleven MCs (plus Willie Hayes's Bar), five DCMs, three GMs, twenty-nine MMs (plus William Evans's Bar), one MBE, three BEMs, two Croix de Guerre and a score of mentions in Despatches and Commander-in-Chief's Commendations. Later, on 16th March 1945, Speedy Bredin and nineteen other officers and men of the 1st Dorsets attended an investiture at Buckingham Palace to receive the decorations they had won in North West Europe. Exceptionally, instead of being presented to the King in the usual order of protocol based on the hierarchy of the awards, the Dorsets followed each other – a privilege enjoyed previously by 617 Squadron after the Dambusters' Raid and by the 11th Hussars.

The survivors of the 1st Battalion could hold their heads high in any company. But they needed a rest.

The Memorial to the 43rd Wessex Division on Hill 112

7

THE 4TH AND 5TH BATTALIONS, NORTH WEST EUROPE 1944–45

BOCAGE TO BREMERHAVEN

FOUR MEMORIALS

On a hill at Chedington, near Crewkerne, just in Dorset but looking west across the fields of Somerset, stands a stone memorial. There is an identical one on a hill overlooking Mere in Wiltshire. A third, again identical, stands on a hill above Maltot in Normandy. A fourth, of different design but the same purpose, is in Cornwall a-top Rough Tor on Bodmin Moor. All four commemorate a single infantry division, the 43rd Wessex Division, who in the eleven months from June 1944 until May 1945 fought their bloody way through Normandy, across the Seine, into the Netherlands during the Arnhem operation, around Geilenkirchen, up to and over the Rhine, and all the way to Bremerhaven.

It is appropriate that these memorials should stand on the Dorset–Somerset border, in Wiltshire and in Cornwall because battalions from all four counties fought in that campaign. There were three brigades in 43rd Wessex Division: 129 Brigade, which included the 4th Somerset Light Infantry and the 4th and 5th Wiltshires; 130 Brigade, which consisted of the 4th and 5th Dorsets and the 7th Hampshires; and 214 Brigade, comprising the 7th Somersets, the 5th Duke of Cornwall's Light Infantry and – the only non-Wessex and non-Territorial Army battalion among them   the 1st Worcesters.

It is appropriate too that the memorial in Normandy should stand where it does, near the village of Maltot. The hill on which it stands was known to the British Army in July 1944 as Hill 112. Although not especially high, it dominated the land for miles around it. The British had to capture it if they were to advance towards the River Orne and encircle Caen, where the Germans still held the south bank of the river; the Germans had to hold it if they were to contain the British Second Army within its bridgehead. The result was a First World War-style bloodbath, which in character if not in scale has been likened to Verdun. Before Hill 112 the men of the 43rd Wessex Division had trained and served together in England for several years. After Hill 112 many of them were recently arrived reinforcements.

The Division would fight in other battles in which they would again suffer heavy casualties, but Hill 112 would overshadow every other battle. It would provide their yardstick of horror: nothing would be as bad again. Yet, despite this devastating first battle and their heavy losses throughout the campaign, they would maintain their reputation to the very end in Germany, prompting their Corps Commander, Sir Brian Horrocks, to write: *I doubt whether any other Division has had so much hard fighting during the campaign and been so successful.* Two battalions of Dorsets – the 4th and 5th – played their part in winning this reputation and are commemorated by those memorials in today's rural landscapes of Wessex and Normandy.

IN THE BEACH-HEAD

The Dorsets' two Territorial battalions arrived on Gold Beach on the anniversary of the Battle of Plassey – 23rd June, seventeen days after the 1st Battalion had fought their way ashore there. The 4th were led by Colonel Howard Cowie, who was now returning to France having been posted away from the 2nd Battalion during the frustrating days of the Phoney War. The 5th were commanded by Colonel Aubrey Coad, an officer of the Wiltshire Regiment who had been Commandant of the Division's Battle School. The other battalion in 130 Brigade were the 7th Hampshires, commanded by Broke Ray's younger brother, Donald, a Regular officer of the Royal Fusiliers. Commanding the Brigade was Brigadier David Leslie, who until recently had been the senior staff officer of 51st Highland Division. Neither these four commanders nor most of their officers and men had yet had any fighting experience in the present war. Within five weeks, none of the four senior commanders in 130 Brigade would still hold their appointments. Colonel Cowie would have been replaced and posted elsewhere, Colonel Ray would be dead and Colonel Coad would temporarily have replaced Brigadier Leslie, who would also have been posted away. Nor was the Brigade exceptional in this respect. By the end in Normandy, not one of the original commanding officers of the Division's nine infantry battalions remained in place.

Having landed on D+17, 130 Brigade concentrated near Cheux, where each Dorset battalion relieved a Canadian battalion in a reserve area. Sad news arrived of old

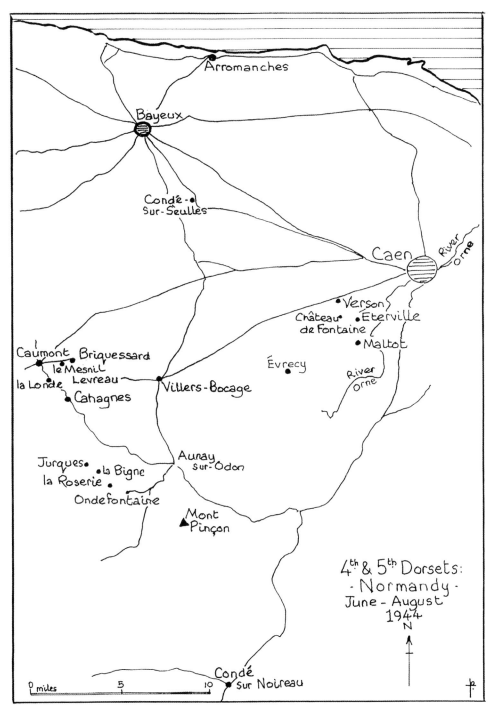

4th and 5th Dorsets' Campaign in Normandy June–August 1944

friends now in 214 Brigade. Colonel John Atherton, who had served with the 4th
and 5th in England, and Major Peter Riddle, late of the 4th, had both been killed.
Atherton had been commanding the 5th Duke of Cornwall's Light Infantry while
Riddle had been attached to the 1st Worcesters. The 5th Dorsets also lost their first
officer, Major Harry Jesty, their Motor Transport Officer, who was wounded by a
shellburst.

On 29th June the Brigade were ordered to move south-east of Cheux towards
the River Odon and to take up position with the 4th Dorsets and 7th Hampshires
forward and the 5th Dorsets in reserve. The 10th SS Panzer Division were expected
to launch an attack to recapture Cheux.

On arrival the 4th Dorsets found the 5th DCLI hard-pressed. They had lost their
CO, and Colonel Cowie tried to bolster them by placing B and C Companies of
the 4th Battalion under their command. He then held A and D Companies back
to act as a counter-attacking force supported by a squadron of Churchill tanks.
The ground the Battalion held was a recent battlefield. The sickly stench of decay
permeated everywhere; the landscape was littered with dead horses and cattle,
bloated and rotting in the summer heat. The atmosphere was oppressively hot and
still, except for the crash of shells and thump of mortar bombs bursting intermit-
tently around them, killing one man and wounding six others.

At 2000 hours Scottish troops – Royal Scots and Royal Scots Fusiliers – began to
form up with squadrons of 11th Armoured Division before moving off south-west
along the Cheux-Noyers road. Two hours later Cowie ordered A and D Companies
forward in support, and went forward himself in his carrier to see what was
happening. Finding the Scots firmly holding a position astride the road, he ordered
his own two companies back to their original positions to begin the relief of the
5th DCLI.

In the first week of July both Dorset battalions relieved, and were relieved by,
units of the 53rd Welsh Division. Private Ron Beale of the 4th Battalion remembered, even back from the line, *the constant noise that was present all the time...
the artillery were firing over our heads almost continuously, their firing would
cause the Germans to return fire, and if it wasn't the guns firing there would be
aircraft roaring overhead. The noise of tanks and transport moving about, night
and day. This particular time it was very hot and consequently very dry – which
caused a lot of dust and clouds of dust invited a shell or two from the Germans.*
Both battalions took casualties from the shelling, the 5th Battalion losing their
Intelligence Officer, twenty-three-year-old Captain John Davies, who was killed
on 2nd July.

The Battle for Hill 112 and Maltot

By the 3rd they were under orders for a forthcoming brigade attack to capture Hill 112. General Paul Hausser, veteran of the First World War, France in 1940, the Russian front and Italy, now commanding II SS Panzer Corps in Normandy, asserted that *he who holds Hill 112 holds Normandy.* It was consequently heavily defended by infantry and armoured units from the SS, Wehrmacht and Hitler Youth. On 29th June 29 Armoured Brigade had occupied the north side of the Hill 112 plateau, but the Germans had clung on to the reverse slope and prevented 4 Armoured Brigade from advancing on 29 Armoured Brigade's right. The 44th Royal Tank Regiment had lost sixteen tanks in the attempt and, on the night of 29th June, 29 Armoured Brigade had withdrawn from their positions on the summit. Now it was 43rd Wessex Division's turn. The Division was reinforced by an additional infantry brigade from 15th Scottish Division and supported by two armoured brigades and a colossal weight of artillery.

The attack's first phase involved the whole of 129 Brigade, whose objective was to capture Hill 112 while the 5th Dorsets took the high ground around Château de Fontaine. The 4th Dorsets would then take Éterville, followed by the 7th Hampshires taking Maltot and two companies of the 5th Dorsets the orchard west of Maltot. Finally, 4 Armoured Brigade would pass through the other brigades and advance towards the River Orne.

The recent wet weather had cleared and, at 0500 hours on the bright morning of 10th July, under heavy shellfire from the German artillery the two forward companies of the 5th Dorsets crossed their start-line. Soon afterwards C Company signalled that they had taken the first objective – the farm at Les Daunes. A few minutes later D Company reported Horseshoe Wood clear of enemy. A and B Companies moved forward to pass through, but at this point wireless contact with C Company was lost when their wireless set was destroyed. D Company reported their commander, Major John Roe, was wounded, that they were suffering heavy casualties and that one of their platoons was missing. The defenders had lain low, letting Lieutenant John Hayes and his platoon pass them before opening up with their Spandaus from behind them.

The Adjutant, Captain Maurice Edwards, followed C and D Companies and remembered *walking quite slowly through a field of corn... with the amazing noise of shells passing overhead – smoke, mortars, tank guns and every other gun within 5 miles seemed to be directed just ahead of the leading companies. We soon found our first casualties, many dead lying in the corn... we all knew each other pretty well.*

It was quite a shock to find bodies so soon after the start line. A White scout car with a 22 set linked to Brigade followed me and some signallers as part of the 'I' section. RSM Horton accompanied me carrying a Bren gun. We were soon at Horseshoe Wood and started to dig in and generally set up HQ. Soon after there was the most tremendous stonk of shell or mortar fire which burst in the trees above us, so we quickly left the wood and re-established Battalion HQ just clear of the trees.

Going forward to see for himself what was happening, Colonel Coad found that C Company had captured Château de Fontaine. Meanwhile, before they had had a chance to dig in, B Company were attacked by tanks. Their commander, Major Goodrich, temporarily blinded, was evacuated while Captain White gallantly led two sections of the Anti-Tank Platoon forward to confront the German tanks. Standing in his carrier wearing his soft cap and wielding only his cane, thirty-one-year-old Gordon White, known throughout the Battalion as *Crasher*, was killed.

Ordered to withdraw to the slope in front of the Château, at this moment the 5th Battalion heard that the 4th Dorsets had taken Éterville. Later in the morning the 7th Somerset Light Infantry dug in on the left of the 5th Dorsets to strengthen their defence. Despite the heavy casualties and confusion, the plan seemed to be working.

On the 5th Dorsets' right, the 4th and 5th Wiltshires and the 4th Somersets had attacked through waist-high corn up the forward slope of Hill 112 and reached the road from Évrecy to Éterville. But their attack had exacted a heavy price. The Somersets, in the middle of 129 Brigade's advance, lost nearly 200 men killed, wounded or captured. Nor was the objective secure. Not only did the attackers face the inevitable German counter-attack from in front, they now found behind them SS troops whose well concealed positions they had passed unwittingly during the advance and who now continued the fight from their rear and their midst. Some SS troops had even whitened their faces and played dead, allowing the British infantry to pass before shooting them from behind. Casualties mounted.

At 0620 hours Brigadier Leslie had unleashed the 4th Dorsets, who were waiting in the cornfield which was their start-line. When Colonel Cowie gave the order, Lance-Corporal Charlie Butt, Cliff Lloyd's friend from the pre-war Gillingham TA, stood and sounded the charge on his bugle. Supported on their left by a squadron of Churchill tanks from the 9th Royal Tank Regiment and a troop of Churchills with flame-throwers from 141 Regiment, RAC, A and B Companies advanced behind the artillery barrage towards Éterville.

Major Joe Symonds, commanding B Company, later described his impressions of the attack.

As we breasted the top of the hill we overran a German platoon dug in in the corn immediately in front of my company. They offered practically no resistance, surrendering immediately, and we continued the advance to the edge of the village, where we had to lie down and wait for the artillery and the RAF to cease shelling and bombing Éterville. We were very close to the barrage, and still in excellent formation, having suffered only a few casualties from enemy shelling during the advance up to this time.

The end of the supporting fire was marked by blue smoke shells, and I gave the signal to assault as soon as these fell. No sooner had we begun the assault than about four fighters came over, presumably a little late, and dropped two bombs in the middle of my company whilst we were still in the open field. We could see the bombs falling so had time to lie down, but we suffered a number of casualties from these, including Sergeant Fowler, who was killed, and all three of our No 18 sets were put out of action.

The weight of the supporting fire had been so great that the enemy offered no resistance at first, the assault coming before he had had time to recover, and we reached the objective, the road beyond the village, without much difficulty. A number of Germans surrendered, some withdrew, and some had yet to be mopped up. The mopping up, which was done by C and D Companies, was not so easy as the garden and field hedges were high and the foliage thick, and soon some enemy troops, who had been quiet to start with, opened fire on us. The enemy then began to shell and mortar us very heavily, and he kept this up all the time we were consolidating, making the whole job very difficult. The attack had gone quite a long way into the enemy positions and they were now very close to us on our immediate front.

I could see A Company, under Major Upton, on my right during the advance and assault, and with their Crocodile flame-throwing tanks in action they looked quite irresistible. They reached their objective on our right about the same time as we did, and probably in rather better order as they did not get the benefit of our own bombs as we did.

The village church became the Regimental Aid Post, where the MO, Captain John Thompson, and the stretcher-bearers worked at full stretch to tend the wounded. The Padre set off in search of help and returned with a German MO (Dr Moeferdt), who worked alongside his British counterpart. Meanwhile, Sergeant Cleal of 4th Battalion Headquarters saw Tiger tanks continuing *to pump shells into the church... killing several of the wounded as they lay on their stretchers. The CO was only about 20 yards away directing operations over the R/T from his carrier.*

After the capture of Éterville, Major Douglas Gaye of the 4th Dorsets was standing by a farmhouse with his batman, Private Cliff Lloyd. When bullets began to ping around them, Gaye reassured Lloyd.

"Don't worry. It's only a sniper getting rid of his ammo."

At which point, Cliff Lloyd remembers, *Major Gaye received a bullet wound in his arm.* Like so many infantry company officers, Douglas Gaye's experience of Normandy was brief. His batman would not survive him long. Wounded by shrapnel, Cliff Lloyd would also be evacuated to England.

By 0745 hours Éterville was firmly in British hands. The 4th Dorsets had captured seventy prisoners and a Tiger tank had been knocked out. The cost, initially low, rose as the Germans relentlessly mortared and shelled their positions. Two company commanders, Major Douglas Gaye and Major Symonds, and the Anti-Tank Platoon commander, Captain Baker, were wounded. For his courage in the attack, Joe Symonds was awarded a Military Cross and, for his bravery tending the wounded during the heavy shelling, Captain John Thompson, the Battalion's Medical Officer, was similarly honoured.

The attack continued. At 0815 hours the 7th Hampshires and A and B Companies of the 5th Dorsets, supported by a squadron of Churchills from the 9th Royal Tank Regiment, advanced between Éterville and Château de Fontaine to capture Maltot. The artillery barrage rolled in front of them as they breasted the crest but, as they moved down the hill towards the village, the barrage outpaced them and the advancing infantry found themselves exposed to German mortar and artillery fire. Despite this, they reached the village and reported its capture. They had walked into a heavily defended German position with tanks dug in all around them. The surrounding orchards hid well-sited machine gun and mortar positions, and a great many German infantry. In the resulting close-quarter shoot-out, the Hampshires and Dorsets lost heavily and the Hampshires' wireless truck was destroyed, severing all communication with 130 Brigade Headquarters. Although company, platoon and section battles continued all morning in the village and in the surrounding fields and orchards, it was not until early afternoon that Brigadier Leslie learnt that Maltot was not yet in British hands.

Some time after 1400 hours, still believing that he was reinforcing success, Brigadier Leslie ordered the 4th Dorsets with tank support to reinforce the men fighting in Maltot. But at 1600 hours, as the leading companies of the 4th approached Maltot and when it was too late to recall them, Colonel Cowie heard that the Hampshires were being withdrawn.

As they advanced through the tall corn and closed on the village, a hurricane of machine gun and anti-tank gun fire burst upon them. Sergeant (later Captain) Wally Caines remembered: *It was hell, none dared to put his head above the corn, as soon as Jerry observed the slightest movement a burst of fire would be the reply. This firing kept up for some time, everything seemed to open together, self-propelled guns fired practically unceasingly.*

Major Mike Whittle of B Company later described the battle.

... the enemy had a large number of tanks and self-propelled guns dug in in concealed positions in the orchards and woods surrounding the village. We suffered heavy casualties and many of our tanks were knocked out. As far as I know, all our Anti-tank Platoon guns were destroyed before they had a chance to go into action.

The rifle companies and Carrier Platoon all reached their objective, and began to consolidate by 1645 hours.

The next two or three hours were very unpleasant. We had failed to knock out the majority of the dug-in tanks, and in the partly wooded area they were very difficult to locate; the few Churchills remaining with us were withdrawn, and fighting was going on all the time. Battalion Headquarters lost contact with all the rifle companies, and eventually at 2030 hrs there was a small party, consisting of the CO, Battalion Headquarters, parts of B, C and D Companies, and the Carrier Platoon, dug in on the Northern outskirts of the village. We were under heavy direct fire from several of the dug-in tanks...

The CO reluctantly gave the order to withdraw...

The attack on Maltot had accounted for the whole of A Company, of which not one member returned, and of two-thirds of the other three companies. Major Upton, Major Connor and Major Dawson, commanding A, C and D Companies respectively, were all missing. It was subsequently learned that a large number of the missing were taken prisoner during the night.

The three company commanders were among those captured and would spend the next nine months in the same prisoner of war camp near Brunswick.[21]

---

21   On 16th July Major George Connor's brother, Trooper Arthur Connor of 153rd Regiment Royal Armoured Corps, was killed when his Churchill tank was knocked out near Hill 112. Counter-attacked by Tiger and Panther tanks, his Regiment lost twelve tanks, thirty-nine men killed and fifty-five wounded.

Corporal Chris Portway, who had assumed command of his section when Corporal Bullock had been wounded a few days earlier, had been knocked unconscious by a shellburst.

My first recollection of anything beyond that I was still alive came with the sound of strange guttural voices and the sensation of being dragged roughly across torn grassland. Slowly memory filtered into my aching head, and the events of the day began to take shape, my first observation being that the artillery barrage had ceased. Then with a cold shock I noticed the coal-scuttle steel helmet and the grinning face of my companion... 'Hello, Tommy – for you the war is over.'

... The main street of the village was, as could be expected, a chaotic mess, the houses on each side blazing furiously. German troops, now that our shelling had ceased, had returned in large numbers and took a friendly interest in the dozen white-faced Britishers amongst them, whilst some even offered us cigarettes. Our escort of three tommy-gunners halted us in the ruins of the main square to pick up a badly wounded German lying on a stretcher. About a mile outside Maltot we were halted again, and searched, all our belongings being removed, inspected and in most instances returned, though our cigarette stocks suffered considerably.

... These Waffen SS had treated us very fairly and their conduct had been typical of front line soldiers in any army.

Maltot had cost the 4th Dorsets 348 casualties and the 7th Hampshires 226; the 5th also lost heavily. Among the Hampshires' wounded was their Colonel, Broke Ray's brother Donald. Sadly, he later died of the three wounds he received that day and was buried near his family home in Wimborne Minster. He was succeeded by Major Dennis Talbot, who until now had been Second-in-Command of the 5th Dorsets.

During the afternoon at enormous cost 129 Brigade had repelled a vicious German counter-attack on Hill 112. Now General Thomas ordered the 5th Duke of Cornwall's Light Infantry, his only battalion not yet committed, to complete the capture of the feature by taking the crest and a small wood. Although one of their companies lost more than half their strength to the Spandaus, the Cornwalls reached the top and held the wood against counter-attack after counter-attack. Their twenty-six-year-old Colonel climbed a tree to get a better view of the enemy positions and was hit in the throat by a burst of fire, which killed him. Finally, the survivors of the Cornwalls were forced to abandon the wood – ever after known as Cornwall Wood – and to retreat behind smoke through the 4th Somersets. The Cornwalls had taken more than 300 casualties, ninety-three of whom were later buried on the spot where the Wessex Division's memorial now stands.

The sun set on this bloody stalemate. On and around Hill 112 the previously unblooded 43rd Wessex Division and their Wehrmacht, SS and Hitler Youth opponents had fought each other to a standstill. Neither had the strength to take and hold the entire feature. For both sides the battle had been a fight to the death: some of the German companies were reduced to four or five men while the British suffered more than 2,000 casualties.

Colonel Cowie's 4th Dorsets, now mustering five officers and eighty soldiers, spent the night in a position behind the 7th Somersets, just forward of Horseshoe Wood. These few, plus those who had been left out of battle in reserve, were all who remained of a Battalion once 750 strong. After spending the day forward between Château de Fontaine and Maltot, they were withdrawn to re-equip and to receive desperately-needed reinforcements. A large draft of reinforcements, including several officers, came from the Essex Regiment and formed the new A Company. Two captains – Letson and Roper – were promoted to command C and D Companies. But throughout this period the Battalion remained within range of the German artillery, whose shelling took a further toll, including their Padre and their MO who were both wounded.

The 5th Battalion had also lost their Padre, Captain Kenneth Prebble, who was wounded and removed by stretcher-bearers. While he was being carried to safety a very heavy artillery stonk burst around him and Prebble leapt from his stretcher to throw himself on top of the stretcher-bearers to protect them. Happily, he survived to spend most of his life as a priest in New Zealand. The survivors of the 5th remained for another eight days dug in on the 7th Somersets' right at Château de Fontaine. During that time they were heavily shelled and mortared. On 13th July Lieutenant Richard Adams, commanding the Anti-Tank Platoon, was killed by a shell. The bodies of Lieutenant John Hayes and many of his platoon were found where they had fallen three days earlier, shot in the back by the SS.

On the night of the 15th a reconnaissance patrol was disrupted by fire from two enemy machine guns which had managed to infiltrate just in front of the forward companies. On the 16th and 17th enemy bombers put in an unexpected appearance and attacked Verson; the Dorsets had the satisfaction of seeing two of them shot down over the target. On the 18th four enemy deserters taken by the 7th Hampshires revealed that the 22nd SS Panzer Grenadiers facing them had been relieved and replaced by a fresh division newly arrived from Bordeaux. That night the 5th Dorsets were relieved by the Hampshires and went into brigade reserve, although A Company were sent to strengthen what remained of the 4th Dorsets, who had insufficient men to hold their allotted position near the Château.

THE FORTUNES OF WAR

Both battalions had done well. In the 4th Battalion, as well as Military Crosses for Joe Symonds and their MO, Dr John Thompson, there was a Croix de Guerre for Captain Cottle, who had led a fighting patrol on Hill 112. Cottle had again excelled at Éterville before being appointed Adjutant. The 5th gained MCs for Major Norman Newton and Lieutenant Hugh Wetherbee, and MMs for Corporal Fred Murray and Private Fred Exley, who with Major Gerald Tilly had rescued two men from a burning tank. There was also a DSO for Aubrey Coad, who had acted swiftly and decisively to ensure the ground his Battalion had won was secured and held.

While the CO of the 5th Dorsets won the first of several well-deserved accolades that were to come his way in the course of the long campaign, the CO of the 4th was replaced. Success in war depends not simply upon courage and skill, but also upon luck. A son of the Regiment – his father, Hugh, had died of wounds after Hill 60 – Howard Cowie had been unlucky. His time as Adjutant of the 2nd Battalion had ended before the German invasion of Belgium and he had been returned to England. Now, as Commanding Officer of the 4th, he had been pitched into Hill 112 as his first battle, and had seen his Battalion virtually eliminated. For the Allies Normandy was a testing ground of new troops under untried commanders. Some would succeed brilliantly, some would fail; some would survive, some would die; some would win high honours, some would be replaced. Colonel Cowie and Brigadier Leslie commanding 130 Brigade were in the last category and they were not alone.

The generals above 130 Brigade provided a striking contrast in styles of leadership. Commanding 43rd Wessex Division throughout the campaign was Major General Ivor Thomas. A field gunner who had won a DSO and two MCs in the First World War, he was an efficient, brave and hard-driving commander, but would not be remembered for his human warmth. Known to the troops as *Butch* – short for *Butcher* – there lingered about him a whiff of Somme callousness. But, unlike some of Haig's generals, he knew his business and was unafraid of appearing frequently in the front line. While several divisional commanders – including Charles Bullen-Smith of 51st Highland Division and Bobby Erskine of 7th Armoured Division – were sacked, Thomas not only survived to the end of the war but would also be Monty's choice to command XXX Corps when he packed Horrocks off on sick leave in December 1944.

Above Thomas during this phase of the Normandy campaign was a legend. Sir Richard O'Connor, now commanding VIII Corps, had led a spectacular advance across North Africa in early 1941 and almost won the desert war before it had begun. But the Dorsets were soon moved to XXX Corps, whose commander for most of the campaign was Brian Horrocks. A Middlesex Regiment officer who had spent most of the First World War as a prisoner and won an MC for his persistent attempts to escape, the extrovert, humorous Horrocks was very much a Monty man. He expended great energy selling himself to the officers and men of his Corps. His predecessor at XXX Corps had also been sacked. Gerry Bucknall, another officer of the Middlesex Regiment with an MC and Bar and the patrician instincts of the best regimental officers, had been devastated by the casualties in Normandy. Monty's view was that Bucknall lacked *the great drive and energy required in the semi-mobile battle; he is too slow.* Like Cowie and Leslie, he was replaced.

Above corps level, commanding Second Army, was Miles Dempsey, a reticent, self-effacing, professional soldier, who concentrated on the daunting task before him and seemed oblivious to the cult of personality. And at the top was Monty, whose unique blend of mischief, egotism, paternalism and professionalism permeated 21st Army Group down to the most junior private soldier.

The prevailing culture of sacking senior officers who did not perform was perhaps inevitable. While many of the Germans in Normandy had gained previous fighting experience in North Africa and in Russia, many of the British troops – and almost all the American and Canadian soldiers – had none. They were pitched into the cauldron that was the Normandy bridgehead, where there was no time for new commanders to learn their trade: they swam or they sank. And since, if a battalion, brigade or divisional commander sank, many men's lives would be lost while he floundered, perhaps Monty and his more ruthless commanders like Thomas were right to replace them rapidly.

The experience of the untried soldiers of 43rd Wessex Division had been similar to that of Kitchener's units on the Somme. Thrown into a bloody campaign of attrition in difficult conditions against a well-entrenched, determined, experienced enemy, they were granted no period of adjustment. A courageously honest survivor of a battalion in 43rd Wessex Division described late in life how, once the battle on Hill 112 began, he found he had ceased to function as a leader and had become simply a rifleman in the company he should have been commanding. Given the violence that confronted them, there was no shame in failing. Until they had been tried, how could they or their commanders have known that they were not cut out for the demands of this kind of war? And how many of those of us reading or writing of their experiences seventy years later would have fared any better?

FIGHTING IN THE BOCAGE

On 14th July, having received 360 reinforcements, the 4th Battalion moved back to Château de Fontaine. Surrounded by the sickly stench of the rotting corpses of bloated cattle and dead Germans who littered the hedgerows, they were heavily shelled and mortared, and bombed by the Luftwaffe. Casualties mounted. Mike Whittle, now commanding S Company, later remembered the new commander of the Anti-Tank Platoon, who was wounded in the chest by a bomb splinter half an hour after his arrival. On the 18th Colonel Tim Wood, who had replaced Cowie a few days earlier, was also wounded in the head when a mortar bomb burst beside Battalion HQ. Major Gerald Tilly, an East Surrey officer who had succeeded Wood as Second-in-Command, now temporarily replaced him as CO.

After a long, hard fight, the 4th and 5th Wiltshires of 129 Brigade finally took Maltot. After its capture, Sergeant Cleal of the 4th Dorsets went back into the village, which he found *eerie in its horror and silence* with *enemy dead still crouched behind their machine and anti-tank guns. The smell was atrocious... I felt revulsion, bewilderment and anger.* One of their supporting gunners from 112th Field Regiment, Gunner Ken Stovey, also described the scene. *Hampshires, 4th and 5th Dorsets lay where they fell all mingled together. The smell was horrendous with swarms of flies and wasps.*

On 23rd July a company of the Bedfordshire and Hertfordshire Regiment arrived to join the 4th Dorsets. Commanded by Major Jimmy Grafton, among their number were Lieutenant Mac McDermott and Private Ginger Pearce, who remembered their arrival.

On seeing some men in a field he [Major Grafton] *shouted "Are you the 4th Dorsets?"*
  "Yes", came the reply.
  "Where's A Company?" he asked.
  "We are A Company", was the answer.
  It was a great shock to find out there were only twenty-one of them and a corporal was the senior man in charge... out of 130 men and four officers.

Both Dorset battalions had at last been removed from the battle area for an unexpected week's rest beside the River Seulles, near Bayeux. Here – incongruously after the nightmare experiences of the last fortnight – men from both battalions

The Normandy Bocage by John Worsley

were entertained by homely George Formby and his ukulele. The week was cut short when, on 29th July, both battalions were warned for a move next day to the area of Caumont. Here they would take part in Operation *Bluecoat* and capture Mont Pinçon, which stood between the Rivers Odon and Orne and, like Hill 112, dominated its part of Normandy. This was typical bocage country: tiny villages and farms among small hills and dense woods intersected by sunken lanes and small streams. In this very close country no one could see very far. The hedgerows, woods, banks, cottages and farm buildings provided first-rate, often invisible positions for the German defenders.

The plan required 130 Brigade to capture the village of Cahagnes. The 5th Dorsets would form a bridgehead over the stream through Le Mesnil Levreau, enabling the bridging tanks of 79th Armoured Division to make the stream passable for tanks to support an attack by the 7th Hampshires on the feature. Meanwhile the 4th Somerset Light Infantry, on temporary loan from 129 Brigade, would capture Briquessard. 4th Dorsets would then pass through to take the hamlet of La Londe and push on to Cahagnes.

At 0800 on 30th July, while a force of American aircraft bombed Cahagnes (and accidentally killed some of the Somersets attacking Briquessard), the 5th Dorsets launched their attack with B Company on the left, A in the centre and C on the right. C Company, taking care to avoid a known minefield, stumbled into an unknown one and suffered some casualties, including their Company Commander. B Company made good progress at first before being held up by heavy mortar and shell fire, one shell wiping out Company HQ, although the Company Commander was unhurt. C Company managed to find a way round the minefield but then bumped into an enemy position.

Meanwhile, A Company almost reached their objective before being halted by heavy fire. It was in this action that Sergeant Chivers took over his platoon when his officer was wounded and, according to the citation for his Croix de Guerre, *set an example of courage and leadership to his men, enabling them to reach their objective in exceptionally difficult circumstances. His determination, offensive spirit and cheerfulness were a source of inspiration to his men.* Happily, Ted Chivers would survive to become the 5th Dorsets' sniper sergeant and to return, at the end of the long campaign, to his home in Sandford, near Wareham.

Others were less lucky. Among those killed was twenty-one-year-old Private Oswald Ball from Bedminster, Bristol. Before he had embarked for Normandy, he had left a poem addressed to his father. He had had no illusions about what lay ahead:

> *Things will go hard and friends will be few,*
> *I shall need all your faith, and prayers too.*

But he had no doubts about the justice of the cause:

> *I'll be fighting for you and the peace of mankind*
> *And all the fine things that I left behind.*

And in these vicious battles in the Normandy bocage Oswald Ball was one of many who gave their young lives for exactly these things.

For the moment, all three forward companies were pinned down by heavy fire in a heavily mined and booby-trapped area. The close country made it nigh on impossible to locate the enemy positions and very difficult for their supporting armour to help them. It was plain that no advance could be made without first conducting a time-consuming, gruelling and hazardous operation to clear a path through the mines.

Throughout the day the 4th Dorsets had waited to be able to carry out their attack, all the time being heavily mortared and shelled. Meanwhile the 7th Hampshires were ordered to attack La Londe from the flank.

Overnight the forward companies of the 5th held their ground and sent out patrols to try to locate the enemy machine guns and minefields. During the morning A and C Companies attacked again, but failed to take their objectives until welcome support from tanks finally brought success. Success was in the air because the 7th Hampshires had also captured La Londe and advanced beyond, repelling a fierce counter-attack by the defending Germans.

While B Company of the 5th completed clearing their area, the 4th Dorsets were ordered to move round the right flank of the 5th and clear the ground between the two streams. At 1500 hours on a blisteringly hot afternoon, the 4th attacked from Montmirel, suffering only six casualties and taking eighty-seven prisoners. They too encountered minefields, which were dealt with very effectively by Sergeant Jack Blandamer and his Pioneer Platoon. They were now able to move south and take Point 174 on the ridge south-east of Caumont, where they remained, under heavy mortaring, until 1st August.

By now, despite the intense fighting, it was clear that the Germans were getting the worst of the battle for Normandy, which was broadly conforming to Montgomery's plan. The bulk of the German armour had been held on the British and Canadian front and now, in the west, the Americans had broken out. But, to underwrite the American break-out, Second Army still had to maintain the pressure on the Germans on their front.

On the night of 1st/2nd August, as the 4th Battalion assembled for their next advance, the Luftwaffe lit the area with parachute flares before dropping bombs. Happily, despite the illumination, they missed the main assembly point. Colonel Wood, who despite his head wound had returned to his Battalion, was taken ill and Gerald Tilly took command.

In the early hours of 2nd August the 4th Battalion led 130 Brigade's advance along the road from Cahagnes, via Jurques and La Bigne, to Ondefontaine. Their task was to capture Jurques, La Bigne and Ondefontaine and the briefing reassuringly told them that they could expect no opposition for twenty miles. The Battalion would be supported by a squadron of Shermans, a section of Sappers, a platoon of anti-tank guns and another of Vickers machine guns. The 5th Dorsets and 7th Hampshires would follow.

Recently promoted Lance-Corporal Ron Beale of the 4th Dorsets recalled that *to speed things up we were to be carried on... tanks... A third class ride is better than a first class walk anyday; the problem is hanging on – there are not many places to hang on to on a tank and the place to avoid is the engine cover. The journey was precarious to say the least... It was hot and dry,* [with] *clouds of dust as the long column sped towards the distant Mont Pinçon.*

The advance to Jurques was not without incident. First, the Dorsets encountered two German Tigers, which happily proved to have been abandoned. Then, at 0915 hours and half a mile from Jurques, A Company found mines on the road and, when they stopped to investigate, were fired on by a machine gun. Patrols quickly saw off this opposition, but the Adjutant's scout car ran over a mine. Captain William Goddard was killed and the Signals Officer, Lieutenant Bogan, severely burned.

As they left Jurques they found the road ahead had also been mined and the Sappers had to clear a path through. But resistance was stiffening. The column was fired on from the flank and ran into unexpectedly strong opposition. Ron Beale remembered:

At the sound of the first shell the tanks deviated off the road seeking cover, all the riding troops jumped off, regardless of the danger of jumping from moving tanks. I was in a group that went to the right of the road up a lane to a farm. This lane had high hedges and steep banks. The shelling was now very heavy and it seemed from where we were that they were after the tanks. We were lying on the banks either side of the lane feeling fairly safe. We couldn't be seen so we remained where we were. Suddenly a shell exploded amongst us. It killed two of our number and wounded several. One of those killed was Eddy Snook, who came from Shillingstone and was my Best Man at our wedding – he was also my very good friend.

We did what we could for the wounded and remained where we were but, conscious that another shell could land among us at any time, there were two or three senior NCOs amongst us who organised us in case of a Jerry attack.

Sergeant Wally Caines remembered the enemy opening *up with all he had, self-propelled guns fired like hell let loose, and as if the heavens above were opening upon us, Spandaus rattled the whole area.*

A Company attacked up the hill but on the summit came under heavy fire and lost heavily. Private Bert Haddrell later recalled:

... we were going into the attack and I was Company runner. We had started to advance when the Company Commander said to me, 'Where is No 2 Platoon?' I replied, 'Still in the trenches, sir', and I was told that they should be in the line of advance. I went back to where they were in their slit trenches where I stood facing them and gave them the Company Commander's orders. All the time the Germans were laying down a mortar barrage of six-barrelled mortars which fire six bombs in succession and were known as 'moaning minnies' because they made a screaming noise as they were fired... One bomb dropped behind me and knocked me out and

when I regained consciousness I had been wounded in the back and was bleeding rather badly. All the men in 2 Platoon who were in the trenches and took the full force of the blast in their faces were dead...

After some time the stretcher-bearers, who were very hard-pressed, picked me up and took me back to the medical post where they gave me emergency treatment for my wounds. All the time this was happening the mortar barrage continued and at one stage the medic Corporal Puddy covered me with his body to protect me from further injury. I later learned that he too had been killed.

Twenty-seven-year-old Lance-Corporal William Puddy, from Parkstone, was killed on 15th August, but happily Bert Haddrell survived to return to his native Bristol.[22]

When A Company's attack faltered, Tilly went forward, withdrew the survivors and sent in two companies supported by tanks.

Ron Beale, Second-in-Command of a rifle section, *started across the first of the cornfields well spread out, walking towards the first of the hedges some distance away, firing from the hip as we walked aiming at the hedge in front. There was some incoming Spandau machine gun fire which didn't appear to be aimed at us, when suddenly I was hit and I collapsed to the ground in the midst of the standing corn.*

I felt alone and frightened then. I couldn't see anything but could hear my colleagues firing away in the distance. Cornfields in those days were quite high, waist even chest high... A man wounded, unable to move could get lost and left there; there was the added danger of being run over by a tank or Bren carrier and there was the danger of the corn being set alight, deliberately or by shelling, so you can perhaps realise how frightening it was. To minimise some of the danger, if he was able, the soldier would stick his rifle and bayonet into the ground, butt uppermost with his helmet on the top, which is what I was able to do. I don't think I was there too long before I was spotted by the Padre with a driver and jeep. I was placed on a stretcher and across the jeep there was already a wounded Jerry. We were carried off to the Regimental Aid Post in some farm buildings some distance behind from where we had started earlier that afternoon.

Back in England, Ron Beale's treatment continued for more than a year and it would be seven years before he was fit enough to pass the medical examination and join the Dorset Police.

---

22   Haddrell's friend, Stan Hodge, saw him fall and believed Bert had been killed. Sixty-eight years would pass before, by chance, the two friends met again.

Meanwhile the two-company attack had succeeded and at 1600 hours the 5th Dorsets were ordered to pass through to take Ondefontaine. However, they were held up in the woods by machine guns and tanks, and were ordered instead to take the high ground around La Roserie. While the Colonel was issuing his orders, Battalion Headquarters was heavily mortared. Two officers were wounded and the Padre, Francis Musgrave, who had just rescued Ron Beale, was killed.

In the morning mist of 3rd August, the 5th took their objective. Major Mead's B Company came under heavy fire from two machine gun positions but put both out of action, killing or capturing both crews. That afternoon the approach to Ondefontaine fell to Tilly's 4th Battalion, who attacked south from La Bigne. Despite heavy casualties in the attack, the 4th were able to repel a determined German counter-attack. A Canadian officer of the 4th Dorsets, Captain Ellis Andrews from New Brunswick, and his thirty-one-strong company were attacked by two German self-propelled guns and over a hundred infantry. Andrews, who had been wounded on Hill 112 on 18th July and had since rejoined the Battalion, beat off the attack after a two-hour battle, after which they were heavily shelled and mortared all night.

For their leadership in these battles Gerald Tilly of the 4th Dorsets received the Distinguished Service Order and Kenneth Mead of the 5th and Ellis Andrews of the 4th the Military Cross. Sadly Andrews would not live to receive his medal. He was killed a few days later, searching for one of his men who had not returned from a patrol. Twenty-five-year-old Ellis Andrews's courage and commitment were characteristic of the two dozen Canadian officers who served with the Regiment and enhanced its reputation.

In the next few days 130 Brigade moved south to play a supporting part in 129 Brigade's attack on Mont Pinçon. Meanwhile, not far away at Grimbosq on 6th, 7th and 8th August, Private Cox was maintaining the heroic record of Dorset Regiment stretcher-bearers. A Dorset from South Wales, attached to the Worcestershire Regiment, Cox led a team of their stretcher-bearers as they collected wounded men and carried them to safety 800 yards across ground swept by small arms, mortar and shell fire. At one point he dug out a wounded man who had been buried in a trench. He was later awarded a Military Medal.

By 9th August the 5th Dorsets were on Mont Pinçon itself. On 13th August General Ivor Thomas sacked Brigadier David Leslie and appointed Aubrey Coad to command 130 Brigade until a permanent brigadier arrived. Major Walter Venour, previously Second-in-Command of the 1/8th Middlesex Regiment, was appointed to succeed Coad. Venour was therefore commanding the 5th Dorsets when that

Regimental Sergeant-Major Jack Horton inspecting German prisoners

day they successfully attacked and captured Proussy. Although their casualties were not heavy, the Battalion lost three officers: Captain John Betts and Second Lieutenant Champion wounded and Lieutenant Alec Channell, attached from the Essex Regiment, killed. The 4th Battalion then took Le Fresnes for only two casualties. Brigadier Ben Walton, late of the Royal Warwickshires, now took over 130 Brigade and Aubrey Coad returned to his Battalion.

At heavy cost, Monty's plan had worked. The German army had been soundly defeated in Normandy, where the campaign was all but over, save for the final defeat of the remaining German troops in the slaughter-house known as the Falaise pocket. Now began a time of rapid, unopposed advances across France. The 5th Battalion's war diary recorded that *the move, although long, was interesting and we*

Crossing the Seine

*passed through villages and towns who were seeing British troops for the first time.
We were greeted everywhere by 'V' signs, salutes and gay faces, the troops giving
away many cigarettes to the male population and receiving... gifts of fruit, cider etc.*

The next possible line of defence for the Germans was the Seine, which 129
Brigade crossed at Vernon on 25th August. After a sharp battle for Vernonnet on
the opposite bank, the route north-east lay open and, two days later, both Dorset
battalions had been transported forward and were concentrated on the high ground
across the river. By this time the Germans were putting up only token defence and
both battalions spent the next two days clearing villages on the Division's route
towards Belgium. In one operation D Company of the 5th captured forty prisoners;
in another Captain Grocott was wounded when his carrier ran over a mine.

During a well-earned rest, the Brigade was visited by General Thomas, who
presented medal ribbons to members of both battalions who had survived the
Normandy campaign unscathed. But, by 10th September, they were on the move
again, chasing Second Army's rapid advance up through Northern France and into
Belgium, past places with legendary names like Arras and Vimy Ridge, towards
the Netherlands, where they would return to the battle.

Operation Market Garden

On 15th September Brigadier Ben Walton called a conference for all 130 Brigade's company commanders and above. At the village school in Hunberg near Diest, Walton briefed them on the plan for their part in Operation *Market Garden*, which was to begin two days later. In essence, 130 Brigade was to lead 43rd Wessex Division supporting Guards Armoured Division in the later stages of the advance. Their final objective – once the Waal and Neder Rijn had been crossed and 1st Airborne Division relieved in their positions north of the Neder Rijn – was the high ground south of Appledoorn, sixteen miles north of Arnhem. If the bridges at Nijmegen and Arnhem had been destroyed, they would have to be prepared for assault crossings. If the bridges had been captured intact, they would have to fight their way through the flat land – the island – in between, and then out into Dutch countryside north-east of Arnhem. Thus, while the 1st Dorsets would support the Guards Armoured Division in the initial stage of the operation, the 4th and 5th Battalions would assume the same role in its closing stages.

On 20th September both battalions in DUKWS pushed their way up the jammed road through Eindhoven. The 4th arrived south-west of Grave on the River Maas early the next morning and were ordered to remain there to guard the bridge. Reaching Hechtel, the 5th were ordered with the 7th Hampshires to clear Nijmegen on 21st September.

The warm reception they received was not the battle they had anticipated. The Germans had gone. Cheering crowds of Dutch civilians threw flowers at their vehicles and pressed apples and gifts on the bewildered soldiers. In this carnival atmosphere they pushed through the town and consolidated at the bridge, which had just been captured by the Shermans of the Grenadier Guards and the American 82nd Airborne Division. The road was strewn with corpses, most of them German, while a number of snipers who had climbed the bridge's high metal struts now swung lifelessly, suspended by their straps, high above it. The supports of the bridge were still laced with German explosives, which were being made safe by a courageous team of Sappers. The railway bridge was also unblown and it was discovered that, because of the way the tracks had been set into the ground, it could bear vehicles. There were therefore two functional bridges over the Waal, which was the last river before Arnhem.

By noon the 5th Dorsets were consolidated around both bridges. What none of them knew – or would know for thirty-six hours – was that that morning the Germans had finally recaptured Arnhem bridge. The epic stand by Colonel John

Frost's 2nd Parachute Regiment was over. The bridge over the Neder-Rijn was back in German hands, simultaneously denying XXX Corps an unopposed crossing and enabling the Germans to pour reinforcements southwards onto the island between Arnhem and Nijmegen.

The late morning of 21st September saw a gallant but abortive attempt by the Irish Guards to get up the road from Nijmegen. The island was not tank country. Flat and open, and criss-crossed by dykes, its narrow roads were exposed to the defenders' machine guns, anti-tank guns and artillery. The Irish Guards column reached Bemmel before being halted by German 88s. The only answer to this was a large force of infantry, who could operate off the roads. At this point 214 Brigade's Commander, Brigadier Essame, who had crossed Nijmegen railway bridge, arrived on the island. Essame agreed with the Guards brigadier that he should take Oosterhout, a village to the west of the road, but his leading battalion, the 7th Somersets, were still in Nijmegen and dusk was approaching. Despite their strenuous efforts (and principally because of the congested single road up which they were advancing), the infantry of 43rd Wessex Division had arrived just too late. The question now was whether XXX Corps could still salvage strategic success by forcing their way up to and across the Neder Rijn to reinforce the 1st Airborne Division on the north bank west of Arnhem.

At first light on the 22nd, the 7th Somersets and 5th Duke of Cornwall's Light Infantry advanced west of the road towards the blazing village of Oosterhout. Once the Somersets had taken the village after a tough battle with the SS troops defending it, the Cornwalls formed an armoured column. Riding on tanks of the 4/7th Royal Dragoon Guards, they fought their way through to Driel, south of the river and south-west of Arnhem. Here during the night they made contact with the Polish Airborne Brigade, who had landed on the south bank and were waiting to cross. They were also now within swimming distance of the 1st Airborne Division within their defensive perimeter around Oosterbeek north of the heavily swollen river. Despite the river's breadth and strong current, a senior officer of 1st Airborne had swum across to report his Division's situation. Nothing had been heard from Frost's men on Arnhem bridge for thirty-six hours and the rest of the Division were being relentlessly attacked and forced back towards the river.

The Cornwalls had taken with them two DUKWs loaded with supplies for the Airborne troops, but they were not nearly enough. Now, early on the 23rd, the 5th Dorsets were sent, followed by the rest of 130 Brigade, to join the Cornwalls and deliver more ammunition, medical supplies and food to the increasingly desperate

1st Airborne. Supported by a squadron of tanks from the 13/18th Hussars, the enormous 130 Brigade column made good progress but, as it negotiated a corner and crossed a narrow bridge, it was fired on by German tanks from the direction of Elst. The leading part of the column arrived safely at Driel after a ten-mile dash but the second half, commanded by Gerald Tilly, was held up. Infantry and anti-tank guns had to be deployed and smoke put down before the rear of the column could finally move on.

At Driel Aubrey Coad and his 5th Dorsets made contact with the 5th Cornwalls and reconnoitred the area. Coad positioned A and D Companies 1,000 yards apart, along the south bank of the river with the rest of the Battalion in an orchard half a mile behind. That night the Poles began to cross the Neder Rijn but, because the crossing had been delayed by a shortage of boats, only half got across before dawn. The 5th Cornwalls' DUKWs, attempting to ferry supplies across to the British Airborne troops, got stuck in the mud or were hit by shelling and mortaring. From some higher ground north of the river the Germans were able to see and shell the British positions on the south bank. During the day the shelling intensified while the Luftwaffe, infrequently seen since Normandy, roared low overhead, strafing the Dorsets' and Cornwalls' positions. RAF Dakotas and Halifaxes, flying heroically low despite the German anti-aircraft guns, paid a heavy price for doing their utmost to resupply Urquhart's men.

With Arnhem bridge back in enemy hands, 1st Airborne steadily being destroyed north of the river and it proving impossible to move supplies or reinforcements across the river, it was becoming clear to Miles Dempsey that *Market Garden* must be abandoned. But Brian Horrocks, reluctant to throw in his hand, ordered Butch Thomas to send the 4th Dorsets over the river with the remaining Polish Airborne troops to reinforce 1st Airborne's defensive perimeter. Brigadier Walton sent for Gerald Tilly and passed on the orders. The Dorsets' task was to broaden the base of the perimeter and to hold on until they were reinforced. It is said that General Boy Browning, commanding the Airborne Corps, had remembered his Grenadiers' humiliation at the hands of the 4th Battalion during the Territorials' Summer Camp at Corfe Castle in 1939 and had asked specifically that the 4th Dorsets be given this dangerous and difficult task. It was a peculiar and costly honour.

Several times during the afternoon of 24th September Tilly climbed up Driel church-tower to examine the crossing area by the ferry and the north bank where his men would land. At 1600, when he and his company commanders were up the tower, the German artillery shelled the church and shook the tower beneath them. Major Philip Roper, commanding C Company, remembered that from the tower:

We could see everything up to the trees which came down to the edge of the river on the north bank, but nothing in the trees on the ground which sloped steeply up from the river. Colonel Tilly said, 'Gentlemen, we've bought it this time.' I think he realised it was a pretty hairy operation. As for myself, I thought it unlikely we would get back. When I had my company O-Group I tried to water it down as much as possible and told them we were going to do an important job to help the airborne people.

At 1800 hours Walton sent for Tilly again. His orders had changed. Dempsey's view had prevailed. The 4th Battalion's task now, with the minimum troops required, was to cross the river in assault boats and defend a small perimeter north of the river while the survivors of 1st Airborne were withdrawn to the south bank. The Brigadier made no mention of how the 4th Dorsets themselves would be withdrawn and told Gerald Tilly that he need not go himself but could send his Second-in-Command. His briefing painted an ominous picture and Tilly was deeply disturbed at what his Battalion was being ordered to do. In the circumstances he resolved to go himself and personally chose the men to accompany him, selecting (in his own words) *those veterans who were absolutely sure – essential – leaving the others behind.* It was a good commanding officer's nightmare: having to choose the men who (again in Tilly's words) *were going to certain death.*

Tilly could not be entirely candid about the true purpose of the operation. Even the Battalion war diary records the intention of the operation as enlarging the bridgehead and getting supplies through to the Airborne troops. But he did confide in Jimmy Grafton,[23] his Second-in-Command, so that, if (as he expected) Tilly himself was killed, someone else would know the truth behind the orders he had had to give. *I'm afraid we're being chucked away,* he said.

H-Hour was set for 2145 but, after the 4th Dorsets had moved forward under murderous fire and reached their position south of the river, they found that their assault boats had not arrived. Tilly vented his frustration on the Sapper Colonel before speaking to Aubrey Coad. *Nothing's right,* he said. *The boats haven't come and we haven't been issued rations. If something isn't done soon, I'm not prepared to go.* Coad immediately ordered his own men to give their rations to their 4th Battalion comrades who were waiting for the boats.

This delay was nothing new. Precisely the same had happened to Major Julian Cook of US 82nd Airborne Division when he had crossed the Waal to help Guards Armoured Division take the bridge at Nijmegen. Once again, the congested single

---

23   After the war, Jimmy Grafton owned and ran a London pub – the Grafton Arms – acted as Harry Secombe's agent and wrote some of the early scripts for *The Goon Show.*

The 4th Dorsets near Arnhem

road exacted its toll. At midnight Tilly heard that his boats had reached Driel. When they finally arrived, they had to be carried under enemy fire 600 yards across an orchard and over various obstructions on their way to the river. Before they even reached the water one boat had been set on fire and several others holed.

At 0100 the first flight of boats, containing men from A and B Companies, pushed off from the south bank and immediately came under withering fire from several well-sited Spandaus. As they made the frightening crossing, twenty-year-old Private Alec Taylor of 3 Platoon in A Company confided to a friend that, as a Jew, he would rather be killed than captured.

Major Mike Whittle described B Company's crossing.

The enemy opened up with counter-fire, and at least two of the ten boats in my company group were holed badly before reaching the bank. We were launching the first boat when they opened up with MMG fire from the opposite bank, the boat sank, and we had several casualties. We discovered that this fire was on fixed lines and, by moving a few yards, the remainder of the boats were launched successfully.

There was a strong current, and my two leading boats were swept rapidly towards the west where the factory, about 400 yards downstream, was ablaze, and we should have been beautifully silhouetted. By using spades as well as the quite inadequate paddles we eventually landed about 100 yards east of the factory and got ashore without much trouble.

We moved forward to the edge of the trees about 50 yards from the river bank and waited for the remainder of the Company, but only two further boatloads joined us. It was subsequently discovered that, of our ten boats, three were holed before launching, one was swept downstream and landed below the burning factory, four crossed with us, and the other two were sunk during the crossing. On the spot the strength of B Company was two officers and less than 30 other ranks.

At 0215 the heavy enemy fire forced the Dorsets to stop trying to cross the river. By that time, of the 420 who had set out, some 240 had reached the other bank. Some were killed or wounded as they landed. Among them was Major Crocker, who was severely wounded in the legs. Under continual mortar and small arms fire, his batman, Private Driver, carried him 600 yards back to the river. Here he found an assault boat and brought Crocker back across the river, delivering him safely to the Regimental Aid Post. Later, Lionel Driver was awarded a Military Medal for his bravery.

The survivors, separated in the dark, found themselves under immediate, heavy attack from the well-positioned defending German troops. Scattered groups of Dorsets fought fierce little battles. Corporal Denis Longmate, a Chesterfield man serving in B Company, remembered: *It was sheer hell. German Spandau machine guns must have been in one line; we daren't raise our heads; we were completely bogged down. We were wet, confused, isolated with an illuminated, fast-flowing river behind us and a wooded area directly in front, but we daren't lift our heads to see what lay beyond. Word filtered through that Major Whittle was in a position near a building that was burning and at the sound of his whistle we were to make a bayonet charge up the steep woods to our front. The whistle blew, the charge was made, the Westerbouwing was ours. We had made a foothold, but not without casualties. An officer directed me with a small party into the woods to our right in an endeavour to make contact with the Airborne.*

Advancing into the woods, Longmate's depleted section ran into mortar fire and suffered more casualties. Seeing a German patrol, the three survivors held their fire until they were within Sten gun range. The silence following their sudden burst of fire was broken by a Brummy voice congratulating them on their shooting.

A sergeant from 1st Airborne approached, borrowed some ammunition for his Sten and took command of the little group.

Just before dawn, Colonel Tilly found himself with a party of men, mostly from Philip Roper's C Company, at the foot of a rise occupied by Germans, who began hurling grenades down on them. *Get them with the bayonet!* Tilly shouted as he scrambled up the hill. Wounded in the head, he was finally forced to surrender along with Roper and his men. Private Norman Francis from Manchester remembered that morning.

Dawn came and a jerry armoured car appeared at the end of one of the pathways and a corporal and one of the lads and myself were ordered to shoot him up with the Bren gun. I was very loath to leave the safety of the slit trench to set up the gun in the open, but we did it and gave jerry a full magazine and a half, about eighty rounds, but he just bowled off without returning our fire. I suppose his job was to locate us. We scuttled back into the trench and returned the jerry fire which was now quite heavy. We had pooled all the spare ammo and were running short. We could hear the jerries shouting to each other and the click of their bolts. My rifle was hot, but we kept up a steady fire. Where were our lads? Why didn't they reinforce us? If they didn't come soon, some poor bugger was going to get hurt.

To our astonishment our CO, Lieutenant-Colonel Tilly, shouted to us all to cease fire. He continued that our position was hopeless; our mission had been to draw the Germans away from the paratroopers for three hours whilst they were rescued. We had been in action for six hours and our ammunition was nearly exhausted, there was no way back, or hope of relief. His orders were to surrender. We were stunned; we had expected the might of the British Army behind us to reinforce the bridgehead we had made... and then relief, perhaps we were going to live after all... our officer then sent a prisoner back to his own lines with a message. Shortly afterwards, the jerries came out of the woods swinging their Schmeissers from side to side and we were a bit apprehensive to discover they were SS from the Herman Goering Division.

I flung the bolt from my rifle into the woods and taking a packet of woodbines from my pocket, offered one to a couple of our captors. They were quite pleased with them and I tried my few words of German out on them. One jerry gave me one of his fags; it was terrible and I asked him if they were made of pferde scheissen (horse shit) – this really got them rolling about and they told the other jerries what the Tommy had said about their fags. I didn't think it was that funny myself, but they seemed to be enjoying themselves and it broke the ice. The jerry prisoner passed by riding pillion on a motorcycle – I waved and he waved back. We were marched off. I kept my helmet and small pack for contingencies. We were joined by paratroopers and airborne and glider troops who had also been captured, marching in good order. Someone started singing 'Green grow the rushes o' and we all took it up. The lads straightened up and marched in great style and as we passed through a small village, the people gave us furtive V signs. Our singing upset jerry and they ran backwards and forwards, with rifles raised, to make us stop. Eventually they halted us and read the riot act and threatened us with their machine guns. Our officers, who were still with us, told us to be silent. It was a sight to see those exhausted dirty squaddies march as though they were on parade. We were deposited at an ex-Netherland barracks and issued with some horrible brownish bread and a lump of lard – it lay on the table neglected.

Also among those who surrendered was the pre-war Territorial Private Cliff Lloyd, who had recently returned to the Battalion having recovered from the shrapnel wound he had received on Hill 112. He and his fellow prisoners faced eight months' captivity, deprivation, hard labour and hunger.

Private Ginger Pearce, a Bren gunner, had somehow lost his own section and joined C Company. He recalled that they *found the fighting very confusing. Germans and Airborne all over the place, you had to hold your fire to some extent to try and check who it was, which made it all very dicey.*

Some of the Airborne passed through us the next night, very dark and raining, also very cold. That was the first time we knew the operation was to evacuate the Airborne; we understood we were there to reinforce them, so we were all saying "Where the hell are they going?" But of course everyone soon realised what our mission really was...

Not far away was Private Jackie Matthews, a signaller, who later recalled his capture with his friend Private *Duce* Caliendo.

Duce, the company runner and I started to make our way to the RV through dense woods in absolute darkness. We suddenly stopped, looking down the barrels of German rifles. I quickly turned the tuning dials off frequency on the radio set. We were blindfolded and marched to a house. After being interrogated and asked many questions, all our personal belongings were taken away. We were thrown into a cellar and left for several hours – frozen stiff. The Jerries gave us some water and tiny pieces of bully beef. The following night intense artillery and air bombardment started and Jerry started to retreat.

Matthews and Caliendo were able to slip away, reach the river, row themselves across using a damaged boat and tree branches as oars, and finally rejoin what was left of their Battalion.

Lieutenant Mac McDermott MC

Captain Mac McDermott led his platoon up a hill and, despite taking heavy casualties, fought a fierce battle with the defenders. He then took up a defensive position in a house, which his platoon held until ordered to withdraw the following night. Corporal Archie Smith had been left behind on the south bank when his boat overloaded but had finally managed to find another boat and get his section across. They now fought several encounters before holding a defensive position throughout the following day. Ordered to withdraw, Smith managed to find an abandoned boat and brought his men back. Two nights later, McDermott and Smith both volunteered to cross the river again to search for surviving comrades. Both were decorated, Dennis McDermott receiving a Military Cross and Archie Smith a Military Medal.

Major Jimmy Grafton, whose first boat had caught fire and who had had to board a second, had been told by Tilly to make sure that a letter containing Boy Browning's order to withdraw reached Urquhart. Grafton was one of relatively few 4th Dorsets to reach the 1st Airborne perimeter, where at one stage he was able to call down artillery support from 112th Field Regiment to disperse an attack by German tanks.

Meanwhile, on the south bank, at 1500 hours the 4th Battalion received their copy of Butch Thomas's orders for the withdrawal. Captain R F Hall, known as

Henry after the bandleader, immediately offered to swim the river to deliver the order. The previous day he had been prevented from crossing first when two of his boats were holed by mortar fire and for a third time when his boat was swept downstream. Now, on the following night, he swam the river and searched in vain through the woods on the north bank to find his Colonel and the remains of his Battalion. Finding no one, he finally swam back alone.

The evacuation began at 2200 on 25th September and the Dorsets on the south bank – the 5th Battalion and the remnants of the 4th – prepared to receive, direct, tend and feed the 1st Airborne survivors as they were ferried across. At 2330 the first small party of the 4th Dorsets arrived in an assault boat accompanied by a number of swimmers, including Major Mike Whittle. They brought news that Colonel Tilly was missing and Major Eyre assumed temporary command of the Battalion. When Whittle reported to Brigadier Walton, he found him with both Henry Hall (reporting his lack of success over the river) and General Butch Thomas. Ben Walton congratulated the young officers and told Thomas he would be recommending both for a Military Cross. When Thomas insisted that Mike Whittle should instead be court-martialled for retiring without orders, a stand-up row developed. Whittle and Hall looked on aghast as Walton refused to court-martial Whittle and was duly sacked. Hall received his MC; Whittle did not.[24] Months later, the unforgiving Thomas would even use the citation for the Bar to Aubrey Coad's DSO to criticise the previous commanders of the Brigade.

Major George Hartwell of the 5th Battalion described the task faced by those organising the evacuation.

The tremendous difficulties... can hardly be imagined. No lights could be used and the night was so dark that men had to walk in front of the vehicles, and even then could scarcely be seen by the drivers. Many vehicles slipped off the narrow roads into the ditch and had to be overturned in order to keep the way clear. Torrential rain was falling the whole time and the enemy continued to harass the area with shell and mortar fire. The guns fired a continuous barrage to cover the evacuation and tracer was used as a directional guide to the boats crossing the river.

During the evacuation the boat crews suffered severe casualties and the 5th's Pioneer Platoon played a major part in helping the courageous Sappers man the boats and keep them in action. Commanding the 5th's Pioneers was Sergeant Bob

24   The Dutch later corrected this injustice, appointing Mike Whittle an Officer of the Order of the Lion.

Rigler, who was mentioned in Despatches and later awarded the Dutch Order of the Bronze Lion for twice crossing the river under heavy fire and rescuing two boat-loads totalling twenty Airborne soldiers. Returning from his second trip, Rigler was surprised to find a German prisoner in one of the boats and asked him what he was doing there. It appears he had made friends with his Airborne captors and had chosen to stick with them.

The main reception point for the evacuees, which was D Company's area, was intensively mortared, receiving 200 bombs in thirty minutes. The 5th's Intelligence Section set up an observation post in an attic to try to spot Dorsets on the north bank while, as we have heard, Captain McDermott and Corporal Smith went back across the river to search for their missing comrades.

General Horrocks recalled: *When I returned, at 10am next day* [26th September]*, from a meeting with the Second Army Commander, I found a very gloomy atmos-phere awaiting me. About 300 men of the 4th Dorsets had crossed under annihi-lating fire but all communications with them had now ceased. I learned afterwards that they held on grimly for thirty-six hours and I am certain that this very gallant battalion had a lot to do with the fact that on the next night we managed to evacuate some 2,400 paratroops to the south bank. Alas, very few of the 4th made that night-mare return trip.*

Some 315 men of Gerald Tilly's Battalion had fought their way across the river and had sacrificed themselves to evacuate 1st Airborne's survivors. Only seventy-five who crossed the river came back. Among those who returned was Corporal Denis Longmate. During the long day of 25th September his new-found friend the Airborne Sergeant had collected an officer and other lost souls, and their group had grown to platoon strength. On the 26th, having lost their officer, they were lucky enough to find a boat back across the river. About 250 officers and men of the 4th Dorsets had been killed, wounded or captured. For the second time in ten weeks, the 4th Battalion had effectively been destroyed. Among the dead was Private Alec Taylor, the Jewish soldier from Stoke Newington who – as he had predicted – had chosen death rather than capture.

On 28th September Brian Horrocks visited the 4th Dorsets and spoke to all the surviving officers, warrant officers and sergeants. Nor did Boy Browning, the Airborne Corps Commander, overlook their sacrifice. He awarded the 4th Battalion the unique distinction of an Airborne Pennant, embroidered with the Dorset regi-mental crest, to be carried with the Colours. The 4th Dorsets would be the only non-Airborne battalion to win the battle honour *Arnhem*. Their courage and sacri-fice had earned this honour in full measure.

Among the Airborne troops captured at Arnhem was another Dorset, Lieutenant Raymond Bussell, who had been commissioned into the Regiment in 1937. Put on a train to Germany with other wounded prisoners of war, Bussell and another officer escaped. Recaptured, on 10th October 1944 they were shot by Untersturmbahnfuhrer Heinemann of the Sicherheitdienst. After the war Heinemann was tried and executed for this and two score other murders he had committed.

Operation *Market Garden* had fallen at the last fence, failing in its strategic purpose and costing eighty per cent of the 1st Airborne Division at Arnhem and in the perimeter north of the river. In the process it had liberated a large area of the Netherlands, including the island between Nijmegen and Arnhem which was still hotly contested and which 43rd Wessex Division now had to hold.

Between 28th September and 4th October the 5th Dorsets faced repeated attacks from their right by the Germans from 116th Panzer Division while, to the south-east, 214 and 129 Brigades confronted a similarly close and aggressive enemy. One of these attacks was described in a piece which appeared in a Liverpool newspaper.

A platoon commanded by Lieutenant K [Ken] Homer, of 122 Waldegrave Road, Liverpool 15, gave valuable help from a flank with its Bren guns when the Dorsets were holding positions on the south bank of the River Lek in Holland.

A platoon led by Lieutenant P I [Peter] Thorpe, of Chiswick, was situated right under the dyke road on the river bank, with a railway embankment running down the right flank. Some 250 yards in the rear of the platoon positions was a cabbage field from which our Bren gunners had periodically opened up in order to deceive the enemy as to the exact location of our forces. After firing several bursts the Bren gunners would withdraw again to the platoon's real position.

This ruse was completely successful. When the German attack came in over the railway embankment, it was this cabbage field which they made for. 'I was shaving at the time', said Lieutenant Thorpe. 'Somebody shouted "Look!" and there was a mass of field grey pouring down the embankment. At once our Bren gunners opened up on the Germans as they made for the cabbage field. They had crossed our flank, and were within 300 yards of us. We opened up with everything we'd got, and shot them up.'

Containing the enemy in the cabbage field, Lieutenant Thorpe got his Bren gun carrier section up and thickened up the fire. The artillery was brought to bear on the target with great success, in spite of the close proximity of our own men. Two tanks also came in to support the infantry, while a platoon commanded by Lieutenant Homer gave valuable help from a flank with its Bren guns.

'We never lost a man in that attack', said Lieutenant Thorpe. 'The Germans had been deceived by our manoeuvre with the Bren guns. At one stage two Germans came forward waving white flags. We shouted to them to come in, but they suddenly made a dash for it up the embankment when they were 100 yards away. We shot one, and the other was pretty heavy by the time he disappeared over the top.'

Of the attacking force of some 150 Germans, the platoon of the Dorsets killed approximately 45, wounded many others and took six prisoners without a casualty to themselves.

Firing from a flank with his Bren gun, Private J Harrison, of Birmingham, was wounded in the arm, but returned to his Bren to continue to engage the enemy. Later in the evening the platoon was mortared heavily. Private L [Leslie] *Hickling, of Plymouth, went through the mortar fire to help a wounded comrade and stayed with him in the open under the heavy mortar fire.* [Leslie Hickling was later mentioned in Despatches.]

A knocked out Panther near Elst

First to give warning of this surprise attack was Private F Cane of Aldeburgh. He was actually picking pears from a tree when he suddenly saw the enemy appear.

When a German self-propelled gun rumbled along the railway embankment and approached their position, the 5th Dorsets knocked it out before it had a chance to rotate its gun in their direction. Discovering that the Germans were less than a hundred yards away, Captain Jack Gilders of the 112th Field Regiment employed just one of his twenty-five-pounders to snipe them out. His was another display of the professionalism that so often won the Royal Artillery the unqualified admiration of their infantry comrades.

On 4th October the 4th Battalion were withdrawn into reserve to receive reinforcements and a new Colonel, Bill Roberts of the Somerset Light Infantry. Next day the 5th were relieved by a battalion from the US 101st Airborne Division. Aubrey Coad left to take over 130 Brigade and his Second-in-Command, Walter Venour, succeeded him in command of the 5th Battalion.

THE REICHSWALD FOREST

Both battalions now moved to a reserve position in the Reichswald Forest, southeast of Nijmegen, around the village of Groesbeek on the Dutch–German border. They would spend a month here, in and out of the forward positions occupying and patrolling the woods and farmland towards the banks of the Maas. Lieutenant Sydney Jary, a platoon commander in the neighbouring 4th Somerset Light Infantry, later recalled his experience occupying this area.

The countryside was beautiful in its autumn colours and, after Elst, the opposition seemed uninspired. Groesbeek was mostly an area of active patrolling and, because of mortar bombs bursting in the treetops, a place where there was a vital need for headcover over our slit trenches. When mortar bombs burst high above ground level their splintered casings showered into the open trenches and caused grievous wounds to the occupants. To prevent this, we covered one end of our trenches with planks, or perhaps a door wrenched from a building, which we covered with soil removed from the trench. This protected us from splinters from 88mm airburst shells and it kept the rain out too!

I remember nights in defensive positions like Groesbeek, stretched out in a slit trench, trying to get an hour's sleep before going round the Platoon positions to check that everything and everyone was all right. One felt and was dirty and in the small hours of the morning, with boot laces cutting into swollen feet, a foul-tasting mouth and an aching stomach, life had little to commend it.

The Dorsets' experience was similar. During the month, both battalions carried out countless reconnaissance and fighting patrols. On 15th October Lieutenant Peter Thorpe of the 5th led a particularly successful reconnaissance patrol just inside the German border. Two nights later, the 4th sent out a fighting patrol to attack the enemy in a village street. When the leader and Second-in-Command of the patrol were both wounded, Private Hyans took command, personally killed three Germans and withdrew the patrol with only one man missing.

On 22nd October Lance-Corporal Norman Harris from Southampton, who had joined the 5th Battalion with his older brother Frederick, was called to see his Company Commander. He later remembered: *I was told my brother had been killed in the next trench to me by a mortar. I knew I had to do something so I asked if I could have the privilege of burying my brother.*

On the 27th Lance-Corporal Vigg of the 4th Battalion, silently observing German activity from a hidden observation post, crawled forward fifty yards to get a better view before shooting two Germans and wounding two more. He then became involved in a single-handed firefight with twenty more Germans, who threw grenades at him, but he managed to withdraw with valuable intelligence about the enemy strength and dispositions. Peter Thorpe was later awarded the Military Cross and Peter Hyans and Sidney Vigg the Military Medal.

GEILENKIRCHEN

On 11th November, as colder weather set in and autumn turned to winter, 43rd Wessex Division were ordered a hundred miles south to the area north-east of Maastricht around Sittard and Geilenkirchen to what became known as the Roer Triangle. Now on the far right flank of the British and Canadian armies, the Division were to protect the left flank of the US 9th Army as they pushed towards Cologne. With the US 84th Division on their right, their immediate task was to take the town of Geilenkirchen.

The 4th Battalion's history describes their time west of Geilenkirchen as the most frustrating period in the campaign: *every time the 4th Dorsets were ordered to go into action the orders were cancelled.* For Bill Roberts's Battalion it was a period of cold, discomfort and disappointment, which was spent in the dispiriting

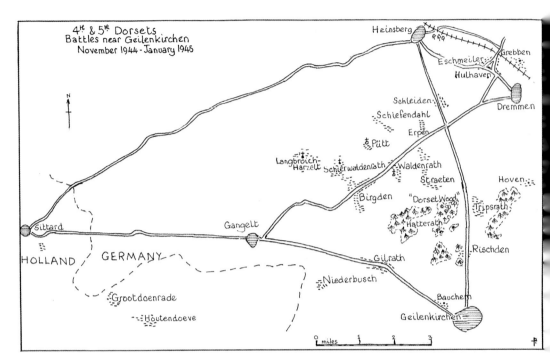

Battles around Geilenkirchen November 1944–January 1945

task of supporting other battalions in the battle. The 5th, however, found itself in the thick of the battle when, on 18th November, they attacked Bauchem, a village beside Geilenkirchen. After a cataclysmic artillery barrage, which killed all the enemy artillery and mortar officers, they advanced against little opposition. The Dorsets captured the line of trenches short of the village before clearing first the outskirts and then the village itself. For only four casualties, they had taken 182 prisoners, but one of the casualties was Sergeant Ted Worth's Platoon Commander. Worth rallied his platoon and led them in a successful charge against the objective, personally accounting for some of the enemy there. His bravery and leadership on that day, and on some of his very successful patrols, led to the award of a Military Medal.

Instead of going into reserve as they had anticipated, the 5th Dorsets received a visit from their new Brigadier, Aubrey Coad. Coad ordered his old Battalion to clear the Germans from the woods west of the village of Tripsrath, where they were counter-attacking the 1st Worcesters. At 1345 hours on 20th November they set off, accompanied by a squadron of tanks from the 13/18th Hussars. Under cover of smoke A and C Companies crossed some open ground and began to clear the

Lance-Corporal Biddy Boyce MM

woods. When crossing a clearing they came under heavy machine gun fire and lost several men killed and wounded. Among the killed was Lieutenant Arthur Kaye, who was attached from the Royal Berkshire Regiment.

Lance-Corporal Les Boyce, who was Number 1 on his platoon's 2-inch mortar, was wounded as they crossed the start line but, despite losing a great deal of blood, carried on throughout the attack providing support for his comrades. At one point he found his friend Norman Harris, who had buried his own brother four weeks earlier at Groesbeek and now was lying severely wounded by an 88 shell fired by a tank. Boyce picked Harris up, propped him against a tree and covered him up. Later both would be evacuated to England and both would recover, although Norman Harris would have a leg amputated above the knee. Biddy Boyce was awarded the Military Medal for his courage and self-sacrifice. The two men remained friends for the rest of their lives.

Another 5th Dorset who won the MM that day was Private Edwin Furey, who was in the six-strong leading section of a forward company in a clearing in the middle of a large wood when suddenly they encountered a party of twelve enemy. On his own initiative, the appropriately named Furey ran at them, shouting as he charged. The terrified enemy, who outnumbered Furey's section two to one, surrendered.

Meanwhile, Colonel Venour ordered George Hartwell to take D Company round to the left to provide fire support for the advance by A and C, but reaching the point from where they could bring fire to bear took D Company several hours and night fell.

Overnight the plan was refined and, in the morning, B Company were moved up beside D, who were now clearing the woods. The 4th Battalion lent their own A Company to provide support behind the companies of the 5th, who were all engaged. During the battle A and C Companies lost heavily, but the Battalion seized the position overlooking Straeten and Waldenrath. Tanks could not reach them because the going was so muddy, but the Gunners as usual turned up trumps and dispersed a number of German counter-attacks before they had got going. Sadly Captain Jack Gilders, one of 112th Field Regiment's gallant forward observation officers who were accompanying B Company, was killed. Despite the appalling ground conditions, a troop of tanks finally managed to reach D Company and Captain Geoffrey Hodgson succeeded in bringing up some of his platoon's anti-tank guns.

That night the 4th Battalion relieved the 5th, who in reserve were visited by General Thomas and Brigadier Coad and told that, in honour of their achievement, the area would now be known as *Dorset Wood*. The honour was hard-earned. The conditions the Dorsets experienced in these winter battles around Geilenkirchen made life almost insupportable. The relentless cold bit to the bone while they lived, moved and fought in a sea of mud. Tanks, half-tracks and carriers slithered and slewed precariously as they battled their way through menacing woods and low-lying ground, waterlogged and pock-marked by shell holes, to complete their grim tasks. Here, in November 1944, the infantrymen of 43rd Wessex Division suffered discomfort and deprivation in a desolate landscape reminiscent of the very worst their fathers' generation had experienced in Flanders twenty-seven years before.

On 26th November Sergeant Richard Gargrave, who had been wounded in July, rejoined the 5th in these appalling conditions. Originally an East Surrey – he had been transferred to the 5th Dorsets in England in June 1944 – he would survive the rest of the campaign and remain a Dorset, soldiering on in peacetime with the 4th and 1st Battalions in Italy, Germany and England until 1953, by which time he was a Colour Sergeant.

Private Ginger Pearce of the 4th's Carrier Platoon, who had also fought in Normandy and crossed the river at Arnhem and returned, remembered

Geilenkirchen as *probably our toughest time in the whole campaign... It was our first fight on German soil and the weather was very wet and freezing cold. The Battalion lost twenty-five per cent of its strength with bronchitis, pneumonia and trench foot alone. We were outside the whole time with no cover, living in holes in the ground. Goodness knows how the Divisional medical people kept up with it all, as there were heavy casualties from the fighting as well.*

We were subjected to heavy shelling for a fortnight from the big guns mounted in the Siegfried Line. These caused many casualties; no one was singing about hanging their washing out on it.

During the 4th's seemingly interminable, eight-day occupation of Dorset Wood, contact was temporarily lost with D Company, who in the bitter cold had to survive twenty-four hours without food or water. The Quartermaster, Captain Sam Titterington, was later appointed MBE for his tireless work supplying his scattered Battalion in these ghastly conditions.[25] Private Mason, a company runner attached to Battalion Headquarters, was awarded the American Silver Star for continually making the 1,400-yard journey back to his Company, carrying messages and guiding patrols and ration parties. Private Victor Lawson of the Signal Platoon also earned a Military Medal for continually going out in these dangerous and unpleasant conditions to repair the lines. He did this under heavy mortar and shell fire and with no cover. Under this shelling Sergeant Edward Harris kept his platoon's morale and fighting efficiency at a high standard – as he had done in Normandy and at Arnhem; his leadership and courage throughout the long campaign would later be recognised by the award of a Military Medal. In these dangerous and testing conditions Colonel Bill Roberts and his Intelligence Officer, Lieutenant John Adams, spent long hours of each day trudging through the mud to visit each company.

On 28th November Dorset Wood was heavily shelled and an ammunition pit containing high explosive and phosphorous bombs was hit and caught fire. Sergeant Percy Hopkins, a Scot from Bridge of Weir, immediately jumped into the pit, removed the burning phosphorous bombs and buried them. His outstanding bravery, which saved the lives of countless men, was later recognised by the award of a Military Medal.

Once again, instead of going into reserve, the 5th Battalion were sent to defend the village of Birgden, where they experienced similar conditions to those endured

25   The Dorsets' experience led to all infantry battalions being ordered to issue 24-hour emergency ration packs to soldiers to avoid a repetition of this level of hardship.

by the 4th. Here their dispersed units lost a ration party and some men from a listening post, who had been snatched by cadets from a German officer training school. The bodies of two of the missing men were later found; they had been bayoneted in the back.

Briefly back in reserve, the 5th were visited by Field Marshal Montgomery, who congratulated them on their recent performance. At one stage they occupied a house as a headquarters. Captain Maurice Edwards remembered investigating the cellar.

As I was poking about I saw two pieces of wire sticking out of the cellar wall... I tried tapping the wood with a stick; this made a hollow sound and I guessed there was some kind of room behind... I set the lads to work pulling the wall out and knocking the wooden partition down and what a surprise we got. Behind the partition was another room and in it was the most amazing collection of loot I have ever seen. Piled high was everything you could think of: pickled eggs which the lads enjoyed every morning for a week, trunks and trunks of new civilian clothing still in boxes, wedding presents, three or four boxes of cutlery, armchairs, cycle tyres, and many more articles, all first class in quality and mostly brand new. The Boches must have spent many hours building their secret store, but they will be very much out of luck if any of them ever return. We have given it to the proper authorities for proper distribution.

When they returned to the line it was to Hoven Woods. In the biting cold and in almost impassable mud, still strewn with the dead of the Cornwalls who had captured it, their days in those dark, low-lying woods must have tested even the most cheerful and resilient among them. But at the end of the first week of December both battalions were withdrawn to prepare for the next part of the Roer offensive.

By 7th December they were back at Hoensbroek between Geilenkirchen and Maastricht. Both battalions received reinforcements from the 1st Dorsets, who had now returned to England. Among them, Lieutenant Frank Shackell, whom we last met on the island with the 1st Battalion, took over a platoon in Mike Whittle's B Company in the 4th. It was here that, on 16th December, they heard of the massive German attack on the Americans in the Ardennes.

Marshal Von Runstedt's plan was to exploit the weakness in Eisenhower's broad front strategy by driving a wedge between his dispersed armies before seizing Antwerp and then encircling four Allied armies from behind. Although many American troops fought bravely, this sudden onslaught threw their higher command into disarray and uncertainty. The German advance punched a substantial salient

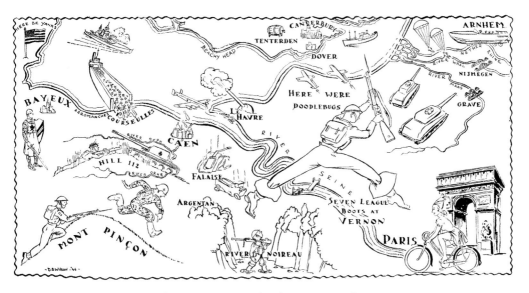

43rd Wessex Division's Christmas card 1944

in the Allied line and threatened worse still. Montgomery, in a characteristic cock-tail of insufferable cockiness and consummate professionalism, urged Eisenhower to put Bradley in charge of the American troops south of the "bulge" and him in charge of those to the north. He then despatched units of XXX Corps to provide a line of defence to block any German advance to the north-west. The units of 43rd Wessex Division therefore found themselves dispersed into defensive positions along and above the River Meuse. Thus it was that the 4th and 5th Dorsets spent Christmas twelve miles north of the Meuse at Waremme in Belgium.

The Germans never came their way. On Boxing Day their advance was halted short of the Meuse and, by mid-January, the Ardennes offensive had petered out, the German forces squeezed between the Allied armies to their north and south. In early January the 43rd Wessex Division returned to its original task in the now snow-covered Roer Triangle. Before each battle, their company commanders were able to take to the air in flimsy Auster aircraft to study the terrain north of Geilenkirchen.

On 21st January, in their first full battalion action since Arnhem, the 4th attacked Schierwaldenrath, three miles north of Niederbusch. In the winter conditions many of the men had been issued with snow suits while the Shermans supporting them sported white sheets. Despite having to negotiate mines in the frozen ground and hidden booby traps, the advancing troops met little resistance, capturing four-teen prisoners for the loss of two casualties themselves.

Once again the Germans were on the retreat. Langbroich Harzelt, the 5th's objective on the 21st, was found to be undefended and was rapidly occupied and consolidated. That night, however, the 4th suffered some casualties from German shelling. Four days later both battalions took their final objectives with little or no German opposition, although in their advance the 4th lost a carrier and one of their supporting tanks to mines.

CLOSING UP TO THE RHINE

These battles proved to be the Dorsets' last around Geilenkirchen. By the end of January the campaign was won and the Division returned north to the area east of Nijmegen, where Monty had prepared his next offensive. Known as Operation *Veritable*, it would breach the Siegfried Line and enable his armies to close up to the Rhine. For this battle Horrocks's XXX Corps would fight under the command of the Canadian First Army.

In the 5th Battalion Major Tim Hope-Thomson, a Royal Scots Fusilier who had been Second-in-Command since November, was promoted to command the 1st Worcesters in 214 Brigade. In his place came Skinny Laugher, whom we last met with the 1st Battalion winning an MC on the island south of Arnhem.

The offensive began on 8th February and, next afternoon, the 43rd Wessex Division concentrated near Nijmegen, which was being heavily shelled. A gasometer was hit and exploded, propelling its top high into the air. Here, while 129 Brigade went first into battle, the men of 130 Brigade waited their turn. It came on 13th February, when they moved through the debris of the town of Cleves, which had been flattened by Bomber Command, and relieved the Somersets and Wiltshires in the Reichswald Forest south of Bedburg. The Dorsets were now firmly on German soil, facing elite German parachute troops and Wehrmacht units, all of whom would fight fiercely to defend their homeland and to prevent the Allies from reaching the Rhine.

At 1000 hours on 15th February the 4th Dorsets assembled to take over the next stage of the advance. Their objective was three hamlets held by a German parachute battalion on the escarpment overlooking Goch.

Major Joe Symonds[26] of A Company recalled the unprecedented weight of German artillery fire on the Battalion as it formed up. His Company then advanced,

---

26   Having recovered from his wounds sustained in Normandy, Joe Symonds had been unable to return to the Regiment. A letter to General Thomas asking for help resulted in a posting to the Cameronians in Scotland. He then returned with them to Belgium, where

Battle for the Rhineland, Rhine Crossing and Advance to Bremerhaven
February–May 1945

led by Lieutenant Girardot of 2 Platoon, who *came under heavy small arms fire from the houses and gardens on the high ground to our front before we had gone far, and was pinned to the ground, Lieutenant Girardot being wounded and Sergeant Gregory killed. After locating the enemy positions with some difficulty, I launched an attack with No 1 Platoon under... Lieutenant Pope. No 3 Platoon had got somewhat broken*

---

he found himself within four miles of the 4th Dorsets. He simply took himself over to join his old Battalion. As he explained to his son, years later: *As a major with an MC you can do what you like.*

up by the enemy defensive fire and could not be got into the attack, so the remaining members supported No 1 Platoon's attack with two-inch mortar smoke and small arms fire.

Supporting artillery fire could not be as heavy as usual because of the shortage of shells resulting from the flooded roads behind them. Meanwhile the 300 guns the German artillery had mustered seemed to suffer no such shortage and, augmented by their mortars, maintained a murderous barrage on the Dorsets throughout the battle.

No 1 Platoon assaulted with splendid courage but was badly shot up... by the German paratroopers, who were dug in in the cellars of the houses...

By this time we had been able to get a troop of Shermans up... so I launched another assault on the enemy positions with the available members of No 3 Platoon and... remaining members of Nos 1 and 2... This assault... went well and the Germans ran out of the rear of the houses as we rushed in through the front gardens. We were able to shoot down a good many of them as they withdrew across the open fields...

C Company on our right met equally stiff opposition and had to fight very hard to capture the houses on the high ground to their immediate front... Although neither A nor C Companies had yet reached their allotted objectives, they did in fact overcome the enemy and capture his principal positions, and the remainder of the Germans withdrew.

As both my officers were badly wounded and my company much depleted, I consolidated on the captured ground at about 1220 hours, as did C Company for similar reasons.

The citation for the Bar to Joe Symonds's Military Cross describes what he omits from his account: that *he was everywhere about the battlefield inspiring his men by his own total disregard for personal safety...* He was finally badly burned when one of the Shermans from which he was directing the battle was knocked out by a Panzerfaust but, despite intense pain, he refused to go back until the position was consolidated.

When C Company's commander was wounded, the Second-in-Command, Captain John Kirkwood, led the Company forward, through machine gun, mortar and shell fire, and secured its objectives. Meanwhile, Lieutenant Tilling (attached from the South Lancashire Regiment) led his platoon forward to cover, from where they returned the enemy's fire. He then ran back, under heavy fire, to bring up the troop of supporting tanks. Riding on the leading tank, he directed its fire against enemy positions in the houses before rejoining his platoon to lead them to clear a number of buildings. Miraculously unwounded, Ronald Tilling was later given a Military Cross. For his bravery here and later, across the Rhine at Millingen, John Kirkwood also received an MC.

Meanwhile, one of C Company's stretcher-bearers, Private Apps, went out time and again under relentless fire to rescue and tend the wounded, single-handedly carrying several of them back to the shelter of a building, until finally he too was wounded. Harold Apps was awarded a Military Medal. So was Corporal Stan Hodge, a nineteen-year-old veteran of Normandy, who attacked the German Spandau positions, firing his Bren from the hip.

But neither the 4th Dorsets' gallant efforts nor those of the 7th Hampshires who took on the next phase of the advance kept pace with the ambitious timetable set by General Thomas. The delay required the postponement of the 5th Dorsets' involvement, which had originally been scheduled for the afternoon but now became a night attack. Advancing with little idea of where the enemy were or even the positions of the 7th Hampshires, George Hartwell's D Company were shot at by both sides and suffered several casualties when they arrived on the scene in the midst of a German counter-attack on the Hampshires. With dawn approaching, Colonel Venour decided to renew the attack in daylight when they could see what they were doing.

At 0930 hours on 16th February Major Robert Hewson's C Company picked their way across country, found some German communication trenches and captured their objective with minimal opposition. A Company, under Major Harry Allen, were held up by heavy shelling and suffered severe casualties until their own supporting artillery silenced the enemy fire. Four battalions – 214 Brigade plus the 4th Somersets – now passed through to continue the advance towards and finally onto the Goch escarpment. When that evening B Company moved forward onto A Company's original objective, two of their officers were killed. Today the graves of Lieutenant John Hannam, attached from the Bedfordshire and Hertfordshire Regiment, and Lieutenant Donald Bridgland, attached from the Seaforth Highlanders, stand close together in the huge cemetery in the Reichswald Forest, where so many young men from the 4th and 5th Dorsets found their final resting place.

130 Brigade had now completed its costly role in Operation *Veritable*. 214 and 129 Brigades would complete 43rd Wessex Division's part, which would end on 9th March with the capture and consolidation of Xanten – Siegfried's birthplace – on the Rhine. The German army had been thoroughly defeated in the Reichswald just as it had been in Normandy. The Divisional historian described the Reichswald

as *the greatest ordeal since Normandy. For a whole month in almost unspeakable conditions of danger and exposure the troops were almost continuously in action. At no time were commanders placed under greater strain or for so long. Nevertheless morale and fighting efficiency probably reached its highest level at this time... The Division faced the flower of the German army fighting for their country with fatalistic courage, as all men should fight, and beat them in the open field.*

For Walter Venour, who was attached from the Manchester Regiment, this was his last battle. He was posted back to England, having commanded the 5th Dorsets since Arnhem. During that time he had fought his Battalion successfully in the battles around Geilenkirchen, where he had won a DSO for his leadership and fighting spirit. He was succeeded by Speedy Bredin, who now arrived to find the redoubtable Skinny Laugher as his Second-in-Command. The 5th Battalion would remain in good hands as they and the 4th prepared to cross the Rhine.

Before leaving the west bank of the Rhine, we must not overlook the reappearance of Peter Stephenson – Young Steve. We last met him in May 1940, when his platoon provided the rearguard for the 2nd Dorsets' final retreat onto the beach at Dunkirk. When last we heard of him he had successfully disengaged, hopped on a boat and brought his men safely back to England. Since then he had gone up in the world. Transferring to the RAF, he had trained as a pilot and specialised in photographic reconnaissance, first with 4 Squadron, where he won a Distinguished Flying Cross. Now he was commanding 268 Squadron, flying American Mustangs fitted with Rolls Royce engines. The citation for the Bar to his DFC tells his story.

On 4 February Squadron Leader Stephenson's Squadron was ordered to photograph a 3-mile stretch of the Rhine at ground level, beginning at Emmerich, one of the most strongly defended sections of the river. He undertook the task himself.

Owing to low cloud his section flew to Emmerich at ground level over an area which is known to be full of anti-aircraft defences. He then ordered his No 2 to fly at a safe height and himself carried out his photographic run past Emmerich down the centre of the river at water level.

Squadron Leader Stephenson carried out the entire photographic run, although the anti-aircraft fire was continuous, intense and accurate and was coming from batteries on both sides of the river. At one stage, in order not to miss any of the river banks, he flew under 8 high tension cables stretching across the river, the pylons showing clearly above the aircraft in the photographs.

This extremely dangerous sortie was flown with very great courage and skill against odds which were theoretically almost impossible.

Had the officers and men of the 5th Dorsets – who were to be the first of the Division's fighting units to reach the east bank of the Rhine – known that a fellow Dorset had risked his life to gather the intelligence to help save theirs, they would have been amused, pleased and proud in equal measure.

ACROSS THE RHINE

A week before the first British troops crossed the Rhine, Speedy Bredin flew home to attend the 1st Battalion's very special investiture at Buckingham Palace. On his return he learnt that on 25th March his new Battalion would be leading the Division across the river, two days after the initial assault by units of the 51st Highland Division. The 43rd Wessex Division's role would be to enlarge the bridgehead, and 130 Brigade's objective would be to capture the small town of Millingen, three miles due north of the crossing place at Rees. Bredin briefed his men on 23rd March and, that evening, 400 guns opened a devastating barrage on the German positions. A little later 227 Lancasters and Halifaxes passed overhead on their way to bomb Wesel. Then a fleet of 4,000 transport aircraft with 1,200 fighters filled the sky en route to deliver the airborne troops to their dropping zones.

Leading the crossing was the 1st Commando Brigade, leading the 1st Commando Brigade was Number 6 Commando and leading Number 6 Commando was a Dorset – Tony Lewis. Lewis led his Commandos with such speed that they had landed, over-run three enemy platoon positions, taken the city of Wesel and allowed the whole Commando Brigade to consolidate its defence before the Germans had been able to react. He won a DSO for his leadership, dash and courage in this whirlwind assault, which epitomised the Commandos' raison d'être. Later, the French would award him a Croix de Guerre. Among Lewis's Commandos was another Dorset, Leonard Penn. Aged twenty and serving as Number One on a Bren gun, Penn served with great gallantry with 6 Commando from Normandy until the very end. During the campaign he was three times recommended for a Military Medal and finally received one thanks to the persistence of Tony Lewis. Lewis will rejoin our story in Japan in 1946 as Second-in-Command to Knocker White: a high-octane combination if ever there was one.

130 Brigade crossed the Rhine during the sunny afternoon of 25th March and, soon after assembling ashore, the 5th Dorsets received orders to attack the villages of Speldrop and Androp. They attacked at 0130 hours on 26th March and took

The 5th Dorsets cross the Rhine

Speldrop without opposition, finding only a few German troops hiding in cellars. But the approach to Androp was overlooked from some high ground and any movement brought down heavy shelling.

Meanwhile, the 4th Dorsets, who had crossed the Rhine in the early hours of 26th March, were able to approach Millingen from a different angle. After a rocket attack by RAF Typhoons and an artillery stonk and smokescreen, the 4th began their attack at 1515 hours. A Company, under Joe Symonds (who had already returned despite the severe burns he had suffered near Goch), took the approach to the village and the bridge over the river. D Company then extended the bridgehead to the right before B cleared the ground for a mile to the south-east.

For the attacking infantry street-fighting was a frightening, frustrating and costly business. Every corner and every room of every house could hide a silent enemy. Many houses had cellars, which could hide a whole platoon – or a group of terrified civilians hiding from the battle above. How to clear them? Sending a man down spelt certain death if the defenders were there and still ready for a fight. Tossing a grenade down the stairs would kill or maim any civilians – perhaps women and children – who were sheltering there.

In the street-fighting and house-clearing in Millingen, Lance-Sergeant Frank Stretch from Wareham was leading a rifle section in D Company. In the battle he killed one German, wounded two more and captured twenty-seven prisoners armed with two Spandaus, two Schmeissers and twenty rifles. He was awarded the Military Medal. Meanwhile, Private Hill, a Bren-gunner in A Company, bounded from house to house, supporting his own section while they cleared the German troops from one building after another.

At the cost of no Dorset lives and a handful of casualties, by 0200 on 27th March Millingen, the Division's first objective beyond the Rhine, had been cleared and consolidated. They had taken 190 prisoners. Colonel Roberts received a Bar to his DSO for his own courageous leadership and his Battalion's performance in this highly successful battle. Newly commissioned Second Lieutenant Wally Caines remembered: *Hundreds of worn-out and bomb happy Germans taken prisoner, many of them running at the double.*

Late on 28th March 130 Brigade captured Landfort, where the retreating Germans had blown the only bridge over the Oude Ijssel. The 5th therefore had to take to assault boats to cross the river at night and take the far bank. Although their advance along the river banks encountered no resistance, some skirmishes developed in the woods and houses beyond. In one such skirmish Sergeant Herbert Foster won the Military Medal attacking and clearing houses. In another Private

Herbert Hill of the 4th Dorsets – who had distinguished himself two days earlier at Millingen – again covered his section in the attack. This time he stood under fire, firing his Bren gun from the hip, until he was wounded. Happily he survived to receive a Military Medal.

During the battle the 5th Dorsets' Pioneer Platoon began erecting a make-shift bridge, enabling Jeeps to bring up some anti-tank guns. Bill Hudson, a Canadian officer with the Battalion, recalled *standing on a road while Speedy Bredin was briefing me on a patrol when I heard incoming shells and went for the ditch. His comment was 'Hudson, what are you doing down there?'*

Overcoming resistance in a series of minor actions, 130 Brigade rapidly completed its part in the operation to enlarge the bridgehead over the Rhine, capturing Anholt and Dinxperlo. Within a week of crossing the Rhine the advancing Allied armies achieved the ultimate prize that had eluded them at Arnhem: the encirclement of the Ruhr. Separated from her industrial heartland, Germany's defeat was now inevitable, her total collapse imminent.

A new, highly mobile campaign developed as the British Second, Canadian First and American Ninth Armies under Monty advanced rapidly north-eastwards through Germany. And then suddenly, at the end of March, without apparent authority from Roosevelt and without warning Churchill, Eisenhower unilaterally allowed Stalin a free hand to take Berlin. Succumbing to political pressure at home and the bruised amour propre of some of his subordinate generals, he now returned all American troops to American command. In his political naivety, he thus handed the German capital and large swathes of Central and Eastern Germany to Soviet control, severely weakened the Allies' long-term position in post-war Europe, and in the short term undermined Montgomery's command's capacity to reach the Elbe and liberate Denmark. For 21st Army Group it had become a race. If the British and Canadian advance did not seal off Schleswig-Holstein before the Russians could reach it, that part of Germany and all of Denmark would fall under Soviet control.

Colonel George Taylor, the thrusting Commanding Officer of the 5th Duke of Cornwall's Light Infantry, described the pressures upon XXX Corps.

The advance was to be sustained by day and by night. Every division of 30 Corps would move forward on a one-brigade front with each brigade fighting its way out of trouble if encountered. Then the next brigade would move up to keep the momentum going. The leading battalion usually moved behind a screen of armoured cars and carriers of the Recce Regiment with a mixed company group of a troop of tanks, 10 armoured Kangaroos carrying infantry sections, 3-in mortars and anti-tank guns. The long armoured column clattered and clanked its way like some centipede across the Dutch-German border. It was exhilarating stuff.

Reflecting both the vernacular and the mood of the time, the operation was named *Forrard On*. After the deadly grind of the Reichswald battles, this style of warfare may have been exhilarating, but it was also costly. Although the retreating Germans were in disarray, in defence they remained as skilful and resourceful as ever. The leading British infantryman, armoured car or scout car approaching the Germans' next defensive position seldom survived the encounter with the hidden Spandaus or 88s.

130 Brigade's next encounters were in Holland, in that part of the Netherlands east of the Rhine where the Germans were defending the line of the Twente Canal. While a motor battalion was deployed to deal with this, Guards Armoured Division pressed on and captured Enschede. 130 Brigade was ordered to take the town of Hengelo and then work back down the Twente Canal to clear it of enemy.

On 3rd April the 5th Dorsets attacked the south of the town along the main road while the 7th Hampshires came in from the north-east. C Company under Major Hewson led, encountering resistance on the outskirts of the town, where the road had been mined. In this fierce firefight with the defenders, Corporal Rudd charged and put out of action a machine gun post while, despite the battle going on all around, Lance-Corporal Holt lay in the road, calmly disarming mines to clear the way for tanks. George Rudd and John Holt were later awarded the Military Medal.

Meanwhile, Hartwell's D Company and Allen's A Company respectively took the centre and south of Hengelo, and Roe's B Company pressed along the canal to clear its banks as far as the blown bridge to the south-west. As would so often be the case in these spring battles, after an initial display of aggression, the defenders withdrew. The 5th Battalion's patrols captured more than a hundred of them trying to make their escape.

The Dutch inhabitants of Hengelo, occupied by the Germans for four years and eleven months, welcomed their liberators with relief, excitement, unrestrained warmth and hospitality. The happy connection thus forged between 130 Brigade and the people of Hengelo has lasted seventy years. A Hampshire and Dorset presence in Hengelo is maintained by memorials and road names. On 3rd April each year Johan and Annelies Koning, who live in Hengelo, place roses and poppy crosses on the graves of the three Dorsets – Corporal Ivan Parkinson and Privates Harry Butler and Clarence Carver – who were killed in the liberation of their town.

The 4th Dorsets liberate Borne

But, so long as the years permit, still more personal links remain. In Winchester in July 2013 the launch of Ian Taylor's history of the 7th Hampshires was attended by a handful of surviving veterans, now in their late eighties or early nineties, and a special guest from Hengelo. Ria Trigg's family and her neighbours have kept in close touch with the young men who returned them their freedom. To this privileged observer at their party, the affection between the members of this special group seemed as solid and tangible as any stone memorial.

By late afternoon on 3rd April the 4th Dorsets were able to advance beyond Hengelo to take Borne, three miles up the road. The customary artillery fireplan had been arranged but, when Colonel Roberts found the town almost undefended, he was able to stand his field gunners down and enter a completely undamaged town. Some thirty prisoners were taken in and around Borne. Once again, the inhabitants celebrated and showed their lasting gratitude to the 4th Battalion by renaming their town square *Dorset Plein*.

Both Dorset battalions remained in this area for the next few days while other units continued the advance but, on 10th April, the Brigade again took the lead in the Division's advance. Up ahead the Dortmund–Ems Canal had been crossed and 130 Brigade were now ordered to continue the push beyond the bridgehead over the Canal in the direction of Bremen. The enemy were putting up token defence:

Sergeant Jack Blandamer MM

firing on the advancing column and then melting away while the British infantry, armour and artillery deployed for an attack. On 12th April, around Lastrup and beyond, this happened twice to the 5th Dorsets, who suffered some casualties from enemy shelling. Next day – Friday the 13th – Robert Hewson's jeep ran over a mine and he too was wounded. That day the 4th Dorsets also lost an officer to a mine when thirty-year-old Lieutenant Tom Worton, a Queen's officer commanding the Pioneer Platoon, was killed at Nicholt. The Germans' skilful defence was still taking its toll and would continue to do so until the very end.

And so the rapid but frustrating advance continued through the towns and villages on the way to Bremen. Many were found to be undefended, some were held by small forces which evaporated after the first contact, while a few required a full-blown assault. Bridges had been blown, roads mined and buildings booby-trapped, and the Sappers and the Dorsets' own pioneer platoons were kept busy clearing the way forward. It was in this kind of work that Sergeant Jack Blandamer, the 4th Battalion's Pioneer Sergeant, won his Military Medal for clearing mines under fire just a few days after the 5th had lost their Pioneer Officer in similar circumstances.

By 19th April 130 Brigade were about fifteen miles from Bremen. The 5th Dorsets could even see the city from their positions in Reida, on the south bank of the Weser. Orders were received that the main attack on Bremen would be carried out by 52nd Lowland Division while 43rd Wessex Division were to play a supporting role. Meanwhile, there were more villages to clear along the way. At Ahausen on 22nd April the 5th faced initial resistance, and Lance-Corporal Watkins earned a Military Medal. While the 5th continued to Oyten and Sagehorn, the 4th moved through Haberloh and found themselves involved in a fierce fight with an enemy supported by self-propelled guns. The 4th Dorsets took 129 prisoners that day but their Colonel, Bill Roberts, was wounded during the afternoon. He was succeeded by his Second-in-Command, Major Maurice Lonsdale, a North Staffordshire Regiment officer who had recently been awarded a DSO.

By 25th April, with 52nd Division fighting in the centre of Bremen, the Dorsets were involved in clearing some of the suburbs and capturing more, bewildered prisoners. While 7th Armoured Division pushed rapidly towards Hamburg, for the next week the 4th and 5th Dorsets were involved in what the history of the 4th later described as a *prolonged mopping-up operation* to clear the peninsular formed by the rivers Weser and Elbe up to the ports of Cuxhaven and Bremerhaven.

On 29th April, in one of these frustrating but still hazardous operations at Tarmstedt, the 5th Battalion lost Captain Peter Thorpe, who had survived since Normandy and won a Military Cross patrolling in the Reichswald Forest. The defending German troops proved unusually determined and finally flame-throwers had to be used to drive them from the buildings. Even then the defenders put in a fierce counter-attack: brave men fighting in an evil cause that by this stage was transparently and imminently lost. For his bravery in the fighting here the veteran Sergeant Albert Mockridge, who had served in India, Malta and Sicily with the 1st Battalion before joining the 5th at Hastings before D-Day, won the Military Medal.

For the 4th Dorsets, the next day held another, similar operation, this time at Rhade. For his skill and bravery leading a long-distance reconnaissance patrol towards Glinstedt on 1st/2nd May, Lieutenant Michael Monfort, attached from the East Surrey Regiment, was awarded a Military Cross. But Monfort was not quite the last Dorset to earn a decoration in the Second World War. On 3rd May Lance-Sergeant Robert Churchill won a Military Medal for the courage and tactical skill he showed when his patrol encountered two Spandaus on the road to Karlshofen. Another veteran awarded a well-deserved MM was Signalman John Rimmer, who had been driver-operator of a Royal Corps of Signals scout car which had supported the 4th Battalion throughout the campaign. His car had been blown up by a mine in Normandy and several men killed, but Rimmer had quickly procured a replacement and returned to his task. His citation spoke of his cold-blooded courage in the most difficult and hazardous circumstances that had enabled him to maintain the essential wireless links between Battalion and Brigade Headquarters, and his unfailing cheerfulness and inspiring example which had made him such a valuable member of the Battalion team.

Lance-Corporal Stan Rickaby was another who had had an eventful campaign. A Durham Light Infantryman, he had found himself switched with his entire company to the 1st Dorsets in Normandy. When the 1st Battalion returned to England, he joined the 5th Battalion, arriving several months before his previous Colonel, Speedy Bredin, assumed command. Rickaby later became a professional footballer and played for England. In his memoirs, *Upover and Downunder*, he remembered his time with the 5th Battalion's Carrier Platoon in these final days of the war.

The saddest incident of all happened just three or four days before the German surrender. Our infantry companies were travelling in 'Kangaroos' (armoured troop carriers), and one went over what was in fact a magnetic sea mine, buried in the road between Wilstedt and Tarmstedt, killing the whole section of about twelve men. A crater about thirty yards wide was created, and the Royal Engineers had to bridge it.

On 4th May we captured Kuhstedt, and we dug in by the side of the road, which led out the other side of the town. It was a beautiful day and it was one when rumours of a complete German surrender were rife. We were in the foremost line of trenches and our CO, Lieutenant-Colonel Speedy Bredin DSO MC, visited us. He came marching down the road, boots highly polished, wearing a soft beret, just as though he was on the barrack square back home in Dorchester. He gave us the latest news, but we were glad to see him go as we were expecting his presence to attract a barrage of shells and bullets from the enemy trenches on the other side of the valley, only about four hundred yards away.

... I had hoped that the bombing of their homeland would persuade the Germans to surrender, but this had not eventuated. Even at this late stage, just make a bit of noise or stick your head up, and you would find that there was still a war on. We had survived all the way from the beaches of Arromanches, and we did not want to spoil our record now.

VICTORY IN EUROPE

Everyone could see that at last the end was not just within sight, but within grasp. It came finally in the evening of 4th May, when 130 Brigade Headquarters telephoned with the news that Montgomery had accepted the Germans' unconditional surrender at Lüneberg Heath.

A delegation of senior German officers had appeared at Monty's Headquarters to negotiate terms for surrender. Arriving with a degree of pomp and Prussian dignity, they were dismayed by their reception. Monty, in pullover and corduroy trousers, had decided to humiliate them. As they approached and saluted, he ordered his interpreter to demand: "What are you doing here?" The interpreter in question – twenty-two-year-old Captain Derek Knee – was a Dorset. Since landing in Normandy on D+4, he had been on Dempsey's staff at Second Army Headquarters but, a few days earlier, he had been sent to Monty's Tactical Headquarters for this express purpose. Now his task was to help Monty browbeat and coax the German generals and admirals into acknowledging that they were thoroughly beaten, that the Russians were very close and that, unless they surrendered unconditionally, the Allied offensive would continue. He and the Field Marshal succeeded. The Germans surrendered unconditionally. The war in Europe was over.[27]

Stan Rickaby remembered the news being received by the 5th Dorsets.

It was a beautiful evening, still broad daylight, and as always our section radio operator was fiddling about with his field radio, trying to pick up any news, when he suddenly shrieked, 'It's over!'

... This was our last night in a slit trench. As the hours slipped away, we did not even try to sleep. We just talked and talked, illuminated as we were by Very lights fired by any who had the wherewithal.

... in the morning we set off with a cavalcade of jeeps, tanks and our three Bren gun carriers. It was the most exciting and the most interesting journey of my life.

A week short of the fifth anniversary of the 2nd Dorsets finding themselves on the Dutch-Belgian border facing Hitler's onslaught through the Low Countries, the 4th and 5th Dorsets had been in at the kill: the final defeat of Nazi Germany. Since Normandy the 4th Battalion had lost 266 men killed in action and the 5th

---

27   In the next three weeks Derek Knee would play a part in the arrest at Flensburg of Admiral Dönitz and the ministers of the caretaker government Dönitz formed after Hitler's suicide. He would also see the body of Heinrich Himmler, who committed suicide after his capture.

The German generals surrender to Monty and Lieutenant Derek Knee

Battalion 218; each had lost some three times that number wounded and captured. Their journey from Cheux to Bremerhaven had taken nearly eleven months of hard fighting, from which the mostly Territorial battalions of the 43rd Wessex Division had emerged, despite devastating casualties, with a reputation second to none. The 4th and 5th Battalions had played a leading role in winning that reputation and, in doing so, had added a new, brave, unutterably sad but ultimately triumphant chapter to the history of the Dorset Regiment.

Today, not far from the entrance to the Dorset Regiment Museum in Dorchester, a gleaming twenty-five-pounder field gun takes pride of place. It belonged to the 94th (Dorset and Hampshire) Field Regiment of the Royal Artillery, who supported 129 Brigade of the 43rd Wessex Division throughout the campaign. A sister regiment, the 112th (Wessex) Field Regiment, spawned from the Somerset Yeomanry but drawn from Wiltshire, supported the 4th and 5th Dorsets and 7th Hampshires in 130 Brigade. The two infantry brigades – 129 and 130 – drew two aces from the pack when they were allocated the 94th and 112th as their supporting Gunners. Any experienced infantry soldier will acknowledge the debt he owes his supporting field Gunners, and countless infantry soldiers of the 43rd Wessex Division owed their success and their survival to the Gunners of these regiments. From the outset, with their sterling support on Hill 112, to the very end near Bremen, they had time and again demonstrated their professionalism, determination and courage. They – especially their Forward Observation Officers, who lived and often died with the forward infantry companies – were part of the exclusive club, in which rank, unit and seniority were irrelevant, whose members faced the greatest dangers and who fought and won the grim infantry battles that had characterised the entire campaign.

8

The Post-War Years 1945–47

The Captains and the Kings Depart

Because the Dorsets' two Regular battalions had been first into battle, it was appropriate that it had fallen to their two Territorial battalions to be in at the kill. Despite their heavy losses, both the 4th and 5th Battalions were in Northern Germany to witness the end of the war that had begun so ominously that Sunday morning in September six years before.

The war had cost the lives of some 1,170 Dorsets; more than 3,000 others had been wounded, and more than 500 taken prisoner. In five years of fighting in six campaigns, the Regiment had won twenty-five new battle honours and its officers and men had been awarded some 500 decorations. Now, the Regiment's 1st, 2nd, 4th and 5th Battalions would be part of the Allied armies occupying the homelands of the defeated Axis powers, Germany, Austria, Italy and Japan.

The 1st and 2nd Battalions Out of Battle 1945

The two Regular battalions, who had first seen action in the late spring and early summer of 1940, had each been withdrawn from the fight after their enemy had been mortally wounded but before his final defeat. We left the 1st Battalion returning to England at the end of 1944 and the 2nd Battalion returning to India in April 1945. What had they been doing between our last glimpse of them and the end of their war in May and September 1945 respectively?

When 50th Division disengaged from the campaign in North West Europe, the 1st Dorsets were broken up. Most of their soldiers – mainly reinforcements since Normandy – were kept in the family by being sent to the 4th and 5th Battalions in 43rd Wessex Division, but in December 1944 Speedy Bredin took the old guard of about 130 all ranks back to England. They were sent to Nawton in Yorkshire, where they acted as instructors, converting Gunners, of whom there were plenty, to become infantry, who after the casualties in France and the Netherlands were in short supply. In February, when Bredin managed to make his escape from what for him was probably an unwelcome posting and take command of the 5th Dorsets in

Germany, he was succeeded by Colonel Alfred Shaw-Ball of the King's Shropshire Light Infantry.

In May 1945 the 1st Battalion celebrated VE Day with an athletics meeting before sending five members to Paris to join 50th Division's Guard of Honour at the British Army Exhibition in June. That month the last group of Gunners completed their training and left for the Far East. The remaining skeleton of the 1st Dorsets became a holding unit for young soldiers. On VJ Day the Battalion held a paper chase. Colonel Shaw-Ball left – he went on to take the 1st Battalion of his own Regiment to Korea – and was succeeded by Colonel Bobby Radcliffe.

The apparently purposeless existence of the dwindling 1st Battalion ended in August 1945, when they were ordered to mobilise. In September two batches of reinforcements arrived, including 120 Dorsets and 150 Devons, doubling their strength to 800. They also received some sailors from the Royal Navy and airmen from the RAF. In November they embarked, via Ostend, to take their place in the British Army occupying Germany.

Meanwhile, the 2nd Battalion, exhausted by their year fighting the Japanese, were withdrawn, by road, rail, river boat and Shanks's pony, to Bandel, north of Calcutta. *Despite the efforts of everyone to preserve our health*, Knocker White remembered, *we were very run down; scratches developed, despite constant care, into septic sores which spread over our bodies, and the slightest malady was apt to raise a fever...*

In June they moved to Kamareddi, north of Secunderabad. Corporal Tom Cattle was not with them. Having got soaked in the monsoon while on leave in Calcutta, he contracted pneumonia, regaining consciousness to find himself in a comfortable bed, in a clean hospital, being attended by *a nice English nurse*. When he recovered and rejoined his Battalion, he was astonished to find that at Kamareddi they were living in bashas (bamboo huts with reed roofs), rather than tents. He did not, however, appreciate the other occupants of his basha: *all sorts of creepy crawlies, snakes, scorpions, spiders and ants.*

In these mixed but less dangerous circumstances, the men of the 2nd Dorsets steadily recovered their strength. When it became clear that his Battalion would not be sent back to Burma for some time, Colonel White left the Dorsets under the command of Major Tony Bridge and returned to Britain on a lecture tour. On 16th August he was able to visit Lyme Regis and attend the presentation to the Regiment of the Freedom of the town. Captain Jock Wilson led a party of 2nd Battalion veterans as they marched with men from the 1st, 4th and 5th Battalions, who had won their victory in Europe. Knocker White was still in England when

Bashas by Jock Murrills

the bombs were dropped on Hiroshima and Nagasaki, and Japan finally surrendered. He flew back to India to rejoin his Battalion.

Tom Cattle probably spoke for most British soldiers when he recalled his feelings on hearing the news of the atom bombs.

Everyone was elated and so glad the war had ended. I know many people questioned the necessity of the atom bomb dropping, but I can assure you had these people been in our position they would have had a different outlook on the matter. Here we were together with thousands of Americans preparing to invade Malaya and their numerous islands in the Pacific Ocean and then finally having to assault the Japanese mainland islands themselves. The casualties would have been astronomical among the allied forces – many, many more than casualties caused by the atomic bomb.

Soon after their Colonel's return, the 2nd Dorsets heard that all those who had been overseas for three years or more were to be returned to Britain. The 2nd Division was to merge with the 36th Indian Division and go to Malaya and Hong

Kong while 5 Brigade was to join the Allied army of occupation in Japan. Within the Brigade, the 2nd Royal Welch Fusiliers would replace the 7th Worcesters. With the 1st Camerons, the 2nd Dorsets and the 2nd Royal Welch Fusiliers, 5 Brigade would now represent the three constituents of mainland Britain.

Under the three-year qualification for repatriation, the 2nd Dorsets lost all those who had fought with it during the campaign in Burma with the exception of men who had arrived with the drafts received in 1943. Only two officers – Captain Jonah Jones and Colonel White himself – would embark for Japan. The others, including Paget Fretts, Clive Chettle, Dick Castle, Tiger Havers, Snagger Highett, Joe Chamberlin and Gus Claxton, were scattered to the winds. Similar sad separations befell the warrant officers, NCOs and men as the veterans, including many of the most memorable characters of the Battalion, returned to England. They were replaced by drafts of 150 reinforcements from the 7th Worcesters and 400 from the 10th Glosters. Among the new officers was John Archer, posted from the 2nd Royal Norfolks who were going home. By the end of the year he would have been promoted captain, formally transferred to the Dorset Regiment and appointed Adjutant. By 1948 he would be a major, by 1965 he would be commanding the 1st Battalion of the Devon and Dorsets and by 1978 he would be Commander-in-Chief, UK Land Forces.

A few old Dorset friends from other battalions arrived, among them Desmond Wakely, who took over C Company, and Hugh Wetherbee, late of the 5th Battalion, whom Knocker White *collected... from some jungle school in India.* Meanwhile, Bobby Nicoll reappeared, post-Staff College, in the guise of 5 Brigade's new Brigade Major. But, despite this injection of Dorset blood, the Battalion that, after much preparation, delay and frustration, set sail for Japan was essentially a new one, sent to undertake a post-war army's policing, peace-keeping and political role occupying the country of their defeated enemy.

THE 4TH AND 5TH BATTALIONS IN POST-WAR GERMANY

On the day before VE Day 130 Brigade found themselves temporarily removed from 43rd Wessex Division and attached to 51st Highland Division while they accepted the surrender of a German corps on the River Ems, disarmed them and took them prisoner. Four days later, on 11th May, the Brigade took part in XXX Corps' Victory Parade at Bremerhaven, where both the 4th and 5th Dorsets marched past their Corps Commander, General Brian Horrocks, who took the salute.

May was spent tidying up the litter – human and materiel – left by a world war and the sudden extinction of a cruel and murderous regime. Dazed soldiers of the Wehrmacht, separated from their units and bewildered by Germany's total collapse, had to be rounded up and sent to prisoner of war camps. Displaced men, women and children, homeless, often stateless, some of them survivors from the camp at Belsen, had to be assembled, treated carefully and passed to the Allied authorities to be cared for in camps while they awaited repatriation. Escaped, some-times vengeful, survivors of the German murder camps and slave factories had to be pacified, occasionally disarmed, and passed to the Allied medical services. It was infinitely depressing but essential work, which can have left the Dorsets in little doubt about the justice of the cause for which they had fought.

On 24th May several Dorsets, including Sergeant Frank Stretch MM and Private Harold Apps MM of the 4th Battalion and Sergeant Herbert Foster MM, Corporal George Rudd MM and Lance-Corporal John Holt MM of the 5th Battalion, attended a 43rd Wessex Division investiture to be decorated by Montgomery. By the end of May both battalions had settled south of Hamburg, the 4th at Oerrel, near Soltau, and the 5th near the villages of Tostedt, Todtglüsingen and Wistedt. In early June General Brian Horrocks visited Soltau and gave a talk about the final stages of the campaign. Skinny Laugher was promoted to lieutenant-colonel and left the 5th Battalion to take command of the 6th Royal Welch Fusiliers. Most of his remaining service would be away from the Regiment. He would serve in Greece – where, quite illicitly for a staff officer, he would fight the Communists in the Grammos mountains – and earn an OBE. And he would fight in Malaya – where he would command the 6th Malay Regiment, who would kill more bandits than any other battalion – and win a mention in Despatches. George Hartwell now succeeded him as Second-in-Command of the 5th Dorsets.

Even the most battle-hardened among the Dorsets were shocked by the scale of destruction wrought by the Allied bombing. The German cities had been devastated, block after block of buildings flattened. Occasionally a single building would seem to have survived but, when one looked closer, it became clear that only a single wall remained standing: behind it there was nothing. Hamburg in particular had never recovered from a series of raids by British and American bombers in the summer of 1943. Over 8,000 tons of bombs had been dropped, and some 45,000 Germans had died, ninety per cent of them in the subsequent firestorm which incinerated the city, devastating acre after acre of military, industrial, commercial and domestic property. Everywhere vast tracts of blackened, rubble-strewn wasteland stood testament to the horror of world war and the price humanity had had to pay to rid itself of the evil that was Nazism. Many British soldiers also glimpsed, and some helped clear up, the horror that was the concentration camp at Belsen. The diseased, ragged, skeletal survivors and the tottering piles of emaciated corpses served to remind any observer that pretty much any price would have been worth paying.

During the summer of 1945 the Pioneer Platoon of the 4th Dorsets, helped by some Luftwaffe prisoners of war, built a church – named *Dorset Church* – in their camp at Oerrel. Their Battalion history recorded that *on Sunday, the 30th September 1945, the Padre, The Rev J E Roberts, held a memorial service in it for the officers and men of the Battalion who had given their lives in the cause of freedom between June 1944 and May 1945. The last CO, Lieut-Colonel W Q Roberts DSO, came out from England to read the lesson, the present CO, Lieut-Col M R Lonsdale DSO, unveiled the memorial, and the buglers sounded the Last Post and Reveille. As far as the 4th Dorsets were concerned, this was the last act of the war.*

In mid-August General Butch Thomas left the 43rd Wessex Division, which he had commanded so successfully throughout its eleven-month campaign. He was replaced by General Bobby Erskine, who had commanded 7th Armoured Division in Normandy. That month the Dorset battalions triumphed at the 130 Brigade Sports day, when the 4th Battalion came first and the 5th second.

Two months later the 4th Battalion were sent to Italy to join the Allied forces there. Their place in the army of occupation in Germany was taken by the 1st Dorsets, who arrived, 800 strong, from England. Characteristically, Speedy Bredin wasted no time in visiting the 1st Battalion to welcome them and to see if he could poach some of his old friends for the 5th Battalion. On Christmas Eve the 1st took their revenge by trouncing Bredin's 5th 4–1 in a football match.

The 5th had just lost their Second-in-Command, George Hartwell, who returned to England, and there was probably a sense of their role winding down as the harsh winter began. The electricity supply failed often and, with coal shortages, the 5th became wood-cutters to keep themselves warm. In February a large group of men were demobilised and, at the end of the month, the whole Brigade were moved to Berlin.

March found the 5th Battalion at the western edge of Spandau, near Berlin, surrounded by a plethora of cinemas, clubs, canteens, theatres and even the opera. They also had access to sport at the Olympic Stadium and sailing and boating on the Havel. In April Speedy Bredin left to attend a course at the RAF Staff College, handing over command to Colonel Bobby Wetherell of the Duke of Cornwall's Light Infantry. Jack Horton, who had been the 5th Battalion's Regimental Sergeant-Major since 1942 and who had recently been mentioned in Despatches for his distinguished service throughout the campaign, was taken ill and left the Battalion to return to England. After a series of three-day company exercises during May, the 5th left 130 Brigade – after nearly seven years – to move to Lüneburg. In June 1946 they were placed in suspended animation and everyone dispersed to other units. It was a sad end for a fine battalion.

The 5th Dorsets had done it again. First created in August 1914, they had fought with distinction at Gallipoli, in Egypt and in France and Flanders before being disbanded after the Armistice. Raised again in August 1939, they had won equal – perhaps still greater – acclaim in the long, hard drive from Normandy to Bremen. Now, seven years later, they disappeared for ever. One of George Hartwell's last tasks in Germany, together with two of his fellow majors, had been to record the story of the 5th Dorsets' campaign in North West Europe. The little green book they produced is still in print and beside me as I write this, nearly seventy years later. The story it tells and the Battalion's Roll of Honour stand as a living memorial to the 218 soldiers of the 5th who gave their lives during the Second World War and to those who fought alongside them and who were lucky enough to survive.

On 3rd April 1947 the 5th Dorsets would make one final appearance when veterans of the Battalion who were now serving in the 1st or 4th or elsewhere formed a Guard of Honour outside the Town Hall in Hengelo. The occasion was the presentation by the Burgomaster, Herr van der Dussen, of a Charter of Deliverance to the Dorset Regiment who had liberated the town two years earlier. Although, sadly, Colonel Sir John Lees (who had raised the Battalion in 1939) was taken ill and was unable to attend the ceremony, it was attended by many distinguished veterans, among them Aubrey Coad, Speedy Bredin, George Hartwell and Ted Chivers. This was the beginning of the lasting and very special friendship between the Regiment and the town of Hengelo, who named several streets after the regiments who liberated them.

Before we leave the Dorsets who were helping to clear up post-war Germany, however, we should briefly mention Major-General Harry Longden. Commissioned into the Dorsets in 1919 but having served away from the Regiment throughout the war, Longden served as President of the Court in the trials of some of the murderers of the fifty men who had escaped from Stalag Luft III. After a long investigation, several of the accused were convicted and sentenced to death or imprisonment. It would be Harry Longden's last job in a long army career. Appointed a Companion of the Bath in 1947, he retired the following summer.

THE 4TH BATTALION IN ITALY 1945–46

On 21st November the 4th Dorsets began a seven-day, 1,700-mile train journey through six countries to Bari, on the Adriatic coast just above the heel of Italy. Here they spent four months on garrison duties which, according to Private Frank Cottam, *meant we were available to do everyone else's odd jobs and dirty work. We provided guards for Area HQ, the military hospital and a vast base supply depot which always contained over 60,000 tons of foodstuffs, mostly in tins, and which Italian gangs frequently tried to break into and steal from. We staffed and ran the town Guard Room, which was a wing of the local prison and which was always well occupied... We were available to be called on by the Military Police to help keep law and order in the area, including assisting with anti-vice patrols, which consisted of going out late at night with the Redcaps and charging into the local brothels shouting 'Stand by your beds!' Then arresting anyone who was daft enough to do so because he was obviously a soldier... Taken all round, it was not work that we very much liked.*

Their work was not all trivial. During their stay at Bari the 4th Battalion helped to clean up a crime wave by enforcing a curfew and using carriers to patrol after dark. They waved the Union flag on every possible occasion. Parades included one to mark the King's birthday; the salute was taken by the Brigadier and a twenty-one gun salute was fired by the 4th Medium Regiment of the Royal Artillery. In January 1946, despite a heavy snowfall even this far south, the Dorsets sent a mobile column 120 miles through the local countryside.

As better weather returned outdoor sports became possible, making use of Bari's impressive sports stadium. The Battalion won the Brigade inter-company competition at basketball and the rugby championship in the area before losing the district final to the 2nd Field Regiment's XV.

In April the 4th Dorsets moved north to Lazaretto, by the sea and eleven miles south-west of Trieste. Here they returned to operational service in an area that was the focus of international political dispute. Once a major seaport within the Austro-Hungarian Empire, Trieste had been annexed by Italy after the First World War despite most of its population being Slovene. During the war its Slovene population had been imprisoned and murdered by the Italians and, after Italy's surrender, its Jewish population had suffered genocide at the hands of the occupying Germans. The city had been liberated from the north by Tito's Communist partisans from neighbouring Yugoslavia and by New Zealanders advancing from the south. Tito's Communists had control of the city for forty days, during which many anti-Communist locals simply disappeared. Under an agreement made between Field

Marshal Alexander and Tito, the partisans withdrew from Trieste and the city came under Anglo-American administration. Nearby, though, was the border with the new Communist Yugoslavia, its eyes fixed on the port and its leaders at every level watchful and resentful of the Allied presence there. The Allies were beginning to get a taste of the ill will and mistrust which would characterise their post-war relationships with the Soviet Union and its satellites and which Churchill had described only a month earlier in one of the defining speeches of the decade.

From Stettin in the Baltic to Trieste in the Adriatic an Iron Curtain has descended across the continent. Behind that line lie all the capitals of the ancient states of Central and Eastern Europe. Warsaw, Berlin, Prague, Vienna, Budapest, Belgrade, Bucharest and Sofia; all these famous cities and the populations around them lie in what I must call the Soviet sphere, and all are subject, in one form or another, not only to Soviet influence but to a very high and in some cases increasing measure of control from Moscow.

In the Trieste area the Dorsets became part of 167 Brigade of the 56th London Division. In the 4th Dorsets' history Major Guy Matthews described the situation confronting them.

The main task of the Battalion was manning the Morgan Line, which marked the frontier between the British-American Zone and Jugo-Slavia, controlling movement across the border at the road blocks, and active patrolling in the hills. Certain posts at strategic points were continuously manned. This was, in fact, the Southern end of the Iron Curtain, which now stretched from the Baltic to the Adriatic. A Company was located at San Dorligo, a village in the hills, inhabited almost entirely by Jugo-Slavs.

There were frequent riots in Trieste, and clashes between pro-Italian and pro-Jugo-Slav sympathisers. Anti-British strikes occurred in Trieste and in the ship-building yards at Muggia, a large village a few miles from Lazaretto. Foodstuffs, particularly UNNRA flour, were being illegally brought across the border from Jugo-Slavia into Trieste to feed the strikers, and so enable the strikes to be prolonged. An operation was therefore planned to impound these foodstuffs, which met with considerable success. A Company, for instance, seized thirty-three smugglers and impounded forty-one sacks of flour.

When the Foreign Ministers of the Great Powers met in Paris in June to decide the future of Trieste, it was considered highly probable that Jugo-Slavia might decide to march in and seize the town, at that time one of the nerve centres of Europe, thus presenting the Foreign Ministers with a 'fait accompli'. The Division therefore prepared for action, and the Battalion was deployed in the hills along the Morgan

Line. Positions were occupied, trenches dug, and platoon localities wired. Active patrolling was carried out, tanks and guns were moved up, defensive fire tasks laid on, and endless 'O' groups held.[28] *Very detailed plans were made to deal with any attack on Trieste and a thorough reconnaissance of the ground was made. At this time an NCO jeep patrol from D Company drove over the line by mistake and was detained by an armed escort of Jugo-Slavs. They were returned safely the following day, after having been escorted back over a circuitous route by the Jugo-Slavs through their own positions, and so enabled to see everything! This situation lasted nearly a month, and when the alarm was over the Battalion returned to its normal routine.*

Sergeant Ginger Pearce was in charge of the Battalion's section equipped with Wasps (carriers equipped with flame-throwers). He recalled: *While up in the mountains we were mostly carrying out foot patrols along the Morgan line and were regularly meeting Yugoslav Partisan patrols. Sometimes they would wave their arms and shout, which seemed to suggest they thought we were on the wrong side of the border. We did the same to them. I do not recall any friendly meetings with them.*

Although we had a map with the Morgan line drawn on it, it was very difficult to be accurate in the mountains. On the patrols I was leading I always made sure we were well spaced out, with a Bren group well to the rear to give cover. We never had to do any fighting on these patrols but, if we had, with a dozen men and three Brens we could have given a good account of ourselves.

During these patrols we were warned that the Partisans now had some Russian T34 tanks, so from then on we also had a PIAT with us...

Another time I had to take the Section to a certain point to escort a Royal Navy party up to the mountains. What on earth are they going to do?... I soon found out when we met up. I saluted when I saw the officer in charge was a commander, who introduced himself as Gunnery Officer from the cruiser HMS Superb... They needed to check various ranging points, mainly roads which could be used if Tito tried to capture Trieste.

Frank Cottam of D Company remembered his platoon being *on permanent duty at the border crossing. The Platoon were billeted in a requisitioned villa... on the seashore. The Section on duty were housed in a Nissen hut by the side of the main road that ran from Trieste, across the temporary border, the Morgan Line, and down the western side of Istria to Pola at the southern end. We had a sentry box by the side of the road and a pole across the road to stop vehicles while we had a look at the*

---

28   O (or Orders) Groups were where a senior officer assembled his subordinate commanders to issue orders.

occupants. Which was a pretty pointless exercise as civilians were allowed to cross freely in either direction. Only military personnel were barred.

The Jugs [Yugoslavs] had their post about a hundred yards up the road... And they were a motley crew. Dressed in all kinds of uniforms, British, American, Italian, even German, and often a mixture of several. About twice a week some big fat fellow in a gorgeous uniform, looking a bit like Marshal Goering, used to ride up on a white horse and give them a pep talk. We never quite knew what that was all about.

They imitated everything we did. If the Orderly Officer came up from the Battalion and turned out the guard, they turned out their guard. If we had a drill parade, they had one. After a fashion. They weren't very good at it. Not exactly Brigade of Guards standard. Not even Home Guard standard. We called it 'Tito's Follies'. One day we dug some slit trenches. They sent a civvy over who measured them and went back. And they dug slit trenches presumably to the same dimensions. Our CO at that time, Lt Col Lonsdale, used to say, 'Keep it up, lads, and we'll make soldiers out of this bloody rabble yet.'

They did everything they could to irritate and annoy us. Even to try to intimidate us, not very successfully...

There was a large copse straddling the border just off one side of the main road. At night they would creep through the copse to our side of the border and commit minor acts of sabotage... We thought we should do something about this...

... During our time in Trieste the type of cigarettes we were getting for free were called 'Superfine Magnum'... So we'd collect a pile of empty Superfine Magnum ciga- rette tins, put a pebble in each one and tie them onto a length of wire or cord and fasten them between the trees at about ankle height. So when the Jugs came creeping through the copse, they'd catch the string and rattle the tins. We'd rattle our rifle bolts and make threatening noises and they'd clear off back to their side of the border. A bit rapid.

... in D Company of the 4th Battalion we always claimed that we designed and built the first Western defence line of the Cold War, aimed at holding back the red hordes of Communism. It was a load of old cigarette tins, tied on strings and stretched between the trees in a copse just outside Trieste.

In September the 4th Dorsets were moved to Mestre, very near Venice, providing guards for forts and installations in the Mestre area and in Venice itself, including one on the Grand Canal and another on one of the islands in the Lagoon. The ancient and beautiful city of pale turquoise water, St Mark's Square and Canaletto's paintings must have been an eye-opener for troops in whose memories the mud of the Reichswald Forest and the snow of Geilenkirchen were still fresh. In winter, though, the bone-chilling cold of Venice, exacerbated by the proximity of the mountains and the city's expanses of numbingly cold water, rivalled even Geilenkirchen. The Dorsets were lucky: they were based in barracks, where they had a better chance of keeping warm during the biting winter months they spent there.

In December 1946 the Battalion were visited by two distinguished Dorsets. One arrived unannounced. Ginger Pearce, veteran of Normandy, Arnhem and Geilenkirchen, was the Guard Commander.

I heard the sentry on guard shout out "Guard Commander!" I was always ready for such a call, just a quick check that I was dressed correctly, as you never knew who was out there, which in this case proved correct. There was a car with a flag with four stars on it and getting out was a full-blown General. I quickly turned out the Guard and we saluted the General.

He thanked me and said "I am General Wood... I was in the area and would like to visit the Battalion. Dismiss the Guard, please."

I sent the Guard runner to find the Orderly Officer. While we waited for them we had a nice chat. I pointed out the various buildings in the barracks. He was very interested in when I joined the Battalion and the actions I had been in, also asking after various officers and men he knew. The runner came back to say he could not find the Orderly Officer, so I sent him for the RSM. When he arrived they greeted each other like long lost brothers.

Their other visitor was Brigadier Harold Matthews, who had once commanded the 4th Battalion. Sadly, Matthews died of a heart attack not long afterwards. It was a time of sad news. Just before Christmas the blow that had struck their sister battalion now struck the 4th. They were to hand over their role to the 1st Battalion and to be placed in suspended animation. The deed was done with astonishing speed in the first week of the New Year and completed by the 7th January. The Battalion's last visitor was General Sir John Harding, who came to wish them well and to praise their work in Italy. And then the Battalion that had been almost destroyed in Normandy and again at Arnhem ceased to exist.

In England, however, plans were afoot to reconstitute the 4th Battalion. Lieutenant-Colonel Joe Weld, a scion of the Lulworth family, was appointed to command. A pre-war Territorial, Weld had been Adjutant of the 5th Battalion in the early years of the war. He had then – unusually for a TA officer – attended the Staff College at Camberley, gained some staff experience then, even more remarkably, returned to the Staff College as an instructor. From 1943 until the end of the war, he had served as a staff Lieutenant-Colonel in the Headquarters of South East Asia Command, where he had earned an OBE. If Weld himself lacked battle and regimental experience, his new Adjutant most certainly did not. Major Willie Hayes, 1st Battalion veteran of Malta, Sicily, Italy and North West Europe, had two Military Crosses to prove it. The Battalion's RSM was Jack Carslake and its Permanent Staff Instructors were CSM Warren and Sergeant Jimmy James, who had won an MM with the 2nd Battalion in the retreat to Dunkirk. By May 1947 it had three companies: A at Bridport, Beaminster and Sherborne, B at Weymouth and C at Poole. Seldom can a phoenix have risen quite so quickly from its ashes, and few at that time would have predicted that the 4th Battalion would survive another twenty years and outlive the Dorsets' last Regular battalion by nearly a decade.

THE 1ST BATTALION IN GERMANY AND AUSTRIA 1945–47

Only the 1st Battalion were in England to see at first-hand the state the country was in after six years of war. For the men of the 2nd, 4th and 5th Battalions, the news came principally through army channels or in letters from home. In the July 1945 election they cast their votes in India or Germany and the election results were delayed three weeks until the ballot papers could be collected and the count conducted correctly. When the result came it dealt a shattering personal blow to Churchill, who everyone knew had done more than anyone to win the war. His indomitable figure still towered over the international scene but, after six years of loss, hardship and sacrifice, perhaps the British people wanted a government that would put their own, urgent domestic needs first. Clement Attlee's Labour Party was elected with a massive majority and its policies would directly affect the Dorset Regiment both immediately – in terms of a short-term task that the 1st Battalion would have to take on in Germany – and for the next decade or more as army recruitment was transformed by the new government's policies.

Great Britain and her Commonwealth was the only Allied nation to fight throughout the Second World War – from the first day to the last – and she had almost bankrupted herself in the process. In the latter years of the war economic aid from the United States of America – *Lend-Lease* – had made an important contribution to the British economy, but it ended on VJ-Day. The economy Attlee's government inherited was depressed and geared almost entirely to waging war: trade and investments had been lost and many industries had shrunk in scale and profitability while the workforce had grown by three million. At home, a tired and impoverished population and returning demobilised servicemen wanted employment, free health care, improvements in education and greater social fairness. Abroad, Britain's commitments as a world power – occupying the defeated territories, policing the empire and providing a robust front to the increasingly aggressive Soviet bloc – required extensive armed services. Rebuilding a shattered economy while maintaining these high levels of public expenditure was a daunting, arguably impossible, job. But the most radical left wing government in this country's history set about its task with a will.

How it did so reflects the character of its highly uncharismatic leader and his peculiar mixture of talents and beliefs. Clement Attlee was formed by three influences: his public school – Haileybury – his Socialism and his service as an infantry officer at Gallipoli and in France. These experiences turned an innately conservative son of the establishment into a practically-minded, radical Socialist with the patrician values of the best regimental officers. A brisk chairman of Cabinet and a ruthless sacker of ministers who failed him, Attlee was a skilled delegator and an efficient administrator. As Deputy Prime Minister in the wartime coalition, he had run the home front while Churchill had conducted the war. He was unafraid of big ideas, hard work or government intervention. He re-organised education by rapidly implementing the changes announced in Rab Butler's 1944 *Education Act*. He began to establish the National Health Service, which would become (after the Indian Railways and the Red Army) the third largest employer in the world. In transport, he set up British Rail and in industry the National Coal Board. In the Services he introduced the *National Service Act* 1948, requiring all young men to serve eighteen months in one of the armed forces.

Conscription was an alien concept in Britain. Britons had seen it introduced in two world wars and had recognised its necessity, but maintaining conscription in peacetime was different. National Service was a radical and risky social experiment, and in the next chapter we shall see its impact on some of the young men who undertook it and on the Dorset Regiment who received and trained them.

The second, more immediate, effect on the 1st Dorsets was the demand for housing in post-war Britain and the desperate shortage of building materials, including timber. The coal mines, crucial for providing power for industry and heating for homes through the freezing winter of 1946–47, also needed timber for pit-props. Attlee's government turned to the British Army in Germany for help. One result would be the 1st Dorsets' leading part in a peculiar triumph of planning and execution, Operation *Woodpecker*.

When they replaced the 4th Battalion, the 1st were unimpressed by their surroundings at Oerrel. B Company's diarist wrote that it *leaves much to be desired, but since our arrival we have worked hard to improve it and are settling down.* His opposite number in C Company was more positive. *Now, after Malta, Egypt, Sicily, Italy, Normandy, Holland and Nawton, here we are as a real battalion again, in the BAOR. We are in wooden huts among fir trees. Snow has fallen, but even so we are decorating the insides of the huts with cotton wool for Christmas.*

In January, however, C Company *spent eight weeks on detachment at Wietzendork ex-concentration camp where it did good work in shooting up looting DPs* [Displaced Persons] *and capturing their ring-leader. The camp closed down at the end of February, and the last sight the departing troops had of it was the local Burgomaster jacking up the Camp Commandant's private car and stripping off the tyres. It is now believed that the whole camp later suffered a similar fate.*

In March 1946 the Battalion moved to Berlin, where they saw for themselves the devastation caused first by the Allied bombing and then during the city's capture by the Red Army. Some veterans remained, including Willie Hayes, Pat Chilton, Darts Dartnall, CSM Jack Carslake, CQMS Jack Collins, CQMS Alby Talbot and Corporal Travers, but many would leave in the coming months. On 30th April Pat Chilton commanded the Guard of Honour when Field Marshal Montgomery relinquished his command of the army in Germany. The Guard included detachments from the Royal Marines, the RAF and the 1st Dorsets, and it was fitting that the Dorsets should be thus honoured, having fielded three battalions in Monty's triumphant campaign in Normandy.

June 1946 saw the Battalion move to Hanover, which they found had little *to offer but its ruins*, before they moved to Munster Lager. Here they guarded a prisoner of war camp containing *mostly SS personnel with quite a few high-ranking officers of various German organisations around them. From the watch towers which surrounded the compound, one could see the internees walking around, some still sporting their elegant uniforms.*

While providing secure accommodation for their enemies, the 1st Dorsets also offered a new home for their friends from the 5th Battalion, which sadly had been disbanded. The woods and fields around Munster were found to be packed with red deer, roebuck, duck and hare and the Battalion Gun Club flourished during their stay.

On a bitingly cold day in mid-December the Battalion completed its move to Brunswick. The diarist recalled that *the main body arrived in darkness and in a snow-storm, where we were installed in barracks for the first time, fortunately as it has turned out, with central heating...*

Major George Connor

Brunswick is possibly the least damaged of the bigger towns in Germany, but the inevitable ruins are to be seen almost everywhere. I understand from George Connor [Major D G Connor, then a company commander] *that all the damage one may see occurred during one night raid on the city. George remembers it quite vividly, as he was a prisoner of war incarcerated in the same barracks we now occupy, a strange twist of fate...* George Connor had enlisted in the Regiment in 1931 and served with the 2nd Battalion first in Palestine and then as a Platoon Sergeant-Major in the retreat to Dunkirk. Commissioned in 1941, he was a Major by 1943 and had been captured in Normandy while commanding C Company of the 4th Battalion at Hill 112.

Operation *Woodpecker* began in January 1947 when A Company's Headquarters, under Captain Paddy Riordan and CSM Edward Kenny (who had won the MM at Agira), were sent to Lüneburg to take up forestry. The rest of their Company were Green Howards while the Wiltshires and Royal Berkshires each contributed a company. Although they were based in barracks at Lüneberg, near the scene of the

Operation Woodpecker

German surrender in May 1945, their work lay fifteen miles away in the Ebstorf Forest. Here they worked throughout the bitter winter, losing only half a day's work during a blizzard, and into the spring and early summer. Working with Sappers, they felled trees, cut them into logs and loaded them onto trailers towed by ten-ton trucks. At the end of May the Company moved into summer camp, where they continued the job, now in the longer days working shifts, and their Green Howard workmates were replaced by Dorsets. A Company's diarist described the scene.

At first sight a Woodpecker site looks like a place on which you can only venture at risk of life and limb. Trees seem to crash down without warning and in unexpected directions, axes flash through the air with apparently very little thought for those who may be standing near the axe-man, huge logs swing through the air to be lowered, more or less gently, on to the trucks, and there is the ever-present risk of being run down by one of the tractors, or possibly trampled underfoot by a couple of horses pulling a log under the charge of a Pole or Yugoslav. In spite of these apparent dangers casualties have been light, and in fact no man of the Company has been seriously hurt on the site, though on two successive days someone did manage to get hit above the eye with an iron hook swinging from a crane.

Private Mike Froud from Blandford was a carrier driver and spent a great deal of his time servicing the carriers, which were busy every day hauling trees to various collecting points. Sixty-seven years on, his principal memory of Operation *Woodpecker* is the bitter cold.

In April the new Colonel of the Regiment, Brigadier Charles Woodhouse, visited the rest of the 1st Battalion and attended a Trooping of the Colour before taking the salute at the March Past. In May the Battalion attended Brigade Camp at Paderborn, working its way up from section to platoon to company exercises. At the Division Shooting Competition in July the Battalion excelled. CSM Conlon came first (out of 350 entries) in the WOs and Sergeants Class; Private Butler had the highest score in the Corporals and Under Competition, while the Battalion's young soldiers took first place in the Bren Gun Contest.

By September 1947 the 1st Battalion were back at Celle to take part in another phase of Operation *Woodpecker*. They suffered two sad losses around this time. On 16th September their Motor Transport Officer, twenty-year-old Lieutenant George Smith from Christchurch, was killed in a motor accident. Two months later twenty-three-year-old Lance-Corporal Reid, a Scottish veteran of the 5th Battalion now serving in the 1st Battalion's Regimental Police section, died in a train accident. The whole Battalion were saddened by these losses, which were followed by the news that the 2nd Dorsets, currently in the Far East, were to be placed in suspended animation.

This time, *Woodpecker* would consume the whole Battalion for three months. It was organised, perhaps unsurprisingly, like a military operation and involved "co-operation with all arms". The Dorsets were supported by a Royal Engineers field squadron, a second troop of specialist Sappers, a REME detachment, a detachment from the Royal Corps of Signals, a troop from a horsed transport company of the Royal Army Service Corps, a Transport Group, officials from the North German Timber Control, a NAAFI Mobile Canteen and even the Catholic Women's League Mobile Canteen.

During October, November and December the Battalion worked a five-day week. Their working day ran from 0815 until 1630 and included a half hour break in the morning and a forty-five minute break at lunchtime. Their job consisted of five stages: felling; pulling the felled trees onto banks of earth four to six feet high and thirty to forty yards long; cutting the timber into transportable lengths; loading the lengths of timber onto trailers and transporting them to the railway; and finally loading the timber onto trains.

It was certainly not the sort of work men joining the army hope to do or are trained to do. But the 1st Dorsets excelled, cutting down a total of 35,000 trees, averaging eight trees per man-day and producing more than 13,000 tons of timber, far exceeding the Divisional Commander's targets for them. Their achievements outstripped those of any other unit or lumber group throughout BAOR and, on the last day of the Operation, the Army Commander, General Sir Richard McCreery, visited them and helped fell their final tree.

Two months later, on 5th February 1948, when the 1st Battalion were about to leave BAOR for Austria, Sir Richard would write to Colonel Radcliffe, recording his appreciation of the 1st Dorsets' *splendid service during the war and, since the end of hostilities, in the British Army of the Rhine.* Praising their *magnificent fighting spirit... , devotion to duty and qualities of cheerfulness, endurance and team spirit... , high standard of discipline and soldierly bearing,* the General congratulated all ranks and sent his best wishes in their future role.

THE 2ND BATTALION IN JAPAN AND MALAYA 1946-47

The architect of victory in Burma, Bill Slim, decreed that the 2nd Dorsets, because of their record in Assam and Burma, should be included in the Division sent to Japan. With their old friends the Camerons and their new friends from the Royal Welch Fusiliers, the Dorsets formed 5 Brigade in Major-General *Punch* Cowan's British-Indian Division. Their role in Japan seemed to be to show the British Commonwealth flag in an otherwise exclusively American occupation.

After several postponements and much uncertainty, the 2nd Dorsets finally embarked for Japan on 5th April 1946 aboard the troopship *Cheshire*. Recently promoted Lance-Sergeant Tom Cattle later remembered *the troopship being old and very crowded. We called at Ceylon, Singapore and then entered the Yellow Sea.*

Never one to miss a first for his Regiment, Knocker White clocked up two on this single voyage. This was the first time a battalion of the Dorset Regiment had ever penetrated these seas, and 5 Brigade were the first British battalions to sail to Japan.

The voyage aboard *MV Cheshire* had not been an easy one, as Tom Cattle recalled.

The weather turned really nasty and I have never seen seas like it... mountainous, the ship rolling and dipping – one minute standing on the bow and the next standing on the end of the stern. As the stern lifted out of the water so the screws raced and made the ship shudder even more. I think everyone suffered sea sickness.

On 23rd April, as he caught sight from the troopship of some of Japan's forbidding coastline, their Colonel's reaction *was one of great relief and thanks – thanks for the atom bomb... Remember, it would probably have fallen to the lot of many of us on that ship to have made an assault landing somewhere on the Japanese coast... nowhere have I seen such a naturally impregnable defence line as that presented by the island-studded, rocky coast of Japan. Every island was a potential bunker, and the Creator, in an outburst of tactical enthusiasm, must have designed each island to be mutually supporting, standing out as sentry posts before the even more formidable coastlines of the larger islands.*

They finally arrived on 24th April in the port of Kure, one of the principal ports used by the Japanese navy, which had been heavily bombed by the Americans. Everywhere they looked there was destruction. It was Tom Cattle's twenty-second birthday. He *had been selected as one of three sergeants to escort the King's Colour and Regimental Colour as we paraded off the ship with the rest of the Battalion, along the quay, but unfortunately due to heavy monsoon rains the full parade was cancelled and it was only the colours and escorts who paraded for the first time on Japanese soil. Although soaking wet, it was one episode in which I felt much pride and satisfaction.*

As he stepped ashore at Kure, Colonel White found General Cowan, who gave him another first for his Battalion. He said: "Geoffrey, the Dorsets have had a pretty raw deal on the way out from India, and so I am going to send you to Tokyo first. Be prepared to relieve the New Zealanders there on 15th July." The plans for what, inevitably, White would call Operation *Primus* began to form in his mind.

Even after the Dorsets' arrival, uncertainty still reigned about where they should be based and what they would be doing. Japan was under America's jurisdiction, which in practice meant that it was subject to the autocratic rule of General Douglas MacArthur. The newly arrived British-Indian Division were the sole representatives of the British Empire and Commonwealth. Although the American officers and men the Dorsets were to encounter were friendly, helpful and hospitable, the atmosphere at the highest level of the American command seemed none of these things. Haphazard bureaucratic systems made these early months very difficult, while a recent directive from MacArthur had halted the supply of timber just at the moment when Cowan's Division arrived and needed to construct accommodation. Tom Cattle recalled realising early on that *we were to be the 'Poor Relations', the Americans having been in Japan since the end of the war had all the best of everything.*

After a few nights at Hiro, near Hiroshima, during which they glimpsed the cataclysmic destruction and death delivered six months earlier by a single bomb, the Dorsets moved by train to Matsue on the north coast of Honshu. Here three companies settled into Japanese barracks while B Company, under Major Roy Turner, undertook internal security duties. Japan's first ever democratic elections were being held, and B Company supervised the process to ensure that it was conducted peacefully and correctly. A few days later Turner took his Company further down the coast to Hamada to discourage smuggling and black market-eering in the port there.

Back at Matsue, on the second anniversary of the Battle of Kohima Knocker White ordered a full-blown parade through the town. The Colours and drums were led by the Battalion's gleaming Bren gun carriers and the Dorsets formed a hollow square in the centre of the town below the castle, where the Colonel told the story of the battle. Some twenty-four veterans of Kohima, still serving in the Battalion, took part in the parade, which was very well attended by the local people. White had previously instructed the Chief of Police that local people should *show their hearty welcome and be careful not to fail to salute the Regimental Flag and Commanding Officer.* Colonel White wrote later that the *large number of Japanese present listened attentively but, from their polite applause at the conclusion of this description of their first heavy defeat at the hands of the British, I gathered that not much of what I had been saying had sunk in. After the Union Jack had been lowered and raised and Lance-Corporal Pope had sounded the 'Last Post' and 'Reveille' in memory of those of us who still lie in the compound of the District Commissioner's bungalow, we marched back by a different route.* The Dorsets did not stay long in Matsue as they were transferred to what would be their permanent station at Gomen on the south coast of Shikoku. On 28th May White heard that the New Zealanders were no longer going to precede the Dorsets in the Japanese capital and that therefore his Battalion would have to take over in Tokyo six weeks earlier than planned – in four days' time on 1st June.

After three frantic days of last-minute preparations, the Dorsets arrived at Ebizu Barracks, which would be their home during their two months in Tokyo. Despite the efforts of the Australians who preceded them, the barracks remained inadequate and uncomfortable. They had been heavily bombed by the USAAF and sabotaged by the Japanese before their surrender.

Each day throughout their tour of duty, the Dorsets provided more than 200 men as guards for posts scattered throughout the city, varying in scale from the Imperial Palace to small posts requiring only a handful of men. In the Palace

Americans, Australians and Dorsets Tokyo 1946

the Dorsets shared the guard with American soldiers and often a single Dorset soldier would share a post with a solitary GI, each performing the drill according to his own army's style. White admired the high standard his men maintained, observing later and tactfully that it *is not easy to remain smart and soldierlike by our standards when your companion on the post allows himself a rather more relaxed form of stand-at-ease, and it is most disconcerting to have a doughnut offered you on the end of a bayonet.*

The climax of the Dorsets' tour in Tokyo came on 28th June 1946 when, with the aid of the Royal Welch Fusiliers' Divisional Band and in the presence of several American generals and three British ones, they trooped their Colour on the Plaza of the Imperial Palace. The Dorsets did their Colonel and their audience – British, American and Japanese – proud. The American Eighth Army Commander, General Eichelberger, wrote to White afterwards: *Not only was the ceremony beautiful but its execution was the most exact I have ever seen, and you know I have seen troops all over the world.*

Colour Party from 2nd Dorsets by Jock Murrills

Off-duty, the Dorsets had some time to enjoy the Japanese capital. Sergeant Cattle remembered Tokyo's *main thoroughfare called the Ginza. There of course were numerous beer gardens renowned for the large two-pint glasses used for the beer drinking. There was a strict non-fraternisation order in force; there were the usual one or two squaddies who took little notice of the instructions and found themselves not only in trouble with the Military Police, but the Japanese youths, who objected to our soldiers co-habiting with their womenfolk and one or two squaddies were injured with knives when caught by these youths in the parks.*

The majority of us contented ourselves with the sights, cinemas, canteens and drinking sessions. I did take a trip on the famous Blue Bullet train which was an expe- rience; the speed took your breath away and I found it very comfortable. However the 24 hour guards were very tiring and the more sensible of us spent much of our time sleeping...

The Tokyo tour had been a great success. The Dorsets had shown the flag very professionally and had made many friends among the city's American and

Commonwealth inhabitants, many of whom had been lavish in their hospitality. On 4th July Dorsets helped the Americans celebrate Independence Day and, ten days later, they shared the French celebrations on Bastille Day.

The American soldiers had enjoyed their encounter with the British Battalion that now claimed to have been *First in Tokyo,* and, as the Dorsets handed over to a battalion of Gurkhas at the end of their time, two of MacArthur's generals wrote most warmly of their conduct, appearance and efficiency.

Back at Gomen, the 2nd Battalion settled into their barracks on the narrow coastal strip between the Pacific Ocean and the steep hills and mountains which rose 8,000 feet behind them. This time their base had been a training centre for kamikaze pilots and the disused airfield provided a large, flat area on which they could train, drill and play sport. A few days after their return from Tokyo they were struck by a typhoon. As Knocker White recalled, *the rain, with a hurricane force behind it, poured down with an amazing intensity.* The nearby river looked dangerously as though it was going to burst its banks and swamp the barracks. The relentless wind and rain penetrated the badly fitted windows. The women of the Women's Auxiliary Service (Burma) had to be rehoused in the Dorset officers' quarters and the officers, ever gentlemen, doubled up (with each other) to accommodate them. White remembered that his greatest dilemma, *which we never finally decided, was whether to let the troops remain in upstairs barrack rooms and get blown over with the buildings or order them downstairs and wait for the buildings to fall on them.* Happily none of these disasters occurred: the river remained within its course, the troops remained upstairs unhurt and the WAS (B) ladies remained in the officers' quarters undisturbed by anything more worrying than their windows rattling in the storm.

Tom Cattle described the difficulties in communicating with the local people: *very few could speak English and the only knowledge we had were phrase books which had been issued to us. It was of course the children who were friendly towards us. The adults were very resentful of us living in their country. I enjoyed most of all the Kabuki Theatre; the story was usually simple but very colourful and at times very noisy. The hall in which it was held was quite small and always packed.*

One thing I noticed about the Japanese was their flimsy buildings – all had sliding doors and raised floors. They all lived, ate and slept on the same floor, not much furniture, the odd table but lots of cupboards. Bed rolls were brought out at night to sleep on the floor, with a huge mosquito net covering everyone, slung from each corner of the room.

A Dorset sentry post, Japan 1946 by Jock Murrills

Knocker White found it *difficult to reconcile the Jap against whom we had fought with these peaceful and courteous peasants tilling their fields, the hard-working fishermen on the coast or the cheerful highlander up-country.*

At very short notice in the late summer the Dorsets had to provide the guard at Divisional Headquarters. White sent Major Phil Roberts,[29] then commanding HQ Company, together with a carefully selected guard company of their best drillers and veterans and the Drums. This small-scale reprise of Operation *Primus* went well and was well-received by the General and his staff.

Companies continued their training in the hills behind Gomen and 5 Brigade hosted 34 Australian Brigade in an athletics meeting involving track and field events. At the last event the two brigades were neck-and-neck but somehow the final Australian runner managed to snatch victory for his side. There was little shame in being bested – just – by a brigade fresh from training.

In October the Battalion lost its Colonel. Geoffrey White had joined the 2nd Battalion in Yorkshire in October 1941. He had led it since soon after Kohima

---

29 Phil Roberts was Australian. Later he was ordained and renewed his links with Dorset when he served as a priest in Dorchester.

and had taken it into Burma, back to India and now to Japan. It was very much his Battalion and he had made it his business to get to know his men, whom he regarded with paternal pride and affection. The parting – for Colonel White and his Battalion – must have been an emotional one. Knocker White now returned to England to attend the Army Staff College. After more than three years in the Far East, Sergeant Tom Cattle also returned home to his young wife in Corfe Castle and a new career with the Dorset Police. Only a handful of Burma veterans remained in the 2nd Battalion, including the Quartermaster Major Freddy Edwards MBE, ORQMS Jackie Vaughan, CSM Johnson and Sergeant Henry Jesty MM.

While the Dorsets awaited the arrival of White's successor, Colonel Douglas Gaye (whom we last met when he was wounded with the 4th Battalion in Normandy), Major Tony Lewis (who had joined the Battalion as Second-in-Command shortly before Operation *Primus*) assumed temporary command. Douglas Gaye's arrival on 19th December was greeted first by a fire in the Royal Engineers store and then, early next morning, by an earthquake. The Sergeants' Mess diarist recorded that *at eighteen minutes past four on the morning of twentieth of December, nineteen forty-six, nature decided to interfere with our comfort by providing one of those irritating things called earthquakes. It was like being under a bombardment all over again... Everybody had either to get up or be shaken up. However, there were no real casualties, except maybe for the RSM who, whilst looking for his slacks in the dark, became smitten by what he thought was the bungalow. It was only half the wall really. The wall broke – our RSM soldiers on, but then who would expect a mere wall to put an RSM out of action?*

The barracks were very close to the centre of one of the largest earthquakes that had ever struck Japan. They were extremely lucky not to have suffered any serious casualties.

Two months later the 2nd Battalion embarked on the twelve-day journey to Malaya. Before it left Japan, at the sounding of Retreat on 14th February, the oldest soldier in the Regiment – the Quartermaster Freddy Edwards – hauled down the Union Jack for the last time. This was an echo of an event eighteen years earlier when the 2nd Battalion had left the Rhine and their oldest soldier – again the Quartermaster, Captain Bolly Bolingbroke DCM – had performed the same ceremony.

The Battalion diarist recorded that, by 16th February, *we were on our way to Malaya. The journey was most unpleasant. The ship we were on was very much over-crowded and conditions were really bad... We disembarked at Singapore. Next came the journey to Kluang. The camp we found here was much better than we expected. We had running water, good showers and electric light.*

In March the Battalion sent its twenty best rifle shots to Penang to take part in the Malaya Command team trials. Three – two of them from B Company – were selected and shot in the competition as part of the Malaya Command team against other command teams from India, Ceylon and Hong Kong. The Malaya Command team won and, according to B Company's proud note in the Regimental Journal, *came back triumphant and weighted down with trophies.*

A and C Companies had been on detachment to Batu Pahat, thirty miles south-west of Kluang. Here, much pig-shooting was done and in May C Company put on a military display in the football ground which was attended by many spectators.

Private David Cowan, who had joined the Battalion at Gomen, remembered the intelligence section capturing an escaped Japanese sergeant-major, *who I had to take to Changi Prison in Singapore (accompanied by our RSM and a sergeant). I shall never forget the face of this prisoner – thank goodness he was chained to our burly Sergeant.*

The Regimental Journals of this time record the Battalion losing one old friend after another as they were returned to England. Henry Jesty, the Medical Sergeant with the Military Medal and two mentions in Despatches, went on long leave but returned three months later, when the cholera inoculations were due, wielding his needle with renewed vigour and enthusiasm. The HQ Company diarist recorded ruefully: *RMOs may come and go, but Sergeant Jesty will stay for ever.* In July, as demobilisation continued but few reinforcements arrived, the painful decision was taken to place A Company in suspended animation.

This was curious timing. What would become known as the *Malayan Emergency* was just beginning. It would last twelve years as Communist bandits fought to seize control of the country by terrorising the population and attacking the British garrison. In their last two months in Malaya the 2nd Dorsets had a taste of what was to come. Their diarist recorded a few of the events in the journal.

Banditry, in the form of hold-ups, robberies, ambushes and, in many cases, murder, was on the increase in Malaya from the Siamese border as far south as within a stone's throw of Johore Bahru and on several occasions the local police enlisted our help in patrols and searches on suspected 'hide-outs'. In one instance the trials of one particular patrol were amply rewarded. A local Communist group were believed to have their HQ in a jungle village but four miles from the camp and a patrol led by Captain Taylor and Lieutenant Whittle [Battalion Intelligence Officer] *combined with the police to make a dawn raid. After a long trek by night they moved in on the straw bashas to be greeted by a grenade and a volley of small arms fire. In the fracas which followed two of the bandits were killed and the remaining six severely wounded and safely brought back in irons. The only casualty on our side was Sergeant Jesty... who sustained a severe gun-shot wound in the leg.*

Another account describes how the fight involved *some hand-to-hand stuff* and how the prisoners included *two Chinese girlfriends.* Sergeant Jesty lived up to his invincible reputation, recovering from his serious ankle wound within six weeks.

The diarist continues: *Private Mules was instrumental in saving the life of a Detective Inspector for which he deserves the highest commendation. The combined result was to raise civilian morale to unprecedented heights and more than curtail activities by similar gentlemen in the neighbourhood for some considerable time. It occasioned the following letter from the Chief Commissioner of Police for the State of Johore:*

> 'May I express to you and the Dorset Regiment the sincere thanks of myself and all ranks of the Johore Police for the valuable assistance you so readily gave to the Kluang Police at Niyor on the morning of 25th September.
>
> I enclose a cheque for $1,000 which it is hoped you will accept as a contribution to the regimental amenities fund in appreciation of the occasion.'

In an endeavour to wipe out general banditry the Battalion was employed in Operation Vermin, a process of searching out and mopping up gangs of gunmen by vehicle and foot patrols. For this operation we enlisted the help of a squadron from the 12th Royal Lancers with their armoured cars with whom we formed a strong liaison. Although extensively carried out in addition to our normal duties, we were not rewarded by any action as formerly. It is undoubtedly true to say, however, that banditry in Johore dropped perceptibly owing to our patrols, road blocks and raids on various points.

Apart from the satisfaction inherent in a job well done, the generous gift from the Malayan Police was the 2nd Dorsets' only reward for their part in these early operations. None of their officers or men would qualify for the *Malaya* clasp to the General Service Medal, eligibility for which would begin on 16th June 1948. Instead they received the worst news of all: the 2nd Battalion was to be reduced to "token cadre" and placed in suspended animation. Letters of condolence followed this bereavement from the Commander-in-Chief in the Far East, from their present Brigadier and from Major-General John Grover, their ever-loyal Divisional Commander from Kohima days.

Work continued. In October, D Company (who had replaced C at Batu Pahat) were recalled to Kluang. Meanwhile B Company were despatched to Johore Bahru, where they were attached to the Royal Welch Fusiliers. B's job, under Captain Bill Guinan, was to guard the vast Tebreu Vehicle Park which contained some 10,000 vehicles. They also had to mount the guard at Lord Killearn's residence.[30]

On 3rd December 1947, the remnants of the Battalion sailed for home, leaving behind them some who would be joining other units, and Henry Jesty who would be a witness at the trial of the captured bandits. It was five years and eight months since they had embarked for what they had thought would be Libya but turned out to be India, Kohima, Burma, Japan and Malaya. Their work complete, they were now returning home to face extinction.

Docking at Southampton on 3rd January 1948, the Battalion entrained for Dorchester. The diarist later recorded that, as *we approached Dorchester the sounds of loud and continuous whistles from all the engines in the station and the bangs of fog-signals greeted us and, on drawing up at the platform, we found several hundred Dorchester people gathered, in spite of the darkness and damp weather, to welcome us. On our march to the Depot the streets were crowded with people who kept up an almost continuous round of cheers and clapping. It was a quite unforgettable sight, spontaneous and sincere, one that warmed the hearts of us all.*

Three days later the Mayor hosted a Civic Reception for the Dorsets who, for the first time in history, marched out of the Depot with Colours flying and bayonets fixed. They marched down Cornwall Road and formed line to present arms while their Colonel laid a wreath at the War Memorial. They then marched to High East Street, where the Mayor waited on a platform outside the Shire Hall. The Mayor gave a speech and Douglas Gaye spoke before three cheers were given by the crowds.[31]

Later the Battalion paraded in heavy rain on the square in Dorchester and, having been presented to Lord Shaftesbury, the Colour was trooped for the last time to the strain of *Auld Lang Syne* before being laid up in the Officers' Mess.

---

30   A career diplomat, Lord Killearn was then Special Commissioner in South East Asia.
31   Douglas Gaye – known as *Maisie* – retired in 1951 after nearly thirty years' service and, having taken Holy Orders, became Padre to the Dorset Regiment Association for twenty years. His son, John, became a Regular officer in the Devon and Dorset Regiment.

At that moment 193 years of history seemed to have come to an end. Many feared that the traditions of the 54th Foot, maintained by the 2nd Battalion since the creation of the Dorsetshire Regiment in 1881, would be lost for ever. The announcement, however, that the 2nd Battalion would not disband, but instead would amalgamate with the 1st Battalion, meant that this was not an end after all. The new 1st Battalion (39th and 54th Foot) would inherit the proud history and traditions of both the Dorsets' parent regiments. The spirit of the 54th – and of the 2nd Dorsets – would live on.

ONE NEW COLONEL, FIVE GEORGE CROSSES, THREE GEORGE MEDALS, FOUR HISTORIES AND HITLER'S WRITING DESK

In late 1946, Major-General Sir Hubert Huddleston retired after thirteen years as Colonel of the Regiment. Although sixty-six years old, Sir Hubert was still serving as Governor-General in the Sudan and he felt that his work there made it impossible for him to continue to devote the necessary time to his Colonelcy. As we have heard, his successor, appointed by King George VI in October 1946, was Brigadier Charles Woodhouse, a son of the family who owned the well-known Blandford brewing company. After service in the 4th Battalion, he had taken a Regular commission and, as Machine Gun Officer of the 1st Battalion, had won the Regiment's first Military Cross in 1914. Having been a prisoner in the First World War, in the 1930s he commanded the 2nd Battalion, was appointed OBE and was mentioned in Despatches while serving with them in Palestine. During the Second World War, although he commanded two brigades, his poor health prevented his serving overseas. Now, during a time of severe contraction of the Regiment combined with increasing demands upon the post-war army, Brigadier Woodhouse took over as Colonel.

On 29th July 1947 three Dorsets attended an investiture at Buckingham Palace to receive the George Cross from the King. They were Private Frederick Chant, Private Thomas Miller and Private Frederick Troake. Together with Company Sergeant-Major William Hand and Assistant Surgeon 3rd Class George Rodrigues of the Indian Medical Service, they had distinguished themselves twenty-six years before – during the campaign in Malabar in 1921. At the time they had each been awarded the Medal of the Order of the British Empire for Gallantry. This medal was replaced by the George Cross when it was instituted in 1940, and the gallant few who had received it were invited to exchange their original medal for a GC. William Hand, who had also won a Military Medal while serving with the 1st Battalion in the First World War, attended his investiture in 1942. The three other Dorsets followed five years later.

Today – and with complete justification because it is so rare an event – the award of a single George Cross is front page news. The 2nd Dorsets' achievement of winning four such awards – five if we include the Doctor's – in a single, brief campaign was a unique achievement, which has been too often overlooked by historians. This may be because few recognised the value of their little-known original award – only 126 were ever awarded – or it may be because the George Cross awards (whose value is widely understood) came so late in the day. It seems even more extraordinary that Volume II of the Regiment's own history mentioned only Frederick Chant – and him briefly. I therefore make no apology for including here the citations for these four awards won by four very distinguished Dorsets, whose bravery may fall outside the period covered by this book but whose George Crosses fall squarely within it.

5718234 Sergeant William George Hand, MM

On 24th September 1921, near Nilambur, Sergeant Hand's No 6 Platoon was leading the advance guard, moving along the road through thickly wooded country, when they were ambushed by rebels holding a very strong position. Small arms fire was insufficient to dislodge the enemy and even the temporary withdrawal of the platoon to allow the supporting eighteen-pounder gun of the Royal Artillery to fire on the strong point had no effect. Sergeant Hand then asked his Company Commander for permission to go forward himself to try and dislodge the rebels with hand grenades. Private Miller of No 8 Platoon asked to be allowed to move on the other side of the road to catch any enemy who tried to get away after they had been bombed by Sergeant Hand. The ruse was entirely successful and Miller was able to complete the work, bayoneting those of the enemy who had not been killed by grenades. Whilst subjected to close fire at about fifteen yards range, Sergeant Hand successfully bombed the enemy and by his coolness and initiative materially assisted in clearing up the situation.

5718907 Private Thomas Miller

At Nilambur on 24th September 1921, this man displayed great gallantry by going forward towards a rebel ambush and firing on it at close range. He was instrumental in dislodging several snipers who were causing casualties to our troops.

The other two awards were won on 13th October 1921.

5718784 Private Frederick Chant

Showed rare coolness and disregard of danger. On one occasion, when he had been using his Lewis gun at a range of about twenty yards against the enemy, who were occupying a house and firing at him at the closest range, his gun failed. He calmly got up and fetched a rifle and bayonet and maintained his fire on the target he had been originally given with coolness and deliberation.

5719290 Private Frederick H Troake

This man showed conspicuous gallantry in advancing close up to the fence surrounding a house in which rebels had been located and in covering the rush of Lieutenant X and Corporal Collins who fired the roof... [He] subsequently showed great courage in clearing the gardens and jungle round the house.

Sadly, no citation seems to have survived for Doctor Rodrigues's award.

Eighteen months after the George Cross investiture, the Regiment unexpectedly received three more retrospective awards. Lance-Corporal Edward Read, Private Richard Munday and Private Jack Bagge were each awarded a George Medal to replace the King's Commendations they had been given in June 1940 for their bravery rescuing drowning sailors off the Maltese coast near Valletta.

The original recommendation had been for three GMs, but in the autumn of 1940 this had been reduced by an honours committee to King's Commendations. Now the *London Gazette* cancelled the three Commendations and, in January 1949, published the announcement of three George Medals with the identical citation that had earned their Commendations and appears in Chapter 2. It is entirely possible that the hand behind the late revision of these awards was Brigadier Ivan de la Bere's. Having been the three men's Commanding Officer in 1940, he joined the Royal Household in 1948 and took charge of a substantial part of the administration of the honours system. Whatever the cause, nine years after the incident, justice was done and Reed's, Munday's and Bagge's bravery was properly recognised.

During these first post-war years, each of the Regiment's four battalions who had fought published their history. First to appear – appropriately – was the 1st Battalion's *Three Assault Landings*, written by Speedy Bredin. A brief and admirably clear book, it shares much of the character of its author, whose professionalism as a soldier and whose affection for those under his command shine through its every paragraph. Bredin also provided a preface for the 5th Battalion's history, produced in 1946 and jointly written by three majors who had served with the 5th in North West Europe. G J B Watkins, an officer of the 4th Dorsets who had not served with them in North West Europe, wrote their history, *From Normandy to the Weser*. Finally, in 1948 came Knocker White's account of the 2nd Battalion's war, *Straight on for Tokyo*. The Regiment was fortunate in all its historians, but it was remarkably lucky to have produced two such experienced Colonels who were capable of producing the vivid histories of the two Regular battalions. *Three Assault Landings* is a history any regiment might be proud of while *Straight on for Tokyo* is the work of a gifted writer.[32]

After the war, Ivan de la Bere was not the only senior Dorset to find himself doing a slightly unusual job. In 1944 a contemporary of his, Alec Bishop, had been recruited to the Political Warfare Executive by Churchill's eminence grise, Brendan Bracken. Bishop had been commissioned into the Dorsets in 1915 and had fought in Mesopotamia and Palestine, serving in various parts of Africa between the wars. After an interesting spell in the War Cabinet Secretariat in 1940-41, he was promoted to brigadier and joined Major-General George Gifford in West Africa. He served in Algiers in 1943, helping to plan the Sicily invasion in which his own Regiment would play such a major part. Just after the war, Bishop was promoted to major-general and sent to re-establish a free press, broadcasting, cinema and theatre in occupied Germany. In Berlin, he visited Hitler's Chancellery, which *presented a very grim appearance. The Russians had gone through the place with flame guns, and all the passages and rooms were charred and burnt. One room contained a large number of charred photographs of models of groups of grandiose buildings which were lying scattered on the floor, possibly illustrations relating to the plans for the reconstruction of German cities by slave labour which Hitler is said to have intended to carry out had he won the war. Outside the entrance to the bunker were the shallow graves in which the Russians found the bodies of Hitler and of Eva Braun when they burst into the Chancellery garden.*

Walking about this place a few weeks after the war ended was a strange experience, as was entering the former Gestapo headquarters in Alexanderplatz. This

---

32 In 1992 Norman Havers, Intelligence Officer of the 2nd Battalion in India and Burma, enlarged the Dorset Regiment's oeuvre when he wrote his very moving memoirs, *March On!* Nor did the creative talent of the 2nd Dorsets end there. Soon after the war Jock Murrills FRWS, Second-in-Command of A Company at Kohima, produced several paintings of the battle and some evocative pen and ink drawings to illustrate Knocker White's book. Some of these drawings illustrate Chapter 5 of this book, while his oil of the Kohima battle appears on the dust jacket.

sinister place was completely deserted, with thousands of records and dossiers strewn about the floors, documents which must have related to the persecution, death or perhaps torture of countless victims.

Working with the Red Army Bishop found that *the Russians could be very generous. When I visited what must once have been Hitler's Chancellery, I met the Russian officer who had been put in charge of the building. In the course of conversation I mentioned that we were short of furniture in our billet, and he asked me if I would like to have one of the writing desks in Hitler's study. The next day a Russian Army lorry deposited a large and imposing desk at our mess. It was very useful to us, and has now found a place in the Dorset Regimental Museum at Dorchester.*

It is still there.

9

THE 1ST AND 4TH BATTALIONS, 1948–67

REGULARS, NATIONAL SERVICEMEN AND TERRITORIALS

With their 2nd Battalion's reduction to cadre in 1948, the Dorset Regiment (like most county regiments at this time) became just two battalions: one Regular (the 1st) and one Territorial (the 4th). For all but nine months of its ten remaining years, the 1st Battalion was overseas and its end would come in Germany. Throughout this time its strength would consist of Regular soldiers, who had signed on voluntarily to serve for three years or more in the Regiment, and National Servicemen, who had been conscripted and who would remain for eighteen months or, after 1950, for two years. The Territorials were all volunteers and gave generously of their time and energy in their evenings, at weekends and for a fortnight's summer camp. Among their commissioned and non-commissioned officers, both the 1st and 4th Battalions had many veterans of the Regiment's various campaigns of the war. This chapter tells the story of what these disparate groups – veterans, volunteers, conscripts and Territorials – achieved together between 1948 and 1967 as the world changed dramatically around them.

At home in the late 1940s the Labour government lurched from one financial crisis to another, desperately trying to fulfil its socialist manifesto while staving off bankruptcy. Rationing continued and was even increased. Austerity was the watchword: the British continued to make do and mend. Buoyed up by their victory of 1945, no longer under attack from bombs and V-weapons and at last able to plan a future their families would live to see, the British tolerated austerity. But they would not continue to do so indefinitely.

In Europe the smouldering relationship between the western democracies and the Soviet Union was striking sparks. In 1948 one would ignite dangerously when Stalin attempted to seal off Berlin and to force the withdrawal of the British, Americans and French from their sectors of the city. The Allied response was the Berlin airlift, a triumph of logistical organisation and of determination, professionalism and heroism on the part of American and British aircrews as they strove to equip and feed Berlin from the air. Stalin was forced to abandon the attempt, but the diplomatic relationship would deteriorate throughout the 1950s. Meanwhile, the economic and moral reconstruction of a democratic West Germany was entering a new phase. The British Army of the Rhine (BAOR) would become less an army occupying a defeated nation and more an army manning the first line of defence against an expansionist Communist regime which dwarfed even Nazi Germany in its scale and power.

In 1949 the Soviet Union tested its first atom bomb. The erstwhile "co-belligerents" in the war against Hitler had become opponents in the Cold War. The protocols in this strange, protracted stand-off were unestablished, the weapons more dangerous and the place of conventional forces (including infantry) very unclear. If Russia's vast armies invaded Berlin and West Germany, could the Allies' conventional forces do more than delay their advance westwards? Or would they be forced to retaliate immediately with an atom bomb? These were the hard new questions with unpalatable answers that would dominate diplomatic and military thinking for four decades.

Beyond Europe, the political geography changed as the British Empire shrank. Independence and partition for India and Pakistan in 1947 were followed by the British withdrawal from their peace-keeping role in Palestine as the state of Israel was created in 1948. That year, as we have just glimpsed, also saw the beginning of a twelve-year commitment for the British Army in Malaya. In 1949 Mao Tse Tung's rebels overthrew the corrupt government of China, establishing another immense, oppressive Communist regime that was hostile to the western democracies. One of the Chinese Communists' first actions was to shell and hold captive (until she escaped) the British warship *Amethyst*. Within a year the Chinese would intervene in Korea to prevent the defeat by a United Nations force of the North Koreans, who had invaded the south of their country. Although a major war was ultimately averted, British soldiers would be fighting Chinese troops in Korea until 1953. In a direct response to the increasing demands posed by the Korean War, in 1950 Attlee's government would extend the term of National Service to two years.

It was against these developments that the 4th Dorsets were reconstituted and, on 5th December 1947, turned out in Dorchester for their first Battalion Parade. Commanded by Colonel Joe Weld and with Majors Joe Symonds, George Hartwell and Philip Roper among their number, they remained pathetically under strength. Their summer camp, at Fort Gomer near Gosport, mustered only eighty, including thirteen officers.

In January 1948, having completed his course at the Staff College, Colonel – now Major – Knocker White was given the task of organising the army's part in the 1948 Olympic Games which were due to begin in London on 29th July. An

The Dorset Regiment Olympic Team 1948
(Sitting l to r: Maj H F Crawley MBE MM, Lt-Col O G W White DSO
and Maj R G R Chilton; Standing l to r: Capt H Smith MBE,
Capt R H B Feltham and Capt W F R Burton)

accomplished athlete and a good organiser, White was an inspired choice on the part of the Military Secretary. Characteristically, he roped in five Dorset officers to help him, including Captain Bert Smith, an ex-Quartermaster, and Captain Bob Feltham, both 2nd Battalion veterans. The army contribution to the Olympics was therefore organised with military precision based on a strong Dorset Regiment presence.

In the spring of 1948, the Regimental Depot, which had been a training centre since 1939 and had moved to Norwich in 1942, was reformed in Dorchester. A great many boxes were unpacked and the Museum, which had been packed away in 1939, began its new life in a single room in the Keep. Dayrell Stayner, captured at La Bassée in 1940 and now retired, would give generously of his time over the coming months to restoring the Museum.

On the evening of 1st October 1948 the men of the 4th paraded to receive a unique honour, awarded by General Sir Frederick *Boy* Browning, which recognised the sacrifice made four years earlier by the Battalion when they had led the evacuation of the 1st Airborne Division's survivors from the Oosterbeek perimeter. Browning had sent a flag of the kind carried by the Parachute Regiment, which the 4th Dorsets could carry in addition to their own Colours. The flag was presented by Colonel Donald Baxter to Major Philip Roper, who now commanded A Company and who had been captured fighting with the Battalion at Arnhem.

THE 1ST BATTALION IN AUSTRIA 1948–52

Meanwhile, on 25th February 1948, the 1st Dorsets had left Celle and the BAOR to join the British Army occupying Austria. The Regimental Journal records that, having crammed six wagonloads of stores into two wagons *by very fitful station lights*, the Battalion boarded their train, which *grunted and groaned but did not move. The engine was not sufficiently powerful.* Though circuitous, the picturesque journey round the mountains – and especially the stretch between Salzburg and Villach – *fully compensated for the other tribulations of the move.* They arrived in deep snow; the weather was bitterly cold and the roads treacherous.

This part of Austria – Carinthia – had been liberated separately by the Eighth Army and by Yugoslav partisans, who had claimed it for their own. Here, as in Trieste, there had been a degree of confrontation before the Yugoslavs withdrew. But this primarily rural area had now returned to peace, and the Dorsets looked forward to an undemanding stay in attractive farming country.

Men were still being returned to England and reinforcements were arriving, but in insufficient numbers. Among those who left was Victor Lawson, now a corporal, who had won the MM in Dorset Wood with the 4th Battalion. This steady reduction in numbers made it difficult to find the troops to provide the various guards which their duties required. Many of their reinforcements – officers and men – were not Dorsets. The Group system, which began formally with the creation of the Wessex Brigade in 1948, joined together the six non-Light Infantry regiments of the south-west: the Dorsets, Devons, Royal Hampshires, Royal Berkshires, Wiltshires and Glosters. This administrative system would continue unchanged until 1957. Reinforcements came from all the regiments within this Wessex Brigade group – although one memorable group, including Lieutenant Bill

Guinan, two other officers and thirteen soldiers, formed the tiny cadre of 2nd Dorsets' men who now joined the 1st Battalion. Jack Horton, the distinguished RSM of the 5th Battalion, also arrived to take over as RSM of the 1st.

The summer saw separate visits to the 1st Battalion by the Colonel of the Regiment, Brigadier Charles Woodhouse, and the Chief of the Imperial General Staff, Field Marshal Viscount Montgomery. Visiting C Company, now commanded by Captain Oner Bray, Monty watched a demonstration of British infantry being supported by American tanks and artillery before gathering the Company around him and giving them a talk.

In September the Battalion were sent to Vienna, where they provided ceremonial guards as they had done previously in Berlin and the 2nd Battalion had done in Tokyo. To reach its required strength the Battalion had to take under command a company of the 1st Northamptonshire Regiment. The 1st Dorsets would spend the next four years in Austria, moving between Vienna, Poertschach and Spittal.

Bob Reep later recalled an incident when Bill Guinan was on a battalion parade. A soldier moving in the ranks behind him was spotted by the Colonel, who shouted, "Mr Guinan, what's that man's name?" Turning about, Guinan did not know who had moved, and so quickly invented a name. "Private Wilson, Sir," he replied. That evening a comedy of errors ensued as the non-existent miscreant was sought to serve his punishment.

In December 1948 Tim Wood replaced Bobby Radcliffe as Commanding Officer. Wood had briefly commanded the 4th Dorsets in Normandy before being wounded in the head. Later he was mentioned in Despatches for service in Burma. In May 1949 he commanded the parade at which the 1st and 2nd Battalions formally amalgamated. It was a characteristically family affair. The Colonel, Brigadier Charles Woodhouse, attended, accompanied by his son, Jock, acting as his ADC. The 1st Battalion's Colours were marched on; the Colonel took command and ordered the 2nd Battalion's Colours to be marched on. They were laid on a dais while Brigadier Woodhouse reminded all on parade of the distinguished history of both battalions. The 2nd Battalion's Colours then took their place on parade, beside those of the 1st Battalion. The symbolism was clear: the 2nd Battalion had not gone. The history and spirit of both battalions now lived on in the new Battalion, which would be known as the 1st Battalion, The Dorsetshire Regiment (39th/54th).

A page of history had turned, but a fresh one had opened because, while the Battalion were in Vienna in 1949, they received the first National Service Platoon to join them – and the first to be posted to any unit in Austria. One of their number, Lance-Corporal Richards, recorded his experience for the Regimental Journal.

After I had completed my basic training at Bulford, and had returned from two weeks' leave, I was surprised to find myself on a draft to Austria.

It was an even greater surprise to find on arrival in Austria in April that we were the first National Service Platoon to come to Austria. When I left the Wessex Brigade Training Centre at Bulford, I thought I had finished my training as a soldier, but it came as a great shock to find that ten weeks' concentrated training had been prepared for us.

During the first few days of training we were visited by the Zone Commander for Austria and the Commanding Officer. Everybody seemed to be taking a great interest in us and we were regarded as something out of the ordinary. We were also the object of many a curious look from the rest of the men.

Later on the Colonel of the Regiment paid us a visit. He asked us various questions about our training and what we thought of Austria and the Army.

Despite these distractions, we got down to some serious training. I found training in A Company interesting and almost a pleasure. The NCOs were very helpful and considerate and took great pains to see that we settled down properly. Most of our training consisted of elementary lessons on all weapons and drill. This was due to the inability to obtain ground for advanced training...

I spent a lot of my spare time in Vienna sight-seeing...

At the end of the Vienna tour, we returned to St Paul's to complete our training. We immediately settled down to training in the fields and woods around the village... The ten weeks were completed with a three-day scheme at Turner See. At the end of our training we took our star-grading tests and all passed...

Now, with nearly half my eighteen months service over, I think I can safely say that it has not been as bad as I had expected.

Corporal Richards probably did not realise how lucky he had been. As the first National Service Platoon to come to the 1st Battalion, they received a degree of care and attention which many National Servicemen would not enjoy. Richards had joined a battalion that was neither overworked nor kicking its heels in barracks at home. The 1st Dorsets could take particular pride that their NCOs were helpful and considerate: the commonest complaint of unhappy National Servicemen in the decade that followed was about bullying and sadistic NCOs.

David Cowan, whom we last met with the 2nd Battalion escorting an escaped Japanese warrant officer to Changi prison, found his life changed for ever when he served with the 1st Battalion in Austria as Colonel Tim Wood's driver and batman. He met an Austrian girl, Hermi, and they became engaged. When he returned to England in December 1951, Hermi followed a few days later. When David and Hermi married in Plymouth two months later, Tim Wood stood in for Hermi's late father by giving her in marriage. For a Colonel to perform this duty for his batman must have been an unusual occurrence; it is small wonder that David Cowan remembered the Dorsets as *the happy regiment*.

Private Gordon Sheppard remembered his own arrival as a National Serviceman at B Company of the 1st Dorsets, who were then at St Paul's, near the Yugoslav border, where he *rejoined my friends from my original draft. Other companies were outstationed in Graz-Volkermarkt etc. Here I met Sergeant Cornell as my Platoon Sergeant. He finished his service at Chickerell Camp years later.*

B Company moved to Maria Worth on the Worther See, and it was here the Defence Secretary (Emmanuel Shinwell) visited. Private Page (Weymouth) and myself were chosen to talk to him.

Training was at the Joint US Battle Camp near Judenburg and we had continual border patrols with Snow Cat vehicles.

B Company then joined the Battalion at Spittal and der Drau – based in an old SS barracks. From here two tours of duty took place to do international guards in the

Private Gordon Sheppard

British Zone. Guards were undertaken with US, French and Russian troops. Next to our barracks in Spittal was a DP [Displaced Persons] camp crowded with refugees from the war, mostly women and children. We used to pass our chocolate ration over the wire for the kids.

During this period volunteers were requested for a draft to the 1st Glosters in Korea.

After National Service, Gordon Sheppard served in the Wiltshire and Wessex Territorials for many years, rising to be Captain Quartermaster and being appointed MBE.

As the war in Korea was about to begin, the turn of the New Year 1950 saw two services of remembrance. In December 1949 the Regiment's Book of Remembrance, listing every Dorset who lost his life in the Second World War, was dedicated by the Chaplain General to the Forces. At the same service in Sherborne Abbey, the Regimental crest was unveiled in the Lady Chapel. A thousand miles away and a few weeks later, in the Upper Barrakka Gardens overlooking Grand Harbour, the Governor of Malta unveiled a memorial tablet. The tablet bears the names of twenty-seven officers and men of the 1st Battalion who died during the siege that had begun a decade before.

THE KOREAN WAR 1950–53

As the only Regiment in the Wessex Brigade to be sent to take part in the war in Korea, the Glosters took with them volunteers from other Wessex regiments. A number of men from the 1st Dorsets joined them, including twenty-two-year-old Lieutenant Alan Blundell, whose friend, John Milner, was one of the first to volunteer for Korea. At least fourteen Second World War veterans were recalled from the Reserve to join the 1st Glosters. Many of them had served with the 2nd Battalion and two of them – Privates Arthur Gyles and Leonard Tyrell – had spent five years in German prisoner of war camps having been captured before Dunkirk. Another, Private Evelyn Martin, had served in the 1st, 2nd and 4th Dorsets between 1938 and 1947. Now they, and their fellow reservists, were rapidly despatched five thousand miles across the world to fight in a new war.

When the army of Soviet-sponsored North Korea invaded democratic South Korea in June 1950, a United Nations force was sent to repel them. Although predominantly an American effort, the force included five British infantry battalions and supporting arms and services. The 1st Glosters, with whom almost all the Dorsets who fought in Korea served, were in 29 Brigade alongside the 1st Royal Northumberland Fusiliers and the 1st Royal Ulster Rifles. The Argylls, whom John

Milner joined, were brigaded with the 1st Middlesex and an Australian battalion; the Brigade was commanded by Aubrey Coad, who – after his long association with the 5th and 4th Dorsets in North West Europe – had pledged to wear Dorset buttons on his uniform for the rest of his career. Thus it transpired that in the Korean War the Regiment was represented by a number of Dorset regulars and reservists, Bobby Nicoll on the Staff, and a very distinguished Dorset Commanding Officer.

With the growing strength and aggression of the Soviet Union and the Communist revolution in China, the uneasy post-war peace had become more precarious. Stalin agreed to support the North Koreans' initial offensive on the understanding that, should they be needed, any reinforcements would be provided by Mao Tse Tung. When the North Koreans were thrown back far beyond the original border they had crossed – known as the 38th Parallel – the Chinese sent in their troops. For some months the battle centred around the 38th Parallel until, in April 1951, the Chinese launched a massive offensive with 700,000 men.

Lieutenant John Milner, who had joined the 1st Dorsets in Austria fresh from Sandhurst, was sent to the 1st Argyll and Sutherland Highlanders in Korea and took over a rifle platoon. Soon afterwards, on 4th April 1951, two of their companies were advancing to take a ridge in the mountains when the defenders' machine guns opened up. Milner was one of two young platoon commanders the Argylls lost in this relatively minor action. He was twenty-two.

Lieutenant John Milner, the last Dorset officer to die in battle

Three weeks later, 650 men of the 1st Glosters found themselves overlooking the Imjin River facing an attack by 11,000 Chinese troops intent on advancing towards the South Korean capital. Despite the advancing torrents of enemy threatening to swamp them, the Glosters held on grimly for three days until their officers ordered them to retire. Only forty made it back. The rest were killed or captured. Many were wounded, among them at least three Dorsets – Privates Egan, Mortimer and Payton. Among the prisoners of war were at least two more – Lieutenant Alan Blundell and Private Leonard Tyrrell, who (as we have seen) had already spent five years as a prisoner of the Germans. As captives of the Chinese, their experience would be protracted and brutal. Their guards would use abuse, torture and brainwashing to destroy their capacity to resist. They would finally be released in August 1953 when an armistice returned both sides to almost exactly the positions they had held before North Korea's invasion.

THREE GOOD MEN AND A KING DEPART, A QUEEN ARRIVES AND A SESTERCENTENNIAL IS CELEBRATED

Throughout the Korean War the 1st Dorsets remained in Austria, providing ceremonial guards, training and excelling at various sports. In August 1951 the Battalion won the BTA Athletic Crown, which was fiercely contested between the Dorsets, West Yorkshires, Royal Warwicks and an RASC team drawn from the whole command. The programme spread over four days, during which the Dorsets – through good teamwork – managed to take top points in the 5,000 metres although not one of their team finished in the first three. They also won the 4 × 110 metres hurdles and finally snatched overall victory from the 1st West Yorkshires, who had been undefeated for three years.

After the war the Regiment had decided to build houses to stand as practical memorials within the county to the Dorset Regiment's dead. By early 1951 the houses at Broadmayne and Dorchester were ready to be occupied by the wives and children of soldiers who died with the Regiment. They would soon be followed by properties in Sherborne and Upton.

Early 1951 saw the retirement of two prominent Dorsets. In January Lieutenant-Colonel Os Ball finally hung up his boots after more than four decades. Joining the 1st Battalion as a boy soldier in 1909, he had been promoted lance-corporal six months before the outbreak of the First World War, in which he had risen to Regimental Quartermaster-Sergeant, been twice mentioned in Despatches and awarded the Meritorious Service Medal. In 1921 he became RSM of the

1st Dorsets before being commissioned Quartermaster in 1928. He remained Quartermaster of the Battalion for an astonishing fifteen years, until they left Malta after the siege. Later he served at Monty's GHQ 21st Army Group and was appointed OBE. He continued in BAOR until 1948 before his last posting, which was a three year stint as an instructor at the Senior Officers' School at Devizes, where Knocker White and Skinny Laugher were among the students. On Colonel Os's retirement, after more than forty-one years in the army, his longstanding friend and former Commanding Officer Ivan de la Bere spoke rightly of *his loyal and tireless services to the Regiment which he served so honourably and devotedly for so many years.*

Meanwhile, Colonel Joe Weld handed over command of the 4th Battalion to Colonel Joe Symonds. Joe Weld had faced an uphill task, trying to revive a TA battalion during a period when few men wanted to don military uniform voluntarily and when the terms of the *National Service Act* limited the pool of potential recruits. Despite this, he had managed to form and then maintain one of the two strongest battalions in the Division. His successor, Joe Symonds, was a nephew of Carl Richards, who had commanded a company in the 4th Dorsets during the First World War. Symonds himself had been a company commander with the 4th Dorsets in Normandy and in Germany. Twice wounded, he had twice returned to his Battalion and had twice won the Military Cross. It was hard to imagine a better man to succeed Weld as Commanding Officer. In the next four years Joe Symonds would work tirelessly to consolidate and build on the sturdy foundations laid by his predecessor. His command fell during the Cold War when the threat from Stalin's Soviet Union seemed pressing and imminent. Symonds remembered the period from 1951 until 1955: *I felt I could have been working in Dorchester one week and advancing towards the Russians the next. Throughout we remained at seven days' notice to move to Germany on mobilisation.* He recalled: *I was blessed with very fine Training Majors.* He was indeed: they were Tony Lewis and Oner Bray.

This was a time of retirements. In early 1952 the widely respected Brigadier Charles Woodhouse, who had done so much for the Regiment as its Colonel, handed over the reins to General George Wood. February 1952 saw the 250th anniversary of the creation of the 39th Regiment of Foot in Ireland in 1702, and one of Charles Woodhouse's last acts as Colonel had been to plan a programme of events throughout the year to commemorate and celebrate this anniversary. But, a few days before the first of these was to take place, Britain and her Commonwealth were stunned by the death of King George VI on 6th February.

At first glance an unlikely man to have won so many hearts, he had taken on the job unexpectedly and with great reluctance when his brother abdicated. Unprepared for the task and plagued by a nervous stammer, he had felt quite unfitted for the weight of responsibility that fell upon him. But his determination, courage and selflessness – and his equally stout-hearted Queen – enabled him to lead his country through a protracted and bitter war. When he had visited the 2nd Battalion before they embarked for India, the King had quizzed Colonel George Wood closely about the well being and efficiency of his men. He had done the same when visiting the 1st Battalion before D-Day in 1944. At that time he had had to be dissuaded from landing with his army on D-Day – the first king to accompany his troops into battle since George II at Dettingen two hundred years before. It is amusing to speculate, had his will prevailed, about how the 1st Dorsets might have felt as they landed on the beaches with their King in one of their landing craft. In Austria the Battalion attended a memorial service for the late King and there, as in Great Britain and across the Commonwealth, there can have been few who did not feel as a personal loss the death of that shy, brave man.

In response to this sad news, the Dorset Regiment cancelled their earlier commemorative events for the anniversary. The celebrations therefore started after the end of the period of Court mourning, and they began in Vienna.

In March command of the 1st Battalion had passed from Colonel Tim Wood to Colonel Tom Affleck-Graves, who now commanded the parade as the Colour was trooped in the presence of the British Ambassador and an international audience which included French, American and Russian forces and Austrian civilians. The commander of the French garrison later remarked to General Wood: "Underlying the beauty of this ceremonial, I gain the impression of strength, great strength, and this I find most reassuring."

The distinguished historian Arthur Bryant had published in *The London Illustrated News* his own tribute to the Dorset Regiment. Entitled *Primus in Indis*, it celebrated the history and achievements of the Regiment, which he saw – rightly – as rooted firmly in the unique county that was their home. His essay ended, appropriately, with a poem by William Barnes about the people of Dorset which includes the lines:

> *They be sound, an' they will stand*
> *By what is right, wi' heart an' hand.*

In this special year the Dorset Regimental Headquarters were honoured by a visit from the new Queen. On 3rd July 1952, for the first time in history, the Royal

HM The Queen visits the Depot, Dorchester 1952. Escorting the Queen is
Major Philip Roper and behind Her Majesty is Maj-Gen George Wood

Standard flew over the Keep in Dorchester. The 4th Battalion provided a Guard
of Honour, which the Queen inspected, accompanied by Major Philip Roper. The
Queen's Colour was carried by Lieutenant Ken Miles and the 4th Battalion Colour
by Lieutenant Lyndon Moore. Afterwards Her Majesty walked around the sides
of the square and spoke to some of the crowds of spectators before visiting the
Museum, where the Curator, Major Vere Sclater, and ex-Company Sergeant-Major
Dolly Gray DCM MM were presented to her. After a visit to the Officers' Mess, the
Queen left, having stayed beyond her time. Later her Private Secretary wrote to
convey Her Majesty's interest in the Regimental Museum and admiration for the
steadiness on parade and arms drill of the Guard of Honour.

Those who attended the parade at the Keep on that warm July day may have felt
in the summer breeze, and in the presence of their young Queen, a faint softening
of the grim mood that seemed to have prevailed during the six dangerous years
of war and the seven bleak years since victory. The return to 10 Downing Street
of the still immense, reassuringly confident figure of Winston Churchill seemed
to promise an end to austerity and a relaxation in rationing. Inspired by Attlee's
government's swansong, the Festival of Britain, and by their youthful new monarch,

people began to speak of a new Elizabethan age. A whiff of change was in the air.

Shortly before the Coronation, Her Majesty the Queen honoured the Dorset Regiment by appointing HRH The Duchess of Kent as their Colonel-in-Chief. A princess of the Danish and Greek Royal Family, Princess Marina was a cousin of Prince Philip and a great-granddaughter of Czar Alexander II of Russia. In 1934 she had married King George V's son, Prince George, Duke of Kent. When her husband had been killed serving in the RAF in 1942, she had joined the Civil Nursing Reserve under a pseudonym. An energetic member of the Royal Family, Princess Marina was a woman of considerable spirit who would serve her new Regiment well. At the Coronation itself, detachments from the 1st and 4th Battalions took part in the procession at the Coronation, while a third, from the Depot, joined the thousands of servicemen and servicewomen lining the streets en route to Westminster Abbey.

The Coronation Honours List included OBEs for Joe Symonds (for his achievements commanding the 4th Battalion) and Tim Wood (for distinguished service on the staff in Malaya), an MBE for Tony Lewis (for his work training troops in Kenya) and a BEM for WO II Mick Trodd recognising his long and distinguished service.

The 1st Dorsets finally left Austria in July 1952, and returned to Chiseldon camp where, while replacing 300 experienced soldiers with 350 new ones, they spent the summer preparing to join the garrison of Hong Kong. Despite the rigorous demands of these preparations, the Battalion were able to play a part in some of the events to celebrate the Regiment's 250th anniversary, including the Tattoo held over five days at the Depot in Dorchester. On 29th August a hundred of their men marched through the town with their band playing, Colours flying and bayonets fixed. The Tattoo ended on Sunday 31st August with a Drumhead Divine Service attended by both the Regiment's battalions, those serving at the Depot and a large number of Old Comrades. Despite its sad start, the anniversary had been well and truly marked and enjoyed.

THE 1ST BATTALION IN HONG KONG 1952–54

On 4th October 1952 the 1st Dorsets embarked on the *Empire Fowey* and steamed, via Ceylon and Singapore, docking at Kowloon on the 31st from where they marched to San Wai Camp. Twenty-year-old Private Jeff Eckersall, a Bolton lad who had completed his education and apprenticeship in Dorchester, remembered that the camp was overlooked by a large hill, on which were displayed the regimental badges of several regiments who had been based there. The Dorsets were replacing the 1st Wiltshires and one of the first men Jeff Eckersall encountered was a close friend from Dorset who was doing his National Service in the Wiltshires.

The Hong Kong garrison had three principal duties: to provide some sort of defence for the colony (which, had it faced a determined Chinese assault, would have been undefendable), to police its borders and to undertake ceremonial duties and show the flag. The Battalion arrived at the most delicate time in Anglo-Chinese relations. The two countries were still fighting in Korea, and negotiations were being conducted to end hostilities without the West having to resort to the atomic bomb.

Private Patrick Baxter had joined the Battalion during their final months in Austria, having been informed by post that six members of his family, including the grandmother who had brought him up, had been killed in the Lynmouth flood. Arriving in Hong Kong, he remembered: *I was still very much bereaved and was not behaving properly and soon found myself in trouble. Captain* [John] *Freer-Smith showed much understanding and compassion when I should have been in serious trouble. I can see now why he was* [later] *Families Officer for 1st Devon and Dorsets and was awarded the MBE for his excellent work.*

The Dorsets' tour did not begin well. In December their new Commanding Officer, Tom Affleck-Graves, was taken ill and had to be evacuated. Sadly, although he recovered his health, he did not return to complete his time as Colonel of the 1st Battalion. Happily, a worthy successor was found in Knocker White, who was in Malaya, having just begun the task of forming the 6th Battalion of the Malay Regiment. Handing over command to Skinny Laugher, he took passage to Hong Kong to become the first man in the history of the Regiment to command both its 1st and 2nd Battalions. A few months earlier he had commanded D Company during the later days of the 1st Battalion's time in Austria. There he had astonished the Battalion with his prowess on skis. Now he donned tropical kit and prepared for new adventures in the Orient.

An early Hong Kong adventure occurred on an immense parade ground, where the entire Battalion had marched and paraded, company by company. Standing at attention for some time, it gradually dawned on hundreds of minds that someone was missing. Where was the Colonel? The RSM stood them at ease and they stood and waited, staring down a slope towards a distant horizon. Suddenly they discerned a speck on that horizon, which began steadily to increase in size as it

1st Dorsets uniforms, Hong Kong 1953
(second from the left is RSM Jimmy James MM)

approached. It was a horse. It was a man on a horse. It was Colonel White on a horse. Finally – as the approaching object came to within fifty yards – they divined that it was Colonel White on a white horse which was out of control. As it galloped straight for the leading rank of one of the companies, the men parted to allow their Colonel passage through and beyond, where he disappeared from sight. The ranks quickly reformed, but the RSM wisely posted a sentry to observe in the direction in which the Colonel had departed. Sure enough, a few minutes later, a speck appeared and grew, the sentry alerted the RSM and another space was made to enable the Colonel to hurtle back through his Battalion's ranks and to disappear at speed in the direction whence he had first appeared.

In the Battalion's new role in Hong Kong RSM Jimmy James did his professional best to keep them up to the mark. John Hambly, a National Service subaltern in Hong Kong and Korea, recalled an American helicopter landing on the square unannounced. *The RSM erupted from Battalion HQ, complete with pace-stick, requiring the driver of the machine to remove it from MY SQUARE!* If American helicopters succumbed to the RSM's powers of command, subalterns most certainly would, as Hambly remembered.

One morning on my way down to Company Muster Parade I passed the RSM on his way to Battalion HQ. Compliments were exchanged and then "Excuse me, sir, who's your batman?"

He then said, "I must have a word with Harvey. He's not turning you out very well."

After a further exchange of compliments one abashed second lieutenant turned about, and dashed back to his quarters to seek a better turnout.

Early in the New Year a draft of 250 soldiers from the Royal Fusiliers arrived and were accommodated as platoons within the 1st Dorsets. One of these platoons was commanded by Colin Shortis, newly commissioned into the Royal Fusiliers. A close observer of his officers, Knocker White could be fiercely critical; but he could also spot talent and, like Speedy Bredin, was quite shameless in poaching it from wherever he could. He asked Shortis if in the future he would like to transfer to the Dorsets, and Shortis accepted with thanks. Several weeks later Shortis found that, while other Fusiliers were going to join their 1st Battalion fighting in Korea, he was still in Hong Kong with the Dorsets. He asked to see White and asked what was happening.

He was told: "You're one of us now, Colin." Second Lieutenant Shortis tried gently to explain to Lieutenant-Colonel White that he was actually still a Fusilier and did not want to be remembered as the Fusilier officer who had avoided battle in Korea by staying with another regiment in Hong Kong. Moved by this line of argument, Knocker produced from his desk three posting orders ordering Shortis to Korea. Because he had wanted to keep him – and because he thought Shortis wanted to join the Dorsets – he had simply sat on them. Now he bade Shortis farewell, but only temporarily, because happily he would survive the next few months in Korea with his Regiment before transferring to the Dorsets. He will rejoin our story later. Justifying Knocker White's judgement of him, he rose to command the 1st Devon and Dorsets and finally became a major-general, Director of Infantry and Colonel of the Devon and Dorset Regiment.

Privates Tony Marsh and Patrick Burgess remembered one of Knocker White's long exercises – Exercise Pheasant – on Cloudy Hill in August 1953. When they were leaving, Private Regan, an old sweat who *had his own idea about things... simply said "See you, fellas."* He had his back pack full of water and food, blankets and a groundsheet, and he left the hut saying schemes were for young men; he had done too many in nearly twenty years.

Later, high on Cloudy Hill, the ration truck failed to appear for two or three days. *We were starving. Deep in the valley Eddie Sarjent from Tipton Roller Mills, Devon,*

Private Tony Marsh with Vickers machine gun

saw some ducks. He took off to the bottom of the valley, caught three ducks, killed them, plucked and drew them and set about to make duck stew. It went down well.

On return to camp, they found Private Regan asleep on his bed. *On waking he said he had looked after the place for us. Pheasant had been hot and hard. Digging in, digging bunkers and defending the area. Our officers were impressive.*

Private Geoff Eavis joined the Regiment on 5th June 1952 and served three years as a Regular soldier. After basic training at the Depot and continuation training at Exeter, he joined the 1st Battalion in Hong Kong. On arrival he was greeted by *our old Provo Sergeant from the Depot, 'Gracie' Fields. The first thing we had to do was change into shorts and vest and run to the top of Badge Hill. Anyone that has been there will know how hard this is after being at sea for six weeks.*

After a few weeks in C Company, Eavis joined S Company and trained to be a carrier driver under Corporals *Oxo* Upton and Vic Farminer:... *our first manoeuvre was a live firing range at the rear of the camp. We had to go between the tapes to keep out of the minefields where the Assault Pioneers were waiting to blow us up. I was driving the lead carrier with the Medium Machine Gun Platoon Commander Captain* [Tony] *Jelley. I went the wrong side of the tape – all the others followed. Lance-Corporal Happy Harman blew us up. Till this day he has never forgotten this.*

Eavis also glimpsed the scale of the threat faced directly by the troops in Korea and Hong Kong.

... I will never forget doing the border guard at Shau-tau-kok and watching thousands of Chinese soldiers doing PT a few hundred yards away. What ten of us would have done if they had attacked, I don't know.

In 1953 Major Rupert Wheatley, who had been serving in Malaya as a company commander with the Devons, joined the Battalion as Second-in-Command.

Private (later Corporal) Gordon Pratten was another National Serviceman who, after basic training with the Glosters and two weeks with the Wiltshires, was transferred to the Dorsets and posted to the 1st Battalion in Hong Kong. Half a century later he remembered it as *one of the most uplifting experiences of my young life and I was thankful to have been posted out to the Far East because I think a home posting would have been too boring for me.* After *much seasickness en route* and a spell in D Company, Pratten joined the Mortar Platoon.

The six months based here was spent on intensive training and occasionally breaking up Communist inspired riots near the borders with China. The army was always full of rumours and, because the ceasefire situation in Korea was still uncertain, we were convinced that we would be destined for what we thought of as that 'God forsaken country'.

By now the Dorset Regiment was as good as my home and a sense of pride ensured that, whenever we turned out among the civilian populus, our uniforms would be in the best possible order. I wish I could say that our behaviour was of the same standard, but sadly we had been educated to believe that we were the best source of humanity on the planet. Little incidents during our stay proved otherwise.

THE 1ST BATTALION IN KOREA 1954–55

When the 1st Dorsets were told of their forthcoming move to Korea, Private Tony Marsh thought luck was on their side because the two sides were discussing terms for an armistice. He recalled: *Each Company in turn were detailed to turn up at the Medical rooms for jabs, cholera and typhus being two of them. Stripped to our waists, we had hands on our hips, through the second door, a jab in each arm. The syringes were scary: it reminded me of the vet using syringes back home on the farm. Stainless steel, huge and no changing needles; they were not sharp. However, after the first two jabs we carried on through another door only to receive two more jabs. Four in one go; we were given the weekend off.*

Their move, in August 1954, coincided with the bi-centenary of the 39th Regiment of Foot landing in India – *Primus in Indis*. Just as the 2nd Battalion had narrowly missed out on qualifying for the General Service Medal with clasp *Malaya*, so now most of the 1st Battalion set out for Korea just too late to earn the United Nations Korea Medal.

Gordon Pratten remembered: *After two weeks of intensive battle training we were shipped out from Hong Kong on HMT Dunera bound for Korea, where after four or five days we landed at Pusan in South Korea. As we disembarked an American band played 'When the saints come marching in.'*

The sights that met me took my breath away and at the tender age of nineteen I saw immediately the absolute stupidity of warfare. This country had been fought through up and down its length four times and during our two-day train journey to the North, to a point just south of the Imjin River, we passed through countryside and places of habitation that had been blasted to hell. Hardly a tree stood at its full height and we subsequently learned that more ammunition had been expended during the three years of this war than was used during the entire six years of World War Two.

In the Regimental Journal they recorded finding themselves *in a really lively first-class formation – where everyone was pleased to welcome us and help us settle in. In 28 British Commonwealth Brigade we took our places alongside our old friends of Austrian days, the Northamptons and the 1st and 3rd Battalions of the Royal Australia Regiment.*

The hills we found to our joy were not so high or steep as in the New Territories, the weather, although there was a lot of rain to fall, was much pleasanter than that which we had left.

On 17th September 1954 the Battalion commemorated the tenth anniversary of the Battle of Arnhem. Although they had no 4th Battalion veterans there, Captain John Wreford (late of the 5th) was present, as was Sergeant Norman Elgie, who had won a Military Medal on the Island with the 1st Battalion. In October the Dorsets were moved to 29 Infantry Brigade.

Gordon Pratten recalled how:... *The following eleven months were spent policing an area up to and over the Imjin River. We also carried out early morning raids on freezing villages in the depth of winter – and Korean winters are something to behold. I well remember one of our army cooks saying that it was the only country he had visited where you must boil an egg before you can fry it!*

... there was more live ammunition lying around everywhere and no army wants to take back to its own country any ordnance that has been in an active zone; therefore

we had to carry out many exercises using up all dangerous material... We fired off tons of 3-inch mortar bombs, many thousands of rounds of rifle and machine gun bullets, which of course brought about the occasional mishap, but we learned to live with and accept this.

Each battalion from all the different United Nations that were stationed in Korea had to police the Demarkation Zone, otherwise known as the 38th Parallel. It was during one of our tours up there, and I am proud to recall, one night whilst at my station up in the observation tower... I was concerned about the amount of vehicular activity on the Communist side of the border. I therefore alerted the duty officer, who duly arrived and agreed with my concerns. As a result a telephone call was made to alert Battalion Headquarters of our observations and, as a direct result, a message was sent to the White House in America, resulting in the whole of South Korea being roused to the Stand-By position.

The Korean winter of 1954–55 was bitterly cold and in Dorset the new Colonel, General George Wood, launched a Winter Fund to try to help the men of the 1st Battalion. Geoff Eavis recalled: ... *how cold it was, and the red hot chuffers in the middle of the tent made out of 40-gallon drums with diesel oil dripping into them. Every two hours if we were on guard we had to start the vehicles to stop them freezing up. One night, me and my mate Derek White-Rogers were patrolling the perimeters of the camp. The Gooks* [Koreans] *had been breaking into the camp. We thought they were trying to break in. We fired one shot into the air and called out the guard. Corporal Oxo Upton called out the Company. They tried to get their rifles out of the strong room, but the storeman, my old mate Ted Bashford, had gone out for the night, and did not tell anyone. It was Ted trying to get back in. Ted went before the CO and got twenty-eight days' detention. He never forgot that. When I came out of the army Ted lived a few doors away; right up until he died a few years ago he would say: "You bugger, you got me twenty-eight days!"*

Tragedy struck on the last day of February when twenty-two-year-old Private John Eady from Tincleton died of wounds received accidentally during a large-scale exercise. Tiddler Damon from Dorchester was first to arrive on the scene and administered first aid until his friend was evacuated by helicopter. Sadly, despite Damon's efforts, John Eady did not survive.

In March 1955 the Battalion were visited first by the Chief of the Imperial General Staff, General Sir John Harding, and then by the Director of Infantry, Major-General Cecil Firbank.

In my last months in Korea, Geoff Eavis recalled, *I was the Padre's driver. This was a good job but two or three nights a week I would have to take him to the American*

Private John Eady, Korea, the last Dorset soldier to die in an operational theatre

Zone in Seoul. The Padre used to like his red wine. Because the Jeep had no doors I had to hold him with one arm and drive with the other, not easy on dirt roads.

The highlight of our Korean experience was if we had credit of over £30 we went to Tokyo on seven days' R & R [rest and recuperation]. *I managed to go three times. It was a rough ride in an old American Dakota, but well worth it to see Mount Fuji, Ginza Market and Geisha Girls, even if we were broke after the first day.*

Six weeks before the Battalion left Korea some of us left the Battalion and were posted to Kure in Japan. We sailed in an old cattle boat called the Wosang. It sailed from Inchon to Kure, where we had a terrific six weeks. We visited Hiroshima to see where the bomb was dropped, then we joined the Empire Fowey, and came home the same route as we went, but docked at Southampton.

WITH THE 1ST ROYAL HAMPSHIRES IN MALAYA 1954–55

Not all the 1st Battalion men went to Korea. Some, including Private Tony Marsh, who had had his four injections for Korea, *were called to Company Office to be told we were joining the Royal Hampshires in Malaya. Private Freeman had just joined us... from Malaya. What he told us was so grim that no one wanted to hear.*

... In just over a week we landed at Singapore. We eventually got a train which took us sixty miles north of Kuala Lumpur, beyond Ben Tong to our training camp called Sungei Penjuring. Here we were to undertake jungle training. Bren guns Mark 1 and Parangs (machetes) were the tools; sign language and no talking. Here we learned how to stay in the jungle for days on end, whilst patrolling every day. These were real bullets and rations were not brilliant.

Towards the end of the fortnight we had to experience our first night in the jungle, not so bad as we were twenty-five in number. However, on the way in, two miles or so, a signal alerted us to bandits. We took up our positions when suddenly bullets were flying too close for comfort. A large piece of bark was ripped off the tree just above our heads; one of the guys said he was going to complain. This training was too dangerous. On being signalled forward, we were looking at three dead Chinese (bandits). One was wounded badly, but never found. We were a bit lucky as they were crossing a stream filling up; their weapons were not the best but they tried to shoot it out. They did not hear us because of the heavy rain.

This exercise came to an end as we had to get the bandits back to the police for identification. Our position was now blown. On our return, HQ was waiting to heap praise on the lads involved. It was duly noted that the Royal Hampshires had been in Malaya for several months but had made no contact with Communist terrorists. We still regarded ourselves very much Dorsets.

Training finished, we were detailed to the four [Royal Hampshire] companies... five of us, Privates Carter, Hunt, Marsh, Neil and Norris, were sent to C Company. The Companies were miles apart; we did not meet up again until it was nearing time to come home.

C Company Commander was... Major Ramsay. By now we were based deep in the jungle. No frills, travelling miles down a huge river by boat. We were close to a railway, always a target for bandits. We initially patrolled from here. Major Ramsay was a good jungle man, keen and precise. He wasn't young but he couldn't get enough of it; personally I would have gone anywhere with him.[33]

He detailed us five Dorsets to mock ambush General Bourne, who was taking over at the top from General Sir Gerald Templer. We saw them and their support, but they didn't see us until they were through our ambush, when we all opened up, firing into the ground. Once more we were thanked for being realistic – we had to show ourselves, they didn't know we were there. We were just five metres from them.

---

33   We last met Ivor Ramsay as he returned with the 2nd Dorsets from Dunkirk on 31st May 1940.

Private David Chant with the Royal Hampshires in Malaya

By this time we were well used to leeches, scorpions and snakes. When possible I preferred using my hammock.

Harry Chandler from Oborne, near Sherborne, was in the same intake as Tony Marsh and also joined the Royal Hampshires in Malaya. Serving in A Company, he was involved in a serious accident while on operations when the army truck he was travelling in went off the road.

Tony Marsh remembered: *We patrolled for months, ending up fifty miles north of Klipis, heading towards the highlands near Siam. Patrols usually lasted a week, never more than three. Weeks turned into months and we were soon thinking of home. Time was so short. They flew us home. We got to Bangkok, then flew to Karachi and stopped, then to Calcutta overnight. Next day we flew to Bahrain, then Nicosia, Cyprus overnight, then Rome next, landing at Blackbushe in good old England. We were put on a mail train ending up in Winchester for some reason. The early hours saw us all put on lorries heading for the Depot, Dorchester. What a welcome sight.*

Three days to go [before discharge]. *It was wonderful to see Sergeant Daniels.*[34] *He even suggested getting our hair cut. It was the weekend; no barber.*

Even back in civilian life it was sometimes difficult for National Servicemen to escape their senior NCOs and warrant officers. Having been discharged in 1954, a year later Jeff Eckersall took his young wife for a day out at the Tower of London. One of the Beefeaters looked familiar and, after some discussion and hesitation, he approached cautiously and enquired.

"Aren't you RSM Webber of the Dorset Regiment?"

He was. John Webber had served twenty-five years with the Dorsets and the Life Guards and had been captured when serving as Company Sergeant-Major of A Company of the 4th Dorsets at Maltot. On retirement from the army and having been appointed MBE, he had begun a new career. Eckersall was pleasantly surprised to find that retirement, age or perhaps his new role had softened someone who had once seemed a terrifying figure. Mr Webber will reappear in our story – as unexpectedly as he reappeared in Jeff Eckersall's life – a little later.

In March 1954 the Colonel-in-Chief, Princess Marina, paid her first visit to the Depot at Dorchester. On parade were detachments from the Depot, the 4th Dorsets, the Cadets and Home Guard, and a large contingent from the Regimental Association. Her Royal Highness was presented with a Dorset Regimental brooch.

In January 1955 Colonel Joe Symonds handed over command of the 4th Dorsets to Colonel Philip Roper. As Second-in-Command to Colonel Joe Weld, Symonds had played a major part in the reconstruction of the 4th after the war. During the four years of his command he had seen the Battalion grow from 200 to 700 men. He now had the satisfaction of passing a thriving concern to a most suitable successor. A son of the Regiment – his father had served in the 1/4th Dorsets in the First World War – Philip Roper had served with the 4th Battalion virtually without a break since he had joined the TA from Sherborne School in 1937. He had trained with it in England, fought with it in North West Europe, commanded a company north of the Neder Rijn where he was captured, and played an important part in the Battalion's post-war reconstruction under the two Joes. The Regimental

---

34 Danny Daniels had fought in France in 1940 with the 2nd Battalion and had been captured. Escaping eastwards, he had encountered the Red Army and been made to serve in it for two or three years before being repatriated.

Journal of March 1955 welcomed Philip Roper's appointment unreservedly and spoke ominously of the dangerous international climate of the mid-1950s with the advent of nuclear weapons and the hydrogen bomb.

The 1st Battalion in Germany 1956–58

The 1st Battalion were not long at home. After six months at Bulford, during which they bade a regretful farewell to Colonel Knocker White and an enthusiastic welcome to his successor, Colonel Bobby Nicoll, they rejoined BAOR at Minden. After twenty-five years' service, Knocker White was now appointed Commandant of the Army Physical Training School. For a distinguished sportsman, which White was, this was an appropriate choice, but it seemed (and still seems) a wasteful appointment for an energetic Colonel who had proved his worth as a leader and commander in peace and in battle.

Princess Marina visited the Battalion shortly before they left Bulford, wished them well and reminded them of their *three great responsibilities. First, the good name of your Country – and of the County whose name you bear. Secondly, the Service to which you belong will be judged by your bearing and behaviour. And lastly, just as every British soldier is – in a very real sense – a representative of this Country, so you have a duty and a responsibility towards those amongst whom you serve; and much may depend in future years upon your tact and consideration for others.*

Bobby Nicoll's 1st Battalion, which arrived at Minden in a snowstorm in April 1956, contained men of past and future distinction. The new Commanding Officer, as we have seen, had served long with the Battalion on Malta, Sicily and Italy before commanding a company and winning a Military Cross on D-Day. The Second-in-Command was Oner Bray, who had won his MC in France in 1940. In time Bray would be replaced by Clive Chettle, who had won the MC at Kohima. The RSM was Jimmy James, who had won the MM swimming the canals between Festubert and Dunkirk. In Headquarters Company were Major Darts Dartnall MC and Company Sergeant-Major Norman Elgie MM. All four rifle company commanders – Charles Metcalfe, Hugh Wyllie, Willie Hayes and Douglas Harris – were veterans of Second World War campaigns. The seedcorn among the subalterns included two future generals and a future brigadier – Tony Jeapes, Colin Shortis and Bill Bullocke. Two more – Brian Edwards and Geoff Brierley – would command a battalion of the Glosters and Parachute Regiment respectively. Colonel Steve's son, Christopher, would spend a distinguished career overseas with the Commonwealth Development Corporation while Nick Speakman would serve in the Tanganyikan Police and the

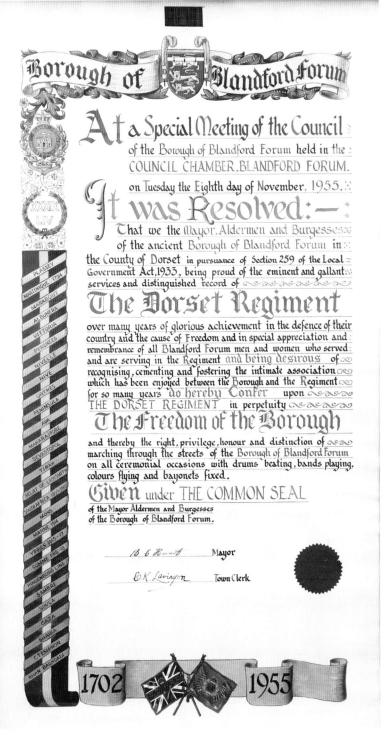

Borough of Blandford Forum

At a Special Meeting of the Council

of the Borough of Blandford Forum held in the
COUNCIL CHAMBER, BLANDFORD FORUM.

on Tuesday the Eighth day of November, 1955.

It was Resolved:—

That we the Mayor, Aldermen and Burgesses
of the ancient Borough of Blandford Forum in
the County of Dorset in pursuance of Section 259 of the Local
Government Act, 1933, being proud of the eminent and gallant
services and distinguished record of

The Dorset Regiment

over many years of glorious achievement in the defence of their
country and the cause of Freedom and in special appreciation and
remembrance of all Blandford Forum men and women who served
and are serving in the Regiment and being desirous of
recognising, cementing and fostering the intimate association
which has been enjoyed between the Borough and the Regiment
for so many years do hereby Confer upon
THE DORSET REGIMENT in perpetuity

The Freedom of the Borough

and thereby the right, privilege, honour and distinction of
marching through the streets of the Borough of Blandford Forum
on all ceremonial occasions with drums beating, bands playing,
colours flying and bayonets fixed.

Given under THE COMMON SEAL

of the Mayor Aldermen and Burgesses
of the Borough of Blandford Forum.

B. C. Hunt   Mayor

C. K. Lavington   Town Clerk

1702   1955

The Freedom of Blandford Forum

Lt-Col Eric Stephenson DSO MC (Mention in Despatches)

PSM Sidney Brown DCM

Private Richard Munday GM

Major Clive Chettle MC

CSM Yorky Seale DCM (Mention in Despatches)

Lieutenant Jock Given MM

Major Bill Pritchard MBE TD (with four clasps)

Corporal Sam Thompson DCM MM

CSM Ted Chivers (Croix de Guerre)

RSM Jack Horton (Mention in Despatches)

Sergeant Jack Blandamer MM

Major Sam Titterington MBE

The 1st Dorsets' Camp in Korea

The Dorsets on exercise with American tanks in Korea

George Le Provost's grave, Imtarfa, Malta GC

Charles Hampton's grave, Taukkyan, Burma

Sam Thompson's grave,
Tilly-sur-Seulles, Normandy

Unknown Dorset soldier's grave,
Normandy

A page from the Dorset Regiment's Memorial Book 1939–45 at Sherborne Abbey

Dorsets Remember: Jig Green Beach, Normandy, May 2014

Probation Service and become a stalwart in the TA, the Regimental Association and the Keep Museum. In the Orderly Room at Minden was Sergeant Bob Roberts who, having earned a BEM, would rise to Lieutenant-Colonel Staff Quartermaster and serve as Assistant Regimental Secretary of the Devon and Dorsets at Exeter.

Among the officers in Minden was Major Nipper Harries. Born in Devon, the younger of two identical twins – hence his nickname – he went straight from school to the RMA Sandhurst and, because his brother chose the Devon Regiment, was commissioned into the Dorsets. During the war he served away from the Regiment with Number 4 Commando and in Italy and Greece. Later he spent much of his career in Africa with the King's African Rifles. But at one stage, while serving with the Dorsets, he and his twin brother introduced some light relief by swapping uniforms and identities and doing each other's jobs for a day. Their prank, which is still often remembered by those who served with them, fooled everyone.

Nigel Salisbury, a subaltern of this era, later became a doctor and served as a Medical Officer in the Territorial Army. More than half a century later, he still regards his posting to Willie Hayes's company as a stroke of good luck. Bill Stevens, who was posted to C Company in late 1956, was also greatly impressed by the professionalism of his Company Commander, Willie Hayes, and the Second-in-Command, Clive Chettle. *What better leadership could an impressionable young*

Private Mike Bugler (on the right) and friend, Minden

soldier have than what those wonderful enthusiastic officers, both holders of the Military Cross, had to offer. The Company Sergeant-Major was Reg Burgoyne. I recall him as lively, slightly rotund, with a big bark, soft heart and considerable fun. This environment seemed to suit Private Stevens, who completed his long career as a major in the Royal Hampshire Regiment and a lieutenant-colonel in the Territorial Army.

Private Mick O'Shea also joined C Company in Minden, where he underwent twelve weeks' continuous training. He recalled: *I must admit I did enjoy it until I was told to raise the Union Jack outside C Company. Unfortunately I only tied a single cord to the flag itself. My CSM Burgoyne made me climb up the pole to bring it back down again. He then ordered me to run round the parade ground with my rifle above my head. In one of the doorways of the Barracks was my Training Sergeant Dinmore. When he recognised who it was, he just shook his head but said nothing.*

[One] reason I signed up as a regular was because I was told by the recruiting centre I would stand a better chance of getting into the Motor Transport Section after finishing my training. Instead I ended up in A Company for the next six months. My Company OC was Major Chettle, who was one of the best and I would have followed him anywhere in the world without question. I became his batman temporarily, mainly because he also wanted me to drive his wife around when she needed to shop! When A Company was disbanded, Major Chettle must have said something because I found myself being transferred to the MT Headquarters at last.

Second Lieutenant Nick Speakman remembered spending a great deal of his time in Germany *footslogging long distances and digging holes*, an impression shared by his contemporary, Tony Jeapes.

We did a lot of exercising, culminating with a major battalion exercise each year on Sennelager or Soltau ranges and the countryside around. Whereas in Britain it was always difficult to get permission to train over private land, if not impossible, German landowners did not seem to have much say in the matter. We moved into their fields and dug trenches. Apparently that was the way the Wehrmacht did it, so nobody seemed to find it strange. Sometimes we lived in the trenches for two or three days. Afterwards we would fill them in, having removed the revetted materials of corrugated iron and angle-iron pickets as best we could, but it certainly did no good to the crops.

The Dorsets' trench digging was something that remained with me for the whole of my service. Remember, all the company commanders were experienced from the Second World War and knew what they were talking about... In the 1st Dorsets trenches always held four men, because with four men one would always be a

Lieutenant Nick Speakman

lance-corporal at least and he would be the trench commander. With four men there would always be one man awake and alert. In battle, if one man was hit there would still be enough fire coming from the trench to make it effective, even if a second man was giving temporary medical support to the wounded man. And with four men it was less likely that they would cower at the bottom of the trench when they came under enemy fire...

It was also drummed into me in the Dorsets that to survive in battle you must not be seen because, with the accuracy of modern weapons, if you were seen you would probably be dead. In consequence you kept low and dug deep... A six-inch shelf was then dug to take your left arm so that only the rifle barrel, the soldier's eyes and the top of his helmet were above ground. The soil that you dug out went behind you, not in front... in what was called a parados... [which] provided cover to prevent your being silhouetted...

It was my experience throughout my career that the further people got from personal knowledge of war the more unsound some of their practices became.

Corporal Robin Gilbert of Nick Speakman's 12 Platoon remembered a large exercise with the Centurions of the 9th Lancers on Lüneberg Heath. It was late summer,

Firing a rocket launcher

hot and dusty. It was also harvest time and the German farmers were less than enthusiastic about the soldiers fighting mock battles among their crops. At first the Dorsets thought riding on the backs of tanks would be restful. They soon realised their error. There was nothing to hold onto and the heat from the engines and the dust being blown into their eyes made it a punishing experience. Every so often they spotted an aircraft and would be ordered to jump off the tank. Once, while they were on foot, their tank sank nose-first into the mud and the Dorsets lit cigarettes and anticipated a long rest. However, with a loud plop, another tank hauled it out and, after only about four drags, the infantry had to remount. When the disgruntled farmers progressed from hurling abuse to hurling missiles, the tank crews simply closed their hatches and the Dorsets became the principal targets.

Second Lieutenant Bill Bullocke and a section from 12 Platoon were chosen to take part in 4th Division's Patrol Competition. This required them carrying out three patrols. When they saw their opponents they were depressed to find that their faces were all properly blacked out with camouflage cream while the Dorset Platoon had simply smeared mud on theirs. Robin Gilbert wryly observed: *They looked the part. We were the part.* And so they proved. Despite being spotlit and nearly arrested by the German police while planting mock explosives on a bridge

The Winners of the Divisional Patrol Competition 1956
(left to right: Sgt Polly Pollock, Cpl Robin Gilbert, Arthur Dunn, Ray Wakely,
Bill Stacey, Jim Floyd and Mick Gollop)

over an autobahn, 12 Platoon won the competition and returned in glory to their
Battalion.

Gilbert felt privileged to be trained by veterans of the stamp of his Platoon
Sergeant, Polly Pollock, who had fought in North West Europe with the 4th
Dorsets. In many ways this wealth of experience was immensely helpful, but –
in the Dorsets as in other regiments – it proved a mixed blessing. Promotion in
the Regular Army had stagnated. For officers who had commanded companies in
fierce battles in a world war, it must have been a challenge to bring similar commitment and energy, eleven or twelve years later, to commanding companies in peacetime Germany. In some respects professionalism and physical fitness suffered.

Those among the 70,000 soldiers serving in the British Army's four divisions in
BAOR who analysed their role must have realised all too painfully that, however
large a conventional army Britain fielded, they could do no more than slightly
delay a determined attack westwards by the Soviet Union's overwhelming forces
in East Germany. NATO's almost immediate response would have to be nuclear. In
such circumstances it must have been doubly hard to maintain a sense of purpose
and professionalism.

The autumn of 1956 brought a chill wind of reality from the East. In Central Europe, Soviet tanks rolled into the streets of Budapest, unopposed by the western democracies, crushing the Hungarian rising. In the Middle East, Great Britain suffered the salutary shock of the Suez Crisis. An ill-judged venture by an ailing Prime Minister had to be abandoned on the realisation – unfamiliar and unpalatable to a Britain accustomed to moral diplomacy and military victories – that their government had been wrong and that their nation could no longer act unilaterally without the co-operation of the United States of America. A relatively minor but shameful incident had created a seismic shock: the Big Three of Yalta had become the Big Two. Great Britain was no longer a major world power.

From the nation's perspective, National Service provided the armed forces with a ready supply of young men with which to perform their still considerable duties at home and overseas. It also eliminated unemployment for two years of each National Serviceman's life, and it is arguable that it played a part in preventing youth crime by occupying and sometimes speeding the transition from adolescence to manhood. On the other hand, it interrupted a generation's progression from education to work and advanced by two years the age at which men settled to work and were able to contribute to the economy.

For the army an unintended consequence of National Service was to damage its professionalism. The rigid constraints of National Service created new difficulties. In A Company, Tony Jeapes was the only platoon commander who was a Regular and, out of every platoon of thirty-six men, perhaps thirty were National Servicemen. Almost all of these would serve only two years, some of which had already been spent before they joined their battalion. This high rate of attrition undermined professionalism partly because, by the time a soldier had gained some useful experience, he was due for discharge, and partly because it drastically reduced the size of the pool of potential senior NCOs; the calibre of sergeants suffered in consequence. The overall picture, therefore, was far less promising than it appeared at first glance. Senior officers within a battalion were less than absorbed by the mundane tasks confronting them, and training often suffered as a result. Fewer good senior NCOs were being produced to replace the excellent veterans of war, although the quality of some of the National Servicemen provided a good supply of junior NCOs. Private soldiers, although some were excellent, did not have long to serve once they had reached a basic level of competence.

From the point of view of the National Serviceman himself, the experience was probably less damaging than it was to the army. Some – a minority – undoubtedly hated the experience, resented the two years that had been taken from their lives and felt they derived little, if anything, from their service. Some – again a minority – relished being exposed to people, places and experiences that otherwise might have been beyond their ken. Most fell between these two extremes. They disliked aspects of the experience but found later that they had derived some benefits from it, such as self-discipline, self-confidence, self-reliance, friendships, a sense of responsibility or just the simple satisfaction of having got through it.

Private Tony Marsh saw the army as *a great leveller.* One of the major benefits National Service veterans often mention was its effect of mixing recruits of all sorts and from very different backgrounds. Private Peter Huxham, a National Serviceman from Poole, was a member of HQ Company in Minden. An unlikely soldier and strongly drawn to the Church, he rapidly acquired the nickname *Padre.* To improve the Company's timing at arms drill, Company Sergeant-Major Reg Burgoyne instructed them to shout "Bugger!" loudly each time part of the drill was completed. After they had done this several times, Burgoyne thoughtfully added: *"Padre,* you needn't swear." Huxham's nickname was prescient: he is now The Reverend Canon Peter Huxham, and remains a keen member of the Regimental Association.

After basic training, ex-Gillingham Grammar schoolboy Tony Coombes was sent on a clerical course. On return to the 1st Battalion, he was posted to the Orderly Room and was surprised by the amount of freedom he enjoyed in his work there and

Private Tony Coombes

with the pay team. The result of National Service for him was a number of enduring friendships and a lifelong connection with his Regiment. His children were later baptised by Peter Huxham, who was by then a curate in Gillingham. Later still, Tony became Mayor of Gillingham, served as Secretary of the Gillingham Branch of the Regimental Association and was appointed MBE in 2013.

Sport loomed large in soldiers' lives but healthy rivalry between the company teams occasionally got out of proportion. Private Alan Brown of the 1st Battalion's Signal Platoon recalled CSM Elgie, horrified that his HQ Company soccer team had lost a match, putting the entire team on guard and fire picquet on Christmas Day 1956.

For some, the army succeeded where school had failed. Jeff Eckersall reported at the Depot in 1952, having completed his apprenticeship as a plumber. A few days later one of his draft shyly asked if he would mind reading him a letter he had received from home. Realising with a jolt that his friend could not read or write, he read it for him and then gently suggested that he might make use of the depot's education centre.

"I'm too old for that stuff," the embarrassed eighteen-year-old replied.

So Private Eckersall offered to go with him. They went together and, by the time the man had completed his National Service, he had mastered basic literacy.

For many the rigidity of hierarchy and discipline sometimes irked. Mick O'Shea, who had signed on as a Regular, remembered: *After my training I thought I would be treated as a regular soldier but it was not to be. For instance, before going on parade for guard duty we would be inspected by our CSM who was very pleased with our turn out, and we proceeded to march to the parade ground for another inspection by the Duty Officer. He asked me if I had polished my boots.*

"Yes, Sir." I replied – they really shone all over.

He then said "Dirty beret. Put him on report, Sergeant."

When I was paraded in front of the Headquarters Company Commander, he said "Have you anything to say?"

I said. "Yes, Sir. You would have been very proud of us."

He then replied. "It was the Duty Officer who charged you. I cannot do much about it."

So I ended up doing seven days' Confined to Barracks.

If the alarm sounded we had to be ten miles away and dug in within two and a half hours. On this occasion it was about two o'clock in the morning when the alarm went off, which meant we had to form up on the parade ground ready to move. It was quite dark at the time and I had to report to the RSM, who asked if I was his Company driver.

"Yes, Sir."

He then said: "By the way, you have a crease in the back of your shirt. Consider yourself on a charge."

I ended up having another seven days' Confined to Barracks.

I know you must have discipline in the Forces so long as it is fair and just, but not one-sided all the time – which it felt like to me at the time. If it had not been for National Service, I would probably have signed on and made a career of it.

Some conscripts were utterly unsuited to army life. One, the son of a senior army officer, was entirely unmilitary and failed to grasp or acknowledge the hierarchy. On his first arrival in his barrack room, instead of tidying away his things, he stretched out on his bed and read a book. When a sergeant arrived and all the other men leapt to stand by their beds, he remained horizontal. The sergeant very soon made his views clear on the subject, but throughout his service the man in question never really seemed to adapt to army ways. A few seemed badly co-ordinated and incapable of marching or picking up even the simplest drill. Most, though, adjusted to a military environment as they had adapted to school, while some found they fitted in comfortably.

Regimental Sergeant-Major Vic Duffield MBE, who trained many National Service Dorsets at the Depot between 1953 and 1955, recalled that: *It was always a very proud day for me, having seen them arrive, untrained as civilians and slopping about, and then to see them leave, smart and upright and fit to face whatever they might be called to do.* Known as *The Voice*, Duffield was an ex Coldstream Guards RSM, and it showed. It was claimed that his commands could be heard three miles from the barrack square. He remembered standing on a horse in the gym, drilling four squads of recruits. *I had just shouted 'Slope arms' and, as I said 'arms', my false teeth flew out. My instinctive reaction was to shout, 'Sergeant Pollock, pick them up.' This was done immediately and the teeth restored to their rightful place. With no more ado, we carried on and I feel sure those recruits will always remember that little incident.*

On one occasion, Mr Duffield was called out in aid of the civil power in Dorchester when a busload of soldiers got drunk, ran riot and broke windows in the town. Assembling a picket of his NCOs, including the eighteen stone Colour Sergeant Ginger Tizzard, the RSM quickly mastered the situation and packed the soldiers back to their unit. In his memoirs he was at pains to point out that they were not Dorsets. Retiring as a Captain after a long and distinguished army career, he served as a Court Usher at Yeovil Magistrates Court for another sixteen years.

On his first day as a National Serviceman, farmer's son Robin Gilbert arrived at Dorchester South Station at the same time as two teddy boys. Viewing them with a degree of caution, he made his separate way to the Keep, where he watched with hidden amusement their effect on the Colour Sergeant. Resplendent in his red sash, he strutted incredulously around the two carefully coiffured teenagers before opining aloud (and in the vocabulary that senior NCOs and warrant officers have made their own) how much effort lay ahead for them and the extent to which their appearance would have to be adjusted if they were to become soldiers. After about three weeks National Servicemen were eligible for passes which would allow them to walk into Dorchester. First, however, each had to pass inspection by a sergeant. Often they were sent back six or seven times before they were passed fit to appear in public. On the first occasion, Robin Gilbert recalled, his friends were finally let out at 2145 hours. Their passes expired at 2200.

Private Mick O'Shea remembers Lieutenant John Ives, then Training Officer at the Depot, who dealt firmly and fairly with some very raw recruits. Nick

The Marabout Gun at the Depot, Dorchester (barrack block behind)

Speakman, who encountered John Ives when he was Adjutant of the 4th Dorsets, envied some of the interesting postings Ives enjoyed in Africa but principally remembered him as an excellent regimental officer. Even after retiring as a major, John Ives took great trouble to maintain contact with his former colleagues and their wives.

So much in the National Serviceman's experience depended on the quality and humanity of his NCOs and company officers. When Private Don Hanney was posted to the Royal Hampshire Regiment, he protested that his father had been in the Dorset Home Guard, his oldest brother had landed with the 1st Dorsets on D-Day, his middle brother had served with the Dorsets in Austria and that his was a Dorset family. He encountered no argument and was transferred to the Dorsets within twenty-four hours. When, after more than a year of his National Service, Corporal Robin Gilbert's mother was taken ill and the family farm was failing, he asked for an interview with Major Douglas Harris, his Company Commander in Minden. Within forty-eight hours Gilbert was on a flight home, where he was given a compassionate discharge.

THE 4TH BATTALION'S SUMMER SUCCESSES

In May 1956 the Band returned from Germany to play in Dorchester on 7th June at the ceremony in which the Colonel-in-Chief, Princess Marina, presented new Colours to the 4th Battalion. After nine days of rehearsal and in the presence of 2,500 guests, relatives and friends, the 4th acquitted themselves with style. Philip Roper, commanding the Battalion, carried the sword his father had carried at the parade in 1909 when the same Colours had been presented by King Edward VII. The old Colours were marched off to the strains of *Auld Lang Syne* before two leading lights of the 4th Battalion – Bill Pritchard and Chips Heron – handed the new Colours to the Duchess of Kent. Her Royal Highness then presented them to the kneeling ensigns, Lieutenants Gibson and Moylan. The rain, which had threatened since the day before, held off until the advance in review order, but it drove hard across the square for the final Royal Salute. Nothing, however, dampened the enthusiasm of the Dorset Regiment that day – or of their Colonel-in-Chief, who visited every Mess and was *immensely impressed with the very high standard of drill and turn-out*. This parade was the last appearance of the 4th Battalion's Quartermaster, Major Sam Titterington, whom we last met earning an MBE in Dorset Wood. Having completed another four year stint with the 4th, he now

HRH The Princess Marina at Bulford 1955 escorted by Major Roy Clarke

left with his wife for Germany to join the 1st Battalion. Other notable figures on parade that day included Majors Mike Sanders, Dennis Worrall and Eric Elford, RSM Russell and CSMs Stubbington and Chivers.

The Regimental Journal later recorded: *1956 must surely be one of the best in our 4th Battalion's peacetime record. In June, when they received their new Colours, they showed us what an extremely high standard they had reached in ceremonial drill and organising ability, and now they have won the China Cup at Bisley with the second highest score ever obtained in that competition.*

The immensely impressive – and impressively immense – China Cup was first presented in 1864 and was awarded annually to regimental teams from army volunteer units. It was usually won by a score of between 360 and 380 from a possible 524. At the July 1956 Meeting the 4th Battalion's eight-man winning team, which included Colonel Philip Roper, RQMS Jim Felton, CSM Ted Chivers (ex-Sniper Sergeant of the 5th) and CSM Jack Stubbington, scored 400. After their historic

The 4th Dorsets' Winners of the China Cup 1956
(Standing l to r: L/Cpl B Ainsworth, Sgt K Nicklen, Sgt B Bearne, Cpl R Goodwin
and Pte A Wareham; sitting l to r: CSM E Chivers, Lt-Col P Roper,
RQMS J Felton and CSM J Stubbington)

victory, four members of the team were selected for the TA Fifty to compete with the team from the Regular Army.[35]

Meanwhile, in Minden the 1st Battalion had been honoured on Kohima Day by a visit from Padre Gus Claxton, who conducted a service for the whole Battalion in the gymnasium. As always, the anniversary brought an opportunity to exchange greetings with old friends, and Bobby Nicoll exchanged telegrams with the 1st Royal Norfolks, the 1st Camerons and the ever-faithful General John Grover.

---

35   The Dorset Territorials had a proud tradition of excellent shooting, which seems to have been hereditary. Ted Chivers's son, Ken, was in the Wessex Regiment teams that won the China Cup in 1979 and 1982. Another member of those teams was Lance-Corporal Robin Price, later Champion Shot of the TAVR and winner of the Queen's Medal in 1982, whose father Tom had done National Service with the Dorsets in Austria and had been in the 4th Dorsets' China Cup squad (but not in the team on the day) in 1956.

The wartime generation were moving on. Peter Brind and Speedy Bredin were both brigadiers and Tim Wood a full colonel. Knocker White was still at the Army School of Physical Training, from where he would emerge with gusto to make his unique contribution to the Keep Museum. Skinny Laugher, having excelled with his Malay battalion during the emergency, was retiring. Tony Lewis was an instructor at the RMA Sandhurst, and Darts Dartnall was attached to the Royal Army Pay Corps at Devizes. Meanwhile, Jock Woodhouse, the son of Brigadier Charles, had been in Malaya as Second-in-Command of 22 SAS. His appointment secured two legacies: an effective system of selection for the SAS (some of whom had acquired a doubtful reputation at this time) and strong links between the Dorsets and the SAS. Woodhouse's influence was such that Colonel David Stirling and General Sir Peter de la Billiere would later claim he was the founder of the modern SAS. He was followed by two more Dorsets, Mike Hawkins and Roger Woodiwiss. They in turn would influence Tony Jeapes (who had married Knocker White's daughter), who would spend much of his career with the SAS and win a Military Cross serving with them in Oman.

AMALGAMATION

At home in January 1957 Harold Macmillan replaced Sir Anthony Eden as Prime Minister, and his new government set about rebuilding the damaged relationship with the United States of America. Overseas, Macmillan recognised that Britain could no longer play with Russia and America at the big table. Instead, he began to carve a relationship with America based on Britain being the elder, experienced statesman and wise counsellor to a youthful friend and ally who was new to international affairs. At home he celebrated low unemployment, a return to economic growth and a new, albeit relative, affluence. *You've never had it so good*, he told the British people.

The Defence White Paper, published in April 1957 by Macmillan's Minister of Defence Duncan Sandys, rebalanced Britain's defences, reducing the size of its army and increasing its nuclear capability in what was becoming known as the missile age. Promising an end to National Service by 1960, the White Paper presaged a reduced international role for a smaller, better trained army. The price was the loss of four armoured regiments, twenty-one gunner regiments and fifteen infantry battalions. The armoured and infantry reductions were to be achieved by amalgamations, but for some months it remained unclear which regiments would be affected.

200th Anniversary of Plassey Parade, Minden 1957
(Company Commander: Major Douglas Harris)

In the summer the Colonels of the Devons and the Dorsets – Colonel Monty Westropp and General George Wood – were called to see Field Marshal Sir Gerald Templer, the Chief of the Imperial General Staff, who told them that their regiments were to amalgamate. They were not alone. Thirty regiments faced amalgamation. Among the Southern county regiments the Queen's and the East Surreys, the Buffs and the Queen's Own Royal West Kents, and the Royal Berkshires and the Wiltshires faced the same fate.

It came as a bitter blow to them all but, in the main and as the Dorsets realised with relief, their partners had been well chosen. The Devons were a fine regiment with proud traditions which went back even further than their own. They were not just the Dorsets' neighbours to the west; they had also been long-standing comrades in two world wars and in campaigns dating back to Wellington. In the First World War their battalions had shared many experiences and in the Second, as we have seen, the 1st Dorsets and 2nd Devons had together faced bombing and deprivation during the siege of Malta before landing together on the beaches of Sicily, Italy and Normandy. The 1st Devons had even fought in Burma when the 2nd Dorsets were there. In the eyes of most Dorset soldiers, the Devon Regiment were almost as good as them, just as their county was as near as it was possible to get to being as beautiful as Dorset...

The two regiments approached amalgamation sadly but with good will and a determination, while preserving as many of their own traditions as possible, to make it work. General Wood referred to it as a marriage which had been arranged, and duly worked very effectively and amicably with Colonel Monty Westropp to ensure that both families were properly honoured and represented. HRH The Duchess of Kent became Colonel-in-Chief of the new Devonshire and Dorset Regiment while George Wood became the first Colonel of the Regiment. The first Commanding Officer, Colonel Guy Young, was a Devon, whose father had commanded a battalion of Devons and grandfather a battalion of Dorsets. Continuing this remarkable family tradition, his son, Simon, would later command the 1st Devon and Dorsets.

Relinquishing command of a battalion is always a highly emotional event. For Bobby Nicoll, handing over as the last Commanding Officer of the 1st Dorsets must have been a deeply upsetting business. One great comfort was that the 4th Battalion would continue within the Territorials, wearing the Dorset badge. In January 1958 Colonel Philip Roper, who was appointed OBE for his period of command, was succeeded by the first Regular officer to command the Territorial Battalion, Colonel Oner Bray. The Regimental Journal hastened to reassure any of its readers who might be concerned at this appointment by pointing out that *no one who has seen Colonel Bray at a 4th Battalion guest night will doubt that he is full of the Territorial spirit.* Although ambiguous and tongue-in-cheek, this remark was close to the mark. Joe Symonds remembered Bray as one of two outstanding training majors who had supported him during his period in command. As well as losing Philip Roper, the Battalion also said farewell to Chips Heron who, like Oner Bray, had won a Military Cross with the 2nd Battalion in 1940.

On a pouring wet day – 21st May 1958 – the 1st Battalion, The Devon and Dorset Regiment paraded for the first time at Minden in the presence of the Chief of the Imperial General Staff, the Commander-in-Chief and their own Colonel. Fifty-six years on, John Cobb, who was the Ensign carrying the Regimental Colour, has three vivid memories of the amalgamation.

As a subaltern platoon commander in the 1st Dorsets with the additional responsi-bility of being the Wines Member for the Officers Mess, my knowledge of the plan-ning for the amalgamation was minimal save for the fact that I was to be given the honour of carrying the Regimental Colour of the Dorset Regiment, for the very last time, on the Parade. John Ives carried the Queens Colour. Since the amalgama-tion was to take place at our barracks in Minden much of the time was spent in

Amalgamation Parade, Minden 1958
General George Wood salutes the Colours of both Regiments

the readjustment to new [Devon] companies and platoons and meeting new faces. My recollections are that all of this went surprisingly smoothly despite some in the Devons being unhappy in having to leave their fine barracks in Celle for the less attractive location of Minden.

    Prior to the Parade proper much of every day was spent on the drill square under the instruction and supervision of the formidable Captain Vic Duffield (late RSM Coldstream Guards) now Quartermaster of the 1st Dorsets. The Devons, God bless them, clearly did not know what hit them! He, when not on the ground, conducted each and every drill session from an elevated position (a platform of vaulting boxes had been constructed) in the centre of the square from which he surveyed his charges. No individual officer, NCO or soldier escaped his eagle eye... Although dressed as an officer, he stood impressively before us as only a former RSM of the Footguards could, with a pacestick under his arm. Needless to say, despite the rain, the Amalgamation Parade was a showpiece for footdrill besides being a very happy and memorable event.

More Devon officers resided in the Officers Mess than Dorsets because many of the Dorset captains and lieutenants were married and lived away from barracks in married quarters some thirty minutes away at Buckeburg. On the eve of the Parade I, together with some fellow Dorset officers, decided that what was required was a party in which we, as the host regiment, would not be outnumbered! We made a call to Buckeburg and enlisted their support. In a short time we were joined by the fun-seeking Buckeburg Brigade of Gerald Blight, John Ives, John Reynolds, Bill Tong, Paul Woodford and Roger Woodiwiss. If any present had reservations about the amalgamation they were dispelled that night.

A new regiment was born with a shared history drawn from two great West Country regiments. The extent to which that history would continue to influence the officers and men of the Devonshire and Dorset Regiment shines through a letter sent to members of the Devon Regiment and Dorset Regiment by John Archer, who was commanding the 1st Battalion of the new Regiment when the Dorset cap badge finally disappeared nine years later.

Since amalgamation in 1958, even though many of us today in the Regular Army have only known the one Regiment, we have always looked and will still look to the tradition of our Parent Regiments for example and inspiration. This history is recorded on our Colours and remains a living symbol of many generations of loyal service which nothing can erase... we who perpetuate the names of your Regiments will do all we can to measure up to the same standards of devoted service which you have always displayed.

THE FINAL YEARS 1958–67: THE DORSET TERRITORIALS

In the three decades – the forties, fifties and sixties – described in this book Great Britain changed dramatically. By 1967 the generation who had gone to war in 1940, and who had listened at home on bulky wireless sets to *A Nightingale Sang in Berkeley Square* or *Two Sleepy People*, were in their fifties. The tiny transistor radios of their young successors now blasted out the Rolling Stones' *Let's Spend the Night Together* or Jimi Hendrix's *Purple Haze*. The late 1950s and 1960s saw a social revolution which had many of the faults and virtues of the young who led it.

Sherborne School Combined Cadet Force
Wearing the Dorset cap badge are Paddy King-Fretts (standing left) and John
Wilsey (sitting centre). The sons of Dorset officers, both would be commissioned into
the Devon and Dorsets and both would later command the 1st Battalion

Its blend of idealism and rebellious foolishness, instant and often transient culture, reduced formality and increased social tolerance had been made possible by the new generation's growing affluence and greatly widened access to state education.

The giants of the previous two decades – Churchill and Attlee – had gone. By 1963 Harold Macmillan's government, under an elderly and increasingly infirm leader, had run out of steam. Meritocrats replaced patrician politicians. Standing at the Commons' despatch box were two men from the grammar schools, Harold Wilson and Ted Heath, but neither became the face of their decade as their predecessors had been. That place, on the front pages and on the televisions that now dominated most sitting rooms, had been seized by Twiggy, Peter Cook, the Beatles, Mary Quant, David Hockney and other youthful leaders of the cultural revolution in art, fashion, design, entertainment and popular music in which sixties Britain now unexpectedly led the western world. Meanwhile, Britain's unavoidable retreat from her unaffordable empire continued after 1964 under a Labour government committed to withdrawal from everywhere east of Suez.

In this less hierarchical, less traditional, more sceptical, often satirical society, and in a world in which Britain's role internationally was much reduced and far less clear, the modern army faced a more difficult task to maintain its discipline and purpose. The sense of national purpose provided by the necessity to defeat Nazism had gone. Despite the continuing Soviet menace and the jolt of the Cuban Missile Crisis in 1962, to many young people of the mid-sixties the threat from Russia seemed remote and too massive to confront. A naive but often admirable idealism led many towards pacifism and to protest against Britain's nuclear weapons. While many of the young men of the forties and fifties had been brought up to respect and obey, their successors were more likely to question and decide for themselves. And yet the army – Regular and Territorial – continued to recruit, particularly in Dorset, whose rural community was perhaps less affected by social and cultural changes that were mostly metropolitan.

It was fitting that the honour of being the last to wear the Dorset cap badge should fall to the Dorset Territorials in 1958, which saw the fiftieth anniversary of the creation of the Territorial Army. In those five decades the TA, including the 4th and 5th Dorsets, had fought magnificently in two world wars and given solid service in the years between and since. Their proud tradition, together with the Dorset badge, would survive for a just a little longer.

Like the 4th Battalion, the Dorset Regiment TA were drawn from and spread throughout the county. Battalion Headquarters and HQ Company were based at Dorchester, A Company at Bridport and Sherborne, B at Weymouth, C at Wareham and Swanage, D at Poole, and Support Company split between Gillingham, Blandford and Wimborne. Although most of the body of the Battalion was Territorial – and their Commanding Officer could be either a Territorial or a Regular – their skeleton came from the Regular Army, including a Training Major, an Adjutant, a Quartermaster and an RSM. Attached to each company was a Permanent Staff Instructor who was usually a sergeant from the 1st Devon and Dorsets.

Oner Bray, the first Commanding Officer of this period, had been commissioned into the Regiment in 1937 and fought in France in 1940 before joining the Commandos. His successor, Tony Lewis, was another Commando, who (as we have seen) won a DSO as an astonishingly youthful Commando Colonel in 1945. Tony Lewis was succeeded by Lieutenant-Colonel John Smith, known as *J B*, an Indian Army officer who had led Sikh troops in Burma before joining the Dorsets after

Indian independence. He was no stranger to the 4th Battalion, with whom he had served before as their Adjutant. In 1965 Smith was followed by Eric Elford, who had been commissioned into the Regiment shortly after VE Day. A long-serving Territorial officer, to him would fall the sad distinction of being the last officer in history to command a battalion of Dorsets.

The demands on TA soldiers, on top of those of their civilian jobs, were considerable. On weekday drill nights they trained in map reading, .22 rifle shooting, drill, first aid, signals and minor tactics, and prepared for forthcoming weekend activities and exercises. At weekends they shot on the ranges at Chickerell and Sydling St Nicholas and trained all over the south-west, practising platoon and company tactics in defence and attack. The training highlight of the year was the annual camp, when the entire Battalion went on exercise together. The camps of these final years were held on Salisbury Plain, in Wales at Sennybridge, at Folkestone and on Alderney, where Colonel Tony Lewis famously became a casualty, breaking his leg.

Territorials were different from Regulars. Time and opportunities for training were far more restricted. Experience and ability within a battalion varied and it took longer to raise new recruits to the required standard of professionalism. In this period, however, there were still a number of officers and NCOs who had precious battle experience and a clear idea of what infantry warfare entailed. Drawn from a wide range of trades and professions, a TA battalion was a very diverse organism which could muster from within its ranks all sorts of skills that would not have been found in a Regular unit. They were amateurs in the best sense: they gave their free time generously for the privilege of doing something they loved. They required less formal discipline and a gentler form of leadership. A very experienced Territorial officer, who had also served two years with the 1st Dorsets, remembers still how important it was to ensure that everyone returned home from their evenings, weekends and annual camps having enjoyed the experience.

Among their number were many stalwarts who determined the character of the Battalion. Ted Chivers, who had so distinguished himself at Cahagnes and then – alongside Philip Roper – had helped win the 4th Battalion the China Cup in 1956. Sergeant Legs Thorne, who joined the 4th after a long career as a Regular, and earned a BEM for his service to the TA. Bill Pritchard, commissioned into the 4th Battalion in 1932, who served as Brigade Major of an Indian infantry brigade in North Africa, returning after the war to serve until the very end in 1967, earning an MBE.

The Dorset Regiment TA's first annual camp was in May 1958, and 250 members endured a fortnight of the wettest and coldest weather conditions as they trained on Dartmoor. In one full-blown brigade exercise the Battalion played the defenders against the two other battalions' assault. Several evenings in various hostelries in Plymouth and Tavistock enabled them to warm up and dry out. Two weeks later they carried out an assault landing on Alderney with the Royal Marine Commandos and Royal Naval Volunteer Reserve. A series of parades across the county were devoted to encouraging recruiting and transmitting the message *The spirit is the same.*

In February 1959 they were back on Dartmoor, trying to capture members of 21 SAS (the Artists' Rifles), the Special Boat Section and 44 Independent Parachute Brigade. With the SAS was one Major Jock Woodhouse, who, much to his own delight and the Dorsets' chagrin, successfully evaded the pursuers from his old Regiment. Twelve of his SAS comrades were less wily. B Company occupied a most satisfactory position in a sheltered valley outside the Fox and Hounds Inn on the main Tavistock-Okehampton road, which enabled them to maintain a high standard of living throughout. John Freer-Smith, then Adjutant, assumed disguise and converted himself into Colonel Freervitch Smithsky, ring leader of a gang of spies which included Lieutenant Michael Aherne, who rather overdid the theatrical aspect of the affair by donning clerical collar and Archbishop's gaiters. Later that year at the Rifle Meeting at Sydling St Nicholas Colonel Bray's wife won the Ladies' Competition, prompting some entertaining speculation about the integrity of the scoring and of the winner's relationship with a husband whose nickname was a permanent reminder of his once memorably having achieved a grand total of one.

Exercise *Black Night*, in February 1960, involved a hundred men travelling 300 miles in motor transport, carrying out two night occupations and manning part of an escape route being followed by 300 SAS troops who were making their way south between Dartmoor's High Tors in drifts of snow often four and five feet deep. They bagged two parties of prisoners and gained some experience of night-driving, patrolling and operating and feeding in harsh conditions in the field. In more clement summer weather, under their new CO Tony Lewis, a group took part in a three-day exercise on Guernsey with the Royal Hampshire Regiment TA, sailing from Portland on the minesweeper HMS *Bronnington*. Once ashore, after a five mile march they engaged dissident elements who had taken control of the golf links; their leading platoon, under Lieutenant Philip Daubeney from Abbotsbury, saw some action against a small party of enemy occupying a rocky hill to their right. The Company then had to engage and extract the remaining enemy who had taken up positions in some of the bunkers and underground passages constructed by the Germans during the island's occupation.

After the amalgamation, the Colonel-in-Chief, Princess Marina, maintained her keen interest in Dorset affairs in addition to those of her Devon and Dorsets. In October 1961 she attended the dedication of the Memorial Screen and the Laying-Up of the Colours of the 2nd and 3rd Dorsets in Sherborne Abbey. A year later at Plymouth Her Royal Highness presented the new Colours to the 1st Devon and Dorsets.

On Friday 11th September 1964 the 1st Dorsets' Colours were laid up in Sherborne Abbey. Originally presented to the Battalion at Sialkot, India, on 14th November 1936, they had travelled with the 1st Dorsets to Malta in 1939. During the siege and throughout the war they had been locked away, rejoining the Battalion in Germany in 1947. Since then they had accompanied the 1st Battalion to Austria, Hong Kong and Minden. After brief service with the Devon and Dorsets in Germany, Cyprus and England, they had been kept at Dorchester awaiting this ceremony.

The Dorset Regiment TA provided the Colour Party and a detachment of fifty officers and men who lined the path to the Abbey's West door. The two ensigns in the Colour Party were Second Lieutenants John Tinsley and Michael Bull, who were escorted by CSM Bob Lamb and Colour Sergeants Richard Riglar and Tom Price.

Laying up the 1st Battalion Colours 1964

Seven hundred people filled the pews in the Abbey, and receptions were held at the TA Centre and, by the kind invitation of Bob Powell – late of the 9th Dorsets and now Headmaster of Sherborne – in the Big Schoolroom at the School. Everywhere were familiar faces on a day resounding with echoes of the past. The four subalterns who had played the leading role at the presentation of the Colours in 1936 – Lieutenants Symes, Hamblin, Wakely and Worrall – had all survived the intervening world war, all retired as lieutenant-colonels and now all lived within fifteen miles of each other in Dorset. All attended this last ceremony. So did Colonel Steve, Knocker White, Skinny Laugher, Bobby Nicoll, Broke Ray, Joe Symonds, Philip Roper, Os Ball and Top Knapp. Joe Weld attended in his new role as Lord Lieutenant. Commanding the standard parties was Major Bolly Bolingbroke. It fell to Brigadier Speedy Bredin, Deputy Colonel of the Devon and Dorsets, to hand the Colours to the Vicar at the Chancel steps.

Reverend Sir, on behalf of the Officers, Warrant Officers, Non-Commissioned Officers and men of the Devonshire and Dorset Regiment, I beg to offer these Colours of the Dorset Regiment to be deposited in perpetuity upon the walls of our Abbey Church of Sherborne as a memorial of past services rendered to the Sovereign.

The year 1964 saw two welcome awards to senior officers of the Dorset Regiment TA. Major Eric Elford, Second-in-Command, was awarded the Territorial Decoration while Major Bill Pritchard, now Paymaster, was awarded an astonishing fourth clasp to his TD. It was also announced that Eric Elford would succeed J B Smith in command. Elford had joined the 4th Dorsets in 1952 and would be the first Territorial CO since Philip Roper. Sadly, he would also be their last Commanding Officer of any kind.

The 1964 annual camp was in Norfolk, where the Battalion camped alongside their sister units in 128 Infantry Brigade, which was then commanded by Brigadier Graham Mills. It was the last camp for Captain John Ives, the Adjutant, whom we last met at the Amalgamation Parade in Minden, for Captain Ken Marquis, the Quartermaster, and for CSM Felton, the Regimental Quartermaster Sergeant, who was a veteran of India, Malta and the campaign in North West Europe.

Training for the TA sometimes offered short attachments to regular units in the British Army of the Rhine. In April 1965 Captain Peter-John Robson took a party of twenty-two Dorsets to train at Sennelager with Y Company of the 1st Royal

Dorset TA group depart for BAOR 1965
(Left to right: Cpl Pat Denty, Ginger Taylor, Michael Chant, Private Biggs,
L/Cpl Ken Parker, Sgt Danny Cole, Cpl Joe Mercer, Capt P-J Robson and Col J B Smith)

Hampshires, gaining experience in field firing by day and night and in the employ-ment of the Saracen armoured personnel carrier. During the Summer Camp at Penhale, near Newquay, the Dorset TA were visited by Major General Halford, then commanding 43rd Wessex Division, and by Lieutenant-General Darling, GOC-in-Chief of Southern Command. Speedy Bredin, Joe Weld and Philip Roper, now Second-in-Command of the Brigade, also called in. It was a bitter-sweet occasion as this was the last camp for J B Smith, who had been posted overseas.

In 1966, a Defence White Paper announced the end of the Dorset Regiment TA and the final disappearance of the Dorset cap badge. The White Paper reorganised the Territorial Army, renaming it the Territorial and Army Volunteer Reserve. Abolishing the regimental and divisional structure of the TA, it divided the new force into four categories, depending upon where the units in each category might be called upon to serve. The White Paper spelt the end not only of the Dorset Regiment but also of the 43rd Wessex Division, in which the 4th and 5th Dorsets had so excelled.

Five Dorset Territorial Commanding Officers
(Left to right: Eric Elford, Joe Weld, Donald Baxter, Joe Symonds and Philip Roper)

All this was desperately sad for surviving Dorsets of all ages who had served in all the Regiment's battalions. Those who feared that, with the disappearance of the Dorset badge, the Regiment might be forgotten drew some reassurance from the knowledge that, commanding the 1st Devon and Dorsets was Lieutenant-Colonel John Archer, who had joined the 2nd Battalion in the Far East in 1945 and served his apprenticeship as Knocker White's Adjutant. More reassurance still lay in the appointment early in 1967 of a new Colonel of the Devonshire and Dorset Regiment. Everyone recognised him as a man who had Dorset Regiment running through his every bone like *WEYMOUTH* through a stick of rock. His name was Speedy Bredin.

The last serving Dorsets began their final farewell on Alderney with parties and parades and the presentation to the Regiment of the Alderney Flag. In late 1966 and early 1967 marches and presentations took place in the towns which had honoured the Dorset Regiment with their Freedom: Poole, Blandford, Lyme Regis and, finally, Dorchester. In February a new Freedom was granted – this

HRH The Princess Marina at the laying up of the 4th Battalion Colours 1967
Colonel Eric Elford and Yeoman Warder John Webber flank the Colonel-in-Chief

time by the town of Bridport – and was accepted on their behalf by Brigadier
Bredin.

Princess Marina's last public appearance on behalf of her old Regiment came at
Sherborne Abbey in March 1967 when Her Royal Highness attended the Laying-Up
of the Colours of the 4th Dorsets which, for the last eleven years, had been carried
by the Dorset Regiment TA. The Colonel-in-Chief was escorted to Sherborne by
Colonel Joe Weld, Honorary Colonel of the Regiment and Lord Lieutenant of Dorset.
Preceded into the Abbey by Yeoman Warder John Webber MBE, who had joined
his old Regiment for this sad but very special occasion, Her Royal Highness was
greeted by Brigadier Bredin and the Dorsets' last Commanding Officer, Colonel Eric
Elford. Her path to the Abbey door was lined by members of the Regiment, a detach-
ment from the 1st Devon and Dorsets (then in Germany), another from the Brigade
Depot at Exeter and a third from the Dorset Army Cadets. After a Royal Salute, the
Colour Escort, commanded by Major Martin Evans, was inspected and the Princess
entered the Abbey to music played by the Band of the Queen's Own Dorset and West
Somerset Yeomanry and the Corps of Drums of the Dorset Regiment TA.

Passing between twelve Branch Standards of the Dorset Regiment Association, the Colonel-in-Chief was escorted to her pew. Behind her sat more than 300 Old Comrades and a large number of Dorset officers past and present.

After the first hymn (*O valiant hearts*), the organist played the Regimental March. The Colour Party marched in slow time up the aisle with Lieutenant Peter Sanguinetti carrying the Queen's Colour and Lieutenant David Hyde the Regimental Colour, escorted by CSM Ted Chivers, CSM Richard Riglar and Colour Sergeant Tom Price. Colonel Elford took the Colours from the Ensigns and gave them into the charge of the Vicar, Canon Basil Wingfield Digby. Gus Claxton's Regimental Collect was read, Brigadier Bredin read the story of the Colours and the Vicar gave a moving address.

At the end of the Service Princess Marina, accompanied by Speedy Bredin and Desmond Wakely, inspected the twelve Standard Bearers and their Escorts. Represented by their Standards on this last day of the Regiment's illustrious life were: Blandford, Bridport, Dorchester, Gillingham, Halstead, London, Poole, Portsmouth, Sherborne, Southampton, Swanage, Wareham and the 1/4th Association. Among the veterans presented to the Colonel-in-Chief at the Lenthay Drill Hall were Major Bolly Bolingbroke, a Norset who had won his DCM at Barjisya in April 1915, and Colonel Sir Mervyn Wheatley, who had gone to the Second Boer War with the Dorset Volunteer Company. In the spirit of a family regiment, Sir Mervyn was the son of one Dorset officer (who had commanded the Volunteers) and the father of another – Rupert Wheatley.

VALE ATQUE AVE

Thus ended the 265-year life of the Dorset Regiment and its predecessors, the 39th and 54th Foot, and with it ends this final volume of the Regiment's story. Since the amalgamation of the 39th and 54th in 1881, Dorsets had served all over the world: in the Tirah campaign, in the Second Boer War and the First World War, in North Russia, Ireland, Malabar, Egypt, the Sudan, Palestine and the Khyber Pass, and throughout the Second World War. In the First World War six Dorset battalions had fought throughout the four-year campaign in France and Belgium, at Gallipoli and in Egypt, Mesopotamia and Palestine. As the earlier chapters of this book recount, four Dorset battalions had played their full part in the Second World War, helping to turn almost certain defeat into total victory and, in the process, winning new honours for their Regiment. The Dorset soldier could hold his head high in any company. In defence – at Festubert, in blitzed Britain and on beleaguered

Dorsets Remember: Regimental Remembrance Day, London
Gus Claxton, Speedy Bredin, George Wood and Skinny Laugher

Malta – he had demonstrated an unbeatable, dogged resilience. In the attack – in the landings and the subsequent advance in Sicily and in the D-Day landings – he had shown great flexibility and dash. In the most gruesome and threatening circumstances – amid the stench of rotting bodies at Kohima, the carnage on Hill 112 and the freezing horror of Dorset Wood – he had stubbornly maintained his offensive spirit and faced up to a determined and skilful enemy. In victory and in the troubled post-war peace he had shown magnanimity to the defeated and offered protection to the vulnerable. The Regiment had entered the second half of the twentieth century with a reputation second to none. It was a triumphant but sad ending to an inspiring story.

But endings often create beginnings. In 1881 the infant Dorsetshire Regiment had sprung from the union of two previously separate regiments, the 39th and 54th, each with a long, proud history. This was equally true in 1958 when they in turn amalgamated with the Devons. Since 2007 the Rifles have been heirs to the spirit and traditions of the Devons and the Dorsets. The fifty years' service of the Devon and Dorsets created new stories and, while I have been writing this book, the Rifles have been creating more in what we hope will be the successful end of the British Army's long campaign in Afghanistan.

The passing of a fine regiment is unutterably sad for all who loved it. But the spirit of a regiment is drawn mainly from its history and, like history, it has no end.

Today at the Top of Town in Dorchester the Keep still dominates the skyline, but behind it – where once stood barracks and parade ground – now stands a Post Office sorting office. The Keep itself which, during the period covered by this book, flourished as the Dorset Regiment Museum under the care of Knocker White, Desmond Wakely, Hugh Wyllie and the redoubtable Sid Avery, is now the Museum of eight regiments: the Devons, the Dorsets, the Devon and Dorsets, the Dorset Yeomanry, the Queen's Own Dorset Yeomanry, the Dorset Militia, the Royal Devon Yeomanry and the 94th Field Regiment, Royal Artillery. Time has brought change but the Museum still prospers. Whenever the proud shades of distinguished Dorsets such as Colonel Steve, Speedy Bredin or Knocker White revisit their old home, they will find it remains a fitting memorial to a magnificent county regiment with a unique history.

Bill Chutter of the 1st Dorsets on D-Day plus 70 – 6th June 2014 –
soon after his 100th birthday, with Chris Copson, curator of the Keep Museum

COLONELS OF THE DORSET REGIMENT

MAJOR-GENERAL SIR HUBERT JERVOISE HUDDLESTON, GCMG, GBE, CB, DSO, MC

COLONEL OF THE DORSET REGIMENT JULY 1933–FEBRUARY 1946

Born in Suffolk in January 1880, Sir Hubert was the second son of a banker, a major in the Volunteers who died during his sons' early childhood. After Bedford School Hubert enlisted, aged eighteen, in the Coldstream Guards and went with them to the Second Boer War. After more than two years in the ranks, he was commissioned into the Dorset Regiment and joined the 2nd Battalion.

Having served throughout the Second Boer War, Huddleston remained in Africa, joining the West African Frontier Force in Nigeria. In 1909 he was seconded to the Egyptian army and posted to the Sudan, where he campaigned in South Kordofan in 1910.

In March 1915 he was awarded a Military Cross for his bravery in an action, in the early months of 1914, against the Mandal Sabai natives in the Nuba Mountains Province of the Sudan. By 1916, as a substantive major, he was commanding the

Camel Corps and played a decisive part in the expedition against the Sultan of Darfur. Awarded a DSO in the New Year's Honours List of 1917, he received a Bar two months later:

> *For conspicuous gallantry and the masterly manner in which he handled*
> *the final assault when light was failing, and a decision had become vitally*
> *necessary. He directed and led the final assault in the most gallant manner,*
> *and was directly responsible for its successful finish.*

In May 1917 (while still a substantive Major), he was promoted Temporary Brigadier-General and commanded a brigade in Allenby's army until 1918. At the end of the war he was appointed CMG and Brevet Lieutenant-Colonel. He had been four times mentioned in Despatches.

A staff appointment in North West Persia, which was threatened by Bolshevik insurgents, provided an interlude before Huddleston returned to the Egyptian army in 1922. His initial task was to quell disturbances in Upper Egypt but in 1924, on the murder of the British Governor General of the Sudan, Huddleston organised the evacuation of Egyptian troops from the Sudan. In the process he handled a mutiny in the Sudanese army and was supported by the 1st Dorsets. When the Sudan Defence Force was formed in 1925 he became its first commander.

Huddleston married Moir Corbett in Kensington in 1928. Rejoining the British Army, he commanded 14 Infantry Brigade at Catterick for three years from 1930. In 1933 he was promoted Major-General and appointed Colonel of the Dorset Regiment. After four years serving in Assam and Baluchistan, Huddleston retired in 1938 and was appointed Lieutenant-Governor of the Royal Hospital, Chelsea.

Retirement did not last. The Second World War first took the fifty-nine-year-old General Huddleston to Northern Ireland before returning him in 1940 to the Sudan, this time as Governor-General. On his way to take up this appointment, he visited the 1st Dorsets in Malta during the early days of the siege.

Back in the Sudan, Huddleston first organised its defence against the Axis threat from the north and then played an important part in operations, mounted from the Sudan, against the Italians in Eritrea and Abyssinia. He spent seven more, punishing and politically precarious, years in the Sudan before retiring in 1947. He died, aged seventy, in London in October 1950.

BRIGADIER CHARLES HALL WOODHOUSE,
OBE, MC, DL, JP, MA

COLONEL OF THE DORSET REGIMENT FEBRUARY 1946–FEBRUARY 1952

Born in 1891, Charles Woodhouse was a member of the Blandford family who owned the Hall & Woodhouse Brewery. Commissioned from Cambridge University into the 4th Battalion in 1911, he transferred to the 1st Battalion in 1913.

On the outbreak of war, the 1st Dorsets went to France on 16th August 1914 and took part in the fighting retreat from Mons. In mid-October the Battalion took part in the Battle of La Bassée and suffered more than 400 casualties. Twenty-three-year-old Lieutenant Charles Woodhouse survived but was captured on 22nd October at Violaines. His nine weeks as a subaltern in action had earned him a mention in Despatches and one of the first awards of the Military Cross. There followed more than four years as a prisoner of war.

Immediately on his release Woodhouse volunteered to command the Dorset Company in the 2nd Hampshires, who were being despatched as part of the North Russian Relief Force to fight the Bolsheviks. Landing at Archangel in late May 1919, Woodhouse's Dorsets found themselves embroiled in a confused, unwinnable campaign in swampy forests where they were plagued by flies, betrayed by mutinous White Russian allies and sporadically shelled, before they were withdrawn four months later.

In early 1921 Charles Woodhouse married Stella, the daughter of Lieutenant-Colonel Charles Evelyn Fairlie who had served with distinction in South Africa during the Second Boer War and First World War. During the 1920s Captain Woodhouse served at the Depot, with the 2nd Battalion in Khartoum (under Colonel Huddleston) and Cairo, and as Adjutant to the 4th Battalion. Promoted Major in 1928, he rejoined the 2nd Battalion in Germany and commanded the Depot for three years from 1929. In 1932 he rejoined the 2nd Battalion and served with it – on Portland and in Dover, Egypt, Palestine and Aldershot – until 1938.

As Commanding Officer from 1935, he took the 2nd Battalion to Palestine during the early stages of the Arab Revolt. He led from the front. On 9th October 1936 he personally took a column, comprising B and C Companies, two mortar detachments, a section of machine guns and a section of RHA, to Kefr, south of

Tulkarm, to try to capture a band of rebels. Lieutenant-Colonel Woodhouse was later appointed OBE and again mentioned in Despatches.

In the Second World War persistent ill health precluded Woodhouse from serving overseas, but he commanded and trained two brigades – 128 Brigade in 43rd Wessex Division and 211 Brigade, which was a home defence brigade – before becoming a Staff Officer responsible for the Home Guard. A Colonel since 1938, he was promoted Honorary Brigadier in 1944. Two years later, in February 1946, he was appointed Colonel of the Regiment he had joined thirty-five years before as a Territorial officer.

No fewer than five members of the Woodhouse family served in the Dorset Regiment, a tradition which began a generation earlier with Charles's uncle Frank, who was commissioned into the 4th Dorsets in 1893. Charles's cousins, Harold and Louis (known as Lakri), served in both world wars. Harold fought in Mesopotamia in the First World War, commanded the 4th Battalion between the wars and in 1940 was appointed to command 130 Brigade, which included the 4th and 5th Dorsets. In 1943, while commanding the Blandford Garrison, he died of a heart attack during a raid by the Luftwaffe. Harold's younger brother, Lakri, served in France, Mesopotamia and Palestine in the First World War, winning a Military Cross. He saw action in the Malabar campaign and in Palestine in 1936 before serving in North Africa, Italy and Burma during the Second World War. He reached the rank of Brigadier and was six times mentioned in Despatches. All three Woodhouses of Charles's generation therefore held brigadier's appointments during the Second World War. Finally, as we have seen, Charles's son Jock was commissioned into the Dorsets and became the third member of the family to win a Military Cross, which he earned while fighting in Italy with the East Surreys. Like his father, Jock was captured but proved a troublesome prisoner. After the war he was a driving force in the creation of the modern Special Air Service.

Charles Woodhouse returned to civilian life and was appointed a Justice of the Peace in 1945 and, four years later, a Deputy Lieutenant for the County of Dorset. His generosity in buying and donating medals won by members of the Regiment laid the foundations for the Keep Museum's extensive collection. He died, aged seventy-one, in June 1962.

MAJOR-GENERAL GEORGE NEVILLE WOOD,
CB, CBE, DSO, MC, MA

COLONEL OF THE DORSET REGIMENT MARCH 1952–MAY 1958
AND OF THE DEVON AND DORSET REGIMENT MAY 1958–FEBRUARY 1962

The son of a commercial traveller, George Wood was born in Bristol in 1898. From Colston's School he passed top into the RMC Sandhurst and was commissioned into the Dorset Regiment in January 1916. Joining the 1st Battalion on the Somme, he was promoted Lieutenant and served briefly as Adjutant before being severely wounded in March 1917.

Although the seriousness of his wounds precluded further regimental service in the First World War, in 1919 he served in South Russia with the British Military Mission to the White Army, fighting on the River Don and on the Kharkov and Crimea fronts. He was appointed OBE, awarded the Military Cross and the Russian Order of St Anne and twice mentioned in Despatches. In 1920 he was attached to the Greek army in the Greek-Turkish War but rejoined the 1st Battalion in Ireland. Appointed Adjutant, he served with the Battalion in Malta, Egypt and in the Sudan (under the command of Brigadier Huddleston).

Captain Wood married Mary Izard in 1928. They would have two children: a son and a daughter. After Staff College and a home staff appointment, he was appointed Brevet Major and Brigade Major of the Landi Khotal Brigade on the North West Frontier, where he acquired a love of India. After a brief spell with the 2nd Battalion at Dover, he commanded the Officer Training Corps at Oxford University, where he gained an honours degree.

Returning to the Regiment on the outbreak of war, after a staff appointment he was given command of the 12th Battalion of the West Yorkshire Regiment before rejoining the 2nd Dorsets as Commanding Officer. Before taking the Battalion to India he twice turned down promotion to Brigadier and was instrumental in preparing the 2nd Dorsets for their arduous, savage campaign in Burma. When promotion proved unavoidable, he served as Brigadier General Staff of XXXIII Indian Corps and witnessed his old Battalion's hard-won triumph at Kohima. He reported on them: *They couldn't have done better.* He himself was advanced to CBE and mentioned again in Despatches.

Given command of 25th Indian Division on the Arakan Front, he excelled in his planning and execution of the capture of Akyab and in later operations, and was awarded an immediate DSO. Later he was appointed Companion of the Bath and again mentioned in Despatches.

General Wood commanded 3rd Infantry Division in Palestine during the post-war troubles and then took command of 53rd Welsh Division. In 1952 he retired from his last appointment as Director of Quartering at the War Office. That year he was appointed Colonel of the Dorset Regiment until their amalgamation with the Devons in 1958. He continued as Colonel of the new Regiment until 1962.

He died in January 1982, having enjoyed the unique distinction of being the last Colonel of the Dorset Regiment and the first of the Devon and Dorset Regiment.

APPENDIX 2

HONOURS AND AWARDS

(This list includes awards made between 1939 and 1967 to members of the Regiment and to members of other corps and regiments who earned them serving with the Regiment. A number in brackets after the name shows the Dorset Battalion with which each was serving when he earned the award. If no number is shown, either the recipient was not serving with a Dorset battalion at that time or it is not clear which battalion he was with.)

GEORGE CROSS (GC)

After the institution of the George Cross in 1940, the following five GCs replaced Empire Gallantry Medals won in the Malabar campaign in 1921.

5718784 Pte F Chant (2)

5718234 Sgt W G Hand MM (2)

5718907 Pte T Miller (2)

Asst Surg 3rd Class G D Rodrigues IMS (2)

5719290 Pte F H Troake (2)

KNIGHT COMMANDER OF THE ORDER OF ST MICHAEL AND ST GEORGE (KCMG)

11689 Maj-Gen W H A Bishop CB CMG CVO OBE

Maj-Gen H J Huddleston CB CMG DSO MC

KNIGHT COMMANDER OF THE ROYAL VICTORIAN ORDER (KCVO)

5792 Brig I de la Bere CB CVO CBE

COMPANION OF THE ORDER OF THE BATH (CB)

11689 Maj-Gen W H A Bishop CMG CVO OBE

5792 Brig I de la Bere CVO CBE

17955 Maj-Gen H L Longden CBE

Maj-Gen R L Petre DSO MC

13820 Maj-Gen G N Wood CBE DSO MC

COMPANION OF THE ORDER OF ST MICHAEL AND ST GEORGE (CMG)

11689 Maj-Gen W H A Bishop CVO OBE

COMMANDER OF THE ROYAL VICTORIAN ORDER (CVO)

5792 Brig I de la Bere CBE

11689 Maj-Gen W H A Bishop OBE

176902 Lt-Col V A J Heald DSO MBE MC

COMMANDER OF THE ORDER OF THE BRITISH EMPIRE (CBE)

5792 Brig I de la Bere OBE

17955 Brig H L Longden

24917 Brig H A E Matthews MBE

13820 Maj-Gen G N Wood OBE MC

37208 Col L J Wood OBE

9475 Brig L J Woodhouse OBE MC

BAR TO DISTINGUISHED SERVICE ORDER

56230 Lt-Col W Q Roberts DSO (4)

DISTINGUISHED SERVICE ORDER (DSO)

52571 Lt-Col J M K Bradford

49794 Lt-Col A E C Bredin MC (1)

509421 Lt-Col P H W Brind OBE

34667 Lt-Col B A Coad (5)

42983 Capt C R A Forsyth
   (A S/Ldr RAFVR)

30854 Lt-Col J Gifford

176902 Capt V A J Heald MC

95626 Lt-Col A D Lewis

751407 Capt R V MacNamara (1)

26073 Lt Col R S McNaught (2)

69156 Capt A C W Martin (1)

52027 Lt-Col E A M Norie (1)

15834 Lt-Col W H B Ray (1)

5486 Lt-Col E L Stephenson MC (2)

14720 Lt-Col B G Symes OBE

90922 Lt-Col G Tilly (4)

32188 Lt-Col W A Venour (5)

66144 Lt-Col R H Wheatley

47671 Lt-Col O G W White (2)

13820 Maj-Gen G N Wood OBE MC

OFFICER OF THE ORDER OF THE BRITISH EMPIRE (OBE)

40376 Lt-Col O V Ball

11689 Lt-Col W H A Bishop

18364 Lt-Col P G Boon

50942 Maj P H W Brind

15516 Lt-Col W M W Collins

15189 Maj R E C Goff MC (2)

34807 Lt-Col G G Green

40478 Lt-Col L W G Hamilton

47616 Lt-Col F F Laugher MC

28305 Lt-Col R D H Radcliffe

71683 Lt-Col P J Roper (4)

14720 Maj B G Symes (2)

78201 Lt-Col G J Symonds MC (4)

26475 Lt-Col F J Trumper

53007 Lt-Col J W Weld (4)

36351 Lt-Col C C I Williams

37208 Lt-Col L J Wood

Member of the Order of the British Empire (MBE)

138872 Lt J F W Barker

796 Lt J R H Bolingbroke DCM

136901 Maj H E Crawley MM

5720606 WO II A J Burden (4)

5719502 WO I F G Drew (4)

131476 Maj L C M Dutot

98557 Lt F J Edwards (2)

261665 Maj J A Fielder

189391 Maj J P Foot

99822 Maj E J Goslin

Maj A Grant

160905 Capt E Hannah (1)

124234 Maj D G Harvey

164725 Capt N Havers (2)

5723313 WO II R G Hayward (2)

176902 Capt V A J Heald DSO MC

9152 Capt R W Hodge MM

93075 Capt J D Home

163031 Capt H J Jefcoate (30)

76315 Maj G A Jones

117629 Maj J Jordan

95626 Lt-Col A D Lewis DSO

5725582 Maj W Luffman

143618 Capt G E Meads (5)

8991 Capt W H Miles

109230 Maj D G Pascall

45411 Capt E R Pound

53449 Maj W P Pritchard (4)

132418 Capt M C Quarmby

775454 WO II W A G Ralph

5721400 WO I H Smith (2)

205509 Capt H A S Titterington (4)

113613 Maj B E Urquhart

5723948 WO I L J Webber (1)

Maj J M Woodhouse MC

Bar to Military Cross

95488 Maj W N Hayes MC (1)

78201 Maj G J Symonds MC (4)

Military Cross (MC)

172272 Capt R J Adams

124567 Maj H C Allen (5)

60 Capt E G Andrews (4)

198226 Capt J L Betts (5)

71164 Capt H A A Bray (2)

49794 Maj A E C Bredin (1)

138725 Capt L G Browne (1)

219867 Capt G W Campion

104576 Capt J A Chamberlin RAMC (2)

138067 Capt C C Chettle (2)

71165 Maj P Chilton (1)

95799 Capt The Rev L E M Claxton RAChD (2)

278356 Maj H R A Dartnall (1)

96425 Capt L E Dawes (5)

137354 Lt D Evans

105574 Capt R F Hall (4)

93937 Maj G R Hartwell (5)

95488 Maj W N Hayes (1)

176902 Lt V A J Heald

55815 Capt J G Heron (2)

189393 Capt L T Highett (2)

78964 Maj G D Hodgson (5)

117629 Maj J Jordan

170473 Capt J F Kirkwood (4)

47616 Maj F F Laugher (1)

162009 Capt P P Lawrance (5)

278550 Capt D E McDermott (4)

126424 Maj K Mead (5)

331203 Lt M M Monfort (5)

57147 Maj N J Newton (5)

62624 Maj R M Nicoll (1)

74660 Capt J A L Peebles (2)

281805 Lt P L Penn

276405 Lt A F B Richards

126426 Lt A D Shireff

117886 Capt J B Smith

143742 Lt S Stoy (1)

78201 Maj G J Symonds (4)

58149 Maj R M Tarrant

149671 Capt J F Thom RA (2)

221859 Capt J Thompson RAMC (4)

295877 Lt P I Thorpe (5)

247784 Lt R Tilling (4)

126928 Lt P N Tregoning

121129 Capt R W Tucker (1)

50940 Capt T G Tucker (2)

63606 Maj D V W Wakely (1)

299401 Lt H H Wetherbee (5)

41527 Capt C R Whittington (1)

235367 Lt J M Woodhouse

53030 Maj D H C Worrall

BAR TO DISTINGUISHED FLYING CROSS

45333 Capt C T P Stephenson DFC (A/S/Ldr RAFVR)

DISTINGUISHED FLYING CROSS (DFC)

45333 Capt C T P Stephenson (F/Lt RAFVR)

COMMANDER OF THE ORDER OF ST JOHN

5792 Brig Sir Ivan de la Bere KCVO CB CBE

DISTINGUISHED CONDUCT MEDAL (DCM)

5725602 L/Cpl D A D Bounsall (1)

5718503 PSM R A Brown (2)

5720440 PSM S Brown (2)

5384577 C/Sgt J F Collins (1)

5724708 Sgt W J Cooper (2)

5725947 Sgt C T Edwards (1)

5721994 PSM E H Giles (2)

5722194 Sgt W F Seale (2)

5882195 Sgt A T Skingley (1)

5724115 Cpl S Thompson MM (1)

GEORGE MEDAL (GM)

5725595 Pte V J Bagge (1)

5719780 WO I E J Legg

2847 Maj G B Matthews MC

5724374 Pte R Munday (1)

5723470 Pte E D W Read (1)

BAR TO MILITARY MEDAL

3907199 Sgt W H Evans MM (1)

MILITARY MEDAL (MM)

5734953 Pte H Apps (4)

5725371 Cpl H G Barnes (1)

5726862 Sgt J W Blandamer (4)

5725038 Sgt G W Blundell (1)

5500455 L/Cpl L F Boyce (5)

5726406 Cpl J E Brandon (1)

5106720 Sgt E Brown (1)

5728866 L/Cpl L W Bunning (1)

5724986 Cpl B E Butel (1)

6087919 Cpl V E Carter (1)

6025436 Cpl R W Churchill (4)

14417029 Pte F J Clarke (2)

5723430 WO II W Coker (5)

4926571 Pte P C Cox (4)

14551906 Pte E Dawes (1)

5725458 Bdsmn W Down (1)

14706830 Pte L Driver (4)

5725697 WO II N Elgie (1)

14291504 Sgt W Else (1)

5725288 L/Cpl S D Ennis (1)

7887185 Pte L Evans (1)

3907199 Sgt W J Evans (1)

5728617 Pte F W Exley (5)

14436023 L/Cpl F G Foreman (5)

5342506 WO II H A Foster (5)

1782717 Pte E Furey (5)

5728400 Sgt R Given (2)

5727062 Pte R Goddard (1)

14218027 Cpl G J Golder (1)

6023331 WO II E J Harris (4)

5728237 Cpl W E Hawkins (1)

5735228 Pte H T Hill (4)

5730229 L/Cpl G C Hockley (1)

14694874 Cpl S Hodge (4)

5728746 Cpl A Holt (5)

3908149 Sgt A Hopkins

5726203 Sgt P B G Hopkins (4)

6146660 Pte P A Hyans (4)

5725676 Sgt R F James (2)

5723746 L/Cpl H C Jesty (2)

5726653 Cpl E G Jones (5)

1117965 L/Cpl L S Jones (5)

5724166 Sgt E T Kenny (1)

14406109 Pte V S Lawson (4)

5725792 Pte K J Leach (1)

4922918 Cpl A E Lewis (1)

5723957 Cpl W Mansfield (2)

5724315 Sgt R Mattock (1)

4643615 Cpl L Metcalfe (5)

6092620 L/Cpl J M Miller (1)

5724619 Sgt A V Mockridge (5)

5729363 Sgt F W Murray (5)

5728242 WO II L W D Northam (1)

5623175 Pte E A Parker (5)

14646360 Pte L W Penn

5725321 Cpl J Redpath (1)

7962298 Sgn J Rimmer R Sigs (4)

5727763 Sgt W E Ring (5)

5734319 Cpl G Rudd (5)

5776788 Sgt C F Scott (1)

5735051 Cpl A C Smith (4)

5726930 Sgt F Stretch (4)

5726158 Pte T Tabb (2)

5722842 Sgt A W Talbot (1)

14572801 L/Cpl R E Thompson (5)

5724115 Cpl S Thompson (1)

5617955 Pte S J Vigg (4)

5730366 Cpl F H Warren (2)

5350609 Cpl G Watkins (5)

5725357 Pte H West (2)

5735508 Cpl K J Willis (5)

5726774 Sgt E J Worth (5)

5345777 Cpl H F V Wright (1)

6343339 Pte J Wynne

BRITISH EMPIRE MEDAL (BEM)

5726102 C/Sgt W F C Anderson

14209709 Cpl J Gibson (1)

3906748 Cpl I Hathaway (1)

5724926 Sgt F E Norman (1)

5723664 Cpl A W Phillips

5732134 Sgt L C Purdy

5723836 WO II C L Siegel (Depot)

Sgt R Thomas (1)

Sgt R F Thorne (Dorset TA)

WO II G F Trodd (1)

4862376 Sgt A R Wheelhouse

TERRITORIAL DECORATION (TD)

Maj D W Butcher

Maj A A P Cotton Thomas

96425 Maj L E Dawes MC

421852 Capt C E Dawkins

Maj W H Dowdeswell

96424 Maj M A Edwards

Maj E D Elford

93937 Maj G R Hartwell MC

55815 Maj J G Heron MC

Capt W J Hicks

9152 Lt R W Hodge MBE

Capt K Holland

Maj H F W Holmes

Lt-Col T Hughes

Maj G E Insley

Maj D L James

162009 Capt P P Lawrance MC

Capt C D Letson

Lt-Col R W Martin

Maj J T Melvin

53449 Maj W P Pritchard MBE

Maj R E J Richards

71683 Maj P J Roper

Maj J Seymour

78201 Maj G J Symonds MC

Maj E W Tory

26475 Lt-Col F J Trumper

53007 Lt-Col J W Weld OBE

36351 Lt-Col C C I Williams

Maj M De L Wilson

KING'S COMMENDATION FOR GALLANTRY

5728898 L/Cpl W I Illiff

5730511 Pte J E Madle

13023400 WO II C Makin

MENTIONED IN DESPATCHES
(ARRANGED WITHIN THEATRES OF OPERATIONS)

BELGIUM AND FRANCE 1940

5722597 Cpl J W Adams (2)
5724455 WO III H D Bowles (2)
5724367 Sgt E H Burnett (2)
5726027 Pte M Dunne (2)
98557 Lt F J Edwards (2)
5723346 Pte J G S Morton (2)

5720640 S/Sgt D S Mullins (2)
5724674 Sgt H J Pearcey (2)
5726146 Pte J J Sinnott (2)
5721482 Sgt F J Smith (2)
6000 Maj D J P P Stayner
5722617 C/Sgt W L Trusler (2)

THE BATTLE OF BRITAIN 1940

6094871 Sgt J R Cowell

THE MEDITERRANEAN 1940–45
(INCLUDING MALTA, NORTH AFRICA, CRETE, SICILY AND ITALY)

323163 Lt G Barker
138872 Lt J F W Barker
5732838 Sgt G H D Brown
78288 Lt-Col F B Colvin
5792 Brig I de la Bere
1678 Maj A Finlay
30854 Brig J Gifford DSO (thrice)
91949 Cap N H Golding (1)
116776 Lt A V Goodspeed
8968 WO II H F W Hallam
49880 Maj S R M Hamblin
57876 Maj H F W Holmes (twice)
12643 Maj F C Jarchow

117882 Maj R I Lawrence
122013 Maj P A Le Sueur
23985 Maj A S Lindsay
23856 Lt-Col L Moore
124788 Capt W F C Pennicott
15165 Col D Percy-Jones
28305 Maj R D H Radcliffe
95487 Maj M J C H Sanders
126426 Lt A D Shireff
91473 Capt J T Tolley
Pte W H C Triance
9475 Lt-Col L J Woodhouse OBE (five times)

INDIA AND BURMA 1942–45

5721199 Sgt F Bagnall (2)
47992 Maj D McL Baynes (2)
57282116 Pte H H Bishop (2)
147177 Maj H D Bowles (2) (second mention)
52571 Lt-Col J M K Bradford
74662 Maj A V N Bridge
104576 Capt J A Chamberlin RAMC (2)

5724973 Cpl G H M Cripps (2)
5728760 Sgt A T Critchley (2)
37773 Maj G N Crowther (2)
5723356 Sgt E A Curtis
5728879 L/Cpl W T Davies (2)
145891 Capt C S H Doran (2)
268906 Lt S S Elvery

5728882 Cpl M J Evans (2)

85714 Maj H P K Fretts (2)

121823 Maj G C Gordon-Wright (2)

165778 Maj E K Govett

5723313 WO II R G Hayward (2)

189393 Lt L T Highett (2)

253961 Capt J A R James

5723746 L/Cpl H C Jesty (2) (twice)

76315 Capt G A Jones

5728027 Sgt T L J Knowles (2)

Capt A C MacKenzie (2)

285402 Capt J R Main (2)

5718457 WO II A Osmond (2)

320404 Lt C G Overman (2)

177749 Lt S H Prebble (2)

334341 Lt V C Pullin (2)

74659 Capt R L M Purser (2)

879662 Sgt D D C Randall

5722194 Sgt W F Seale (2)

5725275 Cpl D E Shearer (2)

5721464 L/Cpl J H Singleton (2)

14720 Lt-Col B G Symes OBE

5727589 Pte R Taylor

50940 Maj T G Tucker (2)

5728786 L/Cpl J Tuckett

5727586 Sgt J D Watling (2)

47671 Lt-Col O G W White (2)

36351 Lt-Col C C I Williams

13820 Maj-Gen G N Wood DSO OBE MC (twice)

14680940 Pte S G Wood

5724356 L/Cpl A E Woodford (2)

NORTH WEST EUROPE 1944–45

5718502 WO II F A Bawcombe

315197 Lt H G P Bear

5723746 C/Sgt J Board

14660189 L/Cpl D W Bradbury (5)

138725 Lt L G Browne MC (1)

18634 Lt-Col P G Boon

5342439 Sgt H C Carroll

5616168 Sgt B J Churchward (5)

5726987 Sgt C G Cleal (4)

14418531 Cpl E Clifford

5731740 Sgt G Coakley (4)

269406 Capt S F Coley (4)

5726811 WO II C Crout

278356 Maj H R A Dartnall MC (1)

1786933 L/Cpl J Dinsley

15147 Maj J R H Dowling

5719502 WO I F G Drew MBE (4)

5574692 Sgt F Driscoll

96424 Capt M A Edwards (5)

261665 Lt J A Fielder (5)

14380007 L/Cpl J M Grimes (4)

5721180 C/Sgt T O Guest (5)

93937 Maj G R Hartwell MC (5)

86253 Capt R W Hewson (5)

14708391 Pte L C Hickling (5)

5729295 Sgt E Hopkins

5723680 WO I J Horton (5)

5727835 Sgt C G Horwood

5726962 Cpl F V Jolliffe

62623 Capt A A E Jones

1117965 L/Cpl L S Jones (5)

256455 Lt A N Kaye (5)

5725836 L/Cpl J E Kingsbury (5)

5727322 Sgt P H Knight

115754 Capt L P Lassman RAMC (1)

14425069 Pte M Lister

17955 Brig H L Longden CBE

5961298 Cpl L MacDonald

5721229 Sgt J Manuel (5)

14731292 Pte W Mardlin

143618 Capt G Meads

66463 Maj K E Meredith (1)

8991 Maj W H Miles

2028585 Sgt W C Newman (4)

5723377 WO II N O'Connell (1)

14269556 Cpl S O'Reilly

109230 Maj D G Pascall

6299918 Pte A R Peacock

5721972 C/Sgt F E Porter

176233 Capt W H Pratt (5)

5625563 Pte N E Redding

5724913 WO II R Rigler (5)

314741 Lt G N Robinson

130709 Maj J H L Royle

5567974 WO II R Scott

184563 Capt R H S Stade (1)

5729250 Sgt L S Thomas

90922 Lt-Col G Tilly DSO (4)

128129 Capt R W Tucker MC (1)

113613 Maj B E Urquhart

5953769 Cpl J H West (4)

143750 Capt J C Whatley-Smith

3660003 Cpl J E Wilson

261671 Lt J F Wreford

AWARDS TO ESCAPED PRISONERS OF WAR IN EUROPE

5726306 Pte J Graham (2)

5723742 Pte C G Knight (2)

189094 Lt E G Lee

3712663 Cpl J Mannion (4)

THEATRE NOT SHOWN IN LONDON GAZETTE

5722299 C/Sgt W H Airey

15516 Maj W M W Collins

5726131 Pte R S Davies

34807 Capt G G Green

5723511 Pte S F C King

5721482 Sgt F J Smith

5570286 Sgt R Webb

THE MALAYAN EMERGENCY 1948–60

49794 Lt-Col A E C Bredin DSO MC

47616 Lt-Col F F Laugher OBE MC

COMMANDER-IN-CHIEF'S CERTIFICATES

124567 Maj H C Allen (5)

5726529 WO II L A Allen (4)

Capt P Aspinall (5)

Pte G Balham (5)

5725387 Pte S G Batten (1)

Sgt G Belan REME (5)

Sgt F Boyt (5)

5723941 Sgt W Brooks (5)

5725291 Pte W J Chutter (1)

5724946 WO II A Corbin (1)

Cpl R Cossins (5)

5728760 Sgt A T Critchley (2)

Pte E Delf (5)

Capt G H Docherty (5)

5722158 C/Sgt H F J Downton (2)

L/Cpl N Fosberry (5)

160905 Capt E Hannah (1)

313428 Lt A W Hatchard (1)

Sgt I Kelloway (5)

5725836 L/Cpl J E Kingsbury (4)

Capt The Rev A R C Leaney RAChD (4)

Sgt A Lloyd (5)

5727810 C/Sgt A H Longstreeth (5)

5729138 Pte W H Mason (4)

5725917 Pte J E Matthews (4)

6343648 Pte J L Merrey (1)

5724868 Sgt F Merritt (5)

Sgt A Milton (5)

Cpl M Newland (5)

5730417 Pte D G Porter

L/Cpl F Powell (5)

Sgt L Radford (5)

5720982 Sgt A Read (5)

Lt W J Rowe (5)

5722194 WO II W F Seale DCM (2)

5721400 WO I II Smith (2)

5725537 Sgt F M Stevens (1)

5727734 L/Cpl R P F Thornell (4)

5350609 L/Cpl I G Watkins (5)

5727049 Sgt H Willimott (5)

L/Cpl E Young (5)

Honours and Awards won by The Dorset Home Guard 1940–45

Officer of the Order of the British Empire (OBE)

Lt-Col C D Drew DSO

Maj R G H Wilson DSO MC

Member of the Order of the British Empire (MBE)

Capt A T Brown

2/Lt A E Gould

Maj G T Ridge MC

Lt J Roper

Maj D C Whitaker

British Empire Medal (BEM)

Sgt T A Allen

Sgt G R Dance

Sgt F J Jordan

Foreign Honours and Awards

French Officer of the Legion d'Honneur

5792 Brig Sir Ivan de la Bere KCVO CB CBE

In July 2014 the French Government announced that all surviving British soldiers who served in the campaign in France on or after D-Day will be awarded the Legion d'Honneur. Some twenty Dorset Regiment veterans, several of whom appear in this book, will be among the recipients.

French Croix de Guerre

148225 Capt A P Babington (1)

5726716 CQMS E J Chivers (5)

5727020 Sgt G H Cooper (4)

285422 Capt W A J Cottle (4)

262166 Capt H W Hitches (5)

95626 Lt-Col A D Lewis DSO

5723973 Sgt E Stevenson (1)

Belgian Commander of the Order of Leopold II

17955 Maj-Gen H L Longden CB CBE

Belgian Commander of the Order of the Crown

Maj-Gen Sir H J Huddleston KCMG CB DSO MC

Belgian Croix de Guerre

17955 Maj-Gen H L Longden CB CBE   5727810 CQMS A H Longstreeth (5)

Dutch Officer of the Order of Orange-Nassau

5792 Brig Sir Ivan de la Bere KCVO CB CBE

Dutch Officer of the Order of the Lion

226 Major Harvey B Spence (5)   137360 Maj W M Whittle (4)

Dutch Order of the Lion Bronze Cross

5724913 C/Sgt R Rigler (5)

Commander of the Order of Merit of the Federal Republic of Germany

5792 Brig Sir Ivan de la Bere KCVO CB CBE

Greek Officer of the Royal Order of the Phoenix

44027 Lt-Col D A Affleck-Graves

GREEK MEMBER OF THE ROYAL ORDER OF THE PHOENIX

103175 Maj T Bruce-Mitford

DANISH OFFICER OF THE ORDER OF THE DANNEBROG

5792 Brig Sir Ivan de la Bere KCVO CB CBE

SWEDISH OFFICER OF THE ORDER OF THE POLAR STAR

5792 Brig Sir Ivan de la Bere KCVO CB CBE

COMMANDER OF THE ORDER OF MERIT OF THE ITALIAN REPUBLIC

5792 Brig Sir Ivan de la Bere KCVO CB CBE

AMERICAN SILVER STAR

5729138 Pte W H Mason (4)   95487 Maj M J C Sanders

AMERICAN BRONZE STAR

149473 Capt H M Payne   41204 Lt-Col D W S Price

THAI COMMANDER OF THE ORDER OF THE WHITE ELEPHANT

5792 Brig Sir Ivan de la Bere KCVO CB CBE

PERSONAL ORDER OF THE SHAH OF PERSIA

5792 Brig Sir Ivan de la Bere KCVO CB CBE

IRAQI OFFICER OF THE ORDER OF RADIFAN

5792 Brig Sir Ivan de la Bere KCVO CB CBE

APPENDIX 3

BATTLE HONOURS WON BY THE DORSET REGIMENT 1939–45

North West Europe 1940
St Omer-La Bassée
Malta 1940–42
Sicily 1943
Landing in Sicily
Agira
Regalbuto
Landing at Porto San Venere, Italy 1943
North West Europe 1944–45
Normandy Landing
Tilly sur Seulles
Villers Bocage
Caen

Mont Pinçon
St Pierre La Vieille
Arnhem 1944
Aam
Geilenkirchen
Goch
Rhine
Twente Canal
Burma 1944–45
Kohima
Mandalay
Mount Popa

APPENDIX 4

FREEDOMS GRANTED TO THE DORSET REGIMENT AND THE DORSET TA 1939–67

1945

Lyme Regis
Poole
Dorchester

1955

Blandford Forum

1967

Bridport

APPENDIX 5

DORSET REGIMENT MEMORIALS IN FRANCE AND THE NETHERLANDS

NORMANDY

Asnelles   Rue Dorset Régiment, Rue Major Martin, and a stained glass panel in the Mairie

Audrieu   Place du Dorset Régiment

Hottot   Place du Dorset Régiment and the 231 (Malta) Brigade Memorial

Maltot   Rue du Dorset Régiment Liberateur and the 5th Dorsetshire Regiment Memorial

Esquay-Notre-Dame   Rue du Dorset Régiment

Fontaine Etoupefour   Rue de Brigadier General Breeden (*sic*)

THE NETHERLANDS

Hengelo   Roads named Bredin and Dorset

Borne   Dorset Plein and the Dorset Mansion House

Westerbouwing   Dorset Regiment badge engraved on restaurant wall

Acknowledgements

Any author of a book of this kind is conscious that, although his name may appear on its cover, it is actually the sum of the contributions of a great many people. I am very grateful to everyone in the list below. Without any one of them, this book would have been the poorer; without all of them, it would not have been possible.

Patrick Baxter
Jean-Pierre Benamou
Alison Bennett
Robin Betts
Alan Brown
Derrick Bunn
Patrick Burgess
John Button
Harry Chandler
David Chant
Ken Chivers
Ian Clark
John Cobb
Tony Coombes
Charles Cooper
Frank Cottam
David Cowan
Peter Cox
Geoff Cullington
Joan Cullington
Charles Debono
Geoff Eavis
Jeff Eckersall
Robin Fraser
Mike Froud
David Gargrave
Robin Gilbert
John Hambly

Don Hanney
Geraldine Harries
Peter Harris
Martin Hester
Bob Hunt
Elizabeth Hunter
Ant Hurst
Peter Huxham
Lois Jary
Tony Jeapes
Christopher Johnson
Vicky Johnson
Helen Jones
Steve Jones
Peter Lacey
Nick Lee
Cliff Lloyd
David Lloyd
Rex Lovell
Tony Marsh
John Martin
Valerie Martin
Peter Metcalfe
Martin Middlebrook
John Murphy
Geoff Nicholls
Jane Nolting-May
Mick O'Shea

Louis Old
Denis Pannett
Colin Parr
Roger Pearce
John Pitman
Hans Pol
Gordon Pratten
Bob Reep
Terry Reeves
David Ridgway
Gary Rogers
Nigel Salisbury
Tim Saunders
John Shackell
Gordon Sheppard
Sherborne School
Colin Shortis
Roger Snook
Richard Spalding
Nick Speakman
Martin Stanley
Christopher Stephenson
Ian Taylor
Derek Thomas
Peter Turner
Michael Woodhouse

Author's Note

I am very grateful to all those who shared their stories with me. This book would be immeasurably poorer without these first-hand accounts, which breathe life into the Regiment's story. A perpetual frustration has been the number of stories which – for reasons of space – I have had to omit. Those which do not appear here, however, are in the archives at the Keep Museum and available to future researchers and writers.

These personal accounts, written and oral, have really helped me to get a feel for the events I have tried to describe. Only one of them troubled me. A brave but embittered man, now dead, frankly recorded more than one occasion on which he was involved in the killing of prisoners. Shameful as well as gallant things are done in war, and those of us who have not faced the danger should be wary of sitting in judgement. But, having known a great many soldiers, I believe that crimes of this kind were rare. His account, therefore, posed a particular problem. Should I ignore it and not tell the exact truth, or should I include it and present an unrepresentative picture? Because I firmly believe his actions to be utterly unrepresentative of the humane behaviour of Dorset soldiers, I have not included these incidents.

Every other account, however, increased my enormous admiration for those who made this history, and I have felt privileged to be able to record many of their experiences.

Bibliography

Published Sources

Archer, Jeremy, *Steely Blue*, privately published 2013.

Arthur, Max, *Forgotten Voices of the Second World War*, Ebury Press 2004.

Atkinson, C T, *The Dorsetshire Regiment Volume II*, Oxford privately published 1947.

Barnes, B S, *The Sign of the Double T*, Sentinel Press 1999.

Benamou, Jean-Pierre, *Gold Beach Normandie 1944*, Orep Editions 2004.

Bredin, Lt-Col A E C, *Three Assault Landings*, Gale & Polden 1946.

Brooks, Stephen, *Montgomery and the Battle of Normandy*, History Press 2008.

Bryant, Arthur, *The Turn of the Tide*, Collins 1957.

—— *Triumph in the West*, Fontana 1965.

Cattle, Tom, *The Road from Corfe to Kohima and Beyond...* , privately published 2003.

Churchill, Winston S, *The Second World War Volumes I–VI*, Cassell 1948–54.

Colville, Sir John, *Man of Valour: Field Marshal Lord Gort VC*, Collins 1972.

Delaforce, Patrick, *The Fighting Wessex Wyverns*, Alan Sutton 1994.

Duffield, Capt C V, *Memoirs of an Old Soldier...* , privately published 1997.

Essame, Maj-Gen H, *The 43rd Wessex Division at War 1944–1945*, William Clowes 1952.

Evans, Bryn, *With the East Surreys in Tunisia and Italy 1942–45*, Pen & Sword 2012.

Forty, George, *Frontline Dorset: A County at War 1939–45*, Halsgrove Publishing 1994.

Gilchrist, Maj R T, *Malta Strikes Back: The Story of 231 Infantry Brigade*, Gale & Polden 1945.

Goddard, Douglas, Rankin, Eric & Vigers, James, *112th (Wessex) Field Regiment RA TA 1938–1946*, privately published 1997.

Haddrell, Ian, *A Bristol Soldier in the Second World War*, History Press 2009.

Hamilton, Nigel, *Monty Volumes I–III*, Hamish Hamilton 1981–86.

Hartwell, Maj G R, Pack, Maj G R & Edwards Maj M A, *The Story of the 5th Battalion, The Dorsetshire Regiment in North-West Europe 23rd June 1944 to 5th May 1945*, Dorset Regiment 1946.

Havers, Norman, *March On!*, Square One Publications 1992.

Holland, James, *Fortress Malta: An Island under Siege 1940–43*, Orion 2003

Jary, Sydney, *18 Platoon*, Sydney Jary Limited 1987.

Keane, Fergal, *Road of Bones: The Siege of Kohima 1944*, Harper Press 2010.

Lewin, Ronald, *Slim, The Standardbearer*, Leo Cooper 1976.

Middlebrook, Martin, *Arnhem 1944: The Airborne Battle*, Viking 1994.

Montgomery, Field Marshal Viscount, *Memoirs*, Collins 1958.

—— *Normandy to the Baltic*, Hutchinson 1947.

Oliver, R Leslie, *Malta at Bay*, Hutchinson 1942.

Pearce, Lance 'Ginger', *Ace of Spades – Lucky for One*, privately published 2013.

Pearce Smith, Brig Kenneth, *Adventures of an Ancient Warrior in Peace, War & Revolution*, privately published 1984.

Pol, Hans, *Our Forgotten Liberators*, privately published.

Popham, Hugh, *The Dorset Regiment*, Leo Cooper 1970.

Portway, Chris, *Journey to Dana*, Kimber 1955.

Proctor, Douglas, *Section Commander*, published for RMA Sandhurst by Sydney Jary Limited 1990.

Rickaby, Stan, *Upover and Downunder*, Britesport 2003.

Ryan, Cornelius, *A Bridge Too Far*, Hamish Hamilton 1974.

Saunders, Tim, *Goldbeach-JIG*, Leo Cooper 2002.

Slim, Field Marshal Sir William, *Defeat into Victory*, Cassell 1956.

Smith, Peter C, *Pedestal: The Convoy that Saved Malta*, Kimber 1970.

Snook, John, *Malta Siege Verse*, Koons 1990.

Sullivan, Bernard, *Sullivan's Stories*, Bernard Sullivan 2007.

Taylor, A J P, *English History 1914–1945*, Oxford University Press 1965.

Taylor, Brigadier George, *Infantry Colonel*, Self Publishing Association 1990.

Taylor, Ian, *The War History of 7th Battalion*, The Hampshire Regiment, Natula 2013.

Thompson, Major-General Julian, *Imperial War Museum Book of Victory in Europe*, Sidgwick & Jackson 1995.

Forgotten Voices of Burma, Ebury Press 2009.

Valentine, Lieutenant-Colonel A W, *We Landed in Sicily*, Gale & Polden 1943.

Watkins, G J B, *From Normandy to the Weser: The War History of the Fourth Battalion, The Dorsetshire Regiment, June 1944–May 1945*, Dorset Regiment 1946.
White, Lt-Col O G W, *Straight on for Tokyo*, Gale & Polden 1948.

REGIMENTAL PUBLICATIONS

Regimental Journals of the Dorset Regiment 1936–58.
Regimental Journals of the Devon and Dorset Regiment 1958–67.

UNPUBLISHED SOURCES

Beadle, George, Memories of Malta and Sicily.
Beale, Ron, Memories of North West Europe.
Chutter, Bill, Memories of Malta, Sicily and North West Europe (audio).
Coogan, Jack, Diary of Malta 1940–42.
Green, Eric, Memories of Malta and Gozo.
Hayes, Willie, Memories of Malta, Sicily and North West Europe.
Lloyd, Cliff, Memories of Normandy, Arnhem and Captivity.
Ramsay, Ivor, Memories of France 1940.
Rigler, Bob, Memories of North West Europe (audio).
Saunders, Tim, Account of the 2nd Dorsets' Battle at Festubert May 1940.
Shackell, Frank, Memories of North West Europe.
Thomas, Derek, Research into history of the Dorset Regiment 1945–58.
War Diaries of the 1st, 2nd, 4th and 5th Battalions of the Dorset Regiment.

INDEX

(Page numbers in bold indicate a picture while those followed by (n) *relate to footnotes)*